WRITING WISELY AND WELL

WRITING
WISELY AND WELL

MARLENE MARTIN

Monterey Peninsula College

MAUREEN GIRARD

Monterey Peninsula College

McGRAW-HILL, INC.

New York   St. Louis   San Francisco   Auckland
Bogotá   Caracas   Lisbon   London   Madrid   Mexico
Milan   Montreal   New Delhi   Paris   San Juan
Singapore   Sydney   Tokyo   Toronto

This book was developed by STEVEN PENSINGER, Inc.

WRITING WISELY AND WELL

Copyright © 1993 by McGraw-Hill, Inc. All rights reserved. Printed in the United States
of America. Except as permitted under the United States Copyright Act of 1976, no part
of this publication may be reproduced or distributed in any form or by any means, or
stored in a data base or retrieval system, without the prior written permission of the
publisher.

Acknowledgments appear on pages 353–354, and on this page by reference.

1 2 3 4 5 6 7 8 9 0   DOC   DOC   9 0 9 8 7 6 5 4 3 2

ISBN 0-07-023472-8

This book was set in Baskerville by Ruttle, Shaw & Wetherill, Inc.
The editors were Steve Pensinger and David A. Damstra;
the designer was Joan Greenfield;
the production supervisor was Louise Karam.
R. R. Donnelley & Sons Company was printer and binder.

Library of Congress Cataloging-in-Publication Data

Martin, Marlene, (date).
    Writing wisely and well / Marlene Martin, Maureen Girard.
      p.   cm.
    Includes index.
    ISBN 0-07-023472-8
    1. English language—Rhetoric.   2. College readers.   I. Girard,
    Maureen.   II. Title.
    PE1408.M386645   1993
    808'.0427—dc20   92-37244

ABOUT THE AUTHORS

Marlene Martin earned her B.A. and M.A. in English Language and Literature at the University of Michigan. For six years, she taught English in secondary school. She also served in the Peace Corps in Honduras where she taught in a teacher training program. Since 1972, she has taught at Monterey Peninsula College where she has served as English Department Chair.

Martin has published extensively in such periodicals as *Christian Science Monitor, Environment, The Los Angeles Times, National Fisherman, Oceans,* and *The San Francisco Examiner & Chronicle.* She has also published two college composition textbooks, *Practicing the Process: A Basic Text,* (Scott, Foresman, 1989) and *Review and Revise* (McGraw-Hill, 1989).

Maureen Girard is an instructor of English and English Department Chair at Monterey Peninsula College. She received her B.A. and M.A. in English Literature from San Jose State University. She taught English composition at San Jose State prior to becoming a member of the English Department faculty at Monterey Peninsula College. She is also the coordinator for the Lindamood Program, a basic reading and spelling program, at Monterey Peninsula College.

CONTENTS

PREFACE

Thomas Riley Marshall was wrong. What this country needs is *not* a good five-cent cigar. What it needs is a freshman composition textbook that is aware of its audience—an audience which has grown up in a McLuhanesque world where the media certainly delivers most of the messages. Most conventional rhetorical texts do not spring to life for students raised in a world where Kermit the Frog and Oscar the Grouch are household words. To appeal to the broad audience of today's college freshmen, a text must reflect real-world concerns in a format that is at once reader friendly and intellectually challenging.

Like *Writing Wisely and Well* and society itself, today's typical freshman composition student is far from typical: the majority of students in this country are over twenty-two; furthermore, the largest collegiate enrollment increase since 1970 has been among students thirty to thirty-four, and the average student age is nearing thirty. More than half these students are women. Approximately a fifth are ethnic minorities.

Currently 10 percent of America's total college population is enrolled in one of California's 107 community colleges, a system whose demographics clearly reflect those of the nation. In the California community colleges, two-thirds of the students are self-supporting, three-quarters are employed, and a quarter work full time. *Writing Wisely and Well* draws from writers and issues important to this changing student population as well as to the traditional model. This text contains subject matter relevant to adults in a complex and rapidly changing world.

To function most effectively in both their private and academic lives, today's students need skill in formulating and expressing ideas about myriad problems. *Writing Wisely and Well* is organized thematically, moving from issues centered on the students' own lives to issues of global importance. Throughout the text, the emphasis is on showing students how to discover and think critically about their ideas and the ideas of others.

Because our knowledge of the world is changing at an ever-increasing pace, finding and evaluating information are cornerstones of an education that will prepare today's college freshmen for a highly uncertain future. Research and interviews are presented as important idea-generating and idea-supporting methods beginning with Chapter Four. Furthermore, two chapters of the book use writing models drawn from the world of science, making use of such little-anthologized journals as *Nature.*

Writing Wisely and Well is process-oriented, ever conscious of the separate functions of the critical and creative sides of personalities—functions the text refers to metaphorically as the "critical brain" and the "creative brain." Because of the text's process orientation, it begins by helping students generate ideas; thus it introduces imagery and figurative language before topic and thesis sentences. In addition, there is a strong emphasis on the importance of playing with ideas by examining their expression not just in essays but in poetry and cartoons as well. John Steinbeck advised a young writer to:

> . . . write poetry—not for selling—not even for seeing—poetry to throw away. For poetry is the mathematics of writing and closely kin to music. And it is also the best therapy because sometimes the troubles come tumbling out.

The text incorporates a variety of genres, from professional and student essays and narratives to cartoons and poems. This mixture helps students understand that creative ideas can be communicated in a number of effective ways, and it helps them understand their own creative processes.

Like a good essay, a good text must contain a web of meaning. Chapters should not be distinct entities without reference to previous chapters; instead, they should interrelate. However, it is often not possible to cover twelve chapters in a semester. Therefore, in our table of contents, we have indicated key concepts within each chapter. Once students have covered the first four chapters, instructors can select a concept from a chapter without teaching the entire chapter. For example, an instructor could dip into Chapter Six and teach introductory techniques without teaching the rest of this chapter.

Assignments in *Writing Wisely and Well* move from prewriting through writing, peer editing, and revising. While the text begins by helping students discover ideas they already have, it moves quickly to show students the importance of considering the ideas of others. By Chapter Four, students are shown how to integrate both library research and interviews into their writing. In each chapter creative prewriting activities are clearly distinguished from critical organizing and editing activities. Chapters also show students the importance of moving back and forth between creative, idea-generating activities and critical thinking and editing activities.

Along with the usual methods of generating ideas, such as clustering, brainstorming, and freewriting, this text emphasizes the importance of working with others to generate ideas. It shows students how to use peer groups both to help generate and clarify their ideas and to help edit their writing. In addition, the text shows students how to integrate the logical principles and organizational patterns of traditional modes such as process, classification, cause-effect, and comparison-contrast. However, instead of using these modes as strait jackets that limit creative thinking and force ideas into rigid, artificial patterns, the text illustrates the use of these modes to help students generate ideas. Acknowledging that these modes rarely are used as the sole means of organization, the text shows students how to integrate useful principles from the modes into their essays.

To keep the primary emphasis on content rather than structure, each chapter focuses on a central theme; instead of miscellaneous examples of essays that demonstrate comparison-contrast, for example, the essays in the comparison-contrast chapter focus on media-related issues. Thus *Writing Wisely and Well* stresses that writing is not merely an academic exercise, but a dynamic means of understanding and communicating a broad range of topics important to students.

Acknowledgments

This book has benefited from the excellent advice of Kathleen Cain, Merrimack College; Michael Hennessy, Southwest Texas State University; Jodi Johnson, Los Angeles Pierce College; Kate Kiefer, Colorado State University; Barry Maid, University of Arkansas–Little Rock; Nell Pickett, Hinds Junior College; Bill Smith, Western Washington University; and Jeff Sommers, Miami University–Middletown.

The hundreds of students who used and contributed to this book in its formative stages deserves great credit for their valuable advice, encouragement, and inspiration. They are indeed the stars of this text.

Monterey Peninsula College librarians Bernadine Abbott, Julia Batchev, Deborah Ruiz, and Mary Anne Teed have been patient, persistent, and precious in their helpfulness. Marguerite Moore, Humanities Division Chair, and Thorne Hacker, Dean of Instruction, have been patient, restrained, sympathetic, and tolerant during the years we struggled to polish *Writing Wisely and Well.*

Among our colleagues on other campuses who have inspired us and demonstrated faith in our work are Edward P. J. Corbett, Nancy Glock, Hans Guth, Marlys Mayfield, and Gabriele Rico.

We appreciate the intelligence and insight of our editor Steve Pensinger, who understood and encouraged our philosophy in writing this text. In addition, the wise counsel and enthusiasm of our editor David Damstra has made the tedious production process more pleasant and expeditious.

Ellen Saxby has furnished friendship, support, and advice.

Our husbands Gary and John and our offspring Amanda, Andrew, Gabrielle, Ian, and Michele have demonstrated forbearance, encouragement, and sympathy as we struggled to meet the demands of being department chair and teaching full loads while writing this book.

MARLENE MARTIN
MAUREEN GIRARD

1

INSPIRATION: DISCOVERING AND EXPLORING IDEAS

CONCEPTS TO LEARN

Helping your creative brain work for you

The importance of images in creative work

Creating and generating ideas with clustering, freewriting, and brainstorming

The advantages of keeping a journal

With all our twenty-first-century technology, you would think that someone could have come up with a surefire way to help writers find good ideas quickly and with little trouble—maybe a computer program that writes your essay after you provide it with a few key pieces of information, or a program with hundreds of ready-made sentences just waiting for you to put them together.

Actually, you already possess the best computer program available to help you with good ideas for writing; you don't have to wait in line to use it, and it won't cost you a penny. All you need is some background information about its operating system and knowledge about how to access it. The program? Your mind. Its operating system? Let's take a look.

YOUR BETTER HALVES: YOUR BRAIN AT WORK

Has it occurred to you before now that you experience two distinct kinds of thinking? "Sure," you say, "on and off." Yet, even as you are reading this textbook, you may have taken a moment to look out the window at the cars passing by or the wind blowing through the trees; you might have closed your eyes and thought back on a conversation with a friend or remembered again the pleasure of winning last Saturday's tennis game. But you caught yourself daydreaming, glanced at the clock, and returned to your studying.

You may think of this mental wandering as unproductive, but in fact this process allows your brain a chance to arrange and bring to the surface the ideas, images, and emotions that are essential to any creative activity, including writing. In the following passage, Professor Gabriele Rico of San Jose State University shows us how the creative process—for birds, bees, and writers—relies on an abundance of raw material:

> Nature operates by profusion. Think of the nearly infinite number of seeds that fall to earth, only a fraction of which take root to become trees; of those five thousand or so drones that exist solely to ensure the fertilization of one queen bee; of the millions of sperm competing so fiercely to fertilize one small egg. Similarly, human beings engaged in the creative process explore an astronomical number of possible patterns before settling on an idea. In the preface to *Becoming a Writer* by Dorothea Brande, novelist John Gardner suggests that writers need some magic key for getting in touch with these secret reserves of imaginative power. What we lack is not ideas but a direct means of getting in touch with them.

Seamus Heaney, a contemporary Irish poet and teacher, describes in the following poem how one teacher helps his students find this magic key. Heaney shows us how music frees a group of students from their customary mental activity, allowing them to explore new avenues of thought and expression.

The Play Way

Sunlight pillars through glass, probes each desk   1
For milk-tops, drinking straws and old dry crusts.
The music strides to challenge it
Mixing memory and desire with chalk dust.

My lesson notes read: Teacher will play   5
Beethoven's Concerto Number Five
And class will express themselves freely
In writing. One said "Can we jive?"

When I produced the record, but now   9
The big sound has silenced them. Higher
And firmer, each authoritative note
Pumps the classroom up tight as a tire

Working its private spell behind eyes   13
That stare wide. They have forgotten me
For once. The pens are busy, the tongues mime
Their blundering embrace of the free

Word. A silence charged with sweetness   17
Breaks short on lost faces where I see

New looks. Then notes stretch taut as snares. They trip
To fall into themselves unknowingly.

For Thought and Discussion

1. In the second stanza of the poem, Heaney sets up an opposition between two forces at work in the classroom. What are those forces? Which is favored by the teacher and which by the students?

2. What is "Working its private spell behind eyes / That stare wide"?

3. Why does the music make it possible for the students to write more freely?

4. What has happened when the students "trip / To fall into themselves unknowingly"?

A Meeting of the Minds

The poem by Seamus Heaney tells a story that all writers want to read: as if by magic, the students in the poem become writers, their "pens are busy," they embrace "the free word," they discover what they want to say. You may have read this and thought, "Oh, sure, all I have to do is put on a Beethoven concerto and I'll automatically start writing the Great American Novel." Not exactly, but you can take advantage of the different kinds of thinking your mind is capable of.

You depend on one kind of thinking—the kind you probably call "real" thinking—to keep track of schedules and information, to make sound decisions, and to organize your thoughts. This logical, businesslike part of yourself is happiest working with material that can be broken down into individual parts and placed into preexisting categories. In order to do this, however, your logical, critical thought process must make judgments about the information it is working with—sorting, organizing, and rejecting ideas that don't fit.

But life would be dull indeed if you were capable only of critical, logical thinking. Fortunately, you also have the capacity to experience emotions, call upon memories, imagine new forms, and create new ideas, patterns, and connections. This playful, creative part of your mind can help when you are confronted with a new situation—for example, the creation of an essay. In addition, this part of your thought process makes it possible for you to conjure up mental pictures (images), and it is where your dreams are played out when you sleep; yet when you are awake, it is the side of yourself that you often ignore.

Your creative thought process—the artist's side—has much to offer, especially when you are involved in an activity that requires imagination and innovation. Brenda Ueland, a teacher of writing, suggests that creative ideas must be given time to grow and develop, that they cannot be hurried or ''willed'':

> Inspiration comes very slowly and quietly. Say that you want to write. Well, not much will come to you the first day. Perhaps nothing at all. You will sit before your typewriter or paper and look out of the window and begin to brush your hair absent-mindedly for an hour or two. Never mind. That is all right. That is as it should be. . . . This quiet looking and thinking is the imagination; it is letting in ideas. ''Willing'' is doing something you know already, something you have been told by somebody else; there is no new imaginative understanding in it.

The character in the cartoon, on the other hand, is having an experience that you may find all too familiar. Rather than ''moodling around,'' as Ueland calls it, he expects inspiration to come as soon as he sits down.

For Thought and Discussion

1. When you begin a writing assignment, how do you approach it? Do you *will* it, trying to force the ideas to come, or do you wait quietly for them to develop?

2. Why do you think a writer might benefit from what Brenda Ueland calls ''quiet looking and thinking,'' rather than getting the job done in a hurry?

3. Discuss an instance when an idea suddenly popped into your mind at a time when you hadn't even been aware that you were thinking about it.

4. What happens when you *try* to remember something, such as someone's name, when you are in a tense or stressful situation?

5. Describe how you felt when you had an experience similar to that

SHOE   **By Jeff MacNelly**

of the character in the cartoon—your mind was completely "dark" when you sat down to write. What happened as a result? (For example, did you give up on the writing assignment, or did you break through the blankness and succeed in completing the task?)

6. When you begin a task that requires concentration, do you feel tense or relaxed? Which state is usually more conducive to good concentration? Explain.

Cultivating Ideas

Brenda Ueland suggests that ideas must be given time to grow and develop, that they cannot be hurried and "willed." When we look at the ancient root word for *create*, the Indo-European word *ker*, we see that it means to grow. The ancient hunter-gatherers who gave us our earliest language witnessed each year the slow, deliberate miracle of creation in nature; it was on this mysterious process that their very lives depended. By contrast, the Indo-European word for *critic, skeri*, means to cut, separate, or sift; at the end of a growing season, farmers ancient and modern must cut, separate, and sift the rice, wheat, and barley they have grown—a process that requires making judgments and decisions. Like farmers, writers must go through a similar process, first allowing their ideas time to grow, then sifting through them for the "pick of the crop."

You will notice that the *critical* thought process handles the kinds of tasks that are usually identified as "academic." It adds and subtracts, it organizes information into charts and graphs, and it makes certain that there is always a logic to the work that it does. You probably learned very early in your life that this is the part of your mind you call upon to take a spelling or algebra test or to come up with the dates of the Civil War during a class discussion.

As a consequence, the "critic" in you begins to think of itself as top dog: whenever you sit down to do any important mental task, whether it is paying the bills or writing an essay, the critical part of your mind dominates and controls the action, while the creative part is left mute, unable to help. Yet, when you allow the critical, businesslike part of yourself to be in control at the beginning of a writing project, you often find yourself simply rehashing old, boring information.

Worse, you may find that as you cast about for new ideas the critical side of your brain simply censors every idea that occurs to you; it is as if you are in the middle of a war zone when you try to write. You have pitted the critical and creative thought processes against one another, and it is not surprising that you cannot think of anything to write.

If you think about it, you can probably remember having the experience of sitting at your desk, pen in hand, paper in front of you, ideas running through your mind, while you say to yourself: "That's no good—what a dumb idea. . . . This won't work because there wouldn't be enough to say about it in an essay. . . . I can't write about *that* subject. . . . My instructor wouldn't like this topic. . . ." Obviously, the critic in you is working overtime, but you feel that because you are being *very* critical and *very* serious and you are working *very* hard, this must be the correct approach to the serious business of writing an essay. Certainly, you would not want to approach writing as if it were a game—or would you?

For Thought and Discussion

Think of an instance in your life when you were "of two minds" about something or when one part of you had lectured or given advice to the other part. (This happens often in sports, on the job, or when you are making a difficult personal decision.) Describe this experience, and discuss how it helped or hindered you in completing your task or making a decision.

CREATIVE SOLUTIONS TO CRITICAL PROBLEMS

The process of sifting through ideas is not confined to writers. It is essential in any creative endeavor. Consider, for a moment, how some of the most important thinkers in the world of science have come up with their ideas. Albert Einstein, whose theory of relativity revolutionized modern physics, conducted what he called "thought experiments," in which he imagined himself riding along on a light wave or plummeting in a falling elevator. He would replay these experiments again and again in his mind until the feelings and images were so clear that he could transform them—first into words, and then into mathematical formulas. Einstein writes:

> The words or the language, as they are written or spoken, do not seem to play any role in my mechanism of thought. The psychical entities which seem to serve as elements in thought are certain signs and more or less clear images which can be "voluntarily" reproduced and combined.
>
> Taken from a psychological viewpoint, this combinatory play seems to be the essential feature in productive thought—before there is any connection with logical construction in words or other kinds of signs which can be communicated to others.
>
> Conventional words or other signs have to be sought for laboriously only in a second stage, when the mentioned associative play is sufficiently established and can be reproduced at will.

It is surprising enough to think of playing your way to a solution, but have you ever thought of *sleeping* your way to a solution? Meme Black tells of the nineteenth-century chemist, August Kekule, whose creative self had the answer to a perplexing problem—but it could only get his attention when he was asleep:

. . . after doggedly struggling to find the chemical structure for the benzene molecule, [Kekule] gave up, went to bed and dreamed of snakes biting their tails. Next morning, the moment Kekule opened his eyes, he realized that the dream held the answer. The benzene molecule, it turns out, was a circular shape.

During his sleep, the critic in Kekule dozed off too, and his dreaming, imaginative, creative self took over. This part of Kekule's thought process had already figured out the answer to the problem, but it couldn't get its message through to Kekule's conscious mind until the critic was "off duty."

You have probably had experiences like Kekule's, in which the solution to a vexing problem has magically presented itself in a dream or after a good night's sleep. Many psychologists believe that dreams, like "moodling," help to work out the problems and puzzles of the day; if we pay attention to our dreams, we will often come up with answers that elude us during our waking hours.

Unfortunately, you can't afford to take a nap in the hope that your creative thought process will automatically write your essays for you. Instead, you need a conscious method for tapping into your creative brain, quickly and efficiently, so that you, like Einstein and Kekule, can assemble the material necessary for some serious thinking. By the time you have finished working in Chapter 1, you will have learned three such methods—clustering, freewriting, and brainstorming—and you will be on your way to discovering which one works best for you.

For Thought and Discussion

1. How much do you allow your own critical brain to be off duty so that you allow room for new ideas to come to the surface? What techniques have you developed for getting around your censoring critic?

2. Review the readings about Einstein's and Kekule's methods of discovery, and reexamine how much they relied on their ability to translate their ideas into pictures and sensations. Why do you think they did so?

A PROFESSIONAL WRITER AT WORK

Back in 1883, when Samuel Clemens (whose pen name was Mark Twain) wrote *Life on the Mississippi*, research into the psychology and physiology of the human brain was in its infancy. Nonetheless, Twain knew that he had two very distinct ways of seeing: the one practical and logical, the other composed of images and feelings. Twain's experiences, not only as a riverboat pilot but also as a newspaperman, gave him an invaluable store of events, memories, and impressions that he could return to again and again in his writings.

As you read his account of navigating the Mississippi during his years as a riverboat pilot, think about the contrast between the creative and critical characteristics of Twain's description.

Two Views of the Mississippi
(*from* Life on the Mississippi)

1   The face of the water, in time, became a wonderful book—a book that was a dead language to the uneducated passenger, but which told its mind to me without reserve, delivering its most cherished secrets as clearly as if it uttered them with a voice. And it was not a book to be read once and thrown aside, for it had a new story to tell every day. Throughout the long twelve hundred miles there was never a page that was void of interest, never one that you could leave unread without loss, never one that you would want to skip, thinking you could find higher enjoyment in some other thing. There never was so wonderful a book written by man; never one whose interest was so absorbing, so unflagging, so sparklingly renewed with every reperusal. The passenger who could not read it was charmed with a peculiar sort of faint dimple on its surface (on the rare occasions when he did not overlook it altogether); but to the pilot that was an *italicized* passage; indeed, it was more than that, it was a legend of the largest capitals, with a string of shouting exclamation points at the end of it; for it meant that a wreck or a rock was buried there that could tear the life out of the strongest vessel that ever floated. It is the faintest and simplest expression the water ever makes, and the most hideous to a pilot's eye. In truth, the passenger who could not read this book saw nothing but all manner of pretty pictures in it, painted by the sun and shaded by the clouds, whereas to the trained eye these were not pictures at all, but the grimmest and most dead-earnest of reading matter.

2   Now when I had mastered the language of this water and had come to know every trifling feature that bordered the great river as familiarly as I knew the letters of the alphabet, I had made a valuable acquisition. But I had lost something, too. I had lost something which could never be restored to me while I lived. All the grace, the beauty, the poetry had gone out of the majestic river! I still keep in mind a certain wonderful sunset which I witnessed when steamboating was new to me. A broad expanse of the river was turned to blood; in the middle distance the red hue brightened into gold, through which a solitary log came floating, black and conspicuous; in one place a long, slanting mark lay sparkling upon the water; in another the surface was broken by boiling, tumbling rings, that were as many-tinted as an opal; where the ruddy flush was faintest, was a smooth spot that was covered with graceful circles and radiating lines, ever so delicately traced; the shore on our left was densely wooded, and the somber shadow that fell from this forest was broken in one place by a long, ruffled trail that shone like silver; and high above the forest wall a clean-stemmed dead tree waved a single leafy bough that glowed like a flame in the unobstructed splendor that was flowing from the sun. There were graceful curves, reflected images, woody heights, soft distances; and over the whole scene, far and near, the dissolving lights drifted steadily, enriching it, every passing moment, with new marvels of coloring.

3   I stood like one bewitched. I drank it in, in a speechless rapture. The world was new to me, and I had never seen anything like this at home. But as I have said, a day came when I began to cease from noting the glories and the charms which the moon and the sun and the twilight wrought upon the river's face; another day came when I ceased altogether to note them. Then, if that sunset scene had been repeated, I should have looked upon it without rapture, and should have commented upon it, inwardly, after this fashion: This sun means that we are going to have wind tomorrow; that floating log means that the river is rising, small thanks to it; that slanting mark on the water refers to a bluff reef which is going to kill somebody's steamboat one of these nights, if it keeps on stretching out like that; those tumbling "boils" show a dissolving bar and a changing channel there; the lines and circles in the slick water over yonder are a warning that that troublesome place is shoaling up dangerously; that silver streak in the shadow of the forest is the "break" from a new snag, and he has located himself in the very best place he could have found to fish for steamboats; that tall dead tree, with a single living branch, is not going to last long, and then how is a body ever going to get through this blind place at night without the friendly old landmark?

4   No, the romance and the beauty were all gone from the river. All the value any feature of it had for me now was the amount of usefulness it could furnish toward compassing the safe piloting of a steamboat. Since those days, I have pitied doctors from my heart. What does the lovely flush in a beauty's cheek mean to a doctor but a "break" that ripples above some deadly disease? Are not all her visible charms sown thick with what are to him the signs and symbols of hidden decay? Does he ever see her beauty at all, or doesn't he simply view her professionally, and comment upon her unwholesome condition all to himself? And doesn't he sometimes wonder whether he has gained most or lost most by learning his trade?

For Thought and Discussion

1. Why does Twain call the river a book? Of what is the river's language composed?

2. List the words in paragraph 1 that help portray the river as a book rather than a body of water.

3. Twain says that he "had lost something" when he learned to read the river. What did he lose?

4. Describe, in your own words, the kind of countryside that borders the river.

5. In paragraphs 2 and 3, Twain responds to the river in very different ways. Make a list of the words he uses to describe what he sees in the river in paragraph 2, then a list of the descriptive words in paragraph 3. Now, go back and see which descriptions reflect Twain's creative brain and which reflect his critical brain.

6. What would have happened to Twain if he had failed to use his critical thought process while navigating the river?

7. What did Twain lose when he used only his critical thought process to see the river?

THE IMPORTANCE OF IMAGES

The capacity to create *images*—mental reproductions of things you ordinarily perceive through your senses—is essential to the creative process. Your memories and dreams are largely composed of images; you would be able to remember very little if you had not stored much of the information in your memory bank in the form of mental pictures. Without images, your imagination would be unable to function; without the help of these pictures, you would be unable to create anything new in your mind.

Do you remember how much you studied details when you were a child? You may not recall the name of the lady next door who used to visit with your mother, but you probably still carry around in your mind the mental picture of a detail that fascinated you—a ring she wore, the way her hair poked out around the edges of her hairnet, or the mole on her chin that moved when she talked.

Good writers make certain that they create pictures and sensations with their words so that their readers can *see, feel, taste, smell,* and *hear* what they mean. As you read the following passage from *I Know Why the Caged Bird Sings* in which Maya Angelou describes a church picnic, be aware of the mental pictures and sense impressions you experience:

> The amount and variety of foods would have found approval on the menu of a Roman epicure. Pans of fried chicken, covered with dishtowels, sat under benches next to a mountain of potato salad crammed with hard-boiled eggs. Whole rust-red sticks of bologna were clothed in cheese-cloth. Homemade pickles and chow-chow, and baked country hams, aromatic with cloves and pineapples, vied for prominence. Our steady customers had ordered cold watermelons, so Bailey and I chugged the striped-green fruit into the Coca-Cola box and filled all the tubs with ice as well as the big black wash pot that Momma used to boil her laundry. Now they too lay sweating in the happy afternoon sun. That summer picnic gave ladies a chance to show off their baking hands. . . . Orange sponge cakes and dark brown mounds dripping Hershey's chocolate stood layer to layer with ice-white coconuts and light brown caramels. Pound cakes sagged with their buttery weight and small children could no more resist licking the icings than their mothers could avoid slapping the sticky fingers.

For Thought and Discussion

1. Using your dictionary, define the word *epicure.* Which thought process dominates the epicure's actions—the creative or the critical?

2. List each of the sense impressions you experienced as you read the

passage by Angelou. Copy down the phrase that triggered each impression. When you finish, compare your list with those of other members of the class to see if your "experiences" were similar.

3. For approximately fifteen minutes, write about a meal that was memorable for you (if you prefer, write about a meal that you would *like* to have). Describe the meal so that someone who was not there could "see," "taste," and "feel" the experience. Share your writing with one or two people in the class and ask them to describe the images and sensations that come to mind as they read your description. *Note:* The paragraph you write for this exercise is not to be evaluated in terms of "good" or "bad." Rather, it is to be read *only* in terms of its effectiveness in creating images for another person—your reader—the audience for this piece of writing.

PREWRITING

In the following pages, you will learn about three methods for getting your creative brain's ideas down on paper quickly and efficiently. While these are not the only methods for sketching out the beginning of an essay, they work well for most writers. In this chapter, we are concentrating on helping you stimulate your creative brain's process. In subsequent chapters, your critical brain will play an important role as you revise and proofread.

HELP IS ON THE WAY: CLUSTERING

As you were writing about a memorable meal, you might have wondered how to keep the all-too-eager critic in your mind quiet while at the same time encouraging your creative thought process to take over for a while. Happily, there is a way, and it is as simple as doodling. In fact, it is a lot like doodling. But if you take it seriously, it can go a long way in helping you unlock the ideas you need to get your essay written.

The technique, called *clustering*, was developed by San José State University composition professor Gabriele Rico. It is a kind of free association which allows you to bypass the aggressive censor, that part of yourself which only wants to organize and criticize. With clustering, you can move directly into the playful, creative part—the part of you that responds best to "moodling around"—your own personal storehouse of good ideas.

Making Arrangements

Your creative self does not organize information hierarchically, from top to bottom, as does your critical self. Instead, it fixes on one controlling idea or theme, then arranges supporting and linking information around that center. Once this is done, the critical brain is free to assess the assembled material and decide on a hierarchical arrangement for the ideas—which topic comes first, which comes second, and so on.

Clustering helps you discover ideas you may not even be aware of, and it permits you to explore those ideas without wondering about correctness or organization. In fact, when you first look at a cluster, it may seem aimless and disorganized, and you might think that an outline would be much more effective and "businesslike." Yet many students find that clustering is the most efficient way to discover what they want to say about a topic when they are planning an essay, taking an essay exam, or trying to decide what to write in a journal entry.

When you are discovering what you think and know, the businesslike approach is the least effective, for it instantly locks you into an organization that may not be suitable for your topic; you will find that within that organization, you are limited in what you can say. You need, therefore, a flexible, open-ended format in which you can write down ideas as soon as they pop into your head.

The student who created the sample cluster in Figure 1-1 (see page 13) was stuck for a journal entry. He started with the word *mud* and began to jot down, quickly and at random, all the associations he could think of. Within minutes, he not only had a topic, but an interesting journal entry.

Mud

Slippery, slimy stuff that's fun to play in. I started my cluster using mud because it reminded me of the time when I was a dirt bike rider. I used to take my yellow Yamaha 80cc dirt bike up into the hills just off Smith Road. There were a couple of trails that seemed to go for miles and miles before crossing a paved road. Since it was a real hilly area, it created quite a challenge.

It was always foggy and damp in the woods. The fog condensed on the trees, the trees dripped on me and my bike, and it was like riding in the rain. There was usually enough moisture to make the top layer of dirt muddy and slippery, yet just under the top layer was enough solid ground for traction and speed.

There was one hill that was next to impossible to get up. I had to get a long, running start at it. The only problem was that the trail was loaded with tree roots and sharp turns that would send me through the brush—and sometimes off my bike. Once I made it through the turns, I could start up the hill—but first, I had to get across two large gullies. I was usually airborne when I came out of the first gully, and with luck, I would fly over the second gully without touching the ground. There were many times when I went through the brush and ended up going over the handlebars while I was attempting to cross the gullies.

If I managed to get across the gullies and build up enough speed, I quickly covered the last fifteen feet of flat trail before beginning the steep climb up the hill. But if it was too wet on the hill, the back tire would often dig into the mud and throw the front of the motorcycle back on top of me.

It probably sounds like a lot of effort and risk for no results, but I'll never

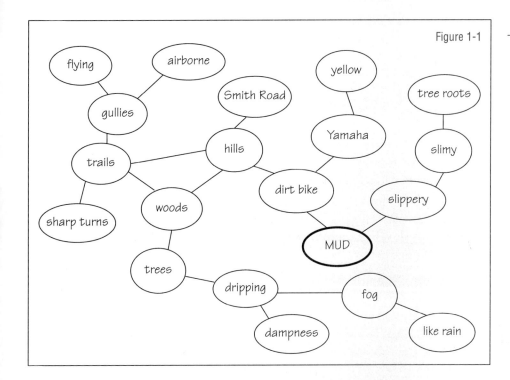

Figure 1-1

forget the first time I made it to the top. I was covered with mud down my back and legs, and I could only see out of one side of my goggles. But I'd made it! I had made it to the top and I was KING.

Clustering for In-Class Journals, Essays, and Exams

Perhaps there is a hotly contested mayoral election going on in your city, and your instructor asks you to write about it in an in-class journal entry. You don't know where to start—you haven't been following the campaign very closely—but you write "campaign for mayor" in the center of a fresh sheet of paper and circle it. Suddenly, words begin to flood into your head and you write them down. You begin to realize that you do know something about this campaign, that you do have strong opinions about some of the issues in the campaign, and that you have some ideas about how the city should be run during the next four years. The two or three minutes of clustering have given you a great deal to write about.

On another occasion, you may be faced with a question about the *Federalist Papers* on a history exam: your brain seems frozen as you stare at the words on the exam prompt, and you feel as though you have forgotten everything you ever knew about those documents. Then you remember clustering. Quickly, you jot "federalist papers" down on a piece of scratch paper and begin to cluster around it. Within sixty seconds, your brain has thawed and you discover that you have a great deal to say about the *Federalist*

Papers. You continue to cluster until you have written down not only your main points but supporting points and ideas for illustrations as well. Within five minutes, you are able to turn from the cluster and begin to write, with a sense of confidence, your response to the test question.

How to Cluster

1. You should work quickly—a cluster should not take more than three or four minutes.

2. Circle each word as you write it down.

3. As you cluster, draw lines between words and ideas that create associations in your mind so that you can return to those connections later and perhaps develop them more fully in a piece of writing.

Organization: Shaping the Ideas in Your Cluster

Usually, when you cluster, an idea will strike you as particularly interesting, and you will want to write about it. This is what Gabriele Rico calls the "Aha phenomenon." You don't have to aggressively search for an idea to get you started—it's there waiting for you. By exploring your thoughts through the clustering process, you will discover ideas and connections that not only will surprise you, but will be genuinely interesting to write about.

Clusters come in all sizes and shapes: they can fill a page, or they can be rather brief. Whatever their size and shape, they are tools to get your creative thought process in gear until you discover where you want to go with a topic. But clusters also help you to organize your ideas, even though they don't appear to be all that organized on the page.

Often, you will be surprised to discover that the ideas you consider most important before you cluster turn out to be of little importance when you look at the whole cluster on the page. Your best idea about your topic may be hiding in your subconscious mind, or it may be an idea that—when it came—you rejected as dull or unworkable. Yet once it was out on paper and combined with other, related ideas, it suddenly made perfect sense as a central focus for writing.

In addition, you will find that the idea-generating capacity in your creative thought process will give you more material than you can possibly fit into one paragraph or essay. You will be able to choose from the ideas in your cluster, selecting those you like best and ignoring the rest.

Moving Deeper: Two Student Clusters

For an in-class assignment, students were asked to cluster the word *deep* for two or three minutes, then write for five to six minutes. They had little time to worry about what to say or how to say it, and they readily turned off the critic-censor in themselves so they could concentrate on what they wanted to say. Figures 1-2 and 1-3 show two clusters from this assignment; the writings that came out of those clusters follow.

The ocean is deep, its dark underwaters hiding the strange creatures who live without the light of the sun. Some people are supposed to be deep, layered with many thoughts and insights. Most people are shallow, though, and are pretty easy to see through. Which is better, to be deep in the ocean or deep inside yourself? I guess it all depends on your point of view. I personally would rather be lost in the dark depths of the ocean, free to move about and to think about whatever I was moved to. But then I would be deep inside of myself, at the same time, wouldn't I?

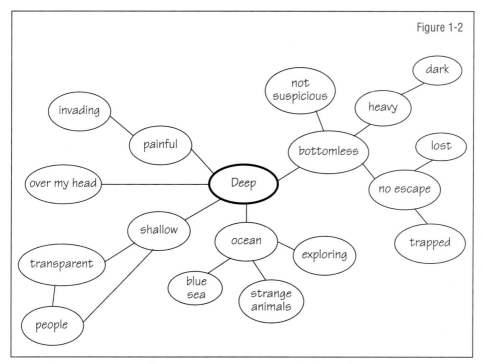

Figure 1-2

One day, I decided to explore the old salt mines that sat a couple of miles from my house. Through time, stories of ill-fate have been passed along, describing the cave-in of one shaft. I explored around the field and came upon a large hole with fencing surrounding it. It was obvious to me that, through the years, the hole had begun to fill in. I realized while looking into this large hole that this was the place that had taken the lives of two men and a pack of mules.

I found myself daydreaming the terror those unfortunate men must have felt: The ground began to shake and rumble, disappearing from my sight. My body begins to descend into this deep and very black hole. It is very frightening, and I continue to fall downward in the hole. Time seems endless and

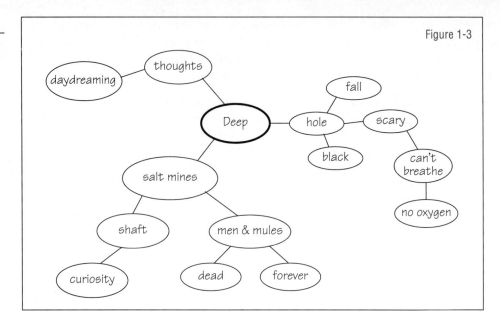

Figure 1-3

I soon realize I am in deep trouble. The earth begins to fall from above, covering me and the mules. I feel myself beginning to gasp for air as the supply of oxygen depletes. I then realize I am beginning to lose consciousness, and feel as though I am falling into a never-ending hole.

The feeling of falling soon snaps me back into reality, and I move quickly away from the fence. Fear envelops me, and I begin to run, escaping the mines, to find security within my home.

Choosing Your Bright Ideas

Like these writers, you won't include everything from your cluster when you write. The cluster is only a means for *getting ideas;* once you have clustered, you can choose to use or not use any of the items you have generated. If you are like most writers, you will discover that your cluster provides more ideas than you can use in a single essay.

You have seen cartoons in which one of the characters gets a bright idea. To indicate what has happened, the cartoonist has drawn a light bulb above the character's head. While it may be a corny way of communicating what happens when ideas and answers pop into our heads, it is nonetheless an accurate representation of the aha phenomenon.

When you cluster, you trigger the ''light bulb'' mechanism in your mind, just as surely as if you had turned on a switch. Once this has happened, it's only a matter of moments before you discover an important idea or a powerful image that you can transform into writing.

For Thought and Discussion

1. *In-Class Super Cluster:* Now it's your turn to try clustering. Because ideas inspire more ideas, and because it is interesting to see the wide range of possibilities that can be generated in a cluster, your first cluster or two should be group efforts.

a. You can cluster almost any word or idea you can think of, but the best kinds of words for you to begin with are those that are basic and not too specific. Colors are excellent cluster words, as are prepositions, such as *in, out, under, up, down,* and *through.*

b. As the instructor writes suggestions on the board, you and your classmates can suggest ideas and associations quickly and without too many second thoughts. Don't worry about sounding silly; your idea may trigger a whole series of new ideas for others in the class.

c. Fill the board with the class cluster.

d. Take about ten minutes for everyone to write individually on one idea or group of ideas from the class cluster. You will probably discover that your topic will leap right out of the cluster at you, and you'll be off and writing.

e. If there is time, your instructor may want to collect the writings and read some of them to the class (keeping the writers anonymous, of course). You will be astonished at the variety of approaches that your classmates take as they write about an idea from the cluster on the board.

f. Figure 1-4 (see page 18) shows a sample super cluster on the cluster word *yellow.*

2. *Ten-Minute In-Class Clustering:* This exercise provides you with an opportunity to see how quickly and efficiently clustering works for you. Choose from the following list of possible cluster words, and spend ten minutes creating your own cluster and writing a brief vignette. Spend about three to four minutes clustering, and five to seven minutes writing. Don't worry about editing—that comes later.

flying	dark	crystal
within	orange	swimming
outside	heavy	white

  LETTING LOOSE: FREEWRITING

Like clustering, *freewriting* allows you to bypass the critical brain censoring mechanism and helps you to get your good ideas onto paper. Also like clustering, freewriting is easy—so easy, in fact, that you may not believe it will work for you. But it is the method that professional writers most often use to explore and discover their ideas when they begin to write.

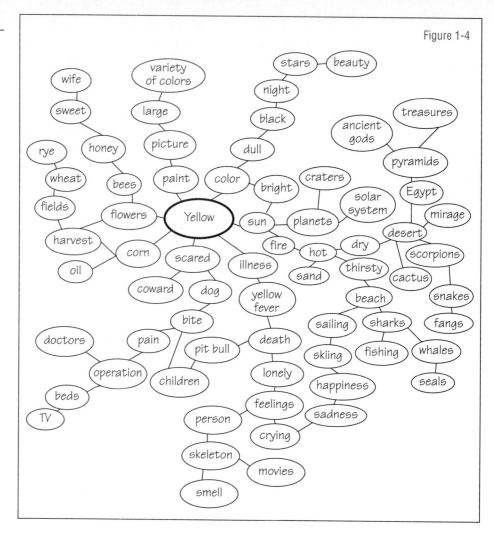

Figure 1-4

In order to freewrite, you need only a few items: a piece of blank paper, a pencil, and a hand (or a computer and two hands). Now, write. Just write. Keep writing. . . . It doesn't matter that your writing seems aimless at the beginning, just stay with it. Your logical, critical self is beginning to object. Tell it to be quiet and keep writing.

You get the idea. The object, as with clustering, is to permit your creative thought process to reveal its store of ideas. You may begin freewriting with a particular topic in mind, or your mind may be a complete blank. In either case, your writing will gradually narrow its focus and you will begin to discover a whole constellation of ideas—as if by magic.

If you keep your hand writing, without censoring or worrying about what is being written, your creative self will begin to gain the ascendancy and provide you with ideas and associations that will surprise you. This is what writer Edmund Wilson means when he says "I think with my right hand."

Take a look at the freewriting of Linda, a first-year composition student:

As I wake I can vaguely remember, ~~j~~ jagged lines dusty ~~piture~~ pictures, old like faces old reel flicks that tears my ears my silent pictures at night *mine* Dreams of mine flash by in quips of color—outlined half-life, all stick to my mind, quickly melting as I reach to snap a shaft of fading ice, it falls and breaks, returning to my mind empty, a dry ~~unforning~~ unforgiving place. ~~Spearding~~ Spreading rummors like seed, they grow & they dance ~~l~~like fairies around my must-up head I reach up to capture one a moment, a strong one slices through my mind, said from beyond. From the second world to have & hold Alternatives play sometimes a whole new life will emerge only to once again fade away. Strangers, faceless pillars, words not spoken, just me here. They take my hand & lead me through the night to another notion. As I try & recall I'm in a ~~theather~~ theater seat pushing everything else aside. I stand in full regatta pushing everything else aside only a bottom view not able to see the screen To be plugged is to be pulled I awake, like, remember, my night world.

Obviously, this is not a piece of writing that Linda would want to hand in as an essay. It is, however, a very interesting collection of thoughts, impressions, and ideas that may help her discover a topic and a focus for her writing; she could, with work, forge this freewriting into an essay or poem of real merit.

LISTING YOUR IDEAS: BRAINSTORMING

You have probably done *brainstorming* with friends or in a class; if you work, you may have engaged in some business-oriented brainstorming, as well. This is a technique that is frequently used in group situations, because it helps to break through the critical brain's dominance and into the group's creativity. Like clustering and freewriting, brainstorming depends on your capacity to make quick associations and to write down whatever comes into your mind—or out of your pen.

When you brainstorm, you simply make an unedited list of your ideas; your object is to get as many ideas onto the paper as quickly as possible, without stopping to evaluate them. You will have plenty of time to evaluate later on. Each idea inspires additional ideas, and your list will likely produce more than one good idea for a journal entry or an essay. Below is a sample of Steve's brainstorming session.

first date
fifteen
scary/exciting

like teetering on the edge of a cliff
Boy Scout hike
Mr. Green
angry with me
saved my life
embarrassed/grateful
conflicting feelings
the anticipation of a new experience is as scary as teetering on the
    edge of a cliff

Notice that Steve discovered a central point at the end of his brain-storm. He was surprised when it appeared, but it served him well; he was able to create a brief essay using this topic sentence. Yet he hadn't even been thinking of this topic when he began his brainstorming exercise.

CREATING YOUR OWN PICTURE OF THE WORLD: THE JOURNAL

There are as many reasons to write as there are writers. Perhaps writers have something on their minds they want to explore on paper. They may wish to re-create experiences they have had in their own lives, or to tell the story of someone else's life experience. Ernest Hemingway says of his craft, ''I am trying to make, before I get through, a picture of the whole world—or as much of it as I have seen.''

Some writers may have special knowledge they want to share with others, or they may want to expose a problem or danger. Brenda Ueland describes the discovery she made about why she chose to write:

> At last I understood that writing was this: an impulse to share with other people a feeling or truth that I myself had. Not to preach to them, but to give it to them if they cared to hear it. If they did not—fine. They did not need to listen. That was all right too.

But most of all, writers simply want the sense of discovery and personal freedom that comes from writing down their own memories, feelings, concerns, ideas, and dreams. In fact, many writers discover and clarify what they think only as they write.

Unfortunately, through your school experiences, you may have learned to think of writing as a chore, something you *have* to do. Worse, you may have come to expect that you will be assigned a grade for your efforts. It is self-evident that this combination of circumstances can lead to negative feelings about writing. But it does not have to be that way.

A journal is an opportunity to escape not only the anxiety of writing for a grade but also the feeling that you will be criticized. Through your journal, you can learn that writing helps you discover what you think. In addition, keeping a journal can become a means for you to paint your own picture of the world, and you don't have to worry at all about how another person (your instructor, for example) might evaluate your writing. Your journal will give you the practice and experience you need to feel comfortable with yourself as a writer so that when you are asked to write an essay or report, you will approach the task as a much more "normal" activity than it seemed in the past.

What a Journal Is—and Isn't

Perhaps you have had some experience with keeping a journal. If so, you know that a journal is a place to write about a variety of observations, memories, experiences, and feelings. These can take any form with which you are comfortable: stories, poems, or mini-essays. Some students even like to include drawings with their writing. There is one thing, however, that a journal is not: a diary. A diary simply records what you *did* today, without elaboration, and without the possibility for new discoveries; it's about as exciting as a grocery list:

> Got up at 7:15 today and was late for my 8:00 class. Went to Sociology and English, then ate lunch with Nancy. Got to work at 2:30—late again—but the boss was out so I didn't get into trouble.

This kind of writing does not reflect a particular human being; rather, it reflects a series of actions that could have been performed by anyone. It is essentially anonymous. Not so with your journal, your own picture of the world.

Your journal records what you *think* and *feel;* it is as individual as your fingerprint—and as exciting as you want to make it. Most of the time, you may, like this writer, be expected to come up with your own journal topics. Yet, as you can see from the example, she discovers within her everyday thoughts and dreams a significant and age-old topic:

> I sometimes think in my mind, in my dreams, that my life is going to be over and I am not going to be in this world any more. It is not death I am talking about, but the fact that I am not living, I am nothing.
>
> If my parents weren't here, or if they had never met, I would not have been born. When I ride the bus, my mind wonders: I would not feel the emotions I feel, or experience my senses. I really can't explain it exactly, but I am going to live my life, get older, do whatever I have time for, and "boom," I am gone. After my life is over, where am I going? Am I going to be reborn and would I remember things before I was reborn?
>
> In a way, it is scary because I won't have the joy, sadness, anger, happiness, depression of the life I am living now. Life seems so short when I think these thoughts. I know I am young to think about these things, but I do wonder, and I wonder where I am going when I am gone. "Boom" just like that and it is gone. Like magic.

How Do I Get Started? What Do I Write?

The first rule of thumb for a successful journal is that you must write in it almost every day. A journal works well only when you are consistent and disciplined about writing on a regular basis.

In the beginning, you may feel rather self-conscious about journal writing, but that feeling will disappear; in fact, you will soon find that you look forward to "thinking on paper." To use the journal most effectively, you should write six journal entries per week, or about one entry per day.

It would defeat the purpose of the journal if you were to write all six entries in one day. The journal is not supposed to be a chore or an afterthought; on the contrary, it should become a welcome respite in a busy day—a place for you to collect your thoughts and record your ideas.

You can write about anything in your journal: last night's movie, a book you just finished reading, a conversation you had with a friend, a situation that occurred at work, a discussion in a class. The ordinary events of your everyday life are always grist for the journal mill. In fact, ordinary events and ideas often lead to some wonderful discoveries about yourself and your world. Notice how the writer in the following example looks at her own, rather ordinary existence in an entirely new light as she sees a connection between her current living situation and the larger concept of rites of passage.

A Student Writer at Work in Her Journal

When Sara Costello was reading about rites of passage in her anthropology textbook one evening, she decided to take a break from her studies and write a journal entry for her composition class. Since the concept was already on her mind, it was easy for Sara to decide to write about rites of passage in her journal; she found the idea intriguing, but it was a fairly new concept.

Sara's logical, critical self wanted her to start writing a coherent, organized journal entry right away, but all she could think to say on the subject sounded like a rehash of the textbook. She had had enough experience with clustering, however, to know that her creative thought process would have many bits and pieces of ideas, many memories and thoughts and feelings that could transform her journal entry into an interesting piece of writing—and an exciting process of discovery.

As ideas flooded into her mind, Sara realized that they were scattered and disorganized. The critic in her said, "Why bother? It's hopeless to sort out this mess." Happily, though, clustering helped her to get ideas out where she could see them and think about them, so she could decide which ones to use and which to discard. And after she did this preliminary exploration, Sara found that she was ready to write with focus and purpose. Take a look at the steps Sara used to generate ideas for her journal entry:

1. First, Sara put the words "Rites of Passage" in the center of a blank page and circled them with a heavy line. This was her starting point, and everything she wrote on the page was connected to this central idea.

2. Next, she jotted down every idea that ran through her head, allowing one idea to generate others, and *not* allowing herself to censor what went onto the page. (This is very important, for once the critical thought process gets into the act, it is likely to take over and put a stop to the action.)

3. As she wrote down her ideas, Sara circled them and connected them to other ideas. (The circles are an important signal to her intellectual-critical thought process to butt out until the creative-experiential part of her has had a chance to express its ideas.) Patterns began to emerge as Sara clustered, more ideas occurred to her, and soon she had a page full of possibilities for her journal entry on rites of passage (see Figure 1-5).

4. After she finished her cluster, Sara looked over the ideas that appeared. She realized that the cluster reflected ambivalence—not only on her part, but on the part of society—regarding the idea of a rite of passage for young people. She began to think about the fact that we have no coming-

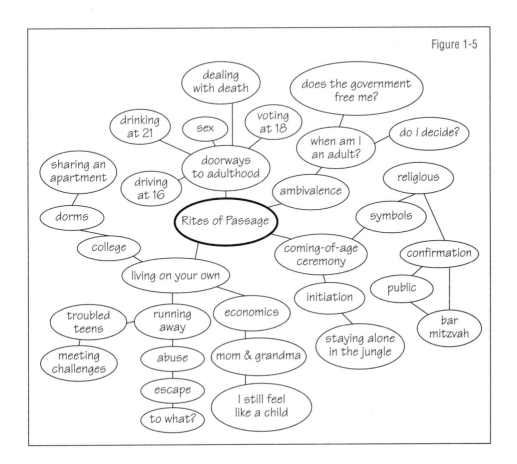

Figure 1-5

of-age ceremony, and she wondered if—perhaps—we should. As a result, Sara decided to write in her journal about the need for a rite of passage in our culture.

Sara's Journal Entry

1   I think our society needs a definite rite of passage, the equivalent of staying in the jungle alone for a week, or something like that. As it is, we spread "growing up" over a long period of time. I don't think one event would instantly mature a person, but I like the idea of some sort of coming-of-age ceremony as a doorway to adulthood, instead of a long gauntlet to be run, with many markers along the way. I'd rather just step over the threshold and orient myself to my status than drag myself through years and years of ambivalence.

2   There are so many times when a person can think, "Wow, I'm really grown up now!" There are the official ones: at sixteen you can drive, at eighteen vote, at twenty-one drink. Yet many people flaunt or ignore these rights (or responsibilities), whether out of a wish to be "grown up" or to devalue what they see as adult privileges—sometimes, even just out of apathy. Anyway, these occasions seem almost demeaning to me, with the government playing the role of a parent who decides that the child is "responsible enough" to do something. There are more personal events that can give someone this feeling—doing something by yourself, coping with death or sex, but they are intangible and depend on the person. It seems silly, but I want something that is more public, that tells yourself *and* everyone else that you've made it.

3   Since marriage happens later (or not at all) than it has in other times in history, moving out on your own can be a symbolic growing up. Still, this isn't totally satisfactory as a rite of passage. Economically, many adult children have no choice but to live at home. Right now, I am living with my mother and she and I with my grandmother, her mother. Going to college blurs the distinction between living at home and on your own—dorms just don't cut it. On the other hand, runaways are children who leave home too soon, though it may be no worse than living in an abusive situation. So considering living on your own as a cut-and-dried rite of passage just doesn't work.

4   What I want is something somewhat difficult, stressful even, but that you do once and are finished—symbolically "grown-up." Most primitive (I hate to use that word) societies seem to have a ceremony to fulfill this function, so do most religions. I do not mean to say that, once successful, you are finished maturing, because I think this takes all of a person's life, but that you swap the role of a child for that of an adult. Then you work on being an adult. Maybe it is because our society is so complex and difficult and pluralistic that we lack one specific rite.

5   I think it is interesting that the programs that seem to have the most success working with troubled or criminal teenagers are ones that involve some sort of rite of passage. I've read about one where the teenager trains a horse or completes an ocean voyage. One way or another, most people cannot escape eventually being thrown into the "adult" world, and I think a clear, definite rite of passage would make the transition easier.

While this is not a perfect, polished piece of writing, it is a very good initial exploration of the topic—and it is a long way from the blank mind that Sara faced as she first pondered how to get started. The clustering enabled Sara to see that she had a great deal to say about rites of passage, and her journal entry gave her some solid material to develop and refine for a future essay.

For Thought and Discussion

1. In the first paragraph, Sara provides several images to explain what she means by a rite of passage. What images did she use? Did they help you to understand her meaning? If so, how? If not, suggest some images that would be more effective.

2. Did Sara use everything that was in her cluster, or did she leave some material out when she wrote? If so, what did she leave out?

3. Write "Rites of Passage" in the center of a clean sheet of paper, circle it as Sara did, and quickly write down as many ideas as come to you in three minutes, circling them and drawing lines from one to another as you go along. Avoid the temptation to look at Sara's cluster for ideas—your cluster should be characteristic of you, and no one else. After you have finished clustering, write for seven to ten minutes.

Guidelines for Getting Your Ideas Down on Paper

During the first week of journal writing, you should reinforce all three of the idea-generating methods that you have learned in this chapter.

1. For your freewriting exercise, spend *at least* ten minutes writing, *without stopping.*

2. When you brainstorm, work for a minimum of three minutes, without stopping. After you have finished your list of ideas and associations, write for ten minutes or more.

3. Your clusters should take you at least three minutes, but no more than ten minutes; if you work too long, the flow of ideas becomes forced and artificial.

WRITING ASSIGNMENT

Below are some suggested cluster words for your journal entries:

purple	velvet	flat
plane	outside	up

Up and *outside* may seem a bit strange to you for such an activity. In fact, Gabriele Rico suggests that prepositions are excellent cluster words because they are open-ended and do not suggest any particular theme; as a result, they give your creative self a chance to really go to work.

After you finish your cluster, write for five to fifteen minutes, using an idea or a group of ideas that interests you. Include this in the first week of journal entries.

STUDENT STARS

Here are some sample journal entries from students.

Lines. Lines everywhere. They line this paper and the words I write contain a series of lines, short and long. Lines are on the carpet, that go all the way to the wall. Lines are created in the sky by an airplane, bird or ball. We are a lined-world, that's all. Lines in our clothing, lines of gray in our hair (most of these we wish were out of there). Lines in our candy. Lines in our food. Lines at the bank can put us in a very bad mood. A curve is nothing more than a bent line. We can't exist without them. We couldn't drive a car without following little yellow lines. Lines help us communicate and lines are created as we kick a ball, lines are on the symbol that stands for justice, one and all.

Have you ever wondered what it's like to walk on six legs? No, I never really thought about it either, before today. But since I spent about thirty minutes observing ants, I've started to think about it.

Nor did I think that ants could be very interesting to write about, but they are. For all their orderliness and social perfection, they are really a peculiar lot. They have uncountable irregularities that I couldn't even begin to explain. And though I watched and followed and peeked and pondered, I still couldn't figure out what 99% of them were up to.

Some days a line of ants will hustle around at top speed as if late for an important appointment; other days (like today) they stroll slowly and lethargically, on their way to church, maybe. Whenever one ant passes another on the busy highways they travel, there is always a split-second pause in their travel to exchange a bit of info with the other guy. They do this through their antenna I guess, since that seems to be the only part that makes contact with a fellow ant. I wonder what they say? It's probably not important stuff, but, just maybe, they exchange brief philosophical observations or gossip, or . . . well, who knows what they talk about anyway.

The hypnotic pulse of the flickering strobe light widens and closes the pupils of my eyes. The vibrations are transmitted to my brain, which draws dizzy conclusions and sends my world spinning. The light's pulse finally dies and the flashing colored lights are its predecessors. Each one throws its shine out to the beat of the wall-tearing music.

I look over at the enormous black houses in which the rhythmic beats live. They shout and screech as they attempt to break the door open, but the house only expands and retracts to the pulse of their screams.

Their shouts become more demanding and I soon feel their breath upon my body. It is as if they have broken their house door down and are now attempting to enter mine!

But my door is much stronger, and they can no longer touch me because it is time to leave the dance floor.

Today was a great day. My son Joaquin had a big birthday party at the park. We had hamburgers and hot dogs, along with potato salad and a green salad. We had plenty to drink, along with a huge cake. I sat on a bench, looking at my second-born, once a baby in my arms, now playing with friends. It is neat to know that he will be growing up some day into an adult.

About a year ago my husband and I decided not to have any more children. We both agreed that having two boys was a handful, and it was difficult enough to keep our sanity intact. That is enough of a struggle—even without raising children.

As I looked at my son playing in the sand (my baby!), I realized how happy I was, but how sad I felt too. I think as a mother I mourn a little that I will never see age three again in my children—that life does move on and people do grow up and change. I have certainly been blessed. However, a part of me will always see my second-born as my baby. I wonder if that changes for a woman over the years, as you watch your children grow into big adults, more and more not needing their parents—especially their mother. As Joaquin keeps reminding me, ''Mom, I am not your baby any more—I am awesome!'' Out of the mouths of babes.

2

DISCOVERY AND NARRATION: MAKING YOUR POINT CONCRETELY

When we are trying to communicate an idea, we are dealing with the elusive. Artists such as painters and sculptors involve their audience's senses through the use of shape, color, and texture. However, a writer cannot pin down ideas or display them in galleries. In order to communicate ideas, then, writers need to translate them into images meaningful to their audience. In this chapter, we will explore several ways to create effective images. Then we will examine how to use images to help us make our points.

Often images are communicated most effectively when they are linked in a story. Take, for instance, the idea of being a celebrity. When Walt Disney was asked how it felt to be a celebrity, he replied:

> It feels fine when it helps to get a good seat for a football game. But it never helped me to make a good film or a good shot in a polo game, or command the obedience of my daughter. It doesn't even seem to keep fleas off our dogs—and if being a celebrity won't give one an advantage over a couple of fleas, then I guess there can't be much in being a celebrity after all.

ABSTRACT IDEAS

29

DISCOVERY
AND
NARRATION:
MAKING
YOUR POINT
CONCRETELY

Abstract ideas such as "How does it feel to be a celebrity?" "What is the purpose of life?" and "What is reality?" need to be explained more fully for people to understand them. Ideas are *abstract.*

The word *abstract* derives from the Latin word *abstrahere,* which means to move away. Unlike the details of a story, such as those in the anecdote about Walt Disney, abstractions are removed from the immediate experiences of our five senses; thus these abstractions draw away from our ability to understand them. We cannot see, hear, taste, smell, or feel abstractions. We cannot perceive abstractions with any of our five senses because abstractions are ideas. Therefore, we have difficulty understanding them ourselves and difficulty in making our readers understand exactly what we mean by an abstract term or phrase. Examples of abstractions include such words and ideas as *kind, cruel, rich, poor, ugly, pretty, old, young, big, little, justice, peace.*

CONCRETE IDEAS

As Walt Disney understood, to communicate an abstract idea effectively, we need to make it more *concrete.* The word *concrete* comes from the Latin word *concretus,* which means to grow together or to solidify. In order to solidify our understanding of an abstract idea, we need to appeal to one or more of our readers' five senses; we need to give a specific example our readers can understand. Disney did this by showing us the impact of being a celebrity on experiences we can perceive through our five senses. Even if we have not been bitten by a flea, even if we do not own a dog, we can sense his point through his brief anecdote.

The more specific—the more concrete—we are, the better able our audience is to understand our point. For example, contrast the abstraction *old* with the concrete statement "The dog is sixteen" or "The woman is 103." Or contrast the abstract statement "She was a kind lady," with "Mother Teresa cradled the head of the poor, starving Indian dying of bone cancer."

Fortunately, when we allow our creative thought process free rein—as we do when we cluster, brainstorm, or freewrite—it almost always will respond with concrete imagery. *Imagery* (you will recall from Chapter 1) means a mental picture or other sense impression such as a smell, taste, feel, or sound. We need to use concrete details to communicate an idea so vividly that we create a powerful impression in our readers' minds.

When we discuss an abstract idea, the people with whom we are talking naturally seek to clarify our point by asking, "For example?"

30

DISCOVERY
AND
NARRATION:
MAKING
YOUR POINT
CONCRETELY

In the following passage, note how Virginia Woolf takes the very abstract term *reality* and gives her readers examples of her point in concrete images that communicate what she means by this abstraction.

> What is meant by "reality"? It would seem to be something very erratic, very undependable—now to be found in a dusty road, now in a scrap of newspaper in the street, now in a daffodil in the sun. It lights up a group in a room and stamps some casual saying. It overwhelms one walking home beneath the stars and makes the silent world more real than the world of speech—and then there it is again in an omnibus[1] in the uproar of Piccadilly.[2] Sometimes, too, it seems to dwell in shapes too far away for us to discern what their nature is. But whatever it touches, it fixes and makes permanent. That is what remains over when the skin of the day has been cast into the hedge; that is what is left of past time and of our loves and hates. Now the writer, as I think, has the chance to live more than other people in the presence of this reality. It is his business to find it and collect it and communicate it to the rest of us.

[1] bus   [2] a central, busy section of London

For Thought and Discussion

1. Review the Woolf quotation. Which of her ideas stem from the intellectual-critical part of her thought process and which come from the creative-experiential part?

2. List the concrete images through which Woolf shows us momentary flashes of reality.

3. According to Woolf, what is the writer's job?

Communicating Concretely

In her novels, Virginia Woolf draws upon her own experiences to create the concrete images that show us what she means by "reality." Woolf, for example, uses experiences stemming from the sudden death of her favorite brother in *The Waves* and *Jacob's Room*. Of course, to communicate effectively all writers must draw upon their experiences whether these experiences are from their own lives or from lives they have read or heard about.

Whether writers are scientists describing their research or students trying to determine what they think about an idea, they are involved in a process that leads to discovery. Often we are uncertain about the significance of an experience; through writing we can first come to understand and then to communicate that experience better.

Our creative and critical faculties are a team. As is illustrated in "Two Views of the Mississippi" from Chapter 1, when we use only the intellectual-critical thought process, we are often unaware of how the feeling, experiencing, creative part of our thought process is reacting to an experience. While the intellectual-critical part of us analyzes and generalizes, the creative part of us sees, feels, hears, smells, and tastes experience.

Your turn

Woolf says that reality is what remains of our thoughts and feelings about our experiences. Select an experience that had a significant impact on your life. Write a journal entry about it. Such experiences might include the birth or death of a loved one, or a topic inspired by your clustering about rites of passage in Chapter 1.

Share your journal entry with your peer group. Group members should (1) point out which passages communicate most effectively and (2) explain what makes these passages effective.

Discussion and the Concrete Reality of Generating Ideas

Ideas—even those you later reject—often inspire yet more ideas. As you saw in Chapter 1, three effective methods of generating ideas by yourself are clustering, brainstorming, and freewriting. Because one idea often inspires other ideas, discussing your thoughts with others and allowing your brain to play uncritically with the ideas that occur in discussion will help you to generate yet more ideas.

As you explore your ideas through clustering, brainstorming, or free-writing, you will probably get some insight into what you want to write about a particular topic, but don't ignore the idea-generating strategy of discussion. Because ideas multiply in the presence of others different from themselves, try discussing your topic. Mystery novelist Robert Campbell says that when he talks about his story ideas, he often suddenly knows what is going to happen. For Campbell, as for many writers, discussion often leads to new insight.

Look at the cartoon on the next page and answer the questions that follow. Then note what additional ideas about the cartoon come to mind after you listen to your classmates' responses.

For Thought and Discussion

1. Why has the climber in the cartoon sought out the guru?

2. Based on the discussion of abstract and concrete, answer the following question: Why is it easier to explain how to get a stain out of cotton than it is to explain the meaning of life or to define reality?

3. In class, brainstorm a list of ways you or other people you know use to create meaning in life.

32

DISCOVERY
AND
NARRATION:
MAKING
YOUR POINT
CONCRETELY

"*I can't tell you the meaning of life, son, but I <u>can</u> tell you how to get India ink out of cotton chambray madras.*"

Your turn

After each of these exercises, share your answers with your classmates. As you share, notice how ideas lead to other ideas.

1. Take a few minutes to cluster one of the following abstract words to see what concrete images occur to you: *love, hate, rich, poor, ugly, pretty, old, young, big, little*.

2. Use brainstorming or freewriting to create a concrete example of each of the following abstractions: a dirty refrigerator, an expensive dinner, a violent movie, a boring lecture, a busy day, an important meeting.

3. In "Two Views of the Mississippi" on page 8 in Chapter 1, find an example of an abstract idea and then find a concrete example or image that helps you understand what Twain meant by this abstract idea.

4. In the introductory quotation, Woolf writes of reality. Review her concrete examples of reality, and then create three examples of your own.

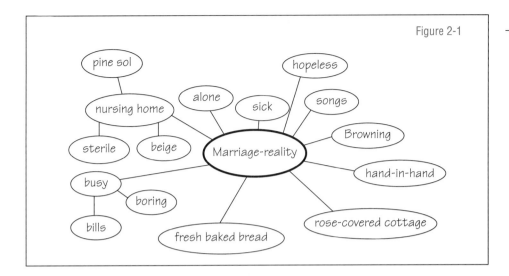

Figure 2-1

33

DISCOVERY
AND
NARRATION:
MAKING
YOUR POINT
CONCRETELY

Explore and discover examples of reality from your own life by clustering or brainstorming. (See Figure 2-1 for a sample cluster of "Reality.")

Writing Inspired by the Reality Cluster

After a few minutes of clustering, the student realized what she wanted to say. She then wrote the following paragraphs.

Marriage

When I think of marriage, I first think of all the songs that promise eternal happiness. In songs, marriage is the gold at the end of the rainbow, the rose-covered cottage filled with the aroma of freshly baked bread. It is walking through life hand-in-hand, always in love.

The reality I see around me is quite different. The song I think of next is the Beatles lyric "Will you still need me when I'm sixty-four?" I think of my grandmother slowly slipping away, sometimes merely forgetful. Sometimes unaccountably angry—even violent. Instead of the rose-covered cottage, there is a nursing home with sterile beige walls and the smell of urine and Pine Sol. There are the old people strapped in wheelchairs staring vacantly.

Teamwork: The Creative and the Critic

Remember that the creative side of us doesn't want to be ordered around, so ordering yourself to produce an idea may not work. Instead, you may need to play with the concept you are exploring. Instead of ordering yourself to produce ideas, sit down and begin to write whatever comes to mind. If your critical brain tells you that this won't work, don't worry. You're normal.

34

**DISCOVERY
AND
NARRATION:
MAKING
YOUR POINT
CONCRETELY**

We all have a critic that makes such suggestions to us. Your job in the initial stages of writing is simply to play with an idea.

Your critical brain will eventually have its chance to monitor your ideas before you share them with others. In fact, your critical brain will eventually have a crucial role to play in polishing your ideas so they communicate effectively. However, when you are generating ideas, the critical part of your intellectual team will get in the way. Just as the defensive squad leaves the football field when the offense has the ball, so too your critical brain must leave the playing field when your creative brain is struggling to score.

Making Abstractions Concrete

One effective way to make an abstract idea such as *reality* concrete is to narrate specific examples of events that illustrate that point concretely. John Updike, author of the following poem, finds in his life the ideas for his novels, short stories, articles, and poems. He discovers in his experiences the concrete examples he uses to develop his ideas. For example, Updike shows his readers his point about an athlete nicknamed Flick through a series of concrete details that make up a story. Updike limits his details to those that illustrate a central point about Flick's life before and after high school.

Poems, because they develop their ideas with imagery, are concrete. They give us specific details to show us the poet's point rather than merely telling us abstractly about the point.

Ex-Basketball Player

Pearl Avenue runs past the high-school lot,
Bends with the trolley tracks, and stops, cut off
Before it has a chance to go two blocks,
At Colonel McComsky Plaza. Berth's Garage
Is on the corner facing west, and there,
Most days, you'll find Flick Webb, who helps Berth out.   6

Flick stands tall among the idiot pumps—
Five on a side, the old bubble-head style,
Their rubber elbows hanging loose and low.
One's nostrils are two S's, and his eyes
An E and O. And one is squat, without
A head at all—more of a football type.   12

Once Flick played for the high-school team, the Wizards.
He was good: in fact, the best. In '46
He bucketed three hundred ninety points,
A county record still. The ball loved Flick.
I saw him rack up thirty-eight or forty
In one home game. His hands were like wild birds.   18

35

**DISCOVERY
AND
NARRATION:
MAKING
YOUR POINT
CONCRETELY**

He never learned a trade, he just sells gas,
Checks oil, and changes flats. Once in a while,
As a gag, he dribbles an inner tube,
But most of us remember anyway.
His hands are fine and nervous on the lug wrench.
It makes no difference to the lug wrench, though.   24

Off work, he hangs around Mae's luncheonette.
Grease-gray and kind of coiled, he plays pinball,
Smokes those thin cigars, nurses lemon phosphates.
Flick seldom says a word to Mae, just nods
Beyond her face toward bright applauding tiers
Of Necco Wafers, Nibs, and Juju Beans.   30

For Thought and Discussion

1. Point out the concrete images in the first two stanzas of this poem. What feeling do these images elicit about Berth's Garage?

2. What concrete images show what Flick was like as an athlete?

3. How do the images in the second stanza relate to Updike's point about Flick?

4. What point is Updike making by contrasting the current Flick with Flick-the-star-athlete? Point out specific passages that illustrate this point concretely.

5. Give an example of information about Flick that Updike omits from this poem because this information is not relevant to the point of the poem.

Denotation, Connotation, and the Concrete

Part of the way artists create the concrete images that communicate feeling is through the emotional impact of hues. We respond differently to a clear, bright blue than to a muddy yellow-green. Similarly, we have an emotional response to a word. This response goes beyond a word's *denotation*—its literal meaning, or dictionary definition. The artist Renoir painted softly round ladies; we think of these ladies as *plump*, comfortable, attractive. Although today's health practitioners might urge them to lose twenty-five or thirty pounds, we do not think of them as *fat*, a word that has a far less attractive connotation but a similar denotation to *plump*.

In making ideas concrete, it is important to consider the connotation of the word we use as well as its denotation. *Connotation* refers to the emotional associations we have with a word or words. For instance, the gas station and the luncheonette in the Updike poem have distinct connotations very different from the phrase *wild birds* at the end of the third stanza.

Because of the importance of connotation, writers must take care to consider their readers' emotional associations with words. Often a writer

36

**DISCOVERY
AND
NARRATION:
MAKING
YOUR POINT
CONCRETELY**

uses connotation deliberately to heighten dramatic effect, as did Updike in comparing the player's hands with wild birds.

For Thought and Discussion

1. Return to "Ex-Basketball Player." Distinguish between the denotation and the connotation of the following:
   a. Trolley tracks
   b. Pinball
   c. Basketball
   d. Bubble-head

2. Working in groups of three or four students, use a dictionary to help contrast the denotation and connotation of the following terms:
   a. Feminist
   b. Black, Afro-American, African-American, white, Caucasian
   c. Liberal
   d. Conservative

3. Which part of your thought process is most actively involved in determining a word's connotation? Which is most involved in the denotation? Support your answer by referring to Chapter 1's discussion of the creative and critical thought process on page 3.

EXPLORING IDEAS IN STORIES

Often it takes us a while to understand the impact of an experience on our lives. Sometimes, if the experience is a complex or profound one, our critical thought process needs help in understanding the importance of the experience to our creative, feeling, experiencing self. To illustrate, let's examine how one person explored an important experience in her life in her journal:

Journal Entry

1   A number of years ago a doctor told me there might be something seriously wrong with my eighteen-month-old son's brain function. He wasn't learning to talk at the usual pace. The doctor wasn't very helpful. He said he didn't have a clue what the problem was. He said my son didn't seem retarded. Perhaps he was aphasic or autistic. I had heard these terms, but I had to scramble to find definitions. I have long believed I should write about this experience. Perhaps I should write an article explaining our successful efforts to help my son; this article would help parents with similar problems.

2   I remember when the doctor first told me I would have to take my son to a medical school for several days of tests. The doctor said there was definitely something seriously wrong with my son.

3   At the time, my critic self responded very strongly.

4   Critic: "Nonsense. Many children, especially boys, don't talk until they are much older than eighteen months. Einstein didn't talk until he was three. Anyway somewhere I read autistic children usually combine acting out with withdrawing. This is a relaxed, affectionate, happy child. The doctor is over-reacting. I totally reject the idea there is anything seriously wrong with my child. I'm not worried."

5   My critic came on loud and strong on this issue—so strong I believed it reflected my "reality"—how I really felt. Then one night, thought processes controlled by my creative self inspired a dream in which my son was alone in a white room, empty except for the hospital bed upon which he lay. He was crying, frightened in the empty room. No one responded to the crying. I wanted to help him, but I couldn't get into the room.

6   It is now many years since I had that dream. After surgery on his soft palate and a great deal of speech therapy, my son is talking normally. But as I write about this time, a lot of details come flooding back into my memory—details about the years of worry, about all the good and bad advice everyone had for me. I had forgotten how upsetting it was when people told me someday my son would talk and talk and talk, and I'd wish for the time when he couldn't talk. Many people said this to me. I tried to listen politely, but I had to keep reminding myself these people were well-meaning. I knew I would never wish for the time my son couldn't talk.

7   Before I started writing, I was sure this was a time that is in an emotionally safe section of my memory. Then I suddenly noticed tears streaming down my cheeks.

8   Evidently a powerful part of me doesn't view this experience as an interesting intellectual exercise. A part of me views this with anguish I have never fully recognized.

For Thought and Discussion

1. What concrete details from the dream create imagery to show how the author felt?

2. When the author started freewriting, what did she think her point would be?

3. What important discovery did she make in freewriting?

4. During writing, what memories recurred that the author had previously forgotten?

Story Telling: Doing What Comes Naturally

The idea of discovering and communicating reality by narrating incidents as stories is deeply embedded in human nature. Note that the previous journal entry is really a story. Its author naturally turned to a narrative to make sense of her experience. Columbia University professor Carolyn Heilbrun, who writes mystery novels under the pen name of Amanda Cross, uses stories to illustrate many of her ideas about the importance of feminist principles in women's lives. In her nonfiction book *Writing a Woman's Life*

38

**DISCOVERY
AND
NARRATION:
MAKING
YOUR POINT
CONCRETELY**

(1988), Heilbrun says: "What matters is that lives do not serve as models; only stories do that." Lives are vast expanses of time filled with many events. Stories, because they are focused, illustrate a central point.

In ancient times, long before they could read and write, humans told each other stories which they imagined using their natural, creative thought processes. In most of these stories an abstract principle is made concrete. For example, in the Old English epic *Beowulf*, evil monsters wreak havoc, but a good and brave hero eventually slays the monsters—just as Dirty Harry destroys the crooks in the modern-day version of this narrative.

Also ancient is the concept that we communicate most effectively when we make abstract ideas concrete. By their very nature, stories are concrete. They clearly and vividly examine abstract ideas such as what is the purpose of life: Should our goal be to pursue self-centered happiness, status, money, and adventure, or to serve others? Walt Disney used story-telling techniques to analyze the impact of being a celebrity on his day-to-day life.

Often in the course of a conversation, speech, or essay, a narrative is the most effective method to make a point. From parables such as that about the Good Samaritan to fables such as "The Fox and the Grapes," narratives have the added bonus of enhancing interest in and giving concreteness to the point you are trying to make. Narratives show their readers the concrete information necessary to make sense of experience.

Unity: Sticking to Your Story

When you write a narrative, it is important to keep in mind a point Chet Meyers makes in *Teaching Students to Think Critically:* "There is nothing more boring than a rambling, anecdotally burdened professor telling his or her sad tales. The very power of stories makes it important that they be carefully chosen to teach or illustrate a point."

As you read the following two excerpts from narratives, notice that the authors select their concrete details carefully. They do not include all the details that occur to them about a person or event. Instead, they select those details that illustrate the central point of their writing. For example, in "Ex-Basketball Player," we do not know what Flick eats for breakfast or what kind of soap he uses. Updike would include such information only if it reinforced the central point of the poem. Similarly, Maya Angelou, in the following narrative, carefully limits her details to those relevant to the point.

A PROFESSIONAL WRITER AT WORK

Maya Angelou is a contemporary African-American author who grew up in strictly segregated Stamps, Arkansas, a society in which minorities were regarded as second-class citizens regardless of their financial status, intelligence, or character. In relating the following incident from her past, Angelou uses vivid images painted with concrete details to show us a point she did not fully understand until long after it occurred. Because she writes for an audience not familiar with the culture in which she grew up, she begins her narrative by reflecting on the importance of using proper titles in that culture.

Confrontation
from I Know Why the Caged Bird Sings

1   The impudent child was detested by God and a shame to its parents and could bring destruction to its house and line. All adults had to be addressed as Mister, Missus, Miss, Auntie, Cousin, Unk, Uncle, Bubbah, Sister, Brother, and a thousand other appellations indicating familial relationship and the lowliness of the addressor.

2   Everyone I knew respected these customary laws, except for the powhitetrash children.

3   Some families of powhitetrash lived on Momma's farm land behind the school. Sometimes a gaggle of them came to the Store, filling the whole room, chasing out the air and even changing the well-known scents. The children crawled over the shelves and into the potato and onion bins, twanging all the time in their sharp voices like cigar-box guitars. They took liberties in my Store that I would never dare. Since Momma told us that the less you say to whitefolks (or even powhitetrash) the better, Bailey and I would stand, solemn, quiet, in the displaced air. But if one of the playful apparitions got close to us, I pinched it. Partly out of angry frustration and partly because I didn't believe in its flesh reality.

4   They called my uncle by his first name and ordered him around the Store. He, to my crying shame, obeyed them in his limping dip-straight-dip fashion.

5   My grandmother, too, followed their orders, except that she didn't seem to be servile because she anticipated their needs.

6   "Here's sugar, Miz Potter, and here's baking powder. You didn't buy soda last month, you'll probably be needing some."

7   Momma always directed her statements to the adults, but sometimes, oh painful sometimes, the grimy, snotty-nosed girls would answer her.

8   "Naw, Annie . . ."—to Momma? Who owned the land they lived on? Who forgot more than they would ever learn? If there was any justice in the world, God should strike them dumb at once!—"Just give us some extry sody crackers, and some more mackerel."

9   At least they never looked in her face, or I never caught them doing so. Nobody with a smidgen of training, not even the worst roustabout, would look right in a grown person's face. It meant the person was trying to take the words out before they were formed. The dirty little children didn't do that, but they threw their orders around the Store like lashes from a cat-o'-nine-tails.

10   When I was around ten years old, those scruffy children caused me the most painful and confusing experience I had ever had with my grandmother.

11   One summer morning, after I had swept the dirt yard of leaves, spearmint-gum wrappers and Vienna-sausage labels, I raked the yellow-red dirt, and

40

**DISCOVERY
AND
NARRATION:
MAKING
YOUR POINT
CONCRETELY**

made half-moons carefully, so that the design stood out clearly and mask-like. I put the rake behind the Store and came through the back of the house to find Grandmother on the front porch in her big, wide white apron. The apron was so stiff by virtue of the starch that it could have stood alone. Momma was admiring the yard, so I joined her. It truly looked like a flat redhead that had been raked with a big-toothed comb. Momma didn't say anything but I knew she liked it. She looked over toward the school principal's house and to the right at Mr. McElroy's. She was hoping one of those community pillars would see the design before the day's business wiped it out. Then she looked upward to the school. My head had swung with hers, so at just about the same time we saw a troop of the powhitetrash kids marching over the hill and down by the side of the school.

12   I looked to Momma for direction. She did an excellent job of sagging from her waist down, but from the waist up she seemed to be pulling for the top of the oak tree across the road. Then she began to moan a hymn. Maybe not to moan, but the tune was so slow and the meter so strange that she could have been moaning. She didn't look at me again. When the children reached halfway down the hill, halfway to the Store, she said without turning, "Sister, go on inside."

13   I wanted to beg her, "Momma, don't wait for them. Come on inside with me. If they come in the Store, you go to the bedroom and let me wait on them. They only frighten me if you're around. Alone I know how to handle them." But of course I couldn't say anything, so I went in and stood behind the screen door.

14   Before the girls got to the porch, I heard their laughter crackling and popping like pine logs in a cooking stove. I suppose my lifelong paranoia was born in those cold, molasses-slow minutes. They came finally to stand on the ground in front of Momma. At first they pretended seriousness. Then one of them wrapped her right arm in the crook of her left, pushed out her mouth and started to hum. I realized that she was aping my grandmother. Another said, "Naw, Helen, you ain't standing like her. This here's it." Then she lifted her chest, folded her arms and mocked that strange carriage that was Annie Henderson. Another laughed. "Naw, you can't do it. Your mouth ain't pooched out enough. It's like this."

15   I thought about the rifle behind the door, but I knew I'd never be able to hold it straight and the .410, our sawed-off shotgun, which stayed loaded and was fired every New Year's night, was locked in the trunk and Uncle Willie had the key on his chain. Through the fly-specked screen-door, I could see that the arms of Momma's apron jiggled from the vibrations of her humming. But her knees seemed to have locked as if they would never bend again.

16   She sang on. No louder than before, but no softer either. No slower or faster.

17   The dirt of the girls' cotton dresses continued on their legs, feet, arms, and faces to make them all of a piece. Their greasy uncolored hair hung down, uncombed, with a grimy finality. I knelt to see them better, to remember them for all time. The tears that slipped down my dress left unsurprising dark spots, and made the front yard blurry and even more unreal. The world had taken a deep breath and was having doubts about continuing to revolve.

41

DISCOVERY
AND
NARRATION:
MAKING
YOUR POINT
CONCRETELY

18   The girls had tired of mocking Momma and turned to other means of agitation. One crossed her eyes, stuck her thumbs in both sides of her mouth and said, "Look here, Annie." Grandmother hummed on and the apron strings trembled. I wanted to throw a handful of black pepper in their faces, to throw lye on them, to scream that they were dirty, scummy peckerwoods, but I knew I was as clearly imprisoned behind the scene as the actors outside were confined to their roles.

19   One of the smaller girls did a kind of puppet dance while her fellow clowns laughed at her. But the tall one, who was almost a woman, said something very quietly, which I couldn't hear. They all moved backward from the porch, still watching Momma. For an awful second I thought they were going to throw a rock at Momma, who seemed (except for the apron strings) to have turned into stone herself. But the big girl turned her back, bent down and put her hands flat on the ground—she didn't pick up anything. She simply shifted her weight and did a hand stand.

20   Her dirty bare feet and long legs went straight for the sky. Her dress fell down around her shoulders, and she had on no drawers. The slick pubic hair made a brown triangle where her legs came together. She hung in the vacuum of that lifeless morning for only a few seconds, then wavered and tumbled. The other girls clapped her on the back and slapped their hands.

21   Momma changed her song to "Bread of Heaven, bread of Heaven, feed me till I want no more."

22   I found that I was praying too. How long would Momma hold out? What new indignity would they think of to subject her to? Would I be able to stay out of it? What would Momma really like me to do?

23   Then they were moving out of the yard, on their way to town. They bobbled their heads and shook their slack behinds and turned, one at a time:

24   " 'Bye, Annie."

25   " 'Bye, Annie."

26   " 'Bye, Annie."

27   Momma never turned her head or unfolded her arms, but she stopped singing and said, " 'Bye, Miz Helen, 'bye, Miz Ruth, 'bye, Miz Eloise."

28   I burst. A firecracker July-the-Fourth burst. How could Momma call them Miz? The mean nasty things. Why couldn't she have come inside the sweet, cool store when we saw them breasting the hill? What did she prove? And then if they were dirty, mean and impudent, why did Momma have to call them Miz?

29   She stood another whole song through and then opened the screen door to look down on me crying in rage. She looked until I looked up. Her face was a brown moon that shone on me. She was beautiful. Something had happened out there, which I couldn't completely understand, but I could see that she was happy. Then she bent down and touched me as mothers of the church "lay hands on the sick and afflicted" and I quieted.

30   "Go wash your face, Sister." And she went behind the candy counter and hummed, "Glory, glory, hallelujah, when I lay my burden down."

31   I threw the well water on my face and used the weekday handkerchief to blow my nose. Whatever the contest had been out front I knew Momma had won.

42

**DISCOVERY
AND
NARRATION:
MAKING
YOUR POINT
CONCRETELY**

32   I took the rake back to the front yard. The smudged footprints were easy to erase. I worked for a long time on my new design and laid the rake behind the wash pot. When I came in the Store, I took Momma's hand and we both walked outside to look at the pattern.

33   It was a large heart with lots of hearts growing smaller inside, and piercing from the outside rim to the smallest heart was an arrow. Momma said, "Sister, that's right pretty." Then she turned back to the Store and resumed, "Glory, glory, hallelujah, when I lay my burden down."

For Thought and Discussion

1. During this confrontation, what does the narrator discover about herself and Momma?

2. List the images—the concrete details of description and action—that show Angelou's point about the "powhitetrash" children.

3. List the images that help to show Angelou's point about Momma.

4. Using your imagination, brainstorm a list of information about this incident that Angelou omitted because it was not relevant to her point.

THE BALANCE BETWEEN EXPLORATION AND UNITY

As we mentioned earlier, narratives are "single-minded": they have a central point, and all concrete material illustrates that central point. Through the Chapter 1 exercises, you discovered that your creative thought process doesn't always stick to a single point when you unleash it to explore a subject. Similarly, when you start to retell a story, one idea will lead to another—as you saw with the clustering, freewriting, and brainstorming and as frequently happens in discussions.

Let's say you want to tell a story about an important rite of passage—graduating from high school, for example. As you prewrite about that fateful day when you came to terms with that reality, you may also recall that during the graduation week ceremonies you were assigned to sit next to Won Kim, a biking fanatic. You had never paid any attention to the biking fanatic before that, but as you talked during graduation rehearsals, you became friends. You decided to try biking, and biking has become your avocation. Every day you ride at least ten miles. Someday you want to have your own bicycle touring business. Won now works as a guide in Europe every summer for a bicycling business based in Vermont.

If your point is graduation as a rite of passage, you will have to do a good deal of backpedaling to justify the inclusion of information about Won—or you will have to eliminate that material. When you write a narrative, you first must discover an experience that interests you. Yet once you have selected such an experience, you still may not know what point you wish to make. Most of our experiences are complex enough that we could write several narratives about them.

Once you decide upon the central point of your story through clustering, brainstorming, freewriting, or a combination of these techniques, be alert to the tendency to go off on tangents. It is possible that a better idea than your original idea will occur to you as you write: remember, ideas lead to more ideas. If you discover better ideas as you write, you certainly can decide to change direction and write about them. Do keep in mind, however, that eventually you need to decide which point you want to make in your essay.

Your critical brain gets involved in helping to keep your central point in mind. To aid your critical-analytical brain in making sure that all the material you include is relevant to your central point, try writing a sentence or two to remind you of that point. This will give you a reference to keep you on track. Note that discovering and developing a central point is a back-and-forth process. As you write, ideas will continue to occur to you. Should you decide to change your central point, then of course you will need to change your reference sentence.

When you revise your early drafts, watch for your tendency to include material not relevant to the point you are trying to make in your essay.

Organization: Chronological Order

In the initial stages of exploring your experience, you need not worry about the critical thinking task of organization. Simply let your creative thought processes decide where to go with your story. Let your ideas flow. At first, bits and pieces of information may pop willy-nilly into your consciousness. Once you have explored your subject through clustering, brainstorming, or freewriting and discovered what you want to say, then you should write your first draft, allowing your critical brain to red-flag any material that seems irrelevant.

When you have an initial draft of your essay, it is time to examine the organization you have used. You are ready to start the revision process. This is the time to put on your critic's hat and get into your readers' shoes, an outfit that would clearly restrict your creativity if you donned it when you were trying to discover ideas.

As in the journal entry about the son with speech difficulties, stories are usually told in *chronological order*, that is, in the order in which they occurred. Occasionally, of course, you will need to insert background information to clarify your point, or you might need to backtrack to fill in some important details. Ask yourself if your readers will follow your point. A good way to gauge whether or not your point is clear is to read your essay to a person typical of your intended audience.

44

DISCOVERY
AND
NARRATION:
MAKING
YOUR POINT
CONCRETELY

Audience Awareness

Your instructor may define your audience for you. If not, you need to determine for whom you are writing. What will your audience know about your subject? For example, early in *I Know Why the Caged Bird Sings*, Maya Angelou lets her audience know about the cultural, social, and political realities of life in a segregated community in the South in the 1930s.

Similarly, you need to ask yourself what background material or vocabulary your audience needs to understand your point. For example, if your point involves an understanding of the geography of Central Park and your audience includes people who have never escaped the confines of California, you will need to include enough information so that audience can follow your point. On the other hand, you do not want to waste time and risk boring or insulting your audience by overexplaining a point that will be obvious to them.

For Thought and Discussion

1. What information in "Ex-Basketball Player" (page 34) needs further explanation for an audience of first-year college students in the 1990s?

2. In addition to the information in the first paragraph of the excerpt from *I Know Why the Caged Bird Sings*, what information does Maya Angelou include that is directed toward audiences not familiar with the culture of Stamps during her childhood?

Transition Time

Transitions are signpost words that help keep your reader from getting lost. When you are revising your initial draft, check to make sure you have included such signposts where necessary. Since stories are usually written in chronological order, the transitions you will use most frequently in a narrative are the transitions that indicate time sequence.

Signal to your readers where you are in your time sequence with such transition words as *after, always, at the same time, before, by then, later, meanwhile, next, now, previously, prior to, subsequently, then, until then, when,* and *while.*

Sometimes a single word or phrase will not be an adequate transition. You might have to write a sentence or more to ensure that your reader follows your point. For example, you might say "after the prisoner had reached shore safely" or "as she reached the ledge just below the summit."

We will discuss transitions at greater length later in Chapter 4. For now, remember to use appropriate time transitional words where necessary to help your readers follow the sequence of events in your narrative.

For Thought and Discussion   **45**

**DISCOVERY
AND
NARRATION:
MAKING
YOUR POINT
CONCRETELY**

1. Point out the transitions Maya Angelou uses in "Confrontation" to ensure that we follow her narrative.

2. Discuss how those transitions keep the narrative moving.

WRITING ASSIGNMENT

Write a narrative that illustrates a central point—just as Maya Angelou illustrated a central point in "Confrontation." Note that you are not going to merely recall as much as you can about an episode; rather you are going to select details in your narrative to illustrate a central abstract idea. Your own life and the lives of those around you contain plenty of material for such a story. In this essay be sure to do the following:

1. Use a prewriting technique to help you explore your ideas.

a. Begin by brainstorming a list of all the experiences that you think might be appropriate. During this stage do not criticize or evaluate your ideas; simply record them.

b. Next reread your list, eliminating those experiences that seem least promising as topics. Discuss your list with classmates. In your group discussions, ask your group to identify the abstract idea they think that you are attempting to illustrate. Remember, even if two people decide to write about a similar topic, their experiences will still be different.

c. If after these steps you still are unsure which experience you wish to write about, spend a few minutes clustering or freewriting about the experiences on your list. This will help you decide.

2. Once you have selected a topic, cluster or brainstorm to help jog your memory for concrete details. Ask yourself what sounds, smells, tastes, and sights were part of your experience. If you aren't accustomed to using a prewriting technique to inspire ideas, you will be astounded at how much you remember by allowing your brain to play with ideas uncritically. Record sensations of touch; for example, was the atmosphere warm or cool? Include specific examples that show your reader your story. When people talk, use dialogue. Don't just say "colorful." Show your readers the van you painted purple with orange and red flowers. In this step, you may once again wish to discuss your experiences with classmates. Talking about your experience may help you discover its significance. The questions your classmates ask will indicate what kinds of information you must include for them to understand your point.

3. When you begin to write your essay, be careful to stay with the central point of your story. Do not get sidetracked. Your creative brain works

46

DISCOVERY
AND
NARRATION:
MAKING
YOUR POINT
CONCRETELY

by association, so you may be tempted to digress. While you are exploring your subject in your initial prewriting, digression is normal. Once you decide upon your point, however, put your critical brain to work making sure you stick to your central point. This means, of course, that you will not be able to use all the ideas you generated in steps 2 and 3. Use only material relevant to your point.

4. When you use the prewriting techniques discussed in Chapter 1, you are not concentrating on coming up with a specific number of words. Rather, you are concentrating on generating and then illustrating an idea. For writing assignments, however, students need an approximate goal. This essay should contain approximately 500 words. After you complete your prewriting exercises, if you discover your paper is only 300 words long, you need to play with your idea longer. Return to a prewriting exercise to more fully explore your idea.

5. After you have written your essay, put it away for a day or two; distance helps foster objectivity. Then go back and revise your essay's content. Ask yourself if your concrete details actually illustrate the point they are supposed to illustrate.

6. When you are happy with the contents of your paper, proofread it for mechanical errors.

Suggestions for Topics

First experiences are good candidates for narrative essays—taking your first driving lesson, buying your first car, dealing with your first accident, going on your first date.

Experiences that involve rites of passage are good topics. For example, you might write about leaving home for the first time, about the birth of a child, or about the death of a beloved person or pet.

Conquests make good narratives—overcoming your fear of heights or your fear of flying (or of writing essays), conquering a mountain, overcoming a handicap.

Read the student star essays at the end of the chapter before you begin to write; they will help inspire your creative brain.

An Important Note about Revising

As you learned in Chapter 1, we block the flow of new ideas when we try to edit our ideas as we write. However, we eventually need to edit both our ideas and our mechanics. For example, in this assignment, you are asked to illustrate a single central point. So you must check to make sure you have not gotten off track and introduced an unrelated idea, and then you need to make sure you have given specific examples that show your readers your point.

47

**DISCOVERY
AND
NARRATION:
MAKING
YOUR POINT
CONCRETELY**

In addition, you must examine your essay for mechanical errors. Note that you will have to reread your paper several times in the revision and editing process. Once the content of your essay is in order, you need to check for mechanical mistakes such as mistakes in spelling, diction, punctuation, and grammar. As you generate and organize your ideas, if you stop to check for such mechanical errors, you will be distracted from your task and you might block the flow of your ideas. Once you have finished capturing those ideas, then it is time to ensure that the mechanics of your writing are those of standard English.

Proofreading Tips

1. To give yourself a fresh perspective, proofread your papers out loud—preferably to a friend, classmate, or small group of classmates. Reading papers aloud will help you to listen for what you actually wrote as opposed to what you thought you wrote. In addition, reading your essays to other people will help you gauge whether or not your message is clear.

2. To help your concentration and help you spot typographical and spelling errors, read your papers backward line for line; place a ruler or sheet of paper under each line before you read it.

3. Another error-catching technique is to exchange papers with a friend or classmate and have that person point out trouble spots. However, do not automatically make the changes this reader suggests. Rather, think about the suggestions and check their validity; look up suspect words in a dictionary and mechanical rules in a handbook.

Peer Editing: Help! For Further Work

Peer editing is a process during which students read each other's papers and make constructive suggestions to help the author improve the writing. Peer editing has several advantages. It is, of course, easier to be objective about the writing of others than it is to be objective about our own writing; peer editing provides an opportunity for such an objective view. Furthermore, the direct feedback of the peer editing sessions helps authors better understand the reactions of their audiences.

To help you hone your peer editing skills, each chapter in this text contains a "Help! For Further Work" essay. Working with these essays will help you recognize the elements of good writing and alert you to possible pitfalls in your own writing.

48

DISCOVERY
AND
NARRATION:
MAKING
YOUR POINT
CONCRETELY

Read the following draft of an essay written for this chapter's writing assignment. Then, working with a group of your classmates, answer the questions following the essay.

The Race

1   The sun was very hot that day, hotter than any sun I have ever seen. The coaches were nervous that the heat would affect our races and were trying to encourage us. Hopefully we could do our best. They reminded us of the horror they made us face daily after school, no matter how tired we were. The nine-mile runs to the water tower, the runs on Veterans Park and worse yet the UCSB relay. I often wondered who the cruel person was that discovered the novel idea of making five-person teams and dividing the track into four one-hundreds. The way it worked is as follows: five people would spread themselves out on the track, two at the starting line and the other three at the chalked-off spots. The first person would take off at a hundred percent and pass on to the second and so on, so to make it all the way around the track we had to make four successful passes and four successful times. After months of this training, I felt the coaches need not worry. I can't say I wasn't worried. Usually I worry about almost everything from what I said at the last party to what I should wear to the next one, so it isn't surprising I was worried.

2   Well, anyway, it was my first time to run a coed relay as well as my first time to run the four-mile-death relay. Each runner in a series of four runs a mile that is four laps long.

3   Kimmy was up first and left at the bang of the gun. She ran a successful mile at 5:48. Next Jason went, he ran a very good time with a 5:02 then it was my turn. I remember grabbing the baton as it came flying into my hands at great speed. As if it were a bullet just fired from one of Rambo's machine guns. Not only was I passed the baton, but a great amount of Jason's perspiration as well. I felt as though I was running the track holding a giant candy cane left in the sun to melt. It was hot and sticky. I was hot and sticky. My jersey clung to me making it look as if the name of the school had been tattooed to my chest. My legs went round and round the track. I thought the race would never end, but at last it did. At last it was over. I have never been so hot and tired in my life.

Peer Editing Checklist

Each peer editing group should respond to the following questions for the preceding essay, "The Race." When the group has practiced peer editing on "The Race," it should go on to work with papers written by group members.

Since it is difficult for more than two readers to share a paper, the writer should submit enough copies of each paper so that everyone in each peer editing group has access to a paper.

1. Indicate any ideas, passages, or other aspects of this essay you thought were especially effective. Positive reinforcement is a powerful tool.

2. What is the central point this narrative illustrates?

3. Point out any places where you do not understand how the narrative illustrates this central point.

4. List the concrete details that develop this central point.

5. Point out any places where dialogue could be used effectively if such places exist.

6. Ask the author about any concrete details you would like to know to strengthen or clarify the point for you.

7. Ask about any passages where you are confused about the time sequence.

When writers have revised the contents of the essay to their satisfaction and are ready for feedback about mechanics, point out but do not correct any problems you suspect exist with spelling, grammar, and punctuation. It is the writer's responsibility to make such corrections.

49

DISCOVERY
AND
NARRATION:
MAKING
YOUR POINT
CONCRETELY

Model Editing Practice

To fully appreciate the final, polished version of a paper, it is helpful to examine the author's initial effort. Read the following early draft of "Jet Blast Blues," and then respond to the "For Thought and Discussion" section following it before you read the polished version in "Student Stars."

An Early Draft of "Jet Blast Blues"

1   I don't think I have ever been so confused as I was the day I had to make the decision whether to reenlist or get out of the military. I wanted to get out really bad; military life wasn't agreeing with me any longer. I had already spent nine years of my life under Uncle Sam's wings and needed a change. Although, I wanted to get out, I was scared to do so. The military was my security blanket. Another concern was the fact that in just eleven more years I could retire. The thought of throwing away nine years and starting over seemed like a pretty stupid idea. Although the fright was overwhelming, all I could think or talk about was turning in my combat boots and starting a new life. I wanted relief—relief away from the everyday bullshit the military dishes out.

2   I think what frightened me most of all was the loss of job security. It felt good knowing that paycheck would be in there every two weeks and that I would not get fired or laid off. My last three years in the military were spent in Okinawa, Japan, so I had no idea of the job situation in the States. To compound the confusion, the only marketable skill I possessed was aircraft maintenance, and I knew there was not a high demand for fighter jet mechanics in the civilian world.

3   Another fear was the loss of medical benefits. I had been through a series of operations while in the military and knew more might be needed. The astronomical cost of medical surgery in the civilian world shocked me.

50

DISCOVERY
AND
NARRATION:
MAKING
YOUR POINT
CONCRETELY

4 With all the frightening thoughts swirling through my head, I still knew I wanted and needed to get out. I needed to get away from that military bullshit. I liked the money I was making, but I hated the job I was doing. Twelve and fourteen hour days on the blazing hot flight line with jet blasts blowing in my face is not my idea of a good time.

5 I also had four or five different bosses barking orders; this made work seem too chaotic. A typical day on the flight line for a jet mechanic begins with a 35-10 inspection of uniform appearance. Mechanics were always reprimanded for having oil and hydraulic fluid stains on their uniforms. This made no sense to me—mechanics naturally get dirty and those kinds of stains don't wash out. After the embarrassment of the inspection, work assignments are made. I remember with disgust one assignment I was given to drop the engine bay doors on a 235, and after I finished I was told they made a mistake. Put the doors up and drop them on a different 235. All that work for nothing. I was so mad I told the sergeant, "Ya know, Brood, they ruined a perfectly good asshole when they put teeth in your mouth."

6 I signed the paperwork for my separation on January 5th. They set my separation date for March 17th. I felt great, but I worried if I had made the right decision. I've been a civilian now for two years. I still haven't established the security I want, but I am happy. Civilian life has its share of bull, but it is not comparable to the bull I experienced in the Air Force. I'm glad I made the decision. I feel a lot better now about myself. —Patricia Smith

For Thought and Discussion

1. Make a list of possible topics the author could focus on in this essay.

2. Suggest changes the author should make for this essay to meet the criteria for a narrative theme.

3. Some of the language is profane. Should the author keep this language or revise it to make it less profane? Defend your answer.

4. Point out places where a civilian audience needs more information to better understand and appreciate the author's point.

5. Make a list of the changes the author made in the following revised edition of "Jet Blast Blues," and then compare the changes to those you suggested in response to number 2. Explain whether or not you think the author has adequately revised her essay.

STUDENT STARS

The students who wrote these essays did the following:

1. Prewriting
2. Writing

3. Revision of content

4. Proofreading and revision of mechanics.

51

DISCOVERY
AND
NARRATION:
MAKING
YOUR POINT
CONCRETELY

Jet Blast Blues: Revised Edition

1   I do not think I have ever been so confused as I was the day I had to make the decision whether to reenlist or get out of the military. I wanted out badly. I had spent nine years of my life under Uncle Sam's wings, and I desperately wanted to fly by myself. Certainly the thought of throwing away nine years of seniority along with a secure paycheck and excellent medical benefits seemed stupid.

2   However, I needed to get away from the military baloney that came with the life of a jet mechanic—twelve- and fourteen-hour days on the blazing hot flight line with jet blast scorching my face was not my idea of a rewarding career. Neither was crawling around on airplanes with metal skins so hot you could fry an egg on them. How I hated my job!

3   A typical day on the flight line for a jet mechanic began with a 35-10 (uniform appearance) inspection. Flight chief desk jockeys were always reprimanding mechanics for having oil and hydraulic fluid on their uniforms. This was frustrating to me: of course a mechanic gets dirty, and all the Stain Sticks and Dynamo in the country won't budge those stains. After the embarrassment of the inspection, work assignments were given. I can remember with disgust one typical assignment.

4   "Sergeant Smith, drop the engine bay doors on 235. We have to roll the engines out. Its compressor stalled yesterday," Sergeant Brood said. We referred to our airplanes by tail numbers.

5   "OK," I said.

6   Two-three-five was about a quarter mile out on the flight line. I picked up my seventy-five-pound toolbox and headed toward the airplane—the whole way wishing that toolbox had wheels.

7   I crawled under 235 (its belly was about four feet from the ground) and started unbolting the doors. Dropping engine bay doors is not an easy task. The F4E aircraft has two engines, each having three doors. Each door weighs about seventy pounds and is fastened with six bolts which are safety wired together to ensure they do not vibrate loose while in flight. Removing this safety wire almost always results in slashes and jabs to the hands.

8   After receiving my share of cuts and jabs dislodging the safety wire, I started to extricate the bolts. Oil and sweat oozed into the cuts which sent searing protests to my aching brain. The first five doors came down with relative ease, but when the last bolt on the sixth door let loose, I lost my grip, and the door swung down knocking me to the ground. As I crawled painfully out, Sergeant Brood yelled and motioned for me to come over to him.

9   "Sorry, Sergeant Smith, I gave you the wrong tail number. Put the doors back up on 235 and drop 236's," he said.

10   Bruised and furious, I felt my muscles tighten. Blood rushed to my head, and everything around me glowed with a reddish tint. *Damn I hate this job.*

11   Sergeant Brood knew I was about to explode. "If you want to remain a sergeant, I advise you to not say a word. Just do as I say," he said with a superior smirk.

52

**DISCOVERY
AND
NARRATION:
MAKING
YOUR POINT
CONCRETELY**

12   This made me even more furious. *The man is threatening my rank, and he is the one who made the mistake,* I fumed. Before I knew it, a disparaging remark involving some of his cherished body parts had somehow escaped my lips.

13   For my comments I was given a letter of reprimand and put on three months of extra duty. The duty consisted of four hours each day cleaning around picnic areas on base—after a grueling day as a flight mechanic.

14   And thus ended another of the days that prompted me to hang up my uniform—hydraulic stains and all—for the last time.   —Patricia Smith

The Chip in the Windshield

1   A few years ago I was in the market for a new truck. After much searching and dickering, I found a plain white, economical Ford Courier. It was six years old, but it was clean, and it had only 36,000 miles on its odometer. Best of all, it cost only $2,000. The only thing that really annoyed me about the truck was an intrusive chip in the windshield—right in the middle of the driver's view of the road. The chip was so annoying that I strongly suspected some person with a lot more money than I might have traded the truck in out of sheer frustration with that one flaw. Promising myself that when finances permitted I would replace the windshield, I paid for the truck and drove it home.

2   At that time I was stationed in Biloxi, Mississippi, a quiet area except for its rambunctious summer and fall visitors, hurricanes. To top it all off, the one bedroom cottage I rented was right on the beach, and I was unable to secure tenant's insurance.

3   My landlords, Audrey and Tom, were sympathetic to my uninsured plight and eagerly offered the hurricane safety advice gleaned in their fifty-plus years of living on the Mississippi coast. When Hurricane Elena was about to make landfall, Tom told me, ''Yeah, she'll come in just like Freddy [Hurricane Frederick] did. If you go up on base to the shelter, just park away from the trees and on the northeast corner of a building, so the gravel doesn't blow down on your truck.''

4   Soon there I was, sitting in a shelter on base literally watching a Kawasaki 750 blow across the courtyard like a discarded Styrofoam cup. Gravel, trees, Kawasakis—a parade of debris roared past. The wind howled, and the lights went out.

5   When the storm blew over and we were released from the shelter, I drove through Biloxi on my way home, surveying the damage and thinking about fishing my stereo out of the gulf. Just as Audrey and Tom had promised, however, my truck had survived unscathed, snug in its northeast corner. My house, which had weathered storms since the Civil War, also came out undamaged.

6   Many other people had not fared so well. Almost every window on base, whether in a car or in a building, needed to be replaced, and we were without electricity off base for nearly a week. The National Guard was called out to prevent looting, and a 9 p.m. curfew was announced.

7   In the face of all the damage from the storm, a number of my acquaintances encouraged me to submit a claim to the government for my windshield. At long last it could be replaced—at Uncle Sam's expense. The base security

police went around writing down license plate numbers of vehicles damaged by the storm. It was a very simple matter to add my truck to that list.

8   I must confess that the idea was tempting, but I just wasn't comfortable with the idea. Besides, I considered myself very lucky for not incurring more damage. Everyone seemed to think I was foolish, but like George Washington, I could not tell the lie.

9   It's now three years later. I still have that truck, and yes, the chip is still right there in the middle of the windshield. I can't move it to the left; I can't move it to the right. It's always right there in the middle. But, you know, every time I see that chip, instead of feeling annoyed, I feel strengthened.

—Skip Davis

EXPLORATION AND UNITY: DISCOVERING A UNIFYING POINT

One of the paradoxes of writing is that we should know our topic well; however, when we know a topic well, there are often many aspects of that topic we could write about. Our first writing step in such cases is to discover just which direction we want to take, what points we wish to make of the many we could make.

This chapter will focus on writing about a person because such a topic provides an excellent opportunity to confront the choices writers must make. As Robert Burns put it, most people "have enough hooks and crooks, depths and shallows, good and evil to puzzle the devil"—and fill several volumes. Since this chapter's assignment is to write a 500-word essay about a person, the chapter will discuss methods of discovering and focusing on a central point and then developing that point in a convincing fashion.

The length of an essay is one of the factors that helps to determine which aspect a writer selects. For instance, Cynthia Griffin Wolff spent years researching the life of Emily Dickinson. Then Wolff wrote *Emily Dickinson*, a 537-page biography that explores the influences leading Dickinson to write her remarkable poetry. Still, Wolff had to cut and sift. Despite her lengthy biography, she says there is much more to write about the influences that shaped Dickinson's ideas.

Through prewriting techniques such as brainstorming, clustering, free-writing, and discussing, we can narrow our topic; we can discover which point we wish to make about a person. Once we decide upon a point, we writers then show our readers that our point is a valid one by creating vivid images and concrete details. In *Pentimento*, from which the following excerpt is taken, playwright Lillian Hellman uses such vivid images and details to make her point: that writing would help her reflect about the people in her life and discover their significance to her.

> Old paint on canvas, as it ages, sometimes becomes transparent. When that happens it is possible, in some pictures, to see the original lines: a tree will show through a woman's dress, a child makes way for a dog, a large boat is no longer on an open sea. That is called *pentimento*, because the painter "repented," changed his mind. Perhaps it would be as well to say that the old conception, replaced by a later choice, is a way of seeing and then seeing again.
>
> That is all I mean about the people in this book. The paint has aged now and I wanted to see what was there for me once, what is there for me now.

The first two chapters of this book emphasize the idea that writing is first a process of discovery. On any subject we often have a multitude of thoughts, feelings, and other impressions that are not directly related to each other except that they were inspired by the subject we are writing about. In this initial exploration phase of writing, the writer should listen to the ideas that bubble up from the subconscious mind, to see "what was there for me once, what is there for me now," in the words of Lillian Hellman.

Like painting, writing provides an opportunity for vision—and later for revision—for examining and then reexamining our thoughts. While writers may have begun writing with one idea in mind, during the exploration phase they may well change their minds or at least fine-tune their thinking. Eventually, however, there comes a time that a focused central idea should crystallize. This idea gives a piece of writing unity and direction.

As you read the following poem, notice how poet John Frederick Nims sorts through a variety of images of his "clumsiest dear" to arrive at a unified point about her.

Love Poem

My clumsiest dear, whose hands shipwreck vases,
At whose quick touch all glasses chip and ring,
Whose palms are bulls in china, burs in linen,
And have no cunning with any soft thing

Except all ill-at-ease fidgeting people: 5
The refugee uncertain at the door
You make at home; deftly you steady
The drunk clambering on his undulant floor.

Unpredictable dear, that taxi driver's terror,
Shrinking from far headlights pale as a dime   10
Yet leaping before red apoplectic streetcars—
Misfit in any space. And never on time.

A wrench in clocks and the solar system. Only
With words and people and love you move at ease.
In traffic of wit expertly manoeuvre   15
And keep us, all devotion, at your knees.

Forgetting your coffee spreading on our flannel,
Your lipstick grinning on our coat,
So gayly in love's unbreakable heaven
Our souls on glory of spilt bourbon float.   20

Be with me, darling, early and late. Smash glasses—
I will study wry music for your sake.
For should your hands drop white and empty
All the toys of the world would break.

For Thought and Discussion

1. John Frederick Nims shows us several different impressions of his "clumsiest dear." What are these impressions?

2. What point does the poet discover is most important about his "clumsiest dear"? He states this point in the last stanza.

3. Explain the significance of the last two lines of the poem.

4. Do you think the relationship between the poet and his "clumsiest dear" is a recent or a long-term relationship? Support your answer.

5. Examine the cartoon, and then explain how the point of the cartoon relates to a writer's problem in writing about people.

DISCOVERING YOUR POINT: TOPIC AND THESIS SENTENCES

Like most of the subjects we must write about, people indeed do have personalities like multilayered onions; that is why when we write about a topic, such as a person we know, we need to discover a unifying point. Of course, when we begin to explore a topic, we may not know what our point is. Discussing our miscellaneous thoughts and impressions with others and then recording our ideas during the prewriting process will help us discover what we want to say. Novelist Lia Matera recognizes this when she says, "If you sit down to write and find you can't create, you *can* work." This work, the process of getting words on paper or on screen, will help you discover the meaning you wish to create.

During prewriting, you should discover a central point to make about

"I'd say we're <u>both</u> multilayered onions."

a subject. Once you are satisfied you have found such a point, you have
found your *topic* or *thesis* sentence. A *topic sentence* expresses the central point
of a single paragraph or a cluster of closely related paragraphs. A *thesis
sentence* is the central point of a longer, more complex essay. A thesis sentence will often have several topic sentences supporting it.

Sometimes a topic or thesis idea is spread over more than one sentence.
Occasionally the idea is implied throughout an essay and not stated specifically. The implied-but-not-stated topic or thesis idea is frequently used in
poetry—for example, as we saw in "Love Poem"—but infrequently used in
essays. In an essay, most often unifying ideas are captured in a single topic
or thesis sentence.

Usually a topic or thesis sentence appears very early in an essay—most
often in the first paragraph or at the beginning of the second paragraph.
It is also common for the topic or thesis idea to be stated at the end of the
essay. However, less experienced writers find it best to put the topic or thesis
idea up front to help both themselves and their readers stay on track.

In the examples that follow, we will first examine thesis sentences and
then go on to topic sentences. However, note that both topic and thesis
sentences do three essential things.

1. They introduce your central point to your audience.

During your prewriting exploration to discover a thesis, you need to find something worth saying, some new information or a fresh way of looking at a subject. Both you and your reader should learn something from your writing.

In her article " 'Sweet Alice' Harris," Julianne Malveaux gives us a brief introduction before moving into her thesis:

> "Everybody can be great, because anybody can serve,"said the Reverend Martin Luther King, Jr. "You don't have to make your subject and your verb agree to serve. . . . You don't have to know the second theory of thermodynamics in physics to serve. You only need a heart full of grace. A soul generated by love."
>
> In the Watts section of Los Angeles, where the need for servers and services is acute, a woman with "a heart full of grace" is serving in astonishingly effective ways.

2. They limit your subject; they decide which aspect of your subject you will develop concretely, which layer of the subject you will focus on.

How narrowly you need to limit your subject depends upon the length of the essay you plan to write. If you set out to write a book-length biography of your subject, you can have a very broad thesis. If you are going to write a 500-word essay, you will need to limit your subject more narrowly.

For example, Joseph P. Lash wrote two books about Eleanor Roosevelt—*Eleanor Roosevelt: A Friend's Memoir* and *Eleanor: The Years Alone.* In addition, Lash wrote *Eleanor and Franklin*, in which Eleanor Roosevelt played a starring role. These books focus on different aspects of their central figure. For example, in *Eleanor and Franklin* Lash explores Eleanor Roosevelt's relationship with FDR, whereas in *Eleanor: The Years Alone* he limits the subject to the contributions she made after FDR's death.

3. They state an attitude or opinion that you can support concretely.

In Chapter 2, you used concrete details to show your reader your point. Topic and thesis sentences are abstract generalizations; to convince your reader your generalized point is valid, you need a topic or thesis sentence that you can support with facts, statistics, or concrete details.

Your topic or thesis sentence expresses an attitude or opinion—an angle—to give your essay unity; therefore, a fact is not a thesis. "Douglas MacArthur was a general" will not do. Instead, you need to say something about MacArthur that you can then spend the rest of your paper clarifying and proving. MacArthur biographer William Manchester writes: "He was a great thundering paradox of a man, noble and ignoble, inspiring and outrageous, arrogant and shy, the best of men and the worst of men, the most protean, most ridiculous, and most sublime." Manchester chose a broad thesis, and in *American Caesar* he used 708 pages to develop that thesis—to show his readers his point was a valid one.

On the other hand, MacArthur biographer Michael Schaller focuses on a more limited aspect of the general's life in the 296 pages of *The Far Eastern General.* Schaller's thesis contends: "Driven by measures of talent, opportunism, vision, egotism, and jealousy, MacArthur's life exemplifies an era in which the United States government as well as an individual American tried to shape the destiny of Asia." By citing examples from MacArthur's two decades in the Orient and examining United States policy in the Orient during those decades, Schaller develops his thesis.

The angle of a thesis sentence provides an argument which the writer must then support. This thesis angle or argument is an important help to the writer. Once writers discover such an angle, their job is greatly simplified. The thesis serves as a guide to remind writers of what must be proved concretely and what is irrelevant to the essay.

Getting It Together

In a short piece of writing with a central point, you may have only a topic sentence. In a longer, more complex piece, you may subdivide your thesis into several sections, each controlled by a topic sentence.

In "Hiding in the Spotlight," Molly Haskell states the thesis: "No one has more steadfastly refused to look like a dish or ask for audience identification than Meryl Streep. . . . The determination to be different—each role not only different from the other but different from what we assume Meryl Streep to be—is the one constant of her career." (Notice that Haskell's thesis is not confined to a single sentence.)

Haskell develops part of her essay with a series of paragraphs that show the unusual, often unsympathetic roles Streep has chosen to play so that she continues to challenge herself as an actress. Each paragraph develops a different facet of Haskell's thesis. Several paragraphs discuss Streep's very different roles in a series of movies, for example, Streep's roles as "the feisty lower-middle-class troublemaker and whistle-blower of *Silkwood*, the sanctimonious idealist in *Plenty*, and the derelict of *Ironweed*."

For Thought and Discussion
Read the following paragraph from "Hiding in the Spotlight." Then answer the questions that follow:

> Her heroines, like Streep herself, are masters of secrecy and evasion. Think of the furtiveness of the wives who become ex-wives in *Manhattan* and *Kramer vs. Kramer;* or the multiple enigmas behind the startling facade of Sophie, the Polish "shiksa" who is concealing not only the truth about her anti-Semitic father, but her betrayal of her own daughter.

1. Identify the topic sentence.

2. How does the topic sentence support the essay's thesis?

3. What concrete support does the author give for the topic sentence?

Topic Sentences: Single Paragraphs

When your point is limited to a point you can cover in a single paragraph or paragraph cluster, you will need only a topic sentence. Remember, the topic sentence

1. Introduces your central point to your audience

2. Limits your point enough that you can develop it in a single paragraph or paragraph cluster

3. States an attitude or opinion you can support concretely.

Note how Russell Baker states and develops his topic sentence in the following excerpt from his autobiography, *Growing Up.*

> When our class was assigned to Mr. Fleagle for third-year English I anticipated another grim year in that dreariest of subjects. Mr. Fleagle was notorious among City students for dullness and inability to inspire. He was said to be stuffy, dull, and hopelessly out of date. To me he looked to be sixty or seventy and prim to a fault. He wore primly severe eyeglasses, his wavy hair was primly cut and primly combed. He wore prim vested suits with neckties blocked primly against the collar buttons of his primly starched white shirts. He had a primly pointed jaw, a primly straight nose, and a prim manner of speaking that was so correct, so gentlemanly, that he seemed a comic antique.

For Thought and Discussion

1. What is Baker's central point about Mr. Fleagle?

2. List the concrete details Baker uses to develop his point.

3. Ordinarily the repetition of a single descriptive word robs writing of its effectiveness. Why is Baker able to repeat *primly* and still make his point so effectively?

Topic Sentences: Paragraph Clusters

Sometimes a topic sentence serves as a unifying point not for just a single paragraph but for a cluster of paragraphs. Note how Eudora Welty introduces her point, limits her subject, and states an idea which she then develops concretely in the following excerpt from *One Writer's Beginnings:*

1   I never knew anyone who's grown up in Jackson without being afraid of
     Mrs. Calloway, our librarian. She ran the Library absolutely by herself, from

the desk where she sat with her back to the books and facing the stairs, her dragon eye on the front door, where who knew what kind of person might come in from the public? SILENCE in big black letters was on signs tacked up everywhere. She herself spoke in her normally commanding voice; every word could be heard all over the Library above a steady seething sound coming from her electric fan; it was the only fan in the Library and stood on her desk, turned directly onto her streaming face.

2   As you came in from the bright outside, if you were a girl, she sent her strong eyes down the stairway to test you; if she could see through your skirt she sent you straight back home: you could just put on another petticoat if you wanted a book that badly from the public library. I was willing; I would do anything to read.

3   My mother was not afraid of Mrs. Calloway. She wished me to have my own library card to check out books for myself. She took me in to introduce me and I saw I had met a witch.

For Thought and Discussion

1. What is Welty's central point about Mrs. Calloway?

2. Which concrete details of appearance and action show us Welty's point?

3. Point out the images in this excerpt.

4. Review the information about transitions on page 44 in Chapter 2. Then point out the transitions Welty uses to help her readers follow her ideas.

FIGURATIVE LANGUAGE: CREATING UNIFYING IMAGES

Thinking involves creating images in our minds: Our minds convert abstractions such as words or groups of words into images. If someone says "war," our brain conjures up images of fighter planes or tanks or wounded people.

When we seek to understand our feelings and ideas about a subject, it is helpful to find out what images our brain naturally calls up. When Lillian Hellman wanted to understand the people in her life, she "wanted to see what was there for me once, what is there for me now." *Imagery,* the mental reproduction of things we perceive through one of our five senses, helps us to understand our own thinking and then to communicate it to others.

We can often discover our point for ourselves and make that point clearer to our readers by exploring the imagery that occurs to us when we cluster, brainstorm, or freewrite. For example, thinking about our boss may generate several images: she is a hard-driving workaholic who devotes much of her scarce leisure time to helping abused children. Furthermore, she works late at night but gets up at 5 a.m. because her cat likes to eat at that hour. Our boss, you see, has a myriad of layers to her personality.

Like the characters in the cartoon, writers often find that an image using *figurative language* is the most effective way to communicate ideas. Figurative language compares something readers are less familiar with to something they are more familiar with, thus producing a vivid image in their minds.

Figurative language is not literally true. People do not, in fact, have layers in the same sense that onions have layers, for example. However, just as onions have layers of flesh, people have layers of personality. Unlike the layers of an onion, we cannot literally sort through the layers of personality, but figuratively we can think of the different layers of personality that comprise all of our characters.

Similarly, using figurative language, the poet Christina Rossetti communicates how she felt by saying "My heart is like a singing bird." Of course, Rossetti didn't literally mean her heart had feathers and a beak; instead she meant she felt the elation we associate with a bird in song.

As you read the following sections about figurative language, it is vital to remember that figurative language is not just an artificial, academic device. It is a natural mode of thinking: we see mushrooms in nuclear explosions and hawks and doves in Congress. We see black holes in space, a greenhouse in our atmosphere, and military defense strategies in our own immune systems. When we allow our imagination to explore without criticism, we often create figurative language, and through this language we understand and then communicate abstractions.

There are many kinds of figurative language we can use to help make our abstract ideas more concrete. The most commonly used devices are *similes*, *metaphors*, and *personification*.

Similes

A *simile* is a comparison in which the author uses a specific comparison word or words such as *like, as, seems to be, seems like*. When Annie Dillard wants to communicate the experience of seeing a frog attacked from beneath by a giant water bug, she writes:

> I knelt on the island's winterkilled grass, lost, dumbstruck, staring at the frog in the creek just four feet away. He was a very small frog with wide, dull eyes. And just as I looked at him, he slowly crumpled and began to sag. The spirit vanished from his eyes as if snuffed. His skin emptied and drooped: his very skull seemed to collapse and settle like a kicked tent. He was shrinking before my eyes like a deflating football. I watched the taut, glistening skin on his shoulders ruck and rumple, and fall. Soon, part of his skin, formless as a pricked balloon, lay in floating folds like bright scum on top of the water.

In *West with the Night,* author Beryl Markham uses similes to show her readers her points about living in Africa.

> The Bwana when he runs very fast is like the trunk of a great boabob tree rolling down a slope.

> He [Markham's horse] never trudges, he never jolts; he is as smooth as silence.

Metaphors

A *metaphor* is a type of figurative language closely related to a simile. However, instead of using a comparison word as similes do, a metaphor implies the comparison by saying the one thing *is* the other. Note how Emily Dickinson uses metaphor in the following poem:

> Hope is the thing with feathers
> That perches in the soul,
> And sings the tune without the words,
> And never stops at all.

As with similes, metaphors are not literally true. Hope isn't really a feathered creature that sings cheerily, and the soul isn't literally a place.

Often metaphors force readers to pause and think for a moment to get the point. Such a pause gives the writer's point extra emphasis. For example, note the emphasis Philip Larkin gives his point when he uses metaphor to ask:

> Why should I let the toad work
>   Squat on my life?
> Can't I use my wit as a pitchfork
>   And drive the brute off?

Like similes, metaphors are as effective in prose as they are in poetry. William Zinsser illustrates this in the following excerpt about sports writer Red Smith from *On Writing Well:*

> I remember countless times when Smith, a devout angler, baited his hook and came up with that slippery fish, a sports commissioner, gasping for air.

Personification

Personification means attributing human characteristics to animals, objects, or ideas. Death is frequently pictured as the grim reaper, for example, while the new year is represented as a chubby baby. The poet Andrew Marvell used personification when he wrote of "Time's winged chariot hurrying near'' as Time becomes a figure driving a chariot. Note how Laura St. Martin uses personification throughout the following poem.

the ocean

the ocean is a strange
midnight lover
skinny dipping when the beach patrol has left
she is a cool seduction
wrapping blue thunder around slick brown shoulders
raising great foam-fringed arms to a steel sky
rushing over us
sometimes tumbling us to the shore
licking the rocks passionately
only to retreat into swirling
indecision
tense
always prancing
and the moon casts a furious gleam on the many-
knuckled sea

For Thought and Discussion

1. Review ''Love Poem,'' and then point out the similes, metaphors, and personification. Explain what impression the poet is trying to create with each use of figurative language.

2. Read the following excerpts and point out the similes, metaphors, and personification. Explain what impression the authors are trying to create with each use of figurative language.

> At the Lake, Oma wore cotton sundresses and low-heeled sandals. She relaxed there; we all did. She barely resembled the formidable woman she was in Pittsburgh the rest of the year. In Pittsburgh, she dressed. She wore jewelry by the breastful, by the armload: diamonds, rubies, emeralds. She wore big rings like engine bearings, and vast, slithering mink coats.
> —Annie Dillard, *An American Childhood*

> Across the years I remember countless phrases in Red Smith's columns that took me by surprise with their humor and originality. It was a pleasure to read about a quarterback who was ''scraped off the turf like apple butter.''
> —William Zinsser, *On Writing Well*

> When the ambulance came, the injured passenger, sheathed in a cocoon of blankets, was handed out of the cabin. Still more onlookers arrived; the animals, conceding armistice, but not peace, had returned in cautious groups, their eyes burning like lanterns in a poorly lighted dream.
> —Beryl Markham, *West with the Night*

3. Return to Chapter 1 and point out the figurative language in ''Two Views of the Mississippi.''

4. What kind of figurative language is used in the cartoon that appears on page 57?

How to Create Figurative Language

In "The Play Way" in Chapter 1, Seamus Heaney talks of his students "falling into themselves unknowingly." Generating figurative language is one of the best ways to get in touch with the "unknown" self of your creative thought processes. When you are searching for figurative language, try clustering or brainstorming. As you play with your ideas, ignore your critical brain; you will probably come up with ideas that may in fact be silly, but do not criticize your thoughts. Simply record them until you think of a figurative comparison that works for you.

Your turn
Take a few minutes to cluster one of the following to create a metaphor, a simile, or personification:

1. History
2. A flag on a flagpole
3. An aspect of your bedroom's appearance
4. How you feel after hours of studying, working, or watching television
5. A descriptive detail about a person you know
6. An event or a feeling of your choice

See Figure 3-1 for a sample student cluster that inspired the first excerpt quoted in the next section.

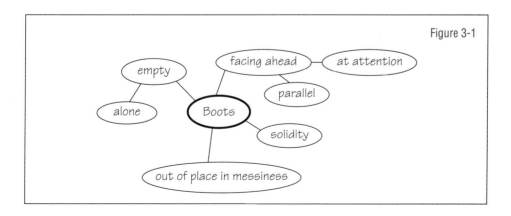

Figure 3-1

Student Stars of Figurative Language

Compare your creative efforts with those of the following student stars:

The boots stood wide and straight, defying the disorder of the clothes-strewn room.

If all the world's a stage, and all the men and women are actors, then I must be an extra.

Depression is a dark pit that slowly but surely caves in on you.

The flag arches like a vigilant Doberman.

History repeats itself like a scratched record.

The dirty clothes lie on my floor like the shed skins of different personalities I have worn.

After watching three straight hours of television, my mind refuses to get up and walk. It is content to spread out lazily like a thick slime drooling slowly over a table edge.

My weekend schedule whirled before me like a runaway merry-go-round.

 ## GETTING IDEAS ONTO PAPER

Let's examine how one author explored her ideas, decided upon a thesis, and then wrote an essay about a person who had influenced her life. Notice that the author made use of three idea-generating techniques: she first clustered (see Figure 3-2), then brainstormed, and then freewrote her initial draft.

Brainstorming—Marika

Immigrant
> Overcame outsider status, became admired, emulated, sought after; sad story of stolen diamond watch; unable to communicate about in English; sad, confused soul

Businesswoman
> Started small; intelligence, integrity, knowledge
> Sharp, shrewd but kindly
> Extensive collection of fans; one of largest dealer collections of eighteenth- and nineteenth-century French, Chinese, and Spanish fans

Human
> Intense; unique way of reacting; not syrupy sweet—honest

Intensely alive; perfectionist
> Couldn't settle for less; had to be ever energetic
> Well read; widely traveled; not cutesy places only

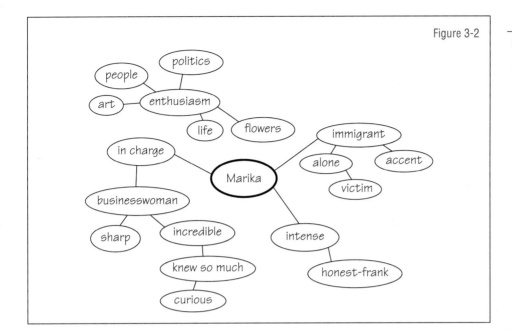

Figure 3-2

Couldn't stand being tired at age 86 after working eight hours
Her flowers; her photographs of her night-blooming flowers
Her little-kid Christmas Eve excitement

Rough Draft—Marika

As you read the following rough draft, notice how the writer continues to play with her ideas. The writer is still open to new ideas, though sometimes these ideas are dead ends.

1   Marika was one of those people few meet in a lifetime. Despite her petite stature—she needed a good inch heel to stretch to the five-foot mark—she was the sort of person one noticed immediately. She had that magic, that charisma impossible to really define but electrifying when you actually encounter it. She had a personality like a magnet, a personality reflected in her blue eyes, eyes that encompassed and defied all clichés—like cornflowers, like the sky over Hawaii, like blue topaz.

2   But this attraction was odd in its way. Capturing her on paper is a little like trying to capture Niagara Falls in a thimble. Like spreading a net of words to catch a star. She certainly wasn't a sweet, little-old-lady type. She was unique; she was careful and exacting; she was intense; she was genuine. Take, for example, the time my son, then about six, sat in her apartment, high over Boston and wrote for her all the letters of the alphabet and all the numbers to a hundred. In the middle, he had drawn a heart; in it he had written "I love you Marika." She didn't gush or exclaim how wonderful—as most would have done automatically. She didn't do much automatically. Instead she stud-

ied the sheet for a full minute. Then she looked up and said, "Andrew, you haven't forgotten a single letter or number. They're all here. I was sure you must have forgotten at least one." Andrew glowed. Had he been praised without such scrutiny, Andrew would have been pleased, but he would not have lighted the whole room with his glow of pride and pleasure at this genuine, careful praise.

3   She was a determined lady. When her parents opposed her trip to the United States from her native Hungary so she could marry a fellow Hungarian who was a student at Columbia, she sold some Oriental rugs left to her by her grandparents to raise the fare. Then speaking almost no English she came to New York City on a student visa and married the student of whom her parents did not approve. When, several decades later, she wanted to help Hungarian refugees fleeing to the United States after the Hungarian revolution of the 1950s, she again turned to selling antiques. Her single table at an antique fair evolved into a million dollar business and earned her feature articles in the *Christian Science Monitor* and *The Wall Street Journal*. Before the fair even opened, she sold her entire stock to other dealers. Her knowledge of antiques was encyclopedic. Museums like Smithsonian turned to her for advice on antiques.

4   Even her death reflected her grace and determination. In her early eighties, she began to complain about not being as sharp as she once was. When pressed for examples she would confess that after a busy, eight-hour day working at her antique shop, she sometimes fell asleep while watching television. She was a person determined to control her life; if she fell asleep it should be because she decided to fall asleep. And so, quite suddenly it seemed to those around her, she decided her time had come. She lay in the hospital for a few weeks while doctors struggled to revive a heart that she had decided should stop, but she did not respond. Her son said she took several weeks to die because she wanted to give her family time to get used to the idea of her death—to break them in gradually and not to shock them too quickly. Shortly before her eighty-sixth birthday, Marika left a world she had made a brighter, kinder, more vibrant place with her presence.

For Thought and Discussion

1. What is the central attitude or opinion about Marika?

2. Point out places where the author got off track. Suggest appropriate revision for these passages.

Final Draft

Thus far the entire writing process has taken the author little more than an hour. Of course, the author knew her subject well and did not have to use any outside sources to supplement her information. As you have learned in Chapters 1 and 2, when the critical thought process is quieted, the creative process can act quickly to generate a myriad of ideas.

After the prewriting, the author sensed what she wanted to say about Marika. Because the author's point is complex, notice that she has subdivided her thesis into separate topics which she develops concretely.

Marika

1   Marika was one of those people few meet in a lifetime. Despite her petite stature—she needed a good inch heel to stretch to the five-foot mark—she was the sort of person one noticed immediately. She had that magic, that charisma impossible to really define but electrifying when you actually encounter it. She had a personality like a magnet, a personality reflected in her blue eyes, eyes that encompassed and defined all clichés—eyes with the beauty and durability of blue diamonds.

2   Capturing her on paper is a little like trying to capture Niagara Falls in a thimble. She certainly wasn't a sweet, little-old-lady type. She bristled with energy, ideas, and opinions. She was unique; she was careful and exacting; she was intense; she was genuine. For example, one time my son, then about six, sat in her apartment, high over Boston, and wrote for her all the letters of the alphabet and all the numbers to a hundred. In the middle of his writing, he had drawn a heart; in it he had written, ''I love you Marika.'' Marika didn't gush or exclaim how wonderful—as most would have done automatically. She didn't do much automatically. Instead she studied the sheet for a full minute. Then she looked up and said, ''Andrew, you haven't forgotten a single letter or number. They're all here. I was sure you must have forgotten at least one.'' Andrew glowed. Had he been praised without such scrutiny, he would have been pleased, but he would not have lit up the whole room with his pride and pleasure at this genuine, careful praise.

3   She was a determined lady. Her parents opposed her trip to the United States to marry a fellow Hungarian who was a student at Columbia. Although she spoke scant English, she defied her parents, sold some Oriental rugs left to her by her grandparents to raise the fare, and left the security of her comfortable home. When, several decades later, she wanted to help Hungarian refugees fleeing to the United States after the Hungarian revolution of the 1950s, she again turned to selling antiques. Her single table at an antique fair evolved into a million-dollar-a-year business and earned her feature articles in the *Christian Science Monitor* and *The Wall Street Journal.* Museums like the Smithsonian turned to her for advice on antiques.

4   Even her death reflected her grace and determination. In her early eighties, she began to complain about not being as sharp as she once was. When pressed for examples she would confess that after a busy, eight-hour day working at her antique shop, she sometimes fell asleep while watching television. She was a person determined to control her life; if she fell asleep it should be because she decided to fall asleep. And so, quite suddenly it seemed to those around her, she decided her time had come. She lay in the hospital for a few weeks while doctors struggled to revive a heart that she had decided should stop. Medical expertise was powerless against her resolve. Shortly before her eighty-sixth birthday, Marika left a world she had made a brighter, kinder, more vibrant place with her presence.

For Thought and Discussion

1. What is the central attitude or opinion about Marika that the writer developed in the final draft of the essay?

2. Review the brainstorming and clustering for the Marika essay. What other attitudes or opinions might have been developed as the central focus?

3. List the concrete details that illustrate the thesis.

4. What topic sentences help support the thesis about Marika?

5. Point out and identify the type of figurative language used in this essay.

UNITY AND CREATIVITY IN TITLES

Creating titles provides an excellent opportunity to see how ideas pop into your consciousness when you turn off your critical thinking processes. Remember that although titles come at the beginning of a work, they cannot be created until you are sure of what you want to say. Once you have decided upon a thesis and written a draft of your essay, take a few minutes to work on a title. Your title should accurately reflect your central point; therefore, creating a title will help you see if you have, in fact, adequately identified your central point.

Because the brain works by association, with one idea leading to other ideas, clustering and brainstorming are effective ways to create titles. The important thing to remember is not to criticize titles that seem silly or inaccurate. If you turn off your critical thought processes, some of the titles that occur to you undoubtedly will be silly or inappropriate. Relax and enjoy experimenting with title ideas; give yourself permission to be less than perfect while you experiment. Once you have generated a list of titles, you can put your critic into gear and mow down inappropriate, inaccurate, or ineffective titles.

The type of title you need depends upon your purpose and intended audience. Your title must harmonize with the rest of your paper. If you intend your writing for a formal, scholarly audience, you will want a more formal, scholarly title than if you are directing your writing to a less formal audience.

There are a number of techniques you can use in creating titles.

Questions

A title can pose a question whose answer becomes your thesis:

"What Ever Happened to Energy Conservation?" from *Sierra*
"What's Killing the Palm Trees?" from *National Geographic*
"Unpleasant Surprises in the Greenhouse?" from *Nature*

Two-part titles using a colon create a dramatic impact and condense ideas into a few words:

> "Paloma Picasso: Living Up to Her Name" from *Lear's*
> "Charles L. Tiffany: A Life of Luxuries" from *Smithsonian*
> "Sharks: More Threatened Than Threatening?" from *Sea Frontiers*

Alliteration

Alliteration is the repetition of similar sounding sounds at the beginning of words (for example, *s*imilar *s*ounding *s*ounds). Because alliteration gives phrases emphasis and helps make them memorable, movie stars and cartoon characters often have alliterative names, as the following evidence: Marilyn Monroe, Robert Redford, Minnie Mouse, Woody Woodpecker. Alliteration can give your essay titles special sparkle by adding emphasis to your ideas and making them more memorable:

> From *Smithsonian:*
>> "W. Graham Arader III: The Maverick Main Line Print Man"
>> "Fred Harvey: The Righteous Restauranteur"
> From *Newsweek:*
>> "Diplomatic Dunces"
>> "Noriega: Strongman in Stir"
>> "Bush and Baker: Prisoners of the Past?"
> From *Natural History:*
>> "Mollusks in Midstream"
>> "A Seabird in the House of the Sun"

Allusions

An *allusion* is a reference to something real or literary. With just a few words, by using an allusion, an author suggests the complex ideas associated with the source of the allusion. For example, with *For Whom the Bell Tolls*, Ernest Hemingway alludes to John Donne's "Any man's death diminishes me, because I am involved in Mankind; And therefore never send to know for whom the bell tolls; It tolls for thee."[1] Thus, with his allusion, Hemingway suggests the mortality that all humans share.

"Do I Dare to Eat a Peach?" an article about the dangers of pesticide residue in the foods we eat, alludes to T. S. Eliot's "The Love Song of J. Alfred Prufrock," in which Prufrock asks, "Shall I part my hair behind? Do I dare to eat a peach?" With its allusion, the title thereby evokes Prufrock's own inability to make decisions.

---

[1] From *Devotions upon Emergent Occasions*, no. 6.

Not only do allusions provide a short, emphatic means of communicating, they also give their readers a sense of belonging; readers who "get" an allusion derive a similar satisfaction to people who get a joke, and, in fact, a punchline is often based on an allusion.

Of course, allusions draw from sources other than literature. We often allude to rock or film stars, lines from movies, or even cartoon characters. In fact, getting such an allusion can make your day—if the allusion isn't to Mickey Mouse.

While allusions are often used within an essay or article, they also make excellent sources for titles. As you read the examples below, note that some of them combine title techniques:

From *National Wildlife:* "The Importance of 'Tweety Birds' "
From *Lear's:* "Sidney Poitier: In the Heat of His Life"
From *Smithsonian:* "Behold the Age of Aquariums"
From *Newsweek:*

   "What's in a Name? A Graceful Debut for *Mirabella*"
   "John le Carré Comes in from the Cold with *Russia House*"
   "Off with Their Heads: Killing Walrus for Ivory"

Mechanical Rules for Titles

Once you have created your title, it is time to proofread to make sure you have followed the conventions governing spelling and punctuation so that your reader does not trip over any mistakes in your title.

1. Capitalize all words in titles except for prepositions, the articles *a, an,* and *the,* and coordinating conjunctions *and, or, but, for, nor, yet, so.* The first and last words of titles are always capitalized even if these words are articles, prepositions, or conjunctions. The word following the colon in a title is always capitalized even if it is an article, preposition, or conjunction.

2. Do not italicize or use quotation marks around titles when you are actually using them as titles. Italics and quotation marks are used only when you are referring to a work of writing. For example, in *Emily Dickinson,* a biography of that poet by Cynthia Griffin Wolff, the author discusses a broad variety of Dickinson's poems, even little-known poems such as "Always Mine." When *Emily Dickinson* and "Always Mine" were used as titles—of the book and a poem, respectively—they were not punctuated; the reader could see they were titles. However when you write *about* these titles, as we have done here, your punctuation helps your readers understand they are titles.

For Thought and Discussion

1. To assess the difference between the impact of a title without a colon and one with a colon, transform the following titles with colons into

titles without colons; for example, "The Mighty Himalaya: A Fragile Heritage" from *National Geographic* could become "A Fragile Heritage Exists in the Mighty Himalaya."

> "Paul Vincent Wiseman: Refined Romantic" from *San Francisco Focus*
> "The Royal Anniversary: Elvis Presley's Fiftieth" from *The Wall Street Journal*
> *Isak Dinesen: The Life of a Storyteller*
> *Beethoven: Biography of a Genius*

2. Work with your classmates to explain the allusions in the titles which use allusions.

3. Discuss the following brainstorming list of titles for the essay about Marika with your classmates or peer editing group. Which title do your prefer? Why?

> Marika: Hungarian Refugee
> Refugee Role Model
> Refugee Makes Good
> Marvelous Marika
> Magic Marika
> Magnetic Marika
> The Magic and Magnetism of Marika
> Marika

Your turn

1. Experiment with brainstorming to create three alliterative titles on a subject of your choice. After you have created a list of titles, properly capitalize and punctuate them.

2. Once you have discovered a thesis for this chapter's writing assignment, use brainstorming and clustering to experiment with a title for your essay. Write one title using alliteration, one with an allusion, and one with a colon.

PROFESSIONAL WRITERS AT WORK

As you read the following two essays, note how the authors use topic and thesis sentences to make their points about their subjects. Also note their use of figurative language in developing those points.

Gloria Steinem, author of the first essay, is a pioneer of the feminist movement. The founding editor of *Ms.* magazine, Steinem is the author of numerous articles published in magazines from *Vogue* to *Esquire.* In addition, she has written three books, including *Marilyn,* a biography of Marilyn

Monroe. The following excerpt, "The Mystery of Uncle Ed," was taken from *Outrageous Acts and Everyday Rebellions*, a book of essays.

The Mystery of Uncle Ed

1   Happy or unhappy, families are all mysterious. We have only to imagine how differently we would be described—and will be, after our deaths—by each of the family members who believe they know us. The only question is, Why are some mysteries more important than others?

2   The fate of my Uncle Ed was a mystery of importance in our family. We lavished years of speculation on his transformation from a brilliant young electrical engineer to the town handyman. What could have changed this elegant, Lincolnesque student voted "Best Dressed" by his classmates to the gaunt, unshaven man I remember? Why did he leave a young son and a first wife of the "proper" class and religion, marry a much less educated woman of the "wrong" religion, and raise a second family in a house near an abandoned airstrip; a house whose walls were patched with metal signs to stop the wind? Why did he never talk about his transformation?

3   For years, I assumed that some secret and dramatic events of a year he spent in Alaska had made the difference. Then I discovered that the trip had come after his change and probably had been made because of it. Strangers he worked for as a much-loved handyman talked about him as one more tragedy of the Depression, and it was true that Uncle Ed's father, my paternal grandfather, had lost his money in the stockmarket Crash and died of (depending on who was telling the story) pneumonia or a broken heart. But the Crash of 1929 also had come long after Uncle Ed's transformation. Another theory was that he was afflicted with a mental problem that lasted most of his life, yet he was supremely competent at his work, led an independent life, and asked for help from no one.

4   Perhaps he had fallen under the spell of a radical professor in the early days of the century, the height of this country's romance with socialism and anarchism. That was the theory of another uncle on my mother's side. I do remember that no matter how much Uncle Ed needed money, he would charge no more for his work than materials plus 10 percent, and I never saw him in anything other than ancient boots and overalls held up with strategic safety pins. Was he really trying to replace socialism-in-one-country with socialism-in-one-man? If so, why did my grandmother, a woman who herself had run for the school board in coalition with anarchists and socialists, mistrust his judgment so much that she left his share of her estate in trust, even though he was over fifty when she died? And why did Uncle Ed seem uninterested in all other political words and acts? Was it true instead that, as another relative insisted, Uncle Ed had chosen poverty to disprove the myths of Jews and money?

5   Years after my uncle's death, I asked a son in his second family if he had the key to this family mystery. No, he said. He had never known his father any other way. For that cousin, there had been no question. For the rest of us, there was to be no answer.

For Thought and Discussion

1. What is Steinem's thesis about Uncle Ed?

2. List the topic sentences from this essay and explain how they help to develop Steinem's thesis.

3. Under each topic sentence, list the concrete information that develops it.

4. Point out examples of figurative language that help Steinem make her point.

Banesh Hoffmann was a writer and mathematician who served with Albert Einstein on the faculty of the Institute for Advanced Study at Princeton University. Hoffmann and Einstein coauthored an article on the theory of relativity. In the following excerpt from *Albert Einstein: Creator and Rebel*, Hoffmann seeks to capture the essence of this brilliant thinker.

My Friend, Albert Einstein

1   He was one of the greatest scientists the world has ever known, yet if I had to convey the essence of Albert Einstein in a single word, I would choose simplicity. Perhaps an anecdote will help. Once, caught in a downpour, he took off his hat and held it under his coat. Asked why, he explained, with admirable logic, that the rain would damage the hat, but his hair would be none the worse for its wetting. This knack for going instinctively to the heart of a matter was the secret of his major scientific discoveries—this and his extraordinary feeling for beauty.

2   I was in awe of Einstein, and hesitated before approaching him about some ideas I had been working on. When I finally knocked on his door, a gentle voice said, "Come"—with a rising inflection that made the single word both a welcome and a question. I entered his office and found him seated at a table, calculating and smoking his pipe. Dressed in ill-fitting clothes, his hair characteristically awry, he smiled a warm welcome. His utter naturalness at once set me at ease.

3   As I began to explain my ideas, he asked me to write the equations on the blackboard so he could see how they developed. Then came the staggering—and altogether endearing—request: "Please go slowly. I do not understand things quickly."

4   In school, though his teachers saw no special talent in him, the signs were already there. He taught himself calculus, for example, and his teachers seemed a little afraid of him because he asked questions they could not answer. At the age of 16, he asked himself whether a light wave would seem stationary if one ran abreast of it. From that innocent question would arise, ten years later, his theory of relativity.

5   Einstein failed his entrance examinations at the Swiss Federal Polytechnic School, in Zurich, but was admitted a year later. There he went beyond his regular work to study the masterworks of physics on his own. Rejected when he applied for academic positions, he ultimately found work, in 1902, as a

patent examiner in Berne, and there in 1905 his genius burst into fabulous flower.

6   Among the extraordinary things he produced in that memorable year were his theory of relativity, with its famous offshoot, $E = mc^2$ (energy equals mass times the speed of light squared), and his quantum theory of light. These two theories were not only revolutionary, but seemingly contradictory: the former was intimately linked to the theory that light consists of waves, while the latter said it consists somehow of particles. Yet this unknown young man boldly proposed both at once—and he was right in both cases, though how he could have been is far too complex a story to tell here.

7   Collaborating with Einstein was an unforgettable experience. In 1937, the Polish physicist Leopold Infeld and I asked if we could work with him. He was pleased with the proposal since he had an idea about gravitation waiting to be worked out in detail. Thus we got to know not merely the man and the friend, but also the professional.

8   The intensity and depth of his concentration were fantastic. When battling a recalcitrant problem, he worried it as an animal its prey. Often, when we found ourselves up against a seemingly insuperable difficulty, he would stand up, put his pipe on the table, and say in his quaint English, "I will a little tink" (he could not pronounce "th"). Then he would pace up and down, twirling a lock of his long, graying hair around his forefinger.

9   A dreamy, faraway and yet inward look would come over his face. There was no appearance of concentration, no furrowing of the brow—only a placid inner communion. The minutes would pass, and then suddenly Einstein would stop pacing as his face relaxed into a gentle smile. He had found the solution to the problem. Sometimes it was so simple that Infeld and I could have kicked ourselves for not having thought of it. But the magic had been performed invisibly in the depths of Einstein's mind, by a process we could not fathom.

10   Although Einstein felt no need for religious ritual and belonged to no formal religious group, he was the most deeply religious man I have known. He once said to me, "Ideas come from God," and one could hear the capital "G" in the reverence with which he pronounced the word. On the marble fireplace in the mathematics building at Princeton University is carved, in the original German, what one might call his scientific credo: "God is subtle, but he is not malicious." By this Einstein meant that scientists could expect to find their task difficult, but not hopeless: the Universe was a Universe of law, and God was not confusing us with deliberate paradoxes and contradictions.

11   Einstein was an accomplished amateur musician. We used to play duets, he on the violin, I at the piano. One day he surprised me by saying Mozart was the greatest composer of all. Beethoven "created" his music, but the music of Mozart was of such purity and beauty one felt he had merely "found" it—that it had always existed as part of the inner beauty of the Universe, waiting to be revealed.

12   It was this Mozartean simplicity that most characterized Einstein's methods. His 1905 theory of relativity, for example, was built on just two simple assumptions. One is the so-called principle of relativity, which means, roughly speaking, that we cannot tell whether we are at rest or moving smoothly. The

other assumption is that the speed of light is the same no matter what the speed of the object that produces it. You can see how reasonable this is if you think of agitating a stick in a lake to create waves. Whether you wiggle the stick from a stationary pier, or from a rushing speedboat, the waves, once generated, are on their own, and their speed has nothing to do with that of the stick.

13   Each of these assumptions, by itself, was so plausible as to seem primitively obvious. But together they were in such violent conflict that a lesser man would have dropped one or the other and fled in panic. Einstein daringly kept both—and by so doing he revolutionized physics. For he demonstrated they could, after all, exist peacefully side by side, provided we gave up cherished beliefs about the nature of time.

14   Science is like a house of cards, with concepts like time and space at the lowest level. Tampering with time brought most of the house tumbling down, and it was this that made Einstein's work so important—and controversial.

15   We think of Einstein as one concerned only with the deepest aspects of science. But he saw scientific principles in everyday things to which most of us would give barely a second thought. He once asked me if I had ever wondered why a man's feet will sink into either dry or completely submerged sand, while sand that is merely damp provides a firm surface. When I could not answer, he offered a simple explanation.

16   It depends, he pointed out, on *surface tension*, the elastic-skin effect of a liquid surface. This is what holds a drop together, or causes two small raindrops on a windowpane to pull into one big drop the moment their surfaces touch.

17   When sand is damp, Einstein explained, there are tiny amounts of water between grains. The surface tensions of these tiny amounts of water pull all the grains together, and friction then makes them hard to budge. When the sand is dry, there is obviously no water between grains. If the sand is fully immersed, there is water between grains, but no water *surface* to pull them together.

18   This is not as important as relativity; yet there is no telling what seeming trifle will lead an Einstein to a major discovery. And the puzzle of the sand does give us an inkling of the power and elegance of his mind.

19   Einstein's work, performed quietly with pencil and paper, seemed remote from the turmoil of everyday life. But his ideas were so revolutionary they caused violent controversy and irrational anger. Indeed, in order to be able to award him a belated Nobel Prize, the selection committee had to avoid mentioning relativity, and pretend the prize was awarded primarily for his work on the quantum theory.

20   Political events upset the serenity of his life even more. When the Nazis came to power in Germany, his theories were officially declared false because they had been formulated by a Jew. His property was confiscated, and it is said a price was put on his head.

21   When scientists in the United States, fearful that the Nazis might develop an atomic bomb, sought to alert American authorities to the danger, they were scarcely heeded. In desperation, they drafted a letter which Einstein signed and sent directly to President Roosevelt. It was this act that led to the

22 fateful decision to go all-out on the production of an atomic bomb—an endeavor in which Einstein took no active part. When he heard of the agony and destruction that his $E = mc^2$ had wrought, he was dismayed beyond measure, and from then on there was a look of ineffable sadness in his eyes.

How shall I sum up what it meant to have known Einstein and his works? I can find no adequate words. It was akin to the revelation of great art that lets one see what was formerly hidden. And when, for example, I walk on the sand of a lonely beach, I am reminded of his ceaseless search for cosmic simplicity—and the scene takes on a deeper, sadder beauty.

For Thought and Discussion

1. What is Hoffmann's thesis about Einstein in this excerpt?

2. In what respect were Uncle Ed and Einstein similar personalities?

3. List the topic sentences that subdivided this thesis.

4. Point out concrete details and anecdotes that develop the topic sentences.

5. Why do you think Einstein's early teachers failed to note his genius? Think about what kind of thought processes might have been emphasized in their traditional classrooms.

6. Compare Einstein's behavior when he was trying to solve a difficult problem to the ideas in this text about generating ideas for writing.

 WRITING ASSIGNMENT

Talk to a classmate about a person who has made a significant impression on your life. Then cluster to explore your ideas. After you have clustered for about five minutes, a significant central idea should have crystallized for you. Once you discover this thesis idea, begin to freewrite an essay that will show your readers your thesis. If your discussion and clustering do not generate enough ideas for your development, try brainstorming after you have finished clustering. Freewrite your initial draft.

Do remember that because one idea leads to another, you may change your mind about your thesis as you write and thus discover new insights about your subject. Eventually, though, you need to decide upon a thesis and then support that thesis with concrete details.

Cluster, freewrite, or brainstorm to create an appropriate title. Remember that creating a title can help ensure that you are clear about your thesis. Experiment with the title types listed earlier in this chapter.

If you reach a place in your writing where you need an image to clarify your point, return to a prewriting technique; clustering is an especially effective way to create metaphors, similes, and personification.

Be alert to the power of allusion to carry a complex, powerful message in a few words. These allusions occur when you allow your creative thought process to play with your ideas during your initial writing stages.

Suggestions for Topics

Whom should you write about? Explore the influence one of the following has had on your life: a relative, a teacher, a neighbor, a friend, a boss, a coworker, or a member of the clergy.

To help discover your ideas, brainstorm, freewrite, or cluster about the positive or negative influence this person has had on your life. The influence could be the kind of direct guidance you often receive from a parent or a teacher, or it could be the influence provided by your observation of that person's life.

Peer Editing Checklist

After you have completed the prewriting and the first draft of your essay, meet with a peer editing group so that you can assess the reaction of an audience to your writing. Photocopy enough essays for your peer editing group. Members of the group should do the following:

1. First read the essay through once without stopping.

2. Indicate any ideas, passages, imagery, allusions, or other aspects of this essay you found effective. Positive reinforcement is a powerful tool.

3. Underline the thesis. If you cannot identify the thesis, ask the writer to point it out or to further clarify the thesis in writing.

4. Point out any details or passages that do not seem relevant to the author's point. The author should then decide whether a transition can clarify the connection with the thesis or if the point is truly irrelevant.

5. Indicate any abstract ideas that need further concrete development. Ask the author any questions you would like to have answered to better understand the essay's points.

6. List examples of any of the following included in the paper: figurative language, allusions, alliteration. Are these effectively used? Indicate places where the addition of such devices might be effective.

7. What is your reaction to the essay's title? Explain whether or not the title helps you better understand the author's point. Does the title pique your interest in reading the essay?

When writers have revised the content of the essay to their satisfaction and are ready for feedback about mechanics, point out but do not correct any problems you suspect exist with spelling, grammar, and punctuation. It is the writer's responsibility to make such corrections.

Read the following student draft as if you were its peer editor. Then respond to the points in the preceding peer editing checklist.

Richard: Modern Thoreau

1   A philosophy is the controlling ideas by which one lives. To help you better understand my friend Richard, I need to tell you a few things about him. He was born in February in the depths of the depression. This tall, blonde has maintained a healthy body through a variety of activities such as jogging, cycling, and hiking. His education was typical of the times: his parents wanted him to go to college and he did. He graduated finally after a short break during which he served in the Korean War. By the end of his military service, Richard's philosophy was surely developing.

2   Back in school, in an American literature class Richard met a man who was to become his life-long hero—Henry David Thoreau. Armed now with *Walden*, Richard was ready for the years of what was to be his Walden Pond. Simplicity, simplicity, simplicity echoed from all the things Richard thought or did. Like Thoreau, Richard was determined to be as self-sufficient as possible, so he cut firewood by hand. This attitude carried over even to his car; for Richard its function was to go from Point A to Point B and nothing more. He would not be owned by his car.

3   In the service Richard had witnessed, seen, and partaken in many profound experiences. After the service Richard wanted to retreat from the complexities of life. He knew that the simple, basic things of life gave him the most pleasure. Most important to his future was the desire to be left alone, with no demands from headquarters, no kow-tow to anyone's whistle.

4   After thirty years as a high school instructor, Richard no longer found joy in teaching. Then he had to make a very heavy decision about whether to take early retirement or continue teaching until he was sixty. Retiring early meant a substantial differential in his earnings versus retiring in later years. Ah, but life was very precious to Richard, so he took his early retirement from the school district, and substitute-taught and remodeled houses to earn additional income. Today Richard has more time to smell the roses than he had when he was teaching full-time.

5   I remember on several occasions when Richard took me to his mountain home and we talked, enjoying the beauty of the day. From one of our dialogues came a statement of life I remember to this day. Richard said, ''my way of life must be close to nature, for I want to hear all She has to say.'' The path Richard chose was soon familiar to him. He said he measured his walk by the trees he passed and other friendly signs of nature. He also built his own house on a hill above a friendly creek. From the trees, floor joists were made and a friendly handcrafted door opened onto the beauty of Carmel Valley.

6   A typical day for Richard is summarized by the idea: ''I'd rather do it myself.'' If it is making a new door for his home, or simply cutting firewood, he does it by hand. In building his house, each plank of lumber was hand-planed—beveled on each side and smoothed by an old-fashioned plane. I stated to Richard that it certainly would have been faster and easier using a

fully accessorized, high-tech set of Black and Decker tools. His comment was that God placed these trees on earth for us to enjoy and it took many years to grow them. By using his method of building, he can enjoy the feel of the wood as he handles each piece lovingly and with care.

7   As Richard reflects on his accomplishments there is a certain pride quite unlike the fellow who has solved a company problem with a computer. As Richard stands alone, he says to the passing world, "Give me the simple, natural life and I will be content."

STUDENT STARS

The students who wrote these essays did the following:

1. Prewriting

2. Writing

3. Revision of content

4. Proofreading and revision of mechanics.

Richard: Modern Thoreau

1   Of all the people I have ever known, Richard best exemplifies how a philosophy can impact one's life. Following graduation from college, Richard served in the army during the Korean War. After the violence and pain of Korea, Richard wanted to retreat from life's unnecessary complications. Watching his friends killed or wounded, he had grown to believe the simple things of life gave him the most pleasure.

2   After his discharge from the army, Richard returned to college where he acquired his most important weapon for life's battle: Henry David Thoreau's philosophy as expressed in *Walden*. Almost as soon as he met Thoreau, that philosopher became Richard's hero. Simplicity, simplicity, simplicity echoed from all things Richard did from then on. For instance, to Richard an auto is a necessity, but he never forgets its function is to get him from Point A to Point B. Richard's autos have never been the sleek, glamorous ones of glossy magazine ads. As their dull, often dirty, exteriors attest, Richard spends just enough time, energy, and money on transportation so he can be sure he will get where he wants to go. Why a thousand stitches today, so to speak, to save nine tomorrow?

3   After thirty years as a high school instructor, Richard lost his joy in teaching. To take an early retirement meant a substantial difference in the check he would get if he taught a few more years. However, material wealth was not so important to Richard as the wealth he would get by controlling his own time. So he retired. He has less money now, but—like Thoreau—he has more time to sit in his doorway and feel the sun on his face.

4   Several times I have visited Richard in his mountain home. There we talked and enjoyed the beauty of the day. From one of our dialogues came a statement that has stuck in my mind. Richard said, "I have to be close to nature,

for I want to hear all she has to say.'' Richard told me he measures his walks each day by the trees he passes, by the wildflowers he sees growing next to his path, by the birds soaring in the sky over his land.

5   From the floor joists to the friendly, handmade door that opens onto the beauty of Carmel Valley, Richard's hand-crafted home reflects his love of nature, his desire to be self-sufficient, and his desire to simplify life. He built his home on a hill above a creek—each plank beveled on both sides, smoothed with an old-fashioned plane, and hand-sanded. "It would certainly have been easier and faster using high-tech, Black & Decker power tools," I once pointed out to Richard.

6   His answer? "God placed these trees on earth for us to enjoy. It took them many years to grow. When I finish lumber by hand, I can enjoy the feel of the wood; I can more fully sense its beauty."

7   As Richard reflects on his accomplishments, there is a pride that is quite unlike the fellow who has just won his company's sales competition. Instead, Richard radiates a rare kind of contentment: a contentment in being who he is and where he is, leading an uncomplicated life close to nature.

—Diana Lee

For Thought and Discussion

1. What is the thesis of this essay?

2. List three examples of concrete support for the thesis.

3. What changes did the author make in her final draft?

4. Point out a change that indicates the author's sensitivity to her audience's need for an explanation of her allusion.

Ode to George

1   George is not your typical fifty-year-old grandfather. He is the type of person you get to know once in a life, and you'll take his influence to the grave.

2   During the several years I have worked with George, he has become not just my co-worker but my teacher and friend. Although he has become such a strong father-figure that I have taken to calling him "Pops," at first meeting he seemed like a gruff, loud, dirty old man. However, as I got to know him I discovered that under his tarnished outer layers lies a heart of gold; if Santa had a mind filled with dirty jokes, he would be George's twin.

3   The first thing I noticed about George was his short, squat stature, his burly, salt-and-pepper beard, and his smile that is reminiscent of a jagged comb missing several teeth. Once I got used to his rough appearance, his most noticeable feature became that broad smile that somehow looks a little guilty, a little like the cat that swallowed the canary.

4   George uses that smile a lot. At work he is never at a loss for words or without his sense of humor. He frequently tells co-workers young enough to be his daughters, "Ladies, if I had my teeth capped, my nose fixed [it has been broken several times], my glasses replaced with contacts, I lost thirty pounds and was twenty years younger, those twerps you date wouldn't stand

a chance. One date with The Hook [he calls himself that because of his large, crooked nose] and you beautiful ladies would throw rocks at your boyfriends.''

5   George's sense of humor makes potentially serious problems at work easier to deal with. Recently, for example, George and I received fifty boxes of highly perishable flowers that needed to be shipped out on a flight immediately; the flight had enough room for a scant twenty-five boxes. When our boss angrily demanded, ''Why didn't you load all the boxes on the plane?'' George simply stated, ''You can't fit two pounds of crap in a one-pound bag.''

6   Despite his blustery manner and his sailor vocabulary, George is a devoted family man. He is especially proud of his granddaughter, whose pictures he is ready to show off. Love flows from him as he brags about her latest accomplishments.

7   George's paternal pride and protectiveness extend to his co-workers. When I was new on the job and not confident in my abilities, I was trying to help a passenger at the counter. His flight was delayed, and he was irate because he could not fly out until several hours later that day. I might as well have cut off his arm considering how loudly he was screaming. He demanded a free airline ticket—though he was a regular commuter and knew the ins and outs of the airline system very well. He knew that since the flight was delayed due to weather, he was not entitled to compensation other than being able to depart on the next available flight. As he screamed demands and insults, I was shaking, my palms were sweating, and my heart was racing. I was ready to chuck the whole job and go home. *No job could be worth this!* I told myself.

8   Luckily, George was working with me. He stepped into the conversation thus subjecting himself to some serious verbal abuse. George listened patiently for several minutes, nodding sympathetically from time to time. Within a few minutes, he had the passenger calmed down.

9   After the incident with the irate passenger, George and I became close friends. He is always willing to listen to my problems and always eager to give some friendly, fatherly advice. One time when I was feeling very discouraged about my job, I asked George what I should do. He said simply, ''Dude, you have to do what's going to make you happy, and no one can make you happy except yourself. Life is too short to waste.''

10   Although George continues to have his rough exterior, I have come to realize that he is, in fact, a warm, wise, and sensitive friend and father figure whose only rough edges are on the outside.   —George DeAnzo

A Visit with Uncle Pilo

1   The front door of my uncle's house stands slightly ajar. The escaping aroma of freshly cooked corn tortillas greets me as I knock courteously. Weakened hinges crackle and pop as momentum pries the door open even further—a curtain of redwood drawing back revealing a domicile rich in Hispanic culture and Hispanic pride, full of warmth and hospitality and representative of life-long labor and sacrifice. It is a home that mirrors my uncle's life. It is a home that is my uncle.

2   ''Buenos dias?'' I utter inquisitively, uncertain if Tio Pilo is home. Don Pedro Gaona Perez is my uncle's full name, but I have always called him as Tio Pilo. It wasn't until my First Communion ceremony that I learned my godfather's full name.

3   From the far corner of the living room, partially hidden behind the door, comes an old, familiar cough. A raspy voice from a hastily cleared throat resonates off the walls. "Adelante [come in]," the voice beckons.

4   Entering the room, I spot my uncle seated in his favorite chair. He glances up with dry, squinting eyes that peer through wire-rim bifocals; pronounced crow's feet signify his rank as a patriarch of the Perez family. His time-worn wooden rocking chair creaks and groans like the hull of an old boat as Uncle struggles to right himself. As far back as I can remember, he has experienced difficulties in standing from a seated position: he suffers from chronic back problems resulting from a fall he had as a construction worker more than half a century ago. Despite this affliction, there is still a glimmer of the strength he possessed when as a young man he hauled brick and mortar on his back up and down ladders.

5   Having overcome his defiant back, Tio Pilo proudly stands upright—looking a little like the statuesque Aztec warrior in the canvas painting hanging on his living room wall. Age and pain have reduced Uncle's five-foot-four-inch frame by a few inches and caused him to hunch over. He smiles reassuringly, exposing the gold cap on his right incisor. Extending his right hand, Tio Pilo turns to greet me. His lingering brawn is never more evident than when he shakes hands. The soothing warmth of his palm is in stark contrast to the clamping, vise-like grip that accompanies it. The handshake gives way to the traditional hug and kiss on the cheek. There is no loss of masculinity here; instead, there is the confirmation of respect.

6   Clasping his hands in mine, I am reminded of the arduous life my uncle has led—a life beset by drudgery and sacrifice. The crushed fingertip from a poorly aimed hammer, the scarred laceration courtesy of a runaway power saw, and the third degree burn mark awarded him by a torch's errant flame are but a few of the many medals he has earned for his tireless work ethic. These medals he wears proudly, and for each medal, there is, of course, a tale to be told.

7   Salutations completed, Tio Pilo quickly invites me to have a seat next to his chair. "Dispense me por favor [excuse me, please]," he whispers as he shuffles off into the adjoining kitchen. A minute later, he returns with two bottles of chilled Corona beer. His oversized khaki pants—held aloft by a pair of apple-red suspenders pulled over a washing-machine-ravaged tee shirt—rustle as he walks toward me.

8   With each toilsome step that Tio Pilo takes nostalgia sets in and old memories spring to life. It seems only yesterday that these bottles of beer were bottles of Coca-Cola. As a young boy, I would sit for hours with my uncle talking about life while taking turns belching up the carbonation from the Coke—something my mother frowned on. For these conversations, my uncle would often have a large, juicy ripe watermelon on hand, and we would spit watermelon seeds for winning distances while devouring slice after slice.

9   Whenever family problems involved disagreements between my father and me, Tio Pilo would find a way to smooth things over. Interrupting my father's reprimands, Tio Pilo would look me straight in the eyes and say, "Did I ever tell you about the time your father . . . ?

10   The gelidity of the glass bottle registers shockingly on my fingers and palm

pulling me back to reality as I take the beer from Tio's grasp. Ever so slowly, Tio Pilo lowers himself onto his rocking chair. The grimace on his face is washed away with the first sip he takes from his beer.

11   To look at my uncle is to see what my father would have looked like had he lived to be Tio Pilo's age. At seventy-eight, my uncle still has a respectable amount of hair—though it is rather thin and gray. The deep wrinkles etched by time in his face are revered by all five generations of his family. As I watch my uncle settle into his throne, I can't help but think about my father and how little time we had together.

12   Someday, and I hope not soon, I will miss my Tio Pilo. I will miss his voice, his smile, and his hands. But for now we sit visiting with one another. "How have you been?" I ask Tio in Spanish.

13   "Very well, thank you," he replies. "And yourself?"

14   "Fine, thank you," I reply respectfully.

15   Tio Pilo then raises his bottle of Corona, tipping the top toward me. I respond by doing the same.

16   "Para tu vida [to your life]," he says with a smile.

17   "Para nuestra vidas [to our lives]," I say.

18   He motions for me to come closer and in the soft voice that has become his trademark he asks, "Did I ever tell you about the time your father . . . ?"

—Jesse Perez

AUDIENCE AWARENESS: DISCOVERING UNIFYING TECHNIQUES

CONCEPTS TO LEARN

Inviting your audience in: Unity, purpose, and tone

Appealing to your audience: Figurative language and parallelism

Keeping your audience with you: Transitions

Just as an artist does with brush or camera, a writer must, with words, provide the reader with shapes, colors, and textures in order to represent what Ernest Hemingway calls "the feeling of the actual life." Otherwise, the words are like shadows on the canvas or photographic paper—they hint at something significant, but the reader has a hard time making sense of them.

So far in this text you have learned about techniques that help you explore your thoughts and discover new ideas. In addition, you have learned the importance of focusing on a central idea which, in turn, is expressed in the thesis or topic sentence. You have learned that, like the eye of a painter or photographer, your writer's mind is most effective when it concentrates your attention on a central idea so that you can help your reader experience "actual life" through your words.

Once you have put down your pen or turned off your computer screen, you may think that your work is behind you. But when the essay goes into the hands of its readers, your work will take on a new life as others look at what had been a private matter between you and the paper.

Your words require action on the part of your readers. They are simply marks on a page until they are processed by the mind and translated into concrete images and ideas. Working together, then, readers and writers bring to life the words that lie on the page. If the result of your work is clear and focused, those who look at it will see what you intended them to see. If, however, your work lacks a focus and is missing vital information, if it is repetitive, or if it is off the subject, then you will have created what William Zinsser calls *noise:*

> Noise is the typographical error, handwriting that's hard to read, distortion on the TV screen, the lapse of memory, the slip of the tongue, the wrong neuron fired by the brain—anything that brings disorder to the intended order of the message.

Unity: The Picture within the Frame

William Zinsser is talking here about a lack of unity. In writing, unity requires that each part of the essay (or poem or story) relate to all the other parts, and that the whole essay (or poem or story) have a central focus to which all parts are related. Just as the camera frames a picture that contains a central focus—perhaps your family standing at the edge of the Grand Canyon—so it also contains minor, supporting elements, such as the red rocks in the background, the hood of your car, and a couple of tourists pointing toward the canyon. The photograph frames a unified whole—the picture of your family on vacation at the Grand Canyon—and even the background elements support that central theme. If, however, a double exposure causes the image of the Golden Gate Bridge to appear in the photograph, then you have "noise" and a lack of unity.

In the following excerpt from a letter to his father, Ernest Hemingway explains his efforts as a writer to show "three dimensions and if possible four" in order to make his writing come alive. Hemingway is acutely aware of the importance of unity, for he knows that "the thing" will be meaningless if the "bad and the ugly as well as what is beautiful" do not have a central, unified focus.

> You see I'm trying in all my stories to get the feeling of the actual life across—not to just depict life—or criticize it—but to actually make it alive. So that when you have read something by me you actually experience the thing. You can't do this without putting in the bad and the ugly as well as what is beautiful. Because if it is all beautiful you can't believe in it. Things aren't that way. It is only by showing both sides—three dimensions and if possible four that you can write the way I want to.

Without a central focus, Hemingway's "sides" and "dimensions" will simply become three- or four-dimensional noise.

Similarly, in the excerpt from "Two Views of the Mississippi" in Chapter 1 of this text, Mark Twain provides many small details about the colors and movements of the river, but all of those details are unified around his central theme: that the "face of the water" is like "a wonderful book." Without such unity, Twain's writing would simply wander from detail to detail, and his readers would soon lose interest. Like Hemingway and Twain, you must be certain that the details you include in your writing support a central focus and create a sense of unity and wholeness.

Experienced writers like Ernest Hemingway, Mark Twain, and William Zinsser know that they can rely on certain unifying techniques to hold their audience's interest and attention. The most important of these techniques is a steady focus on the writer's tone, purpose, and attitude; in addition, experienced writers use figurative language, parallelism, and transitions to add to a sense of unity. In this chapter, you will learn how to use these techniques to hold your audience's interest and attention.

For Thought and Discussion

1. Write down the first word that pops into your head, and cluster or brainstorm around it.

2. Look at your cluster or brainstorm list to see how the ideas you came up with are unified—first with the central word or idea, and then with each other. If some of the ideas don't fit, simply cross them out.

3. Write for ten minutes, using those ideas that contribute to the unity of the writing and ignoring those that do not. (Remember: Even though you have put an idea down on paper as a possibility, either in your cluster, brainstorm, or freewriting or in an early draft of your essay, you do not have to include that idea in the final product.)

4. Reread your writing for unity. Is there a central focus? Does everything in the piece of writing support that focus? If not, how can you change it?

5. Bring this exercise to class (including your prewriting) and share it with a peer group, describing the process you went through in sorting out your ideas and in sharpening your focus. Ask your peer editors for suggestions on how to improve your piece.

Capturing the Crucial: Your Audience

Whether you are trying to capture the crucial elements of a scene in a photograph, the important features of a microscopic organism in a lab report, or the essence of an idea in an essay, you must be aware of the key role played by your audience. Sometimes it is difficult to remember that you are writing for anyone other than yourself; yet if you lose sight of this critical element, you are in danger of forgetting about your central focus and allowing "noise" to creep into your writing.

"The object of art," says Jean Anouilh, "is to give life shape." When you write, you take the materials of your medium (words) and shape them into something that has meaning for another person (an essay or story), just as a sculptor might give shape to a piece of wire or a lump of clay; each creation is a reflection of some aspect of the world—a person, an event, or an idea.

During your lifetime, you will write for many audiences—personal, professional, and academic. But in order for each audience to feel "at home" with what you have written, you will need to communicate with that audience in its particular vocabulary and language pattern. In a single week, you may need to write a memo at work, a letter to your best friend, a résumé or job application, and a letter to the editor of the local newspaper. You wouldn't want your letter to the editor to be written in the same informal style as your letter to your best friend, any more than you would want to show up at a black-tie dinner in blue jeans. Your awareness of your audience, as well as of your purpose, will determine key factors in the writing that finally emerges.

The Writer's Purpose and Attitude

Just as Ernest Hemingway explains to his father (a doctor who had difficulty understanding his son's desire to be a writer) that he wants to show "the bad and the ugly as well as what is beautiful" through his writing, you should have reasons for arranging your words as you do. These reasons should grow out of your *purpose* for writing and your *attitude* toward your subject. As you read the following poem by Elizabeth Bartlett, a contemporary British poet, think about how the words she has chosen and the concrete details she has provided help you to understand her attitude and purpose. In addition, notice how Bartlett frames these "photographs" of her mother, creating a carefully thought out portrait of her life.

Contre Jour

Contre jour, he said, a photographic phrase,   1
literally against the day, I suppose.
I'll put a little by, my mother would say,
against the day when we have nothing left.
Limp purse, well-rubbed false teeth,   5
not quite fitting, second-hand clothes,
knees like nutmeg graters. Whatever happened
to those gentle scented mothers sitting in gardens

under a shady hat, the maid mincing across the grass
with a tray for afternoon tea in early June?   10
It was never summer for her. It didn't reach
the dank back yard, the airless little rooms,
where the kitchen range brought a flush
to her face as she perpetually bent over it,
cooking, ironing, shifting sooty kettles round,   15
but never posed for her husband to catch
the tilt of her head against the day,
who never owned a camera anyway.

My inner lens clicks faster, faster,
contre jour, for now her face is fading   20
as her life recedes. You must have known
that once she minced across the lawn
carrying a loaded tray for mothers
like yours, whose photographs have
frames of silver, like the ones   25
she polished every week for twelve
pounds per annum and her keep.

For Thought and Discussion

1. What does the phrase *contre jour* mean?

2. Describe the mother in the poem, adding your mental images to the images supplied by the poet.

3. Does "you" include the entire audience for the poem, or a specific person or group of people? Does Bartlett intend that the poem be read by persons other than "you"?

4. What are the connotation and denotation of "summer," as it is used in the poem?

5. What is the central metaphor for the poem?

6. List the figurative language that describes the mother in the poem.

7. By framing these pictures from her mother's life, the speaker conveys her own attitude toward that life. What is the speaker's attitude? Support your answer with specific examples from the poem.

8. In what ways does Bartlett "welcome" you into the world of the poem? What kinds of details are easy for you to picture in your mind? What kinds of details are not so easy for you to see or understand?

What Do You Mean by That Tone?

When you speak, the tone of your voice conveys as much meaning to your audience as the words you use. Your tone can be suggestive, like the voice Dorothy Parker says is as "intimate as the rustle of sheets," or as irritating as the voice Somerset Maugham likens to "the pitiless clamour of the pneumatic drill." When you write, your tone can make your readers feel "at home" with your writing, or it can make them feel uncomfortable—as if they had walked into the wrong house.

Your tone is a reflection of your attitude toward your subject, your audience, and your purpose—not only when you speak, but also when you write. The speaker in "Contre Jour" tells her mother's story in a tone that is sad, regretful, and slightly bitter. You, as the reader, are left to ponder the details: Why is she sad? What does she regret? Against whom is she bitter? The speaker's tone leads us to ask the questions; the experience created by the words yields the answers.

Your tone may reflect your topic, or it may provide—for a more dramatic effect—a sharp contrast to your topic. This is what Virginia Woolf does when she decides that irony is the most effective tool to help a particular audience—in this case, a group of twentieth-century professional women—understand the bittersweet fact that nineteenth-century women were able to succeed as writers long before they were allowed to pursue any other profession:

> Writing was a reputable and harmless occupation. The family peace was not broken by the scratching of a pen. No demand was made upon the family purse. For ten and sixpence one can buy paper enough to write all the plays of Shakespeare—if one has a mind that way. Pianos and models, Paris, Vienna, and Berlin, masters and mistresses, are not needed by a writer. The cheapness of writing paper is, of course, the reason why women have succeeded as writers before they have succeeded in the other professions.

Woolf's ironic tone creates a deliberate contrast between her serious point that women were prevented from pursuing any work that would make them conspicuous, costly, or controversial, and the "cheapness of writing paper." The members of her audience may smile at the absurdity of the contrast—but they get the point.

On the other hand, a research paper for your sociology professor, detailing the results of your field studies on the problems faced by families of migrant farmworkers living along the U.S.-Mexican border, would probably reflect a serious, scholarly tone. Your tone would be dictated by (1) the kind of material you have included in the essay—information relating directly to your discoveries and conclusions, (2) your purpose—to communicate a great deal of information in a clear and carefully structured manner, and (3) your audience—your professor. A passage from your research paper might sound something like this:

> Although these families are under considerable stress in their daily lives, since they have neither homes nor jobs upon which they can depend, many are able temporarily to relieve some of the tensions through the use of traditional art forms, especially music.

In contrast, your letters from the field to family and friends would likely be informal, descriptive, perhaps humorous, telling about the area you are visiting, the people with whom you are traveling, the food, the accommodations, and the climate. You would discuss the work itself in a more personal tone, perhaps describing your emotional responses to the people and conditions you have met:

> Last night, I had dinner with the Gomez family. After we ate, the children began to sing some traditional Mexican songs, and they insisted that I join in. You know how awful I am at carrying a tune, and my Spanish still isn't very good, so I made some amazing changes in their songs. I was embarrassed! But we all laughed so hard that I couldn't stay embarrassed—and they want me to come for dinner again next week. As I left, Mrs. Gomez said to me, *"Mi casa es tu casa,"* meaning "My house is your house." Needless to say, I think I'm going to find it difficult to leave these warm, generous people at the end of the summer.

While this account would be inappropriate in a scholarly report, it includes the kinds of details that your family would most want to read about.

For Thought and Discussion

1. The following brief excerpts focus on one general topic: parents and children. Yet, each passage is markedly different from the others. As you read these selections, identify each writer's *attitude, purpose, tone,* and intended *audience,* and discuss with your classmates the clues that help you to decide.

a   To the child, abandonment by its parents is the equivalent of death. Most parents, even when they are otherwise relatively ignorant or callous, are instinctively sensitive to their children's fear of abandonment and will therefore, day in and day out, hundreds and thousands of times, offer their children needed reassurance: "You know Mommy and Daddy aren't going to leave you behind"; "Of course Mommy and Daddy will come back to get you"; "Mommy and Daddy aren't going to forget about you." If these words are matched by deeds, month in and month out, year in and year out, by the time of adolescence the child will have lost the fear of abandonment and in its stead will have a deep inner feeling that the world is a safe place in which to be and protection will be there when it is needed. With this internal sense of the consistent safety of the world, such a child is free to delay gratification of one kind or another, secure in the knowledge that the opportunity for gratification, like home and parents, is always there, available when needed.

—M. Scott Peck

b   One of Mama's favorite teaching techniques was comparison—impossible us versus some paragon of elegance. "Does President Coolidge hang his dirty socks on a doorknob? Answer me! Does Rudolph Valentino leave his sneakers on his bed? Answer me! Does Chaim Weizmann chew his tie? Does the Prince of Wales throw newspaper into his mother's toilet bowl?" When all else failed

Mama made the announcement that put fear in our hearts. "All right; enough is enough. Tomorrow the Board of Health is coming to take you all away. Goodbye."

—Sam Levenson

c   God, Papa, ever since I went to sea and was on my own, and found out what hard work for little pay was, and what it felt like to be broke, and starve, and camp on park benches because I had no place to sleep, I've tried to be fair to you because I knew what you'd been up against as a kid. I've tried to make allowances. Christ, you have to make allowances in this damned family or go nuts! I have tried to make allowances for myself when I remember all the rotten stuff I've pulled! I've tried to feel like Mama that you can't help being what you are where money is concerned. But God Almighty, this last stunt of yours is too much! It makes me want to puke! Not because of the rotten way you're treating me. To hell with that! I've treated you rottenly, in my way, more than once. But to think when it's a question of your son having consumption, you can show yourself up before the whole town as such a stinking old tightwad. . . . Jesus, Papa, haven't you any pride or shame?

—Eugene O'Neill

d   Sitting at [my dying mother's] bedside, forever out of touch with her, I wondered about my own children, and their children, and children in general, and about the disconnections between children and parents that prevent them from knowing each other. Children rarely want to know who their parents were before they were parents, and when age finally stirs their curiosity there is no parent left to tell them. If a parent does lift the curtain a bit, it is often only to stun the young with some exemplary tale of how much harder life was in the old days.

—Russell Baker

2. Return to the examples of figurative language beginning on page 62 in Chapter 3, and identify the tone and purpose of each. Next describe how the use of metaphor and simile helps to define the tone and purpose in each of the preceding passages.

3. Identify the unifying theme of each passage.

Peer Editing Practice with a Focus on Your Audience

You may have had the experience of being told by an instructor or a peer editor that your points were not clear, when in fact you knew *exactly* what you meant to say. That last phrase, *what you meant to say*, holds the key to the mystery of what happens between the writer, the text, and the reader; in fact, what your readers perceive in your text may be quite different from what you think you are saying.

It is important to make the distinction between your intentions as a writer and your actual performance. Your audience has only the text—the written piece—to go on, while you have many more ideas, thoughts, shades of meanings, and connections circulating in your head. As you go through the process of writing and revising, you mentally fill in the blanks with connecting words, mental images, even missing punctuation, all of which serve to make the written piece perfectly clear to you. Your audience, how-ever, does not have the same advantage.

This interaction between text and reader is, of course, why we revise and why peer editing is so helpful. The opportunity to have another reader tell you what he or she understands is invaluable. Once you know what another person sees, you will return to the text with "new eyes," seeing your own writing in ways that had not occurred to you before.

Think of your communication with your audience as a triangle (see Figure 4-1), with each element having equal weight in the communication. The information travels in both directions along the sides of the reader-writer-text triangle, and you can see that your piece of writing is, in fact, *six* dialogues, all likely to send slightly different versions of your message—unless you as the writer are especially careful about making your ideas clear.

For Thought and Discussion

1. Choose a past journal entry of at least 250 words in length. Now, imagine that you are going to direct this journal entry to a particular audi-ence. If the entry is about a political issue, you may want to direct it toward your congressional representative. If the entry deals with your job, you may want to direct it to your employer. If it is a story, you may want to direct it to the little boy next door. Revise the entry with this audience in mind. Then make two photocopies and bring both the original and the copies to class.

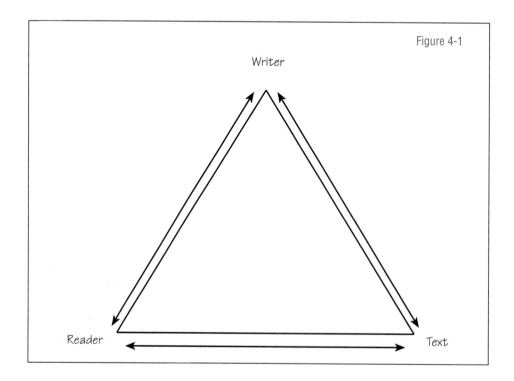

Figure 4-1

Writer

Reader

Text

2. Work in a peer editing group of three. Spend fifteen to twenty minutes reading and discussing each of the three entries.

3. As a reader, identify the audience, tone, and purpose of each piece of writing. Summarize these briefly, in writing; then check your perceptions with the other members of the group: Do your perceptions fit with those of the others? Is the writer's style appropriate for the audience he or she has chosen? Has the writer's tone and purpose been understood in the way he or she intended? If not, why not?

4. As a writer, pay attention to the way the others in the peer editing group perceive your meaning. Compare their perceptions with what you meant to say. What do you need to explain and clarify? What kinds of questions do the others ask you?

CONNECTING AND CREATING: APPEALING TO YOUR AUDIENCE

Only human beings create new objects and ideas out of those which already exist. Our ability to do so derives, in large part, from the fact that we can form new connections between previously isolated and unrelated bits of matter and information, just as Dagwood tries to do with isolated pieces of lumber in the cartoon. Unfortunately, Dagwood is not very successful. His ability to translate his vision into a form that is useful or understandable fails him.

So it is when a writer simply hammers words together into a form that looks as if it ought to hold up, but which lacks the necessary ''joints'' and ''glue.'' There is a lack of unity, a lack of integrity, a lack of clear purpose about the structure of the words; they are simply ''noise'' on paper, not worth a reader's time.

As you learned in Chapter 3, the process of writing helps you see, with the use of figurative language, the interaction between your own ideas—which are often abstract—and concrete images. In fact, you can often be most effective at communicating important ideas when you ''show'' them

to your readers. For example, on page 63, Emily Dickinson's "hope" becomes "the thing with feathers," while meaningless work, for Philip Larkin, becomes a "toad" that he can drive off with a pitchfork. These are familiar images that readers readily understand, but they are also effective in helping readers understand Dickinson's and Larkin's larger ideas about hope and work.

Similarly, writers can help their readers feel at home in a piece of writing by creating a sense of unity, not only with the familiar images created with the use of figurative language, but also with the use of parallelism and transitions. These devices can often tie together abstract ideas to help make the writer's central point, as Mark Twain does by showing us throughout his essay how a riverboat captain must learn to "read" the river, or as Maya Angelou does when she shows us her grandmother's dignity: in the way she carried her body, in the way she kept her composure when the children were mocking her, and even in the way her "apron strings trembled" when the children insulted her. Such images have audience appeal and create a lasting impression; a simple statement such as "My grandmother was a dignified woman" would not have the same effect.

FIGURATIVE LANGUAGE

In Chapter 3 we introduced you to three kinds of *figurative language: metaphors, similes,* and *personification.* Now we want to look at how these devices, along with *parallelism,* can help to create unity in your writing.

Metaphors

When Annie Dillard says that nature is a "now-you-see-it, now-you-don't affair," she is using a metaphor (recall that a metaphor says that one thing *is* another). As you read the following passage, look at the way in which Dillard unifies all of her ideas under this one central metaphor:

> Unfortunately, nature is very much a now-you-see-it, now-you-don't affair. A fish flashes, then dissolves in the water before my eyes like so much salt. Deer apparently ascend bodily into heaven; the brightest oriole fades into leaves. These disappearances stun me into stillness and concentration; they say of nature that it conceals with a grand nonchalance, and they say of vision that it is a deliberate gift, the revelation of a dancer who for my eyes only flings away her seven veils.

Dillard cannot, of course, show her readers *all* of nature's possibilities in a paragraph, a book, or a lifetime of writings. But she can help readers to see one aspect of nature as she sees it; this, in turn, may open her readers' eyes to seeing familiar scenes in new ways.

Vincent Dethier uses a series of metaphors to show his readers that

> A properly conducted experiment is a beautiful thing. It is an adventure, an expedition, a conquest. It commences with an act of faith, faith that the world is real, that our senses generally can be trusted, that effects have causes, and that we can discover meaning by reason. It continues with an observation and a question. An experiment is a scientist's way of asking nature a question.

Similes

A simile says that a thing is *like* or *as* another thing, as when Aldo Leopold says,

> Just as there is honor among thieves, so there is solidarity and co-operation among plant and animal pests. Where one pest is stopped by natural barriers, another arrives to breach the same wall by a new approach. In the end every region and every resource get their quota of uninvited ecological guests.

Leopold helps you to understand the ways pests in nature function as a unit by showing you how they are like human "pests," unifying several pieces of information about pests under one central idea and helping you to create an image of this activity.

Personification

John Muir, writing about the mountain winds, uses a central simile at the beginning of the following paragraph to show how they, like the other forces of nature, perform vital functions in the forest. See how many other similes you can find as you read:

> The mountain winds, like the dew and rain, sunshine and snow, are measured and bestowed with love on the forests to develop their strength and beauty. However restricted the scope of other forest influences, that of the winds is universal. The snow bends and trims the upper forests every winter, the lightning strikes a single tree here and there, while avalanches mow down thousands at a swoop as a gardener trims out a bed of flowers. But the winds go to every tree, fingering every leaf and branch and furrowed bole; not one is forgotten . . . they seek and find them all, caressing them tenderly, bending them in lusty exercise, stimulating their growth, plucking off a leaf or limb as required, or removing an entire tree or grove, now whispering and cooing through the branches like a sleepy child, now roaring like the ocean; the winds blessing the forests, the forests the winds, with ineffable beauty and harmony as the sure results.

For Muir, nature reflects an intelligence, complexity, and planning that humans can only glimpse. He provides one such glimpse in this passage by personifying the wind—portraying it as able to "seek and find" trees, to caress them, to bless them, to pluck off their leaves and limbs "as required," or to remove them altogether. This device further helps to unify the paragraph by making all of the wind's actions like those of a grand gardener.

For Thought and Discussion

1. Find in your reading an example of figurative language that helps to create unity in a passage.

2. Bring this example to class and share it with your peers during a discussion of unity and figurative language.

Parallelism

Lewis Thomas, a physician and laboratory researcher, describes the process of scientific exploration as one in which the researcher is "flung off into blind alleys, up trees, down dead ends, out into blue sky, along wrong turnings, around bends." Thomas creates pictures in his readers' minds that imaginatively "send" the researcher outside of the safety of the laboratory and into the larger world where everyone knows there are risks and surprises. What his readers may not know—and what Thomas wants them to understand—is that there are also risks and surprises in every research laboratory, and his metaphor is one way to show that scientific exploration is not the dull, white-coated experience that it often appears to be to an outsider.

Notice that Lewis Thomas links together the figurative actions with a series of prepositions—*off, up, down, out, along, around*—not only creating a sense of rhythm and motion, but, through his repeated use of the same part of speech, creating unity as well.

This repetition of key words and phrases or of syntax is called *parallelism*. It is a favorite tool of effective writers and speakers because its rhythms make ideas more memorable. Parallelism creates a sense of unity, forging strong, well-defined links along the reader-writer-text triangle. Most commonly, writers use parallelism with single parts of speech—nouns, verbs, adjectives, or prepositions. But longer units of thought, such as phrases and clauses, can also be parallel.

Parallelism is the favorite tool of poets and orators. They know that parallel phrases stick in people's memories, sometimes becoming more memorable than the events that inspired them in the first place. Franklin D. Roosevelt's Depression-era exhortation remains memorable and powerful in its simplicity: "We have nothing to fear but fear itself." Roosevelt repeats only the word *fear*, but since that single word constitutes one-fourth of the sentence, its impact is magnified.

Like Franklin Roosevelt, Abraham Lincoln, and Martin Luther King, Jr., President John F. Kennedy understood the force of parallelism in writing. Even though you may not have been alive when Kennedy was president, it is likely that you are familiar with "Ask not what your country can do for you; ask what you can do for your country." In this example, the second phrase reverses the idea in the first by repeating the *words* but not the *word order,* making the passage stick indelibly in the minds of those who have read or heard it. It is no accident that this sentence remains memorable after more than thirty years.

Parallelism streamlines and unifies a writer's ideas, making it possible to condense and emphasize important points:

> Through the love, stability, discipline, and laughter of parents and siblings, children learn that reality accepts them, welcomes them, invites their willingness to take risks.

Notice that the writer, Michael Novak, uses two parallel series: first a series of nouns—"love, stability, discipline, and laughter"—then a series of verb phrases—"accepts them, welcomes them, invites their willingness." Novak has unified a number of important ideas within a single sentence through the use of parallelism, though he could have said the same thing by using a great many more words, as in the following example:

> Parents should show their children that they love them. It is also important to have a stable home. Discipline is essential for a child's growth. Parents and siblings should laugh together. If they do these things, then children learn that reality accepts them. In addition, it welcomes them and invites their willingness to take risks.

While it may seem that the greater number of words is desirable, experienced writers know that the use of parallelism to streamline a passage creates writing that people enjoy and remember. Which of the two versions above would you rather read? More important, which one would you remember?

Alliteration is often used as a parallel device. In Chapter 3, you saw how alliteration creates memorable titles through the repetition of similar sounding sounds. Such repetition is equally effective in any kind of writing, whether it is a sentence, a paragraph, or an essay. And because it is written to be remembered, poetry often makes powerful use of alliteration, as in Gwendolyn Brooks' poem quoted on page 101.

Whenever we create a parallel between two things, we are focusing on the resemblances between them. So when we create parallelism in our writing, we are asking our readers to focus on the resemblances between the ideas or images. Such similarities may lie in repetition of words, phrases, parts of speech, or sounds, as in alliteration.

Following are some examples of parallelism. You will recognize that some are taken from passages you have already read in this text.

Noun Series:

> In Pittsburgh, she dressed. She wore jewelry by the breastful, by the armload: diamonds, rubies, emeralds.   —Annie Dillard

> All the grace, the beauty, the poetry had gone out of the majestic river.
>   —Mark Twain

100

AUDIENCE
AWARENESS:
DISCOVERING
UNIFYING
TECHNIQUES

Adjective Series:

And that is why these smart, energetic, do-it-now, pushing people so often say: "I am not creative."
—Brenda Ueland

He was said to be stuffy, dull, and hopelessly out of date.
—Russell Baker

Verb Series:

Now the writer, as I think, has a chance to live more than other people in the presence of this reality. It is his business to find it and collect it and communicate it to the rest of us.
—Virginia Woolf

I wanted to throw a handful of black pepper in their faces, to throw lye on them, to scream that they were dirty, scummy peckerwoods, but I knew I was as clearly imprisoned behind the scene as the actors outside were confined to their roles.
—Maya Angelou

Series of Independent Clauses (an independent clause has a subject and a verb):

Old paint on canvas, as it ages, sometimes becomes transparent. When that happens it is possible, in some pictures, to see the original lines: a tree will show through a woman's dress, a child makes way for a dog, a large boat is no longer on an open sea.
—Lillian Hellman

She was unique; she was careful and exacting; she was intense; she was genuine.
—from "Marika"

Series of Prepositional Phrases (a prepositional phrase consists of a preposition plus the noun or pronoun that follows it):

There are so many times when a person can think, "Wow, I'm really grown up now!" There are the official ones: at sixteen you can drive, at eighteen vote, at twenty-one drink.
—Sara Costello

What is meant by "reality"? It would seem to be something very erratic, very undependable—now to be found in a dusty road, now in a scrap of newspaper in the street, now in a daffodil in the sun.
—Virginia Woolf

Parallelism with Modification (you may decide to modify a parallel series in order to avoid monotony or to emphasize a point):

He had a primly pointed jaw, a primly straight nose, and a prim manner of speaking that was so correct, so gentlemanly, that he seemed a comic antique.
—Russell Baker

Repetition:

A very now rock group is playing at all of her parties. A very now underground filmmaker's filming her thumbs. A very now artist is doing her portrait in latex.
—Judith Viorst

Alliteration:

101

**AUDIENCE
AWARENESS:
DISCOVERING
UNIFYING
TECHNIQUES**

The Pool Players
Seven at the Golden Shovel

We real cool.   We
Left school.   We

Lurk late.   We
Strike straight.   We

Sing sin.   We
Thin gin.   We

Jazz June.   We
Die soon.   —Gwendolyn Brooks

In the final example, note how effectively Brooks uses parallelism. Not only does she repeat "We," which creates a strong, almost musical rhythm, but she also repeats certain sounds. Look again at the poem and note how many "W," "L," "S," "ee" and "oo" sounds appear in its brief eight lines.

For Thought and Discussion

1. Return to the passages in this chapter by Sam Levenson and Eugene O'Neill on pages 92–93. One writer uses repetition to heighten the humor in his passage, the other to heighten the sense of sadness and loss.
      a. Point out the parallelism in each passage.
      b. Explain how parallelism makes the writer's points more vivid.

2. Lewis Thomas makes effective use of prepositional phrases in the passage about scientific exploration on page 98. List those phrases, and examine their parallel structure.

3. Make a list of all of the verbs that Annie Dillard uses when she describes the dying frog on page 62. Why is this kind of repetition effective?

4. Clustering and brainstorming generate parallel structure in writing quite naturally, since all three techniques depend upon the similarities and connections between ideas. To discover your own ability to come up with parallel structures, do the following exercise:
      a. Cluster or brainstorm the word *childhood* for three to four minutes.
      b. Write for about ten minutes.
      c. When you finish, evaluate your passage for repetition and parallelism. Look for places where you can add these elements to make your writing even more concrete, vivid, and memorable for your readers; rewrite the passage again.
      d. Bring your first and second drafts to the next class and share them with a small peer editing group (three or four students).
      e. Read the passage out loud, then talk about the process that led to the final version.

102

**AUDIENCE
AWARENESS:
DISCOVERING
UNIFYING
TECHNIQUES**

f. Using the ideas that come out of the discussion with your partners, rewrite the passage again.

5. Make a list of quotations that you know from memory. Which of these contain parallel structure?

 KEEPING YOUR AUDIENCE WITH YOU

The Verbal "Glue": Transitions

Another way to create unity in your writing is to draw on special *transitional words* to guide your readers from one idea to the next. Transitional words are especially important signposts when you move between ideas, helping your readers to follow you from one idea to the next.

Keep in mind that the communication among the reader, the text, and the writer is likely to break down along the triangle we discussed earlier in this chapter if the writer fails to make accurate, clear verbal connections. Without them, you as a writer are at risk of losing or confusing your readers, just as you are likely to become lost or confused when driving in an unfamiliar place where the road signs are missing or pointing in the wrong direction.

There are many transitional words and phrases you can use to mark the logical shifts within or between sentences. With the transition chart below, you will—unlike Dagwood—have at your disposal some of the necessary "glue" and "braces" to hold your essay together.

TRANSITION CHART

With Examples:

for example	in fact	particularly
for instance	in other words	specifically
incidentally	in particular	that is
indeed	namely	thus

With Additions:

again	even	next
also	first*	of course
and	further	second*
and then	furthermore	similarly
besides	in addition (to)	subsequently
beyond that	likewise	third*
equally important	moreover	too

* Avoid the use of "firstly," "secondly," and "thirdly." It is awkward and unnecessary.

In Comparisons:
- as
- in the same way
- like
- likewise
- similarly

With Hypothetical Conditions:
- as if
- as though
- even though
- if

In Contrasts:

after all	even though	notwithstanding
although	however	on the contrary
but	(in) contrast (to)	on the other hand
conversely	in spite (of)	or
despite	instead (of)	still
except	nevertheless	while
even if	nor	yet

Showing Cause and Effect:

accordingly	if . . . then	so that
as a result	necessarily	then
because	of necessity	thereby
consequently	of course	therefore
for	since	thus
hence	so	

Showing Passage of Time:

after	last	since then
after a while	presently	temporarily
afterward	recently	then
at last	shortly	when
lately	since	

With Conclusions or Summaries:

accordingly	in conclusion	so
and so	in other words	then
as a result	in short	therefore
consequently	in summary	thus
finally	last	to conclude
in brief	on the whole	to summarize

Word Choice: Black Tie or Blue Jeans?

Some of the transitions on the list have a polished, sophisticated tone. When you use them, they add to the polished, sophisticated tone of your essays, as well. If you do not already use them, it may seem awkward, at first, to use words like *thereby* or *nevertheless*, since they are not everyday words. Yet, the words we use in formal writing *are* somewhat different from spoken English: there are more rules about what word goes with what; in addition, for many

104

AUDIENCE
AWARENESS:
DISCOVERING
UNIFYING
TECHNIQUES

audiences, we use a larger, more varied vocabulary than that which we use in speech.

M. Scott Peck, in his discussion of children's need for a sense of safety (first quoted on page 92) uses transitions to keep a long sentence organized and unified:

> If these words are matched by deeds, month in and month out, year in and year out, by the time of adolescence the child will have lost the fear of abandonment and in its stead will have a deep inner feeling that the world is a safe place in which to be and that protection will be there when it is needed.

The use of transitional words helps you to keep track of the direction of your thoughts as you write. Watch how Sara Costello, in her informal journal entry about rites of passage, signals additions to her ideas or changes in the direction of her thoughts as she writes:

> There are so many times when a person can think, "Wow, I'm really grown up now!" There are the official ones: at sixteen you can drive, at eighteen vote, at twenty-one drink. Yet many people flaunt or ignore these rights (or responsibilities), whether out of a wish to be "grown up" or to devalue what they see as adult privileges—sometimes, even just out of apathy. Anyway, these occasions seem almost demeaning to me, with the government playing the role of a parent who decides that the child is "responsible enough" to do something.

In addition, transitional words are important signals to readers about where you are going next. The words *however* and *but* alert the reader to a very different direction in thought than the words *so* and *therefore*. Watch how Mark Twain uses transitions to control the direction of his readers' attention in the following excerpt from "Two Views of the Mississippi" (first quoted on page 7):

> The passenger who could not read it was charmed with a peculiar sort of faint dimple on its surface . . .; but to the pilot that was an *italicized* passage; indeed, it was more than that, it was a legend of the largest capitals, with a string of shouting exclamation points at the end of it; for it meant that a wreck or a rock was buried there that could tear the life out of the strongest vessel that ever floated.

Notice that Twain uses an entire phrase—"indeed, it was more than that"— to make a transition between his description of the river as "an *italicized* passage" and as "a legend of the largest capitals."

Sometimes, you may need to use a whole sentence or two in order to move smoothly between ideas. In the following sentence from the essay reprinted in the next section, Ellen Goodman makes a major transition between an idea about age segregation in housing and age segregation in our thinking: "Even when we don't live in age ghettos, we often think that way."

The way you use language sends powerful messages to your audience.

Your choice of words, whenever you speak or write, signals not only your attitude, purpose, and tone, but also your consideration for your audience's needs and feelings, your level of sophistication, and your opinion of yourself.

105

AUDIENCE
AWARENESS:
DISCOVERING
UNIFYING
TECHNIQUES

A PROFESSIONAL WRITER AT WORK

Ellen Goodman is a nationally syndicated columnist who is noted for her ability to examine the impact of worldwide events and political decisions on the everyday lives of individuals. The following selection comes from a collection of her essays, *Coming Home.*

Family: The One Social Glue

1   They are going home for Thanksgiving, traveling through the clogged arteries of airports and highways, bearing bridge chairs and serving plates, Port-a-Cribs and pies. They are going home to rooms that resound with old arguments and interruptions, to piano benches filled with small cousins, to dining-room tables stretched out to the last leaf.

2   They no longer migrate over the river and through the woods straight into that Norman Rockwell poster: Freedom from Want. No, Thanksgiving isn't just a feast, but a reunion. It's no longer a celebration of food (which is plentiful in America) but of family (which is scarce).

3   Now families are so dispersed that it's easier to bring in the crops than the cousins. Now it's not so remarkable that we have a turkey to feed the family. It's more remarkable that there's enough family around to warrant a turkey.

4   For most of the year, we are a nation of individuals, all wrapped in separate cellophane packages like lamb chops in the meat department of a city supermarket. Increasingly, we live with decreasing numbers. We create a new category like Single Householder, and fill it to the top of the Census Bureau reports.

5   For most of the year, we are segregated along generation lines into retirement villages and singles complexes, young married subdivisions and college dormitories, all exclusive clubs whose membership is defined by age.

6   Even when we don't live in age ghettos, we often think that way. Those who worried about a generation gap in the sixties worried about a generation war in the seventies. They see a community torn by warring rights: the Elderly Rights vs. the Middle-Aged Rights vs. the Children Rights. All competing for a piece of the pie.

7   This year, the Elderly Rights fought against mandatory retirement while the Younger Rights fought for job openings. The Children Rights worried about the money to keep their schools open, while the Elderly Rights worried about the rising cost of real estate taxes.

8   The retired generation lobbied for an increase in Social Security payments, while the working generation lobbied for a decrease in Social Security taxes. The elderly wanted health care and the children wanted day care and the middle-aged were tired of taking care. They wanted the right to lead their own lives.

106

**AUDIENCE
AWARENESS:
DISCOVERING
UNIFYING
TECHNIQUES**

9   At times it seemed as if the nation had splintered into peer pressure groups, panthers of all ages: People who cried, not "Me First" but, rather, "My Generation First."

10   But now they have come home for Thanksgiving. Even the Rights are a family who come together, not to fight for their piece of the pie this day, but to share it.

11   The family—as extended as that dining-room table—may be the one social glue strong enough to withstand the centrifuge of special interests which sends us spinning away from each other. There, in the family, the Elderly Rights are also the grandparents and the Children Rights are also nieces and nephews. There, the old are our parents and the young are our children. There, we care about each others' lives. There, self-interest includes concern for the future of the next generation—because they are ours.

12   Our families are not just the people (if I may massacre Robert Frost) who, "when you have to go there, they have to let you in." They are the people who maintain an unreasonable interest in each other. They are the natural peacemakers in the generation war.

13   "Home" is the only place in society where we now connect along the ages, like discs along the spine of society—the only place where we remember that we're all related. And that's not a bad idea to go home to.

For Thought and Discussion

1. List the transitional words that Goodman uses to connect her ideas.

2. Which paragraphs begin with transitional words or phrases?

3. List the parallel phrases and words that Goodman employs in this essay.

4. What are some of the advantages of the extended family? What are some of the disadvantages?

5. What is Goodman's opinion of age segregation? In your opinion, what are the advantages of having the generations segregated? What are the disadvantages?

6. Goodman has alluded to a famous quote from Robert Frost's poem, "The Death of the Hired Man":

> Home is the place where, when you have to go there
> They have to take you in.

In what way has Goodman changed the quote? Why does she still give Frost credit?

WRITING ASSIGNMENT

For this essay, address one of the following topics on the family. Be sure that you do the following:

■ Cluster, brainstorm, or freewrite on the topic you have chosen.

■ Discover your central focus, and be sure that you support it adequately.

■ After you have done your prewriting and a preliminary draft, think about who your audience will be and begin to write with one eye on the essay's potential readers. (Remember the interaction between the points on the reader-writer-text triangle.)

■ Be sure that you include parallelism and transitional words in your essay.

Suggestions for Topics

1. On page 92, Sam Levenson discusses his mother's "teaching techniques." Did your mother (or father) have special teaching techniques, or do you have any if you are a parent? Write an essay in which you state a thesis about the effect of those teaching techniques, and be sure to support your thesis.

2. On page 93, Russell Baker writes about the poignant situation in which children become interested too late in their parents' lives. In an essay of at least 500 words, make a significant point about an aspect of your mother's or father's life that you find particularly interesting or meaningful. Support your central point with illustrations and examples.

3. In her essay beginning on page 105, Ellen Goodman discusses the war between the generations. Do you see aspects of that war in your own family life, or do you think that she is overstating the case? Write an essay of at least 500 words in which you state a thesis and support it with examples and illustrations.

Peer Editing Checklist

After you have completed the prewriting and the first draft of your essay, meet with a peer editing group so that you can assess the reaction of an audience to your writing. Photocopy enough copies of your essay for your peer editing group.

1. First, read the essay through once without stopping.

2. Indicate any ideas, passages, imagery, allusions, or other aspects of this essay you find effective. Positive reinforcement is a powerful tool.

3. Underline the thesis. If you cannot identify the thesis, ask the writer to point it out or to further clarify the thesis, in writing, should this prove necessary.

4. Point out any details or passages that do not seem relevant to the author's point. The author can then decide whether a transition could clarify the connection with the thesis or if the point is truly irrelevant.

5. Point out places where the illustrations and examples are convincing, and where the writer uses concrete, vivid words. Then show the writer where he or she needs to add these strategies in order to add color, life, and variety to the essay.

6. Identify the writer's tone. Tell the writer whether it is appropriate and effective for the topic.

7. Look for parallelism in the essay. If you see opportunities for streamlining ideas through the use of parallelism, point them out.

8. Look for figurative language—metaphors, similes, and personification. Note areas on the rough draft where figurative language would help clarify the point.

9. What is your reaction to the essay's title? Does the title help you better understand the author's point, or does the title pique your interest in reading the essay?

When writers have revised the content of the essay to their satisfaction and are ready for feedback about mechanics, point out but do not correct any problems you suspect with spelling, grammar, and punctuation. It is the writer's responsibility to make such corrections.

Help! For Further Work

Read the following student draft as if you were its peer editor. Then respond to the points in the peer editing checklist.

Easy Things Come Hard

1   The time had come to expand my horizons. I was to step up from my tricycle and ''Big Wheel'' riding days of my younger years. No more senseless trips of circling around our driveway going absolutely nowhere. The time had come to conquer the bicycle, my round trip ticket to our unexplored neighborhood.

2   It was the middle of a sizzling summer day with dusky peach skies. With the aid of my older brother and our next door neighbor at my side, I was to master the bicycle, that musky summer day. As I looked up upon this ominous piece of machinery, towering over me, my puny hands quivered at my sides. Fear raced through my head.

3   It was your typical American hand me down bike of the early 1970's era. It was slightly too large and painstakingly to mount. It was a curvy, glistening shade of orange furnished with an unsightly banana-style seat that glittered purple in the glare of the sun. A seat so oblong I wasn't sure where to lay down my posterior. The awkward U-shaped handlebars were designed more to doom a young boy than to steer a bicycle. Red and white diamond-like reflectors dotted the bike and, of course, wheels—two of them. It was an intangible mode of transportation, but also, my ride to freedom.

4   As was expected, my first attempts were utter disasters. Physically and emo-

tionally painful disasters. While our next door neighbor steadied the shaky bike, my brother would set me off with a push. As we sputtered off down the sidewalk, the bike went one way and my body parts went the opposite way. Ten feet and "crash". I was flat on my face. The bike never went a straight path for a second. I must of been the most uncoordinated seven year old on this planet. My brain was scrambled with mixed emotions. My ride to an expanding, unexplored neighborhood was now my deadliest enemy.

5   So here I lay. Confronted with my future. I was flat on my face. My helpers getting impatient with me. The bike mocking me. Lying there on the edge of the hot sidewalk. My destiny was before me. I was to prove myself worthy or forever walk or saddleride for the remainder of my childhood. Time was running out. The blinding sun was descending downward. Soon it would be time to go in.

6   Determined, I slowly picked up the bicycle off the ground and mounted it. Balancing myself on my tiptoes, I pushed off with all my might. With the front wheel wobbling side to side, I pedalled and pedalled. Finally, steadying the impossible handlebars, I was on my way. Ten feet, twenty feet, thirty feet, a smile came upon my face. My two helpers cheered me on to go faster or to turn around or something. I was too ecstatic to hear anything but a breeze at my side. The world was at my feet as I pedalled onward.

7   From one end of the block to the other end, I proudly rode that bike. All my fears were pedalled away. As I senselessly rode around our neighborhood down the block into the sunset, I was set free.

STUDENT STARS

The students who wrote these essays did the following:

1. Prewriting
2. Writing
3. Revision of content
4. Proofreading and revision of mechanics.

The first essay was written by a student who was forced to leave Vietnam, alone, at the age of ten. He has not seen the family he left behind since that time. This is his recollection of his life—before.

The Bright Past

1   My mother was a gentle woman and a person who did not want to leave the kitchen, but her attitude changed when my father disappeared to the "heaven of joy" and left her with ten young children. Throughout, she was the silk of our clothes, the daily nutrition for our bodies, and the cup of water to fulfill our thirsty moments.

2   When my father died, her feminine attitude changed because she had to

110

**AUDIENCE
AWARENESS:
DISCOVERING
UNIFYING
TECHNIQUES**

deal with the daily life situations that traditional people believed that only men could handle: preparing the new crops, watering the crops manually, and processing the crops into rice that she could then sell.

3 Every morning before sunrise, she was already in the rice fields, checking the crop and praying that the God of Nature would bless us with a year of success. At sunset, she would come home with a muddy body but always with a happy face. At supper, she was never tired of giving us a fascinating description of new events that took place at her worksite.

4 One time, she told us about the day when our neighbors planted their crops. Those who put the crops into the ground sang the traditional song describing the life of a peasant, while those who watered the field made a rhythm out of the water from the well. She told us that the last thing she saw that day was a group of people moving across the field like a school of fish and carrying the food for the workers.

5 Because I was so young, my mother did not want me to help in the fields, so for me, living in the small Bien province in Viet Nam was like living in a fantasy Garden of Eden. Since my mother and older siblings worked all day, I could go off adventuring on my own. At the end of the day, I would have stories to tell the family about what I had seen and done.

6 For example, when I wanted to see what real tea was made out of, all I had to do was just go to the tea farm. When I got there, I could smell the dark green tea bushes, whose scent permeated the air. It always made me close my eyes to inhale the elegant odor, and I couldn't resist picking the leaves and taking a handful home to my mother.

7 Whenever I wanted to release my anger, I just walked to the pond that was filled with lotus. I felt like I was browsing in heaven's garden because of the silence and misty atmosphere. Along the path to the lotus garden, there were many kinds of flowers on both sides, and there was a long bridge connecting the garden to the Chinese style castle that had been built during the Minh Dynasty. My mother had told me stories about that castle, and I imagined how it must have been when it was occupied by noblemen and soldiers.

8 During the fall, I would see bright red apples, ready to be picked, which made the garden look even more colorful. After I visited there, I would always feel better and my mind would be more open. I would walk home and listen to the crickets make noise, the birds sing, and the bees buzz. The natural beauty of this land is always in my heart, and my memory always flashes back when I read the descriptions of the Garden of Eden. Like Adam and Eve, I couldn't resist picking an apple once in a while, even though my mother repeatedly told me not to. Maybe that was a foreshadowing of things to come.

9 I was unaware that my mother worried that this land would not be an Eden for me if I remained much longer. Our family was out of favor with the government, and as such, no member of the family would be allowed to receive an education for the next ten generations. As a consequence, I would have few opportunities in Vietnamese society. My mother was determined that I would not live the life of an uneducated peasant or soldier, so she sent me to this country to give me a chance for an education and a better life.

10 Though I have not seen her since I was ten, I clearly remember that whenever my mother told us a story, she always concluded by saying, "Edu-

cation is the key to a bright future; if you use it wisely, then you will become somebody in any society. I hope that my sacrifice will reflect on the outcome of my children.'' I will try very hard to reach for the very best.   —Tinh Vy

111

AUDIENCE
AWARENESS:
DISCOVERING
UNIFYING
TECHNIQUES

The Lesson

1   I was sixteen years old and the anticipation of driving a car was killing me. My hormones were popping, and all I cared about were boys, getting a driver's license, and being "cool." Then the words spoke to me from my father's mouth: "If you learn how to drive on a stick, you can drive anything." Those words led to an experience I would never forget.

2   My dad was a Drivers Ed teacher at Monterey High School, so he was able to pull some strings to get my best friend, Denise, and me to be his students. We met my dad on the Monterey High School parking lot on a sunny Saturday morning for our first lesson. There my dad stood in front of a white VW bug. As we approached him, his words echoed in my head: "If you learn how to drive on a stick, you can drive anything." God, how I hated those words. The misery of learning to drive a stick was nearly unbearable, but the words "driver's license" rang in my head like a cathedral bell in a tower. I gritted my teeth and took a deep breath, knowing I would have to learn on a stick.

3   We loaded into the VW bug, Denise in back, my father in the passenger's seat, and I in the driver's seat, giggling and squealing. "Now, in order to start the car, you have to push the clutch all the way to the floor and turn the key," said my father. My hands were sweaty as I started the ignition. "Rum, rum," the VW shook. Denise screamed with excitement. There we were, two Monterey High School girls just about to make the cruise; what coolness, what badness, how awesome we were.

4   "Let's cruise down the main drag," said Denise.

5   "Let your foot off the clutch a little and then step on the gas," said my father.

6   "No sweat," I said, feeling cocky. As I started to ease off the clutch and step on the gas, the car jerked forward and died. There was dead silence for a few seconds, then the words rang in my head: "If you learn on a stick, you can drive anything." How I hated learning on a stick, how I hated those words.

7   After that long and miserable day, I swore I would never drive a stick shift again. I was successful in getting my license, but I made sure I drove a car with an automatic transmission for my test, and I drove only cars with automatics for many years after. The pain and agony of learning on a stick eventually left me, leaving only the words my father had spoken: "If you learn on a stick, you can drive anything."

8   On a sunny morning several years later, my husband and I left home for a Rolling Stones concert at Candlestick Park. His van was loaded with blankets, food and drink for the long day, and the concert was as exciting as we had hoped. However, when it was time to head home, we realized that my husband had had a little too much to drink. That meant that I was going to have to drive the stick shift van home.

9   As I approached the van, my stomach felt sick and I started to sweat. I hadn't driven a stick since that day with my dad and Denise in the VW bug.

And I certainly had had no experience with a big, clunky, bulky Ford van on a busy freeway. Fear set in, and as I stood looking at the van, I felt paralyzed. My mind flooded with my father's words—words I hadn't thought of in years: "If you learn on a stick, you can drive anything."

10   I waited in the parking lot for many hours, watching the cars clear out. As darkness fell, I finally drew a deep breath and began to relive that hellish Saturday morning when I was sixteen. I started the ignition and lifted my foot off the clutch, expecting the van to jerk and die. However, the van did not die. Suddenly, I was driving the van. "Yes, Dad!" I yelled, as I drove the van off the lot, stick shifting to the music on the radio.

11   My dad was right. When you learn on a stick, you can drive anything. I am grateful for the lesson I learned on that Saturday morning so long ago. Thanks, Dad.

                                                       —Auburn Velasquez

5

RESEARCH: DISCOVERING AND USING THE IDEAS OF OTHERS

CONCEPTS TO LEARN

Research sources and techniques

Narrowing a research topic

Avoiding plagiarism

Taking notes from research material

Keeping track of your research sources

When and why to quote research sources

Punctuation and other mechanics for quotations

When we generate ideas through clustering, brainstorming, freewriting, and discussing, we produce ideas from information we or our acquaintances already have. While we must begin by examining what we already know, most of the writing we do in the academic and professional world is more formal in tone, less personal in nature than the writing we have done thus far in this text. Most academic and professional writing depends on our ability to research information. Such writing is based not on our personal experience but on the knowledge of experts. In this chapter, we will explore one of the most important methods of generating and supporting ideas: borrowing ideas and information from others.

A major purpose in writing is to inform others about facts and ideas. We live in an age that could be dubbed "the information blitz." Seventy-four thousand scientific journals report the latest findings on a cornucopia of topics ranging from the status of the Antarctic ice caps to the latest uses of zirconium.

Learning about and then borrowing the words and ideas of others is what makes possible the growth and expansion of knowledge. In his essay "On Societies as Organisms," scientist–medical doctor Lewis Thomas writes

114

**RESEARCH:
DISCOVERING
AND USING
THE IDEAS
OF OTHERS**

about sharing ideas and information as an integral part not just of our culture, but of our species.

The phenomenon of separate animals joining up to form an organism is not unique in insects. Slime-mold cells do it all the time, of course, in each life cycle. At first they are single amebocytes swimming around, eating bacteria, aloof from each other, untouching, voting straight Republican. Then, a bell sounds, and acrasin is released by special cells toward which the others converge in stellate ranks, touch, fuse together, and construct the slug, solid as a trout. A splendid stalk is raised, with a fruiting body on top, and out of this comes the next generation of amebocytes, ready to swim across the same moist ground, solitary and ambitious. . . .

Although we are by all odds the most social of all social animals—more interdependent, more attached to each other, more inseparable in our behavior than bees—we do not often feel our conjoined intelligence. Perhaps, however, we are linked in circuits for the storage, processing, and retrieval of information, since this appears to be the most basic and universal of all human enterprises. It may be our biological function to build a certain kind of Hill. We have access to all the information of the biosphere, arriving as elementary units in the stream of solar photons. When we have learned how these are rearranged against randomness, to make, say, springtails, quantum mechanics, and the late quartets, we may have a clearer notion how to proceed. The circuitry seems to be there, even if the current is not always on.

The system of communications used in science should provide a neat, workable model for studying mechanisms of information-building in human society. Zinman, in a recent *Nature* essay, points out, "the invention of a mechanism for the systematic publication of fragments of scientific work may well have been the key event in the history of modern science." He continues:

> A regular journal carries from one research worker to another the various . . . observations which are of common interest. . . . A typical scientific paper has never pretended to be more than another little piece in a larger jigsaw—not significant in itself but as an element in a grander scheme. This technique, of soliciting many modest contributions to the store of human knowledge, has been the secret of Western science since the seventeenth century, for it achieves a corporate, collective power that is far greater than any one individual can exert.

With some alteration of terms, some toning down, the passage could describe the building of a termite nest. . . .

We like to think of exploring in science as a lonely, meditative business, and so it is in the first stages, but always, sooner or later, before the enterprise reaches completion, as we explore, we call to each other, communicate, publish, send letters to the editor, present papers, cry out on finding.

For Thought and Discussion

1. According to Thomas, what is the most basic of all human activities? Explain why you agree or disagree.

2. What types of figurative language does Thomas use to develop his point?

3. Working in a peer group, make a list of activities in our society that involve a team approach to information sharing.

115

RESEARCH:
DISCOVERING
AND USING
THE IDEAS
OF OTHERS

TRACKING DOWN THE TRUTH THROUGH RESEARCH

Many of the earth's five billion residents spend their work time researching topics you may someday need to know about. Whether you need to know the latest techniques for fighting a particular type of cancer or what current research says about the disposal of nuclear waste, somewhere there are experts who can give you information and insight. In this chapter we will discuss the most effective methods for finding and then integrating the ideas of others with your own ideas.

Before you begin to write, you will often have a vague target topic. Perhaps it will take the form of a question such as "What's wrong with acid rain?" To answer this question you may have to backtrack to more basic questions such as "What is acid rain?" To ask intelligent questions about a topic requires a certain amount of knowledge. So before you do your initial prewriting on a research paper topic, you may need to do a little *preresearching*—that is, you may need to read some background information about your subject to help you decide which aspect of a topic you want to research in greater depth.

In general, you can get an overview of your subject from an encyclopedia or from a comprehensive magazine article. Reading this overview is the preresearch that will help you generate and then answer your initial questions about your topic. Research and note-taking for specific information will come after you adequately understand your broader subject and are therefore able to ask the kinds of informed questions that will help limit your topic and research more efficiently.

Encyclopedias

One of the best ways to get a quick overview of your subject is by reading a background article or two in a current, general encyclopedia such as *Encyclopedia Americana, Encyclopaedia Britannica,* or *World Book.* While encyclopedias should *not* serve as your only or even your primary research tool, they can provide a comprehensive overview to help you understand the general issues involved in your topic.

116

RESEARCH:
DISCOVERING
AND USING
THE IDEAS
OF OTHERS

Specialized Encyclopedias

In addition to the encyclopedias such as *Encyclopedia Americana* and *Encyclopaedia Britannica,* which you have used since elementary school days, there are a wealth of specialized encyclopedias. The following is a sample list (*not* intended to be all-inclusive) of these specialized encyclopedias:

Afro-American Encyclopedia
Encyclopedia of American Economic History
Encyclopedia of American Political History
Encyclopedia of Asian History
Encyclopedia of Psychology
Encyclopedia of Religion
Encyclopedia of World Art
Encyclopedia of World Literature in the Twentieth Century
Grzimek's Animal Life Encyclopedia
Kodansha Encyclopedia of Japan
McGraw-Hill Encyclopedia of Science and Technology
New Encyclopedia of Science

To find the specialized encyclopedias, look under your subject heading in the card catalog or its computerized equivalent.

When you have several weeks to gather material for a paper or report, you can turn to sources that sometimes entail waiting for your information. Among the best of these sources is the four-volume *Encyclopedia of Associations: National Associations of the United States,* which is published annually by Gale Research. This encyclopedia contains the names and addresses of organizations dealing with issues ranging from the problems of aging to the protection of zebras. A letter or phone call to such an organization will yield a wealth of information.

The Public Access Catalog

Before you read a comprehensive background article in a magazine or journal, of course, first you have to find such an article. Nowhere is the contemporary information blitz more apparent than in our libraries. Information is changing so rapidly that libraries do not even have a standardized vocabulary for the tools you must use to search for information. A few years ago, the card catalog and *Reader's Guide to Periodical Literature* were primary reference tools for research in most libraries. Now many libraries have on-line computer systems to combine periodical indexes such as *Reader's Guide to Periodical Literature* with the information traditionally listed in the card catalog. In addition, the rapidity of the computer revolution has meant that not all college and university libraries have exactly the same primary reference systems. The key source of information about reference material is the "something," which, for lack of a standard name, we will call the *Public Access Catalog*. Your library may call it the *Card Catalog* or the *Public Access Catalog* or *Melville* or *Socrates* or the *On-Line Catalog*, or something else.

You may find information indexed in an on-line computerized system or in the traditional card catalog consisting of three-by-five-inch cards filed by subject, author, and title—or in a combination of an on-line system and a traditional card catalog. Whatever it is called, it will list a broad range of material on a topic, material that includes not only books, but pamphlets, periodicals, software, photographs, specialized reference sets, and audio-visual material as well.

Periodical Indexes

It is vitally important to get recent information on current topics, as information often changes. This is one reason why encyclopedias can serve only to give you a background; by the time the articles are written, edited, combined into volumes, printed, and distributed, the information they contain could be out of date in our fast-paced world.

On the other hand, *Reader's Guide to Periodical Literature* and its computerized cousins such as *Info-Track* and *Wilsondisc* are excellent sources of up-to-date information if your library's *Public Access Catalog* does not incorporate periodicals. These indexes are updated monthly, and they list the titles of articles published in hundreds of periodicals ranging from *Aging* to *The Writer* and covering a huge range of topics.

Specialized Periodical Indexes

In addition to the general indexes such as *Reader's Guide to Periodical Literature*, libraries also have more specialized indexes that are updated biweekly, monthly, or quarterly. The following list is a sample of those indexes available in most college and university libraries:

Art Index
Biography Index
Biology Digest
Cumulative Index to Nursing and Allied Health
Education Index
Essay and General Literature Index
General Science Index
Humanities Index
Social Science Index

118

RESEARCH:
DISCOVERING
AND USING
THE IDEAS
OF OTHERS

Newspaper Indexes

Many libraries carry indexes that aid users in finding newspaper articles about topics they are researching. The most common of these multiple-newspaper indexes is the *National Newspaper Index*, which indexes the *Christian Science Monitor*, the *Los Angeles Times*, the *New York Times*, the *Wall Street Journal*, and the *Washington Post*. Updated monthly on microfilm, this index also has an annual cumulative index.

Some newspapers provide their own index; many libraries carry the *New York Times Index*, a guide to articles appearing in that paper.

Almanacs

Almanacs summarize a useful collection of information about countries, people, events, and a variety of other subjects. For example, if you wanted to know the number of babies born in Mexico during the past year, you would look in the *World Almanac*.

To locate a particular almanac in the library, look under "almanac" in the *Public Access Catalog*, or look under the subject heading about which you are trying to find information.

Atlases

Atlases are collections of maps, usually of the earth's geography, but some atlases contain maps of other things—for example, human anatomy.

Geographical atlases are listed in the *Public Access Catalog* under the subheading of maps of a region such as "South America—Maps," for example. Nongeographical atlases are listed under subject headings such as "Anatomy—Atlas" or "Obstetrics—Atlas."

Directories

Directories give brief summaries of information about people or groups that have a common principle of classification—for example, people who have telephones.

To find the type of directory you want, look in the *Public Access Catalog* under the subject heading you are interested in—for example, "Consumer Protection—Directories."

Gazetteers

Gazetteers are dictionaries of geographical place names with information about their locations. Often these entries contain brief descriptive facts.

Look under "Geography—Dictionaries" in the *Public Access Catalog* to locate the gazetteers.

119

RESEARCH:
DISCOVERING
AND USING
THE IDEAS
OF OTHERS

Handbooks

Handbooks contain information about particular subjects. In addition, they provide bibliographical references to the sources of their information, so they can help you to compile a list of sources for your own research paper.

To locate a handbook, look in the *Public Access Catalog* under the subject heading in which you are interested—for example, "Chemistry—Handbooks." You probably have used a handbook to look up the mechanical rules for writing—for example, the rules that govern the use of the dash.

Statistical Sources

Sometimes you need to know "how many" or "how often" or "how large." Statistical sources give this information about a wide variety of topics. The *Statistical Abstracts of the United States* is one of the most useful statistical reference sources available. Among other things, it will tell you how many Americans were killed in any given war. It will also give information about parks, education, government, and numerous other topics.

To find a book that will give you the kind of statistics you seek, look in the card catalog (or *Public Access Catalog*) under the subject of your interest combined with the subheading *statistics*—for example, "United States—Statistics."

For Thought and Discussion

1. Suggest library sources from those listed in the preceding sections to help with research about the greenhouse effect.

2. Where in the library could you look to find out how much of the earth's surface is covered by ocean water?

3. What sources would help you research current issues facing the European Economic Community?

SELECTING A RESEARCH TOPIC

As you read the following journal entries by Roberta Tavares, a first-year composition student, note the process that she used to help her find and limit her research topic. Her assignment was to write a mini research paper

120

RESEARCH:
DISCOVERING
AND USING
THE IDEAS
OF OTHERS

about a current controversial issue. The paper was to be 500 to 750 words long.

I want to write about an environmental issue. To help me figure out how to limit my subject, I called up articles under the heading "Environment" today on the computer in the library. Wow! Have we got problems. I could spend the rest of my college years just reading the articles that came up—pages and pages.

What interested me most were all of the articles about the greenhouse effect, so I printed out a list of the greenhouse-related articles. Next I looked up "Greenhouse Effect" in *Encyclopedia Americana* to get a quick overview of this problem.

I learned that the greenhouse effect means that the carbon dioxide content of our atmosphere has been increased by 25% over the last century.

Then I read another article about the greenhouse effect and the hole in the ozone layer. I found this article in—surprise, surprise—*Sports Illustrated* of all places. Since this magazine is for non-scientist audiences, I figured the article wouldn't be too technical for me to understand. And it wasn't. Along with the encyclopedia article, the *Sports Illustrated* article gave me a pretty good understanding of current problems posed by the greenhouse effect.

Since the beginning of the industrial revolution, we've changed the atmosphere of our planet in a fairly major way! That's pretty shocking. To make matters worse, at the same time we're adding tons and tons of carbon dioxide to the atmosphere through burning fossil fuels such as auto exhausts and the exhausts from industry, we've decided to chop down our rain forests. In fact we add a net total of 3 billion tons annually because we burn increasing amounts of fossil fuel at the same time we are reducing the forests that could pull the carbon out of the atmosphere. In a novel that would be too coincidental to fly it seems to me. Sometimes I think *Homo sapiens* is misnamed. This species doesn't act very smart.

The whole problem with the greenhouse effect could take up a book. So next I've got to figure out what I want to write about. I have figured out several questions I want to answer:

1. What sources are the worst contributors to the greenhouse effect?
2. How much does each source contribute?
3. What can we do to cut down on greenhouse gases?
4. Since we are actually increasing the greenhouse gases rather dramatically each year, will cutting down on current levels be enough?
5. Is it already too late?
6. Does science have anything up its sleeve to help solve this problem?
7. How much do scientists agree about the problem?

Next Day

I checked back through the computer printout of articles I got when I started this project. The ones that seemed most intriguing to me had to do with ways of solving the greenhouse problem: cut back on fossil fuel use, stop chopping and start replanting the rain forests, control world population,

121

**RESEARCH:
DISCOVERING
AND USING
THE IDEAS
OF OTHERS**

artificially manipulate how much carbon dioxide gets recycled—this is called "engineering the atmosphere."

That last suggestion really caught my eye. This sounds like Dr. Strangelove in action. How can we manipulate how much gets recycled? It turns out there are a couple schemes to make the ocean plants recycle more carbon dioxide—just the way trees and other plants do on earth. Pretty interesting. How much of the planet is covered with water? I'll have to find out. A quick glance at a globe tells me that there is a lot more water than land.

I guess I knew there were plants in the ocean, but I've never really thought about it before. This seems like a pretty interesting topic: making the ocean absorb more carbon dioxide. After all, we seem to be roaringly unsuccessful in limiting world population growth or cutting down on fossil fuels—we can't even get people out of cars and on to mass transit, so maybe we better start thinking of some alternatives because by the time we wake up to the problems of global warming, it may be too late to stop it.

That Night

I found a really interesting article in the April 1991 *Discover* called "Earth on Ice." It's a really long article—seven pages, and it gives pros and cons about a California scientist's idea. This scientist has already done research that shows large parts of the ocean would recycle more carbon dioxide except there isn't enough iron! I wonder if that's really a legitimate idea. This is definitely interesting. The scientist—Dr. John Martin—sounds pretty colorful too. He says stuff like "Give me half a tanker full of iron, and I'll give you another ice age." Dr. Strangelove couldn't have said it better. I'm going back to the library tomorrow to see what I can find out.

Roberta's Return

Before I returned to the library, I jotted down some questions that occurred to me in my first round of reading:

1. What percent of the earth is covered with ocean water? Since it looks like there is more water than land, it figures that the ocean must have an impact on what happens to our planet's atmosphere.

2. How fast is the world population growing? How fast is population growing in the Third World? How fast is it growing in the industrialized world? One article I read said that as the undeveloped world industrializes, it will add greatly to the greenhouse problem. Because residents of the industrialized world use more resources, they have a greater impact per person than Third World people currently have. Since people are having a big impact on increasing the levels of carbon dioxide in our atmosphere, control of population growth will be important in limiting the amount of greenhouse gases.

I went first to the reference section of our library and checked a couple of almanacs. I looked under "ocean" in the *Universal Almanac* and learned that almost three-quarters of our planet's surface is covered by ocean.

While I was in the almanac section, I tried to find information about population growth. I didn't have any luck, so I looked under "population" in our *Public Access Catalog*. Still no luck, so I asked a reference librarian for

122

RESEARCH:
DISCOVERING
AND USING
THE IDEAS
OF OTHERS

help. She went directly to *The New Book of World Rankings* and looked under "statistics." I learned that in developed countries the population is growing at a rate of 0.6% annually while in the Third World the growth is a whopping 2.1%.

While I was in the library, I checked out the *National Newspaper Index;* I wanted to see if there were any news items about that California scientist who wants to manipulate the amount of carbon dioxide the oceans absorb.

I found articles in the May 20, 1990, *Washington Post* and the November 20, 1990, *New York Times.* Fortunately the library had both papers on microfilm.

I also did another computer search of periodicals now that my topic was narrowed to the role of iron in the greenhouse debate. I came up with a number of articles including two from *Nature*. First I read Martin's May 10, 1990, *Nature* article, "Iron in Antarctic Waters." Then I read Dr. Wallace Broecker's "Unpleasant Surprises in the Greenhouse" from the July 9, 1987, issue of *Nature.* Broecker is a geochemist at Columbia University. (Broecker writes colorfully.) He is also mentioned prominently in the *Sports Illustrated* article. Another especially helpful article was from the September 27, 1991, *Science:* "Report Nixes 'Geritol' Fix for Global Warming." This title was misleading because, in fact, an important group of scientists supports doing the iron enrichment experiments. Evidently the *Science* editor slept through the information in her composition class about making sure titles are accurate.

The same computer search turned up a video tape of the PBS program *The Infinite Voyage*, a source I found by looking in our *Public Access Catalog.* In the program both Martin and Broecker discuss Martin's theory. Even though he is one of the most important critics, Broecker urged that Martin's idea be tested in the open ocean. He said the idea was "important" and the test would help us better understand both the ocean food chain and the role the ocean plays in pulling carbon out of the atmosphere.

At this point, I was feeling pretty well armed with information. It was time to explore my ideas in writing:

Freewriting Draft

Gosh, this whole subject is so complicated. It sounds as though we are in a real mess. It turns out that we are increasing the buildup of carbon dioxide and other greenhouse gases in our atmosphere rather dramatically each year.

In addition the population of the Third World is growing at a remarkable 2.1% annually. Most of these people naturally want the comforts that come from the industrialization of life—from the burning of the fossil fuels to create electricity, to produce manufactured goods, to run automobiles. While the Industrialized World has a population growth of only 0.6% annually, that growth still creates more people to raise more havoc with the environment through burning fossil fuels, and, of course, citizens of the Industrialized World create much more greenhouse pollution per person than people of the Third World.

What is scary is that no one seems to be doing anything to stop this buildup. Politicians talk about energy-efficient public transportation, but it takes only a quick peek at a freeway to discover that those cars are not decreasing in number.

123

**RESEARCH:
DISCOVERING
AND USING
THE IDEAS
OF OTHERS**

In fact, I wonder if I should get some statistics to support the fact that we aren't reducing pollution from auto exhaust. I wonder if that is obvious enough to everyone. I do have statistics to show that we are increasing the amount of carbon we are adding to the atmosphere. The *New York Times* says that according to Dr. Karl Banse, a marine biologist at the University of Washington, we add seven billion tons of carbon to the atmosphere annually due to human activities—especially burning of fossil fuels in auto exhausts, industry, and the burning of the rain forests. These statistics will work, so I won't go back to the library to see how much is from auto exhaust alone.

Of this seven billion tons, plants take up about five billion. (There seems to be a billion ton discrepancy in the figures used by my sources. I'll either have to say "approximately" or admit there is a difference in the figures. I'll watch for additional figures to resolve this problem.) Anyway it is clear that we are adding vast amounts of carbon to our atmosphere. This same *New York Times* article says that there are two basic ways to decrease the carbon buildup: 1) decrease carbon emissions and 2) increase the amount absorbed by natural processes.

It's that second solution I want to focus on. *Science* says that the American Society of Limnology and Oceanography wants a small scale experiment to be done to see what would happen if the ocean was fertilized with iron. This theory that ocean plants don't grow in vast stretches of the ocean because iron quickly sinks out of ocean water is called "the Geritol solution."

This solution seems to have a lot of validity. It turns out that the percent of carbon dioxide in the atmosphere was a lot lower before and during ice ages. With less carbon dioxide in the atmosphere, the earth retains less heat and it is therefore cooler. Of course, there are other gases that make up greenhouse gases, but carbon dioxide is the main one.

Martin has been generating a lot of heat himself with his theory. Folks are lining up in pro and con columns. He is even quoted in *Science* as saying "People were madder than hell at me." Hell is pretty hot too, come to think of it. Of course if the earth's climate gets warmer, life could be hell for much of the globe. Coastal areas would flood as the polar ice caps melt, for example. Areas that were once important agricultural centers could become deserts.

Among those who are pro-Geritol solution are the following:

1. Roger Revelle, former director of the Scripps Institution of Oceanography and a scientist generally recognized as a father of global ocean-atmosphere studies has said, "You've got to go out and find out if it works. It's definitely worth trying" (*The Washington Post*).
2. The University of Texas chemical engineer Adam Heller, member of the National Academy of Engineering: "It is far more economically feasible than other options on the table" (*The Washington Post*).
3. Dr. Wallace Broecker, Columbia University geochemist: "We would learn a lot from such a study; it "definitely should be conducted" (PBS program *The Infinite Voyage*).
4. Dr. Sallie Chisholm, a biological oceanographer at MIT: the experiment would help us better understand the ocean food chain and the global carbon cycle also. "The hypothesis is gathering momentum while the geochemical engineering option is losing momentum" (*Science*).

124

RESEARCH:
DISCOVERING
AND USING
THE IDEAS
OF OTHERS

5. Dr. Richard Barber, Duke University Marine Laboratory: "My equatorial data suggest Martin is absolutely correct" (*Science*).

6. It could work. Dr. Jorge Sarmiento and Dr. Robbie Toggweiler of Princeton: Ancient ice cores reveal atmospheric carbon dioxide levels dropped from 280 to 200 parts per million during ice age 18,000 years ago (*Science*).

What's Wrong with the Theory

1. It could change the kind of plants (plankton) that grow in the ocean. Since these are the basis of the ocean food chain, such a change could be a disaster for life in the ocean (*Discover*).

2. "You don't tinker with a perfectly healthy ecosystem to clean up humanity's mess" (*Science*). (But how healthy is the ecosystem? We've already changed it pretty drastically by increasing carbon dioxide levels by 25% to say nothing of all the other changes humans have made.)

Using Your Curiosity to Guide Your Research

Notice that Roberta moved from a very broad subject—the environment—to a far more limited one—a specific idea about reversing the greenhouse effect. As she read articles, she jotted down the questions that occurred to her. Such questions will ultimately help her to limit her thesis. Also notice that Roberta moved from the very general source of an encyclopedia to the more up-to-date but still general source of magazines.

When Roberta thought about the *Sports Illustrated* article and wrote down her questions, she found she was interested in a still more limited topic. Next she went to a more specialized source—*Discover*, a magazine that contains articles about scientific research for a nonscientific audience. As Roberta's own curiosity and questions led her to narrow her topic, she also narrowed the kind of articles she read.

Like Roberta, when you have read enough background information to help you understand your general subject, you are ready to begin identifying what aspect of that topic you want to know about.

Once Roberta had written her rough draft, she took a break before engaging her critical brain in revision. She had discovered one area she needed to research more carefully. The break would help her gain the objectivity to find out if there were other sections that needed work: Nothing breeds objectivity like a period of time between drafts.

Roberta did not produce her final draft in one fell swoop. Instead she reread her rough draft and moved sections of information around, asking herself if her readers could follow her reasoning. She noted sections that needed additional development, and she questioned any material that seemed too loosely related to her thesis. By the way, because she was writing on a computer, her revision process was much faster and easier than it would have been had she needed to type and retype her ideas.

125

RESEARCH:
DISCOVERING
AND USING
THE IDEAS
OF OTHERS

Roberta's next draft contained 462 words. Her assignment was to write a minimum of 500 words. For her final draft, she needed to reexamine her writing to see if any ideas could use additional support or clarification. In addition, she needed to reexamine her research material to see if she could generate important ideas from that material.

Samuel Johnson, author of the first comprehensive English dictionary, wrote: "Knowledge is of two kinds; we know a subject ourselves, or we know where we can find information about it." In an age during which humankind's treasury of facts is doubling at an ever-increasing rate, the knowledge of where to find information is increasingly important—and in some instances tricky. When the usual sources of information do not yield your answer, ask your reference librarians. Usually, they will know where to find the information you need. For example, when Roberta couldn't find the information she wanted about the rate of world population growth, she turned to a reference librarian for help.

Roberta's final draft is reprinted below.

The Geritol Solution

Columbia University geochemist Wallace Broecker, writing in *Nature*, contends we are conducting a massive experiment with the earth's atmosphere—an experiment Broecker says is like playing Russian roulette with the earth's climate. The *New York Times* quotes Dr. Karl Banse, a marine biologist at the University of Washington, as saying that we are spewing seven billion tons of carbon into the atmosphere annually with human activities—especially the destruction of the rain forests and the burning of fossil fuels.

According to "Forecast for Disaster" from *Sports Illustrated,* of that seven tons, two to three tons annually stays in the atmosphere, so every year the concentration of carbon in the atmosphere increases. Since this carbon acts like a blanket to keep heat from escaping from our planet, the earth is growing ever warmer. Among the problems such climate change will cause is the melting of the polar ice caps, the subsequent raising of sea level, and the flooding of coastal communities. In addition, large, fertile areas such as the U.S. breadbasket could become deserts.

The problem of global climate change is attracting worldwide attention. The *New York Times,* reporting on an international conference in Geneva, declared we have but two choices: to decrease carbon emissions or to increase the amount of carbon our planet absorbs naturally.

The scheme that is currently the leading contender, to increase the amount absorbed naturally, has been proposed in *Nature* by oceanographer Dr. John Martin, Director of Moss Landing Marine Laboratories in California. Martin's research has convinced his colleagues that plants don't grow in vast stretches of nutrient-rich ocean because they lack iron; iron doesn't remain in ocean water. Instead, iron does just what you might expect: it sinks. Martin theorized that if iron were added to barren stretches of ocean, more plants would grow,

126

RESEARCH:
DISCOVERING
AND USING
THE IDEAS
OF OTHERS

thus pulling CO_2 out of the atmosphere. When Martin and his colleagues conducted experiments to test their theory, they discovered two things: large stretches of ocean are indeed iron-poor, and when a minute amount of iron was added to the water, according to *Science*, "productivity soared."

What do other scientists think of stimulating the ocean to absorb more carbon dioxide and thus slow climate change? Martin's research, which has been dubbed the "Geritol Solution," is widely accepted as valid. Among those reproducing Martin's work is Dr. Richard Barber, of Duke University Marine Laboratory. *Science* quotes Dr. Barber as confirming: "My equatorial data suggest Martin is absolutely correct." According to University of Texas chemical engineer Adam Heller, a member of the National Academy of Engineering and another proponent of the Geritol Solution: "It is far more economically feasible than other options on the table."

A number of other highly respected scientists agree with a special panel of the National Research Council: an ocean fertilization experiment of roughly 60 square miles should be conducted to see if the ocean could reduce carbon levels in the atmosphere. Among the supporters of Martin's research, the *Washington Post* quotes Roger Revelle, the former director of the Scripps Institution of Oceanography and a scientist generally recognized as a father of global ocean-atmosphere studies. Revelle said: "You've got to go out and find out if it works. It's definitely worth trying." Even such critics of Martin's theory as Dr. Wallace Broecker, a Columbia University geochemist speaking on the PBS program *The Infinite Voyage*, counsel that such a study "definitely should be conducted."

Now the American Society of Limnology and Oceanography (ASLO) has issued a report suggesting that a small scale experiment of approximately 60 square miles be conducted to see what would happen if tiny amounts of iron were added to the open ocean. However, the ASLO report contends that the experiment should not be done to engineer global climate, but to learn more about the global food chain and the global carbon cycle and thus better understand global climate changes.

Science quotes Dr. Sallie Chisholm, a biological oceanographer at MIT who is working with Martin to conduct an experiment on a 100- to 400-square-kilometer stretch of ocean: "The hypothesis is gathering momentum while the geochemical engineering option is losing momentum." In other words, more and more scientists want to conduct iron-enrichment experiments because such experiments will help them learn a great deal about the food chain and the global carbon cycle. However, many of these same scientists are less enthusiastic about actually trying to manage how much CO_2 is in the atmosphere by encouraging more plants to grow there.

An open ocean fertilization study would also answer a key question: would fertilizing the open ocean change the kind of plants that grow there? After all, plankton, tiny ocean plants, are the basis of the food chain. Changing the kinds of plankton could spell disaster for the animals that depend on these plants—animals that range in size from microscopic zooplankton to whales, the leviathans of the earth.

While Martin himself is eager to conduct open ocean experiments, he is

127

**RESEARCH:
DISCOVERING
AND USING
THE IDEAS
OF OTHERS**

quoted in a *Discover* article as cautioning: "It's scary. I don't want to go down in history as Martin's Mistake—as the guy who advocated adding iron, and they did it, and it completely ruined the ecosystem. What I want is to do the ocean experiment, and prove that iron is limiting."

Regardless of the results, Martin's experiment would provide valuable information about both our planet's food chain and its carbon cycle. Since we are changing the composition of our atmosphere at an increasing rate, it would be indeed wise for *Homo sapiens*—the "wise human"—to understand the basic processes that promote life on our planet before we change the very atmosphere that allows our planet to foster life as we currently know it.

—Roberta Tavares

For Thought and Discussion

1. Reread Roberta's first and final draft. What ideas did she eliminate as she narrowed her subject in her final draft?

2. List two examples of information Roberta had that she did not use in her final draft.

3. Explain why you agree or disagree with Roberta's thesis.

Getting an Objective View through Research

As you learn about your subject, you may change your mind about your thesis. According to Ralph Waldo Emerson: "A foolish consistency is the hobgoblin of little minds." Exorcise any such hobgoblins haunting your mind. Don't hesitate to modify your thesis as you learn more about your subject.

Make sure that you do not limit your research to information written from a single point of view. Note that Roberta discussed the views both for and against the Geritol Solution. As you read articles from sources such as newspapers and magazines, note the information about opposition groups. Then contact both pro and con groups to get their points of view. For instance, if you are writing about the feasibility of clearing land to accommodate equipment that will generate electricity from sunlight, you would need to contact both an electric company involved in such an activity and groups opposing such an action.

In Chapter 10, there will be a more extensive discussion of argument. For now, realize that you will be more convincing to your readers if you acknowledge opposing ideas and do not try to sweep them under the rug. Keep your audience in mind: You will not convince them of the validity of your thesis by ignoring important facts and ideas.

128

RESEARCH:
DISCOVERING
AND USING
THE IDEAS
OF OTHERS

RESEARCH SOURCES: WHERE DID YOU GET THAT IDEA?

When you call in the expert witnesses to support and develop your ideas, you want to make sure those experts have the relevant credentials that will lend credence to their testimony. Whether the moose and his companions in the cartoon are successful in their lobbying effort will depend upon more than their wholesome good looks. They will need to cite facts and statistics to support their fight for clean air. Where they get their ideas and information will have a great deal to do with their ability to convince Congress—just as your source of information has a great deal to do with convincing your readers.

Telling your readers the sources of your facts, quotations, and ideas allows them to decide for themselves how convincing your information is. When you are not the recognized authority in a field, you need to support your ideas by citing those who are and telling your readers enough to make the credentials of the authorities seem trustworthy.

"Looks as if the clean-air crowd turned out in force."

129

**RESEARCH:
DISCOVERING
AND USING
THE IDEAS
OF OTHERS**

If friends told you they read an article claiming that eating six apples each day prevents cancer, you would want to know where they got this information. Had they found the article in the *New England Journal of Medicine,* the *Washington Post,* the *New York Times,* the *Los Angeles Times,* or a similarly reliable source, your response would be very different than if they had read the article in a supermarket tabloid right next to the article "Six-Headed Visitor from Space Seen with Elvis."

Similarly, if a person is the authoritative source of information you use in an essay, let your readers know who this authority is and what his or her credentials are. If, for example, someone were to give you a book entitled *Advice to a Young Scientist,* think for a moment about what information you would want to know about the author in determining the credibility of the advice. Note how much more credible such advice is when you know that its author is Sir Peter Medawar, who was awarded the Nobel prize for his research into the cause and remedy for the rejection of organ and tissue transplants. When you cite a person as an authority, be sure of the following:

1. The person is an authority in the field about which you are writing. An expert on breast cancer is not therefore an expert on the depletion of the ozone layer.

2. You understand and quote or paraphrase the authority correctly.

3. The authority is up to date. In our fast-paced world, technology is changing rapidly. If you quote something an expert wrote a decade ago, even that expert may now disagree.

When you cite an important idea, piece of research, or quotation, your readers want to determine the validity of your source before deciding on the reliability of the information. Just as you need to show your reader your point by using concrete support, so too you need to show your reader that you got your information from a reliable source. Chapter 12 will cover the procedure for writing a research paper requiring formal documentation. However, it is important to tell your readers who your sources are even when you are not writing a formal research paper.

Certainly, you are familiar with informal documentation. Such documentation is used by newspapers and newsmagazines such as *Time, U.S. News & World Report,* and *Newsweek.* Informal documentation simply means that you mention within the text of your essay where you got your information whenever you use a quotation, an idea, or a fact that is not common knowledge. This is what Roberta has done in "The Geritol Solution."

For Thought and Discussion

1. Return to "The Geritol Solution." Point out places where Roberta has indicated the sources of her information.

130

RESEARCH:
DISCOVERING
AND USING
THE IDEAS
OF OTHERS

2. Point out places where Roberta has indicated the credentials of those whose ideas she cites.

Avoiding Plagiarism: When and Why You Must Credit Sources

You must credit your sources for two reasons:

1. To add authority to your points

2. To avoid charges of plagiarism

When you borrow a car, you need permission from its owner. When you borrow words or ideas, you need to credit the creator: stealing words and ideas is a crime, just as stealing a material object is a crime. Furthermore, your ideas gain credibility when they have an authoritative source. The nice thing about words and ideas is that you can and should borrow them to use in your essays without getting the author's permission as long as you credit your source.

Let's take a few minutes to look at proper borrowing versus plagiarism. The following excerpt is from an article entitled "On the Trail of Acid Rain." This article, which was written by Sharon Begley, appeared in *National Wildlife*. First read the excerpt. Then compare the original material to the paragraphs that follow it—and borrow from it.

The Original Material

A study done for EPA estimates that in seventeen states east of the Mississippi River, acid rain and the deposition of dry sulfate-containing particles are corroding buildings to the tune of $5 billion a year. The Washington Monument and the U.S. Capitol are being eaten away by acid. Steel in bridges is being destroyed—the metal corrodes four times faster in sulfur-polluted environments than in areas spared the scourge. Acidic pollution has been identified as one of the prime causes of corrosion of B-52 bombers, a problem costing the Air Force millions of dollars a year to fix. And the recent facelift given the Statue of Liberty was necessitated in part by the acid corrosion of her copper skin.

Note that the author credits her source—an EPA report. This is an adequate credit since this is an informal essay. In a paper using formal documentation, the author would have to tell us enough about the EPA report for us to track it down. (Formal documentation is the subject of Chapter 12.)

Let's look at another excerpt from the Sharon Begley article to see how to borrow her ideas giving her proper credit.

From "On the Trail of Acid Rain"

Despite clear evidence of the damage caused by acid rain, it is unlikely that the political wrangling over solutions will be settled anytime soon. Those in favor of preserving the environment for coming generations will not flinch at the cost of stifling sulfur emissions. Those who regard $150 million for a single scrubber [a device to reduce pollutants] as a steep price will keep arguing for more research before imposing controls. Says Johnson [whose credentials were given earlier in the article], "The issue now boils down to one of values rather than science." And while the debate continues, the problem gets worse.

Now let's examine a plagiarized version of the Begley article:

A Plagiarized Version

Clearly much evidence exists that acid rain causes great damage. However, it is not probable that political arguments over solutions will be settled very soon. Conservationists will not hesitate to spend $150 million for a single scrubber while others will argue we need more research before we try to control acid rain. It is really a question of values, and the problem is getting worse while politicians argue about those values.

In the following paragraph, note how the author has properly credited her source:

Proper Borrowing

As Sharon Begley points out in "On the Trail of Acid Rain" in *National Wildlife*, the political arguments over controlling acid rain are likely to continue simply because clearing up acid rain is a complex, costly process. A single scrubber, for example, can cost $150 million. However, the frightening point is that while politicians, conservationists, and industrialists argue, the problems caused by acid rain are growing ever worse.

For Thought and Discussion

1. Which version, the plagiarized one or the one containing properly borrowed material, is more convincing? Why?

2. For what two reasons must you properly credit your sources?

Integrating Your Research Sources into Your Paper

Integrate your quotations clearly and smoothly. Let your readers know that you are about to quote someone. Furthermore, if you are citing an authority—unless your readers will recognize that person as an authority—you must give not only the person's name but enough additional information to let your readers know why that person is an authority. On the other hand, do not give more information about your source than is necessary to ensure that your readers will recognize the source's authority. The following two excerpts from this chapter's professional essay illustrate proper integration of sources.

132

RESEARCH:
DISCOVERING
AND USING
THE IDEAS
OF OTHERS

Properly Integrated Sources

Dr. James Hansen of the NASA Goddard Institute for Space Studies in New York flatly says that within 10 to 15 years the earth will be warmer than it has been in 100,000 years.

The most outspoken scientist on the ozone depletion is Sherwood Rowland, chairman of the chemistry department at the University of California at Irvine. When Rowland began his investigations at UC Irvine in October 1973, the annual production of CFCs [chlorofluorocarbons] in the U.S. was on the order of 850 million pounds. Rowland did his initial research with Mario Molina, a postdoctoral student who had just received his Ph.D. from Berkeley. In June 1974 they published a paper in *Nature*. As Rowland says, "I just came home one night and told my wife, 'The work is going very well, but it looks like the end of the world.' "

For Thought and Discussion

1. What credentials do James Hansen and Sherwood Rowland have that lend credibility to their views?

2. Where did Hansen and Rowland originally publish their data?

When Should You Quote?

When used sparingly, quotations add authority and interest to your writing. Often a striking quotation provides an excellent starting place for an essay or adds authority and clarity to an important point. Sometimes the most effective way to highlight opposing points is to let the antagonists speak briefly for themselves.

However, before you quote someone's words, ask yourself if you could just as effectively paraphrase that person's words. When used indiscriminately, quotations merely disrupt your ideas. Furthermore, although quotations add authority and variety to your writing, the majority of words in your essay must be your own. A good rule is to use quotations for no more than 20 percent of an essay.

In general use quotations in those cases in which

1. Your source is especially eloquent.

2. You want the idea to get special emphasis.

Transitions to Help Integrate Your Research Sources

The following transitions alert your reader that you are about to use a quotation:

According to Dr. Goldberg . . .

Dr. Goldberg affirms, argues, asserts, attests, avows, believes, claims, contends, propounds, rebuts, refutes, says . . .

133

RESEARCH:
DISCOVERING
AND USING
THE IDEAS
OF OTHERS

PUNCTUATION AND OTHER MECHANICS FOR QUOTATIONS

Punctuation and Indentation for Longer Quotations

1. Poetry quotations of three or more lines and prose quotations of four or more lines must be indented ten spaces from the left margin but not indented from the right margin. Do not use quotation marks around these longer quotations.

> *For example:* Writing in a recent *Sierra*, Stanford University Professor of Biology Paul Ehrlich concluded: "Birds are the only tropical animals that send many representatives into our territory. Not only do they inform us of the quality of local environments critical to our lives, they also bring news from areas remote from the thinking of most North Americans, but crucial to the survival of our civilization."

2. Prose quotations of fewer than four typed lines are not set off from the text by indenting them; instead, these shorter quotations are indicated with quotation marks.

> *For example:* According to Buckminster Fuller, "The most important thing about Spaceship Earth—an instruction book didn't come with it."

Quotations within Quotations

3. Use single quotation marks to indicate a quotation within a quotation.

> *For example:* In "Winged Warning," a recent article published in *Sierra*, Stanford University Professor of Biology Paul Ehrlich wrote: "The poet Rilke called migratory birds 'single-minded' and 'unperplexed.' But on their annual shuttle between hemispheres, they bear aloft a complex—and alarming—ecological message."

Other Punctuation with Quotation Marks

4a. Periods and commas go *inside* quotation marks (," .").

> *For example:* "In nature there are neither rewards nor punishments—there are consequences," Robert B. Ingersoll pointed out. Voltaire put it more succinctly: "Men argue. Nature acts."

134

RESEARCH:
DISCOVERING
AND USING
THE IDEAS
OF OTHERS

4b. Colons and semicolons *always* go *outside* quotation marks ('';'' '':).

> *For example:* I am not sure if Einstein was being ironic when he said, ''The environment is everything that isn't me''; in fact, as Einstein surely realized, we are all part of the environment.

4c. Question marks, exclamation marks, and dashes go inside the quotation marks when they are the punctuation for the quoted phrase or for the sentence as a whole.

> *For example:* Henry David Thoreau wrote: ''Think of our life in Nature— daily to be shown matter, to come in contact with it—rocks, trees, wind on our cheeks! The solid earth! . . . Who are we? Where are we?''

4d. Question marks, exclamation marks, and dashes go outside the quotation marks when they are the punctuation for the entire sentence.

> *For example:* Don Marquis expressed this point well when he wrote: ''Pity the meek for they shall inherit the earth''—after the developers finish with it.
>
> Was it Irv Kupcinet who wrote, ''Air pollution is turning Mother Nature prematurely gray''?

Alterations within a Quotation

5. When you indicate you are quoting someone's exact words, you must stick with those exact words unless you signal to your reader that you are editing or explaining the quotation. Use brackets to signal that you are adding some explanation in the middle of a quoted passage. Brackets look like this: [   ].

> *For example:* '' 'I think it gives people power and moral support to know they're not alone struggling with what appear to be monumental problems', he [John Berger] says.''

Deleting Material from a Quotation

6a. Use ellipses to indicate that you are deleting part of a quotation. An ellipsis consists of three periods with one space before and after each period. An ellipsis looks like this: . . .

> *For example:* It will be fun to restore health, our own and the earth's, and to rediscover mutual respect, . . . a bit of serenity now and then. To hear more silence than we have been hearing lately.

6b. When a punctuation mark occurs immediately before the ellipsis, you can include this mark if you so choose:

> *For example:* and to rediscover mutual respect, . . . a bit of serenity now and then.

6c. If an ellipsis comes at the end of a sentence, follow the end punctuation mark with the ellipsis.

> *For example:* To hear more silence than we have been hearing lately. . . . This is the goal of the environmentalist.

Sic: When Quoting an Error

7. If the quotation you are using contains an error with which you do not want to be charged, indicate the error with brackets and the Latin expression *sic:*

> *For example:* He misquoted Revelations 7:3, "Hurt not the earth, neither [*sic*] the see [*sic*], nor the trees."

Paragraphing with Quotations

8a. Begin a new paragraph with each change of speaker when you are writing dialogue.

> *For example:* Alice stared, astounded. "You mean you've never read Rachel Carson's *Silent Spring*?"
> Bruce frowned defiantly. "No, but I certainly understand her central point."

8b. When you use dialogue not for its own sake but to further a point (as writers often do in an essay), you do not have to begin a new paragraph with a change of speaker if it is clear to your reader who is speaking.

> *For example:* Environmental writer Sarah Pollock points out, "When the damage to the environment has existed long before ecologists get involved, restoration can be much more problematic." According to Teri Knight, a botanist with the Nature Conservancy, "There are so many different ecosystems we're trying to patch up. The idea is there, but we don't know enough about how to do it."

Your turn

1. Read the following excerpt from an article written for *Nature* by Wallace S. Broecker, professor of oceanography at the Lamont-Doherty

Geological Observatory of Columbia University. Dr. Broecker is one of the foremost authorities on the greenhouse effect.

From "Unpleasant Surprises in the Greenhouse?"

The inhabitants of planet Earth are quietly conducting a gigantic environmental experiment. So vast and so sweeping will be the consequences that, were it brought before any responsible council for approval, it would be firmly rejected. Yet it goes on with little interference from any jurisdiction or nation. The experiment in question is the release of CO_2 and other so-called "greenhouse" gases to the atmosphere. Because these releases are largely by-products of energy and food production, we have little choice but to let the experiment continue. We can perhaps slow its pace by eliminating frivolous production and by making more efficient use of energy from fossil fuels. But beyond this we can only prepare ourselves to cope with its effects.

The task of scientists is to predict the consequences of the build-up of CO_2 and other gases. To be useful these predictions must be reasonably detailed, but we are in no better a position to make them than are medical scientists when asked when and where cancer will strike a specific person. Understanding the operation of the joint hydrosphere-atmosphere-biosphere-cryosphere system is every bit as difficult as understanding the factors that determine whether or not cancerous cells will get the upper hand. Because of our lack of basic knowledge, the range of possibility for the greenhouse effects remains large. It is for this reason that the experiment is a dangerous one. We play Russian roulette with climate, hoping that the future will hold no unpleasant surprises. No one knows what lies in the active chamber of the gun, but I am less optimistic about its contents than many.

My suspicion is that we have been lulled into complacency by model simulations that suggest a gradual warming over a period of about 100 years. If this seemingly logical response to a gradual build-up of greenhouse gases is correct, then one can imagine that man may be able to cope with the coming changes. While I do not have any complaints about how these modeling experiments were conducted—indeed they were done by brilliant scientists using the best computers available—the basic architecture of the models denies the possibility of key interactions that occur in the real system. The reason is that we do not yet know how to incorporate such interactions into models.

My impressions are more than educated hunches. They come from viewing the results of experiments nature has conducted on her own. The results of the most recent of them are well portrayed in polar ice, in ocean sediment and in bog mucks. What these records indicate is that Earth's climate does not respond to forcing in a smooth and gradual way. Rather, it responds in sharp jumps which involve large-scale reorganization of Earth's system. If this reading of the natural record is correct, then we must consider the possibility that the main responses of the system to our provocation of the atmosphere will come in jumps whose timing and magnitude are unpredictable. Coping with this type of change is clearly a far more serious matter than coping with a gradual warming.

2. Write a short summary of Dr. Broecker's key point. Compare your summary with those written by other members of your peer editing group.

3. Write a paragraph in which you quote and paraphrase from the Broecker excerpt. Be sure your readers understand Dr. Broecker's authority for making his statements.

 MEMORIES: KEEPING TRACK OF YOUR RESEARCH SOURCES

When you use several sources to document your ideas, you need to keep track of these sources so you can credit them properly. The following methods will help you keep track of your ideas as you take notes, thus saving you a great deal of time plowing through your notes to find information and its source.

Photocopying machines are wonderful aids to research. However, be especially careful when you write directly from an original source. When you do not want to use a quotation, summarize the major ideas from your sources in your own words. Return to Roberta's freewriting draft. Note how she uses her own words to explore her reaction to the ideas she reads. Instead of copying exact words, she summarizes ideas.

Once you know enough about your topic to divide it into subtopics, you can devise a color-coded highlighter scheme to help you keep track of information. In her essay, for instance, Roberta could have used a green highlighter to indicate information favoring the Geritol solution and a pink highlighter for information opposing it. Roberta could have used this scheme both on her own notes and on the material she photocopied.

Using a set of highlighters as you take notes helps you to summarize important facts and ideas in addition to helping you locate useful quotations within your notes. However, when you are writing your essay, you may discover that you would like to look at the original source. Photocopying the material allows you to do this; it also allows you to use highlighters freely on your photocopy to help you spot important information. Furthermore, photocopying material can save you note-taking time if you have a method— such as highlighting—to help you organize the articles you photocopy.

To organize your ideas as you research, keep a list of the subtopics into which you divide your larger subject. When you come to a subdivision not already on your list, simply add it. For example, if you are researching the use of nuclear energy to generate electrical power, you might use the following types of subdivisions: economic considerations, dangers to the environment, problems with disposal of nuclear waste, historical background.

Color-code information as you read. For example, use a shocking pink highlighter to spotlight the shocking effects of acid rain. Use a green one

138

RESEARCH:
DISCOVERING
AND USING
THE IDEAS
OF OTHERS

to highlight economic considerations and a blue one to spotlight dangers to the environment.

When you photocopy an article, be sure you copy the name and date of the source. Often the periodical's name and date of publication do not appear on each page of an article, so you might not have this information in your photocopy. You will need this information for the formal documentation discussed in Chapter 12. Furthermore, you may need to know the periodical's name and date of publication even in informal documentation. The name of the periodical helps readers determine the validity of your information, and the date of publication indicates to readers how current your material is.

Using Note Cards

A more traditional way of keeping track of your notes involves the use of two sets of note cards—one set of approximately four-by-six-inch cards to record your sources and one set of five-by-seven-inch cards on which to take notes. On the smaller cards, write the author, article title, book or periodical title, publisher (for a book but not for a periodical), and date of publication. This will help you organize your material as you take notes. This method of using note and source cards will also help you when you have to write the formal research paper discussed in Chapter 12. See Figures 5-1 and 5-2 for sample source cards.

Use the larger cards for taking notes. Write only one type of information on each note card. On the top of each card, write a title to remind yourself what type of information it contains. If you are using the highlighter system to color-code your ideas, you can highlight the title of each note card. With this system of organizing as you take notes, you will not have to

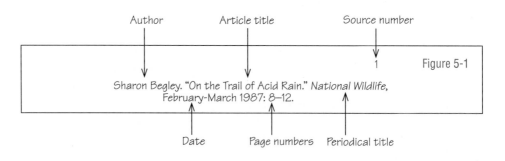

Author   Article title   Source number

1   Figure 5-1

Sharon Begley. "On the Trail of Acid Rain." *National Wildlife,*
February-March 1987: 8–12.

Date   Page numbers   Periodical title

2   Figure 5-2

Jamie James. "Who Will Stop the Acid Rain?" *Discover,*
October 1983: 62–65

139

**RESEARCH:
DISCOVERING
AND USING
THE IDEAS
OF OTHERS**

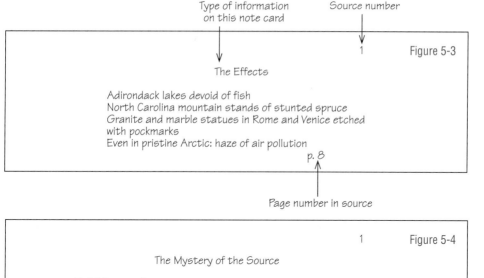

Type of information
on this note card

Source number

1   Figure 5-3

The Effects

Adirondack lakes devoid of fish
North Carolina mountain stands of stunted spruce
Granite and marble statues in Rome and Venice etched
with pockmarks
Even in pristine Arctic: haze of air pollution
                                    p. 8

Page number in source

1   Figure 5-4

The Mystery of the Source

3,000 scientific papers
7 major government reports on causes and effects
Michael Dukakis has called "the silent spring of the 1980s"
(p. 8)
But until recently evidence against any region too tenuous to justify
costly program (millions of $$; thousands of jobs)

2   Figure 5-5

Definition

Distilled water = pH 7 which is neutral
the lower the pH, the more acid
pH more than 7 = alkalinity

wade through your notes searching for information. You will be able to find exactly the information you want quickly and efficiently.

You will find that color-coding your note cards to the photocopied article color code will further help you organize your notes when you begin to write the first draft of your essay.

Write a number in the upper right-hand corner of each note card. This number should correspond to the number on the source card indicating where you got the information you put on your note card. This way you will know whom to credit for the information.

Remember: As you take notes, do not copy ideas word for word unless you plan to use the words in a quotation; instead, summarize ideas and translate these ideas into your own words. When you use note cards written in your own words, you can work quickly to transcribe notes into actual text without risking plagiarism.

Figures 5-3 to 5-7 show sample note cards.

140

**RESEARCH:
DISCOVERING
AND USING
THE IDEAS
OF OTHERS**

---

1   Figure 5-6

The Scientific Detectives

Atmospheric chemists Kenneth Rahn and Randall Borys of University
of Rhode Island

Devised new, patented technique for fingerprinting pollutants in Arctic
air

Discovery came from central Soviet Union, UK, continental Europe

---

Note-Taking Pros and Cons

Some writers find they prefer to use notebook paper instead of note cards. Using notebook paper will give you more room for notes, but you will not have room on your table or desk to lay out all your notes for a particular subdivision of your topic so you can see these notes at a glance. Rather you will have to sort through the stack of notebook paper.

Photocopying articles means you will have these articles to refer to. However, when you take notes, you summarize and translate ideas into your own words, so you can write directly from note cards with less risk of plagiarism.

Experiment to see which note-taking method works best for you. However, regardless of the method you use be sure that

1. Only one type of information appears in each color or on each card or page

2. Each card or page has a title to indicate its contents

3. The source number appears in the upper right-hand corner.

Also, remember to consider color-coding information to save time and aid organization.

 PUTTING THE PUZZLE PIECES IN PLACE

When you have enough notes, you should once again brainstorm, cluster, or freewrite to help discover how to organize your ideas.

Of course, you may find as you begin to write that you need to return to the library to find additional information. Keep a list of information you need so you can capture several facts with one library trip.

141

RESEARCH:
DISCOVERING
AND USING
THE IDEAS
OF OTHERS

2   Figure 5-7

The Effects

Thousands of dead lakes, e.g., Big Moose Lake in Adirondack
20,000 lakes in Sweden alone

Headline journal *Nature*: Too Late for Black Forest?
Kills trees, aquatic life
May have serious effect on crops

Corrosive rain dissolving buildings, stone, bronze
In Chinese industrial city Chongqing, 800-year-old sculptures
now dissolving

Near Los Angeles fog with a pH of 2—more acid than vinegar
Affects drinking water—may threaten drinker's health

Fermenting and Polishing

The best way to gain perspective is to put your paper away for as long as possible—at least two days—and then reread the paper with your critical brain engaged. Ask yourself these questions:

Do I adequately limit my thesis?
Do I stick to my thesis, providing necessary transitions?
Do I concretely, clearly, and logically support my thesis?
Do I cite sources to support my ideas?
Do I explain why the people I cite are authorities?
Do I make any mechanical mistakes in punctuation, grammar, or sentence structure?
Do I make any spelling mistakes or typing errors?

A PROFESSIONAL AT WORK

As you read this article from *Sports Illustrated,* note how author Robert H. Boyle integrates his sources.

Forecast for Disaster

1   And now for the news for July 4, 2030:

2   The second hurricane of the year has struck the East Coast. The 15-foot seawalls built to protect Baltimore, Philadelphia, New York, and Boston held against the 12-foot tides, but a 25-foot storm surge swept over the eastern tip of Long Island, drowning 260 residents who had refused to leave their homes. The 310 fatalities from this hurricane are still far fewer than the 5,600 people who drowned in last month's hurricane in south Florida.

3   Twenty-two inches of rain from the hurricane flooded Washington, D.C.,

142

RESEARCH:
DISCOVERING
AND USING
THE IDEAS
OF OTHERS

breaking the heat wave that had gripped the city for 62 straight days of 90-plus temperatures. This fell short of the record set eight years ago when 72 consecutive 90-plus days caused the move of the nation's capital to the cooler environs of Marquette, Michigan.

4   And now the weather. In the Midwest, Southwest, and West, conditions remain normal—searing heat, drought and dangerous levels of ultraviolet radiation.

5   If this reads like a newscast from *Saturday Night Live,* it isn't. This report has been extrapolated from carefully considered forecasts by a wide variety of scientists as we spin toward the 21st century.

6   Pollutants are saturating our atmosphere. Acid rain, which already has had a devastating impact on parts of eastern North America, central Europe and southern Scandinavia, is one manifestation of this pollution, but its effects tend to be regional. Two similar and interrelated pollutant threats loom even larger, and they may soon affect life on a global scale.

7   The first of these threats is caused by the release of chlorofluorocarbons into the atmosphere. These man-made chemical compounds—more commonly called CFCs—are used as refrigerants and coolants and in the manufacture of everything from pillows to polystyrene boxes for fast food. Ever since their invention not quite 60 years ago, CFCs have been rising into the stratosphere. When they hit the protective cover known as the ozone layer—10 to 20 miles up—they raise hell because their chlorine component devours the molecules that form the thin ozone shell. As that layer is depleted, stronger and stronger doses of ultraviolet (UV) radiation from the sun are able to penetrate to the earth's surface. Skin diseases and plant destruction are only the beginning of the troubles that excessive UV radiation can cause.

8   The other major threat is caused by the continuing buildup of carbon dioxide, nitrous oxide and trace gases, including CFCs, in the atmosphere. In the 150 or so years since the industrial revolution, man's activities have enormously increased the atmospheric concentrations of these gases. The rapidly expanding use of fossil fuels and the vast destruction of the earth's forests have combined to create a great effusion of these so-called greenhouse gases. They are given that name because when they rise into the atmosphere, they form a kind of blanket in the sky that lets in solar heat but prevents heat from escaping the earth's atmosphere—much like a giant greenhouse. The resulting rise in air temperatures could create havoc.

9   This is not the stuff of the far-off future, either. To the alarm of many scientists, a seasonal hole has begun to appear in the ozone layer above the Antarctic. When a significant drop in the ozone level was first recorded in 1978, the scientists who made the observations didn't pay much attention to their own data because no one had foreseen the possibility of such a thing. Unlike the ozone hole, the greenhouse effect was something scientists had anticipated, but it is developing faster than expected. In fact, Dr. James Hansen of the NASA Goddard Institute for Space Studies in New York flatly says that within 10 to 15 years the earth will be warmer than it has been in 100,000 years. Clearly, changes are underway. Whether they will be moderate or catastrophic depends on how man responds. However, when it comes to massive

changes in climate, there are some precedents that may give us signs of what to expect.

143

RESEARCH:
DISCOVERING
AND USING
THE IDEAS
OF OTHERS

10 Over the last 2,000 years, the earth has undergone two major changes in climate. The first was a warm period known to scientists as the medieval warm epoch; it occurred between the years 800 and 1250, when average global temperatures were about the same as they are now. Certain areas, however, were distinctly warmer. During that time barley and oats were grown in Iceland and vineyards flourished in England, where sea levels were gradually rising. In Belgium the rising sea made Bruges, now some 15 miles inland, a seaport.

11 Around 985, the Vikings began to colonize Greenland, which had been discovered by Eric the Red. But by the end of the 13th century Arctic sea ice had spread through Greenland's waters and had become such a navigational hazard that the colonies died out.

12 The medieval warm epoch was soon followed by the Little Ice Age, which lasted from about 1550 to 1850, during which the global climate was generally about 1° C (2° F) cooler than now. In India, the monsoons often failed to arrive, prompting the abandonment in 1588 of the great city of Fatehpur Sikri because of lack of water. The Thames froze over several times in the late 1500s. Year-round snow, now absent, covered the high mountains of Ethiopia. The vineyards of northern France died off.

13 Some scientists who have studied the earth's climatic cycles believe that around 1700, when the Little Ice Age began its gradual decline, the earth swung into a period of 1,000 years of natural warming. This forecast, however, does not take into account the effect of unnatural agents, such as the increasing concentrations of carbon dioxide, nitrous oxide and other greenhouse gases in the atmosphere.

14 What's happening is this. Light from the sun passes through these transparent gases to the earth, where the short-wave radiation (light) becomes long-wave radiation (heat). The heat rises from the earth and ordinarily would escape into space. However, greenhouse gases absorb the long-wave radiation. Thus, the more these gases accumulate in the atmosphere, the more heat they absorb, and the warmer the earth becomes. In time, the planet will come to be like a greenhouse—or a car parked with its windows up on a sunny day.

15 In 1958, Charles D. Keeling, a chemist and professor of oceanography at the Scripps Institution of Oceanography, began measuring atmospheric carbon dioxide on Mauna Loa in Hawaii. Since Keeling's measurements began, the concentration of the gas has increased every year. It jumped from 315 parts per million (ppm) in 1958 to 349 in 1987—a 25% increase from the levels that are thought to have been present before the industrial age. The increase is attributable to a combination of the burning of fossil fuels and the destruction of forests, which serve as reservoirs of carbon. A forest stores about 100 tons of carbon per acre, and in the last 40 years it is estimated that as much as half the world's forests have been destroyed. Given current emission levels, the atmospheric concentration of carbon dioxide is expected to reach about 420 ppm by the year 2030.

16 Two other greenhouse gases, CFCs and nitrous oxide, are double whammies. They are involved in the depletion of the ozone layer (in the case of nitrous oxide this is true only when the gas mixes in the atmosphere with

144

RESEARCH:
DISCOVERING
AND USING
THE IDEAS
OF OTHERS

CFCs or carbon dioxide) and they absorb heat. Measured in the range of parts per trillion, CFC concentrations might seem insignificant, but they are extraordinarily effective heat absorbers. One molecule of CFC-11 or CFC-12 can trap as much heat as 10,000 molecules of carbon dioxide. And CFC levels are increasing at the rate of 5 to 7% per year.

17   Ground-level ozone also qualifies as a greenhouse gas. It is formed by the action of sunlight on nitrogen oxide and hydrocarbon pollutants emitted primarily by cars and trucks. We call it smog. Ozone has a split personality. Stratospheric ozone protects life by shielding the earth from harmful UV radiation; ground-level ozone is toxic. In the U.S. alone, according to a study made by the Environmental Defense Fund, ozone pollution is responsible for annual losses of as much as $2 billion in wheat, corn, soybeans and cotton. Ozone produced on earth cannot be used to replenish the ozone layer in the stratosphere because it has a limited life span before combining into other chemical substances. Therefore it doesn't last long enough to accumulate in amounts significant enough to replace what's being lost in the stratosphere.

18   In the last 100 years, the global mean temperature has gone up by about 0.5° C. Even if all emissions of greenhouse gases were cut off today, past emissions already make another 0.5° C increase likely by 2050. According to computer model estimates done by Dr. Veerabhadran Ramanathan, an atmospheric scientist at the University of Chicago, the global average surface temperature could increase by a total of as much as 4.5° C in the next 40 years, based on current levels of greenhouse gas emissions. That would make the earth almost as hot as it was during the Cretaceous period, the age of the dinosaurs, 100 million years ago. Mind you, that is the global average. The greatest increase in temperatures will occur from the mid-latitudes to the poles, where wintertime averages would be 10° C higher than now.

19   "Other discussions of the practical impacts of greenhouse warming have focused on possible indirect effects such as changes of sea level, storm frequency and drought," Hansen of NASA's Goddard Center says. "We believe that the temperature changes themselves will substantially modify the environment and have a major impact on the quality of life in some regions." However, the greenhouse issue is not likely to receive the full attention it deserves until the global temperature rises above the level of the present natural climate variability. If our model is approximately correct, that time may be soon—within the next decade.

20   Dr. Wallace Broecker, a geochemist at the Lamont-Doherty Geological Observatory of Columbia University, thinks the situation may be even worse than indicated by models, with their supposition of a gradual warming over a considerable period of time. "The earth's climate doesn't respond in a smooth and gradual way," he says. "Rather, it responds in sharp jumps. These jumps appear to involve large-scale reorganizations of earth systems. If this reading of the natural record is correct, then we must consider the possibility that the major response of the earth system to our greenhouse provocation will also occur in jumps whose timing and magnitude are uneven and unpredictable. Coping with this type of change is clearly a far more serious matter than coping with a gradual steady warming."

21   A study by the National Academy of Sciences suggests that water volume

in northern California rivers and in the Colorado River will decline by as much as 60 percent. This would leave much of the West without water. Southern California would run dry and be subjected to an increased incidence of fire, as would forests throughout much of the West and upper Midwest.

22   Within the past 100 years, tide gauges of the Atlantic Coast of the U.S. have documented a 30-centimeter, or one-foot, rise in sea level. Globally, the average is about five inches. Models predict that the level will have risen by another foot in low-lying coastal regions of the U.S. in 2030, and by as much as three feet in 2100.

23   Couple all the greenhouse effects with increased ultraviolet radiation, and we have written the prescription for disaster—ecological, economical and political.

24   Dr. Michael Oppenheimer, a former Harvard astrophysicist who is now senior atmospheric scientist with the Environmental Defense Fund, puts it this way:

> We're flying blind into a highly uncertain future. These changes are going to affect every human being and every ecosystem on the face of the earth, and we only have a glimmer of what these changes will be. The atmosphere is supposed to do two things for us: maintain a constant chemical climate of oxygen, nitrogen and water vapor, and help maintain the radiation balance—for example, by keeping out excess UV. The unthinkable is that we're distorting this atmospheric balance. We're shifting the chemical balance so that we have more poisons in the atmosphere—ozone and acid rain on ground level—while we're also changing the thermal climate of the earth through the greenhouse effect and—get this—simultaneously causing destruction of our primary filter of ultraviolet light. It's incredible. Talk about the national-debt crisis—we're piling up debts in the atmosphere, and the piper will want to be paid.

25   Fortunately, it's still possible to ameliorate the damage. Here's what we must do:

26   *Reduce production of CFCs by 95% world wide within the next six to eight years.*

27   In September [1987] the U.S. and 23 other countries signed a treaty calling for a 50% cut in CFC production by mid-1999, but the new findings from the Antarctic demonstrate that the cut is neither big enough nor fast enough. "We've got to beat the clock," says Rafe Pomerance, a policy analyst who has been following the ozone problem for the World Resources Institute in Washington, D.C., for the past two years. "If the data from the Antarctic continues to build over the next few months, we may have to reconvene and strengthen the treaty."

28   *Reduce dependence on fossil fuels.* "We should focus on incremental steps that limit our dependence on coal and oil," Oppenheimer says. "Let's focus on the do-able. Number one is conservation. The U.S. still uses twice as much energy per capita as the European nations. We're wasting money, we're wasting energy, and we're producing too much carbon dioxide because of our overdependence on fossil fuels."

29   Reliance on these fuels can also be reduced through greater use of non-

146

RESEARCH:
DISCOVERING
AND USING
THE IDEAS
OF OTHERS

polluting alternative sources of energy. Solar power is a prime example, but the U.S. seems to have given up leadership in photovoltaic research, and the Japanese are now forging ahead. Photovoltaic technology promises to deliver energy at a reasonable price without producing carbon dioxide.

30   *Halt deforestation.* "You have to do two things," says Dr. George M. Woodwell, former president of the Ecological Society of America and now director of the Woods Hole Research Center. "First, you have to stop deforestation around the world, not just in the tropics, and you have to do it on the basis of an international protocol. Second, you have to have an equally intensive and imaginative protocol that calls for reforestation so as to store one billion tons of carbon annually. A million square kilometers is 600 miles by 600 miles, and we will probably have to reforest on the order of four million square kilometers per year over good land to do the job."

31   *Establish a national institute devoted to basic environmental research.* Says Oppenheimer: "We need a national commitment comparable to the Manhattan Project, not only so we can understand what the consequences of global change are for man, but so that we can be in the forefront of the development of alternative energy sources that will help limit this problem. I envision a multibillion dollar scientific effort. It's as important as national defense. It *is* the national defense. If we do nothing waiting for the atmosphere to change and for unpleasant consequences to occur, it will be too late for us to avoid disruptive and devastating changes."

32   *Discontinue basic environmental research by or funded by EPA and the Department of Energy.* These agencies are unrealiable because they are heavily influenced by political pressure. Last January, Broecker bluntly told the Senate Subcommittee on Environmental Protection, "I believe that most scientists would agree with me that the handling of research on greenhouse gases by DOE [the Department of Energy] and on acid rain by EPA has been a disaster."

33   Will the world act in time? As Rowland, who won eight varsity letters in basketball and baseball at Ohio Wesleyan and the University of Chicago, puts it, "The key thing about baseball is, there is always next year, another season. The question for the earth now is, will there be a next year?"

For Thought and Discussion

1. Why do you think *Sports Illustrated* ran this article?

2. According to the author, which pollutants may soon have a catastrophic effect on life on earth?

3. How does the author give credibility to his points?

4. List two examples where the author cites authorities to support his point.

5. Reread paragraph 20; then reread "From 'Unpleasant Surprises in the Greenhouse?'" (page 136). How are Broecker's words altered to fit the *Sports Illustrated* readership audience?

6. List two examples of information showing that authorities are credible. (See "Research Sources: Where Did You Get That Idea?", page 128.)

147

RESEARCH:
DISCOVERING
AND USING
THE IDEAS
OF OTHERS

7. Give an example of information the author includes to ensure that his general, nonscientific audience understands his ideas.

Guests at a Continent's Edge

Although the following poem was written more than sixty years ago, it seems to document many of the predictions from "Forecast for Disaster." While poet Robinson Jeffers did not have access to modern scientific thinking, he was an ardent student of both Mother Nature and human nature. Born in Pittsburgh, Pennsylvania, in 1887, Jeffers moved to Carmel, California, in 1913; he lived there at the edge of the Pacific Ocean until his death in 1962. A former forestry student at the University of Washington, Jeffers lamented people's failure to revere nature, whose beauty and grandeur he celebrated in his poetry.

November Surf

Some lucky day each November great waves awake and are drawn
Like smoking mountains bright from the west
And come and cover the cliff with white violent cleanness; then suddenly
The old granite forgets half a year's filth:
The orange-peel, eggshells, papers, pieces of clothing, the clots   5
Of dung in corners of the rock, and used
Sheaths that make light love safe in the evenings: all the droppings of the
    summer
Idlers washed off in a winter ecstasy:
I think this cumbered continent envies its cliff then. . . . But all seasons
The earth, in her childlike prophetic sleep,   10
Keeps dreaming of the bath of a storm that prepares up the long coast
Of the future to scour more than her sea-lines:
The cities gone down, the people fewer and the hawks more numerous,
The river's mouth to source pure; when the two-footed
Mammal, being someways one of the nobler animals, regains   15
The dignity of room, the value of rareness.

For Thought and Discussion

1. How do the summer beach-goers treat nature?

2. What does nature do to repair the damage left by people?

3. According to Jeffers, what will be the impact on humankind when nature's dream of the future comes to pass?

4. Do you agree or disagree with Jeffers' prediction of the future? Support your answer by citing authorities from the article "Forecast for Disaster."

148

RESEARCH:
DISCOVERING
AND USING
THE IDEAS
OF OTHERS

WRITING ASSIGNMENT

Write an essay with a 500-word minimum and a 750-word maximum. In this paper, use at least three sources to help you support a thesis about a current environmental, social, or political problem. To lend credibility to your message and to eliminate the possibility of plagiarism, be sure to credit your sources in your writing.

Suggestions for Topics

The following list consists of broad, general areas which need to be more narrowly focused for a paper of the assigned length. While environmental issues have been the central focus of the writing in this chapter, the research techniques discussed in the chapter are applicable to subjects unrelated to the environment.

> Nuclear power plants
> Arms control
> Acid rain
> The greenhouse effect
> The ozone problem
> Toxic waste
> Reducing pollution through conservation of energy
> Pesticides
> The impact of pollution on the economy
> The death penalty
> Mercy killing (euthanasia)
> Reducing the risk of heart attack
> Reducing the risk of cancer (select a specific type)
> The impact of the balance of payments on the economy

Peer Editing Checklist

After you have completed the prewriting and the first draft of your essay, meet with a peer editing group so that you can assess the reaction of an audience to your writing. Photocopy enough copies of your essay for your peer editing group.

1. Indicate any ideas, passages, imagery, allusions, or other aspects of this essay you found effective. Positive reinforcement is a powerful tool.

2. Restate the thesis in your own words, so the author can see if the thesis was clear. If you are confused about what the thesis is, indicate this to the writer.

3. Point out development you found especially compelling.

4. Point out places where more information should be included to convince readers that the thesis is credible.

5. Point out any section of the paper in which you are confused by the ideas or their development.

6. Indicate any places where the connection between ideas is not clear.

7. Point out any places where you are not clear about the credentials of the authorities cited.

8. Tell the author how you think the introduction and conclusion contribute to the paper's purpose.

9. Point out any places where the use of figurative language or allusion would help clarify the point.

When writers have revised the content of the essay to their satisfaction and are ready for feedback about mechanics, point out but do not correct any problems you suspect exist with spelling, grammar, and punctuation. It is the writer's responsibility to make corrections.

Help! For Further Work

Read the following draft as if you were its peer editor. Then use the peer editing checklist to make suggestions for the next draft.

Action against Pesticides

1   The thought of being exposed to harmful pesticides is an awful one. Yet it is taken for granted that the majority of us will be exposed to harmful pesticides in our lifetime, of course, the pesticides that are considered harmful to some may be considered necessary by others and others may not find them harmful at all except perhaps in the long run. The use of pesticides around our cities, neighborhoods, and in our homes is a subject that we should be concerned with.

2   The growing war on pests with chemical compounds has generated a number of small groups that are busy studying local issues on pesticides. These activist groups in some cases have prevented the use of particular pesticides and sometimes a total ban on pesticide spraying. The reason for these actions taken by these groups is a simple one: some chemical pesticides are considered very harmful to the environment and to human life as well. On numerous occasions effects have closely followed sprayings of neighborhoods. Chemicals such as diazinon, imadin, and oftunol may be responsible for birth defects, serious damage to the nervous system and mutations in cells or cancer.

3   Uses of large amounts of chemicals to eradicate pests like the California med fly have begun to awaken the public to the possible dangers of these campaigns against pests. Local and State Governments have increased the programs against pests like the gypsy moth, Japanese beetle, mosquito, and Mexican fruit fly. The California Food and Agriculture Department believes

150

**RESEARCH:
DISCOVERING
AND USING
THE IDEAS
OF OTHERS**

that once a pest becomes a public nuisance the problem then becomes a type of emergency. The activist groups agree that they should fight these pests but with other safe chemicals or natural alternative methods.

4   The activists groups feel that educating the public is their most important goal. If the public has a greater knowledge of what is being done around them then they will have a more knowledgeable opinion about what should or should not be allowed. The public also needs to know that there are natural insecticide alternatives to chemical pesticides. Bacteria can be used in place of pesticides to attack pests.

5   Another intensified activity of the activists groups is lobbying efforts in local, state and federal governments which is where the National Coalition Against the Misuse of Pesticides in Washington, D.C. really helps out. The coalition is a type of clearing-house for small groups. Its most recent success has been the reauthorization and reform of the Federal Insecticide, Fungicide and Rodenticide Act. This act regulates the manufacture, sale, and use of pesticides.

6   It will take a long while for much to be accomplished in the use and misuse of chemical pesticides. Yet a few determined people have banded together and are determined to make a difference. If not for this generation, then the generation to come.

STUDENT STARS

While the examples thus far in this chapter have centered around environmental issues, the methods discussed in this chapter apply to any writing that requires research. Therefore, the student star essays, like the suggested topics, are on a variety of topics.

The authors of the following essays have done the following:

1. Prewriting
2. Writing
3. Revision
4. Correction of mechanical errors.

Repeal the Fifty-five Miles Per Hour Speed Limit

1   More than a decade has passed since the fifty-five miles per hour speed limit became the law of the land. Now Congress is backing down and allowing drivers on some highways to speed up. Why? The fifty-five law has been praised for saving legions of lives and a tanker armada of fuel. But this law was the proverbial thorn in the paw awaiting a Congressional Androcles to pluck it out. With implementation of the fifty-five law, did the numbers of traffic deaths really diminish?

2   Statistics compiled by the National Safety Council show the fatality rates did drop from 18.2 persons in 1925 to 3.6 per hundred-million vehicle miles in 1974 when the fifty-five limit took effect. Why the drop in fatalities? Auto makers built safer vehicles, drivers became more skillful, and roads improved.

3   In 1983 deaths hit a twenty-year low with 43,000 fatalities. This was a reduction of 2.1% from 1982 and 15.8% from 1980. These figures calculate out to 2.6 persons killed per hundred million miles of travel. But former Secretary of Transportation Elizabeth Dole attributes the decline in deaths to the efforts of state and local governments to crack down on drunk drivers, not to the fifty-five law.

151
RESEARCH:
DISCOVERING
AND USING
THE IDEAS
OF OTHERS

4   In a study of traffic records for primary causes of accidents, Dr. B. J. Campbell of the University of North Carolina, Highway Safety Research Institute, found that only 9% of the accidents occurred above the posted speed limit.

5   After analyzing thousands of crashes in the Midwest, Matthew C. Sielski of the Michigan Auto Club found that speed too fast for the road and weather conditions (not necessarily faster than the posted speed) accounted for less than 5% of the fatal accidents. Eighty percent of the fatal accidents occurred under forty miles per hour.

6   Granted, fatalities did decline an impressive 17% in 1974 with the fifty-five limit; however, part of that reduction is due to fuel scarcity which resulted in fewer people being on the road. In addition, government-required safety equipment and crackdowns on drunk drivers helped lower fatality numbers.

7   If, in fact, the real point of a fifty-five speed limit is to save lives, we must look at the accidents themselves and analyze the part speed played in fatalities. People under age twenty-five account for 22% of the driving population, but they also account for 40% of the auto fatalities. Half of all teenage deaths involve auto accidents.

8   Dr. William Haddon, Jr. of the Insurance Institute for Highway Safety analyzed statistics from the Department of Transportation that showed teen drivers were responsible for five times as many crash deaths than people in the thirty-five to sixty-four age group. Males were responsible for four times as many crash deaths than females in the under twenty-five group.

9   Since a significant part of the traffic fatality problem involves younger drivers, *Road and Track* has two life-saving suggestions: those who want to cut the number of traffic fatalities should raise the drinking age (as fourteen states have done), or they should impose a teen driving curfew (as twelve states have).

10   What about claims that fifty-five saves gas? When an oil embargo hit and fuel prices leaped in the seventies, Congress mandated a fifty-five limit which resulted in approximately a 3% fuel saving. Instead of setting their sights so low, had Congress been serious about saving fuel they could have required auto makers to produce more fuel-efficient vehicles by creating more efficient bodies and engines. Performance tests completed by *Car and Driver* magazine proved car design and not speed was the more important factor in fuel economy. A small car traveling ninety miles per hour is more fuel efficient than a big car traveling at fifty-five.

11   Moreover, Jim Banter, head of the Citizens Coalition for Rational Traffic Laws, claims the national speed limit raises travel time on interstate highways by twenty-one percent. This figure is based on the old speed limit of seventy miles per hour and driving 45,000 to 50,000 miles per year—as truckers do. And these experienced truckers say that fatigue from longer hours on the road causes more accidents than the fifty-five limit avoids. In addition, in

12   many sections of the country the road stretches to the horizon with hardly another vehicle in sight. Carl Sorrentino, spokesman for the Colorado Highway Department, wonders why anyone should stick to a fifty-five limit when the only traffic in sight is tumbleweeds and jack rabbits.

H. L. Mencken once said: "For every complex problem, there is a simple solution—that is wrong." The simple solution of a fifty-five law has cost taxpayers well over two hundred million dollars to enforce. For the complex problems of traffic fatalities and fuel economy we need better solutions than a simple fifty-five speed limit.

—Ronald Green

The Chemicals We Eat

1   Most lists of ingredients on food labels today read like the index pages of a chemistry book. For us consumers convenience is king. We want to spend less time preparing food, we want food to have a longer shelf life, and we want our food to be economical. To achieve these goals, food processors use a broad variety of additives. Few of us are willing to wrestle with oranges when we want a glass of orange juice. Instead we reach for a jar of orange powder which is colored, flavored, preserved, fortified, and instantly dissolving. Ice cream that melts too fast and is then refrozen will develop an undesirable texture. Vegetable gum stabilizer will help to create and maintain a smooth, creamy texture. Oil-containing foods such as mayonnaise and shortening will spoil when oxygen in the air reacts with polyunsaturated oils. But a dash of antioxidant will help preserve these foods and save money by lowering manufacturing costs.

2   Manufactured, emulsified, stabilized, fortified, and preserved foods containing more than $490,000,000 worth of several thousand food additives line our supermarket shelves. What worries food consumers is the effect of these additives. That some of the additives present only a small cancer risk is not reassuring to many consumers. These consumers want to be assured of absolute safety, but, in fact, consumers can't have absolute safety coupled with convenience and economy.

3   How serious is the threat posed to consumers by food additives? The term "chemical" itself has a bad connotation, but this connotation does not stand up to careful scrutiny. The truth is that foods, regardless of their origins, are conglomerations of chemicals. To illustrate, if someone proposed to add acetone, acetaldehyde, methylpropylketone, methyl isovalerianate, isomyl isovalerianate, methanol, *o*-methylpropyl benzene, or *B*-phenylethyleaproate to enhance the flavor or aroma of a food, how would you feel about eating that food? In fact, according to "Chemicals and Engineering News" from *Chemicals,* all of these chemicals and more occur naturally in ripe strawberries.

4   Today many of the substances produced by living organisms can be combined or synthesized in laboratories by chemists. When the synthetic version is produced, the resulting chemical is identical to the one produced by Mother Nature.

5   What about the fear that food additives will cause cancer or other diseases? According to the United States Department of Agriculture, most food-related diseases involve meat. Most disease-causing bacteria come from meat that has been undercooked or has been carelessly handled. In fact, such meat causes

millions of infections annually. According to "Chemicals and Engineering News," studies show that food poisoning may damage blood vessels and contribute to cardiovascular disease.

6   Thus we have to weigh the potential hazard represented by chemical preservatives against the hazard posed by the diseases that may be harbored by food not containing these preservatives. Sodium nitrite is an excellent case in point. Manufacturers add sodium nitrite to ham and lunch meats to prevent the growth of toxic bacteria. There is a slight risk, however, that nitrite can contribute to cancer. The FDA presently believes that the health insurance we receive from nitrite outweighs the chance that this additive is hazardous.

7   So what should the consumer do when faced with the dilemma of the positive and negative effects of food additives? One suggestion is to minimize the use of the potentially hazardous chemicals while manufacturers work to develop less hazardous ones. Avoid additives that offer no nutritional or preserving benefits—for example the sodium nitrate in baby foods has a slight effect on the color and taste, but does not act as a preservative and does not increase the nutritional value of the baby food. Since nitrite is suspected of causing cancer, mothers and public officials are clamoring for it to be removed from baby foods. Remember, read the label before you buy a product so you can weigh the risks and benefits of its additives.

8   Do remember that additives save the consumer a great deal of money. According to John Bailer, author of *Chemicals in Foods*, removal of additives from bread would cost the consumer $1.1 billion annually, from margarine $600 million annually, from meats $600 million annually, and from processed cheese $32 million annually.

9   So we consumers face a big decision when we go food shopping. There is no easy answer to the dilemma about the risks and benefits of the chemicals we eat.
                                                                        —Michael Ousbye

Making the Golden Years Golden

1   Today Americans are leading longer and healthier lives than in the past. Nevertheless, according to a special *Money* report on care for the elderly, "The majority of Americans age sixty-five or older suffer from some kind of chronic disability or acute illness." As a result, middle-aged Americans may be called upon to help their parents.

2   The options available to aid this growing population of elderly have increased in an attempt to meet demand. Choosing the type of care for your parents requires much time, thought, and discussion between you and your parents. Make sure you understand what they want. "Quality of life means different things to the adult child than it does to the parent. The child worries most about the parent's security, the parent about keeping control of his or her life," states Sandra Howell, an associate professor at MIT who specializes in environments for the elderly. Among the options available to care for the elderly are the following:

Your Parent's Home

3   Most parents have an emotional attachment to their home. If capable of living on their own, parents can continue to live in their home if it is retrofitted

154

**RESEARCH:
DISCOVERING
AND USING
THE IDEAS
OF OTHERS**

with simple things like ramps to doors, grab bars in bathrooms, and first-floor bathrooms in multi-story homes. Parents will still be in control of their own lives and maintain their independence under this option. Of course, they may need help with routine chores such as shopping, preparing meals, and house cleaning. If you do not live nearby or cannot meet the heavy demands of caring for a parent, there are community services available to aid you. Most of these services are provided to the senior citizen at little or no cost. Examples include visiting nurses, Meals-on-Wheels, programs that provide low or no-cost home maintenance, and companion and phone reassurance programs (programs that are often staffed by volunteers). To insure that the agency providing help to your parents is reputable, check to see if it is approved by Medicare. According to the article "New Options for the Aging" in *Saturday Evening Post,* nearly 6,000 agencies are thus approved.

In Your Home

4   Approximately 60% of elderly adults needing care move in with their children. However, in these situations, conflict often arises no matter how close the family. Elderly parents are sometimes bitter about giving up their independence and children resent the intrusion. Old roles can cause problems. As Lissy Jarvik, a professor of geriatric psychiatry at UCLA, points out: "Your childhood has deep roots in both you and your parent. Dependency and living together are apt to awaken some old conflicts."

5   Building a self-contained apartment as an addition to your home can help alleviate some of these problems. The cost of such construction varies greatly, with an average range of between $15,000 to $50,000 depending on the design and local labor costs.

6   If you cannot provide daily care, you can tap into the community services mentioned above or enroll your parent in adult day care. These programs are in the vanguard of efforts to keep elderly people out of nursing homes and in their homes and communities as long as possible. Described in the *Newsweek* article "A Home Away from Home" as country clubs, these programs—along with summer camps and social clubs provided by organizations like ElderCare, Inc.—offer stimulation, structure, social life, and self-esteem. For patients with Alzheimer's, the stimulation received at the day care facility seems to help stave off some mental deterioration. Rick Zawadski, principal investigator for the National Adult Day Care Census, points out another plus to these new day care programs. Costing an average of $37 a day, they are in Zawadski's words, "a real bargain—less than the cost of one nursing visit to your home."

Elder Care Communities

7   Group homes and continuous care facilities fall into this category. Group homes are private houses in which six to seven adults with similar needs live together. Continuous care facilities resemble a college campus. Elderly adults live in independent apartments. As the need arises, management will move them to an intermediate or continuous care facility, all on the premises. These facilities are difficult to get into, but the management is obligated to continue care.

8   For the parent who has fallen victim to a severe mental or physical impairment, a nursing home may be the only option available. Unfortunately, many of the best nursing homes have a year-long waiting list. *Money Magazine* writer Lani Luciano urges that if you feel your parents' health is deteriorating and will necessitate placement in a home, get their names on the waiting list as soon as possible. Luciano further cautions that you be prepared for the expense: $18,000 to $50,000 or more annually.

9   When the time comes that a decision must be made for the care of an elderly parent, it will not be easy on either of you. Jo Horne, author of *The Nursing Handbook,* advises, "Take things one step at a time. When you don't know what to do, you just consult your conscience and your heart."

—Ginny Scout

6

DISCOVERING IDEAS THROUGH QUESTIONS: WRITING ABOUT PROCESSES

CONCEPTS TO LEARN

Discovering and organizing ideas about processes by asking these key questions:

How does X work?

What steps must you take to accomplish X?

The analogy

Introductory techniques for capturing your audience's attention

---

We *Homo sapiens* seem to have an instinctive need to create systems that explain experiences for us. "In our beclouded and tempestuous existence," as novelist Joseph Conrad put it, we want life to be more than an accident in a whimsical universe. Art, literature, music, mythology all try to create systems that organize experience so people can make sense of it.

In Chapter 2, we pointed out the basic urge in people to tell stories to make sense of their experience. For example, in some cultures, people have explained through mythology—through fanciful tales of gods and goddesses—why a bright flash in the stormy sky is followed by a loud clap of thunder.

In this century and the last, we have increasingly turned to science to show us that the universe is, in fact, an ordered place with an underlying, predictable organization. "Science," Albert Einstein wrote, "is the attempt to make the chaotic diversity of our sense-experience correspond to a logically uniform system of thought."

In this desire to organize experience meaningfully, scientists turn to writing for the same primary reasons that other people turn to writing: first to make sense of and then to communicate their ideas. Like other writers, scientists begin, not by organizing answers they already know, but by asking questions. In *The Ascent of Man,* Cambridge University mathematician Jacob Bronowski wrote of the value of questioning in the following anecdote about atomic theory pioneer John Dalton:

157

DISCOVERING
IDEAS
THROUGH
QUESTIONS:
WRITING
ABOUT
PROCESSES

> Dalton was a man of regular habits. For fifty-seven years he walked out of Manchester every day; he measured the rainfall, the temperature—a singularly monotonous enterprise in this climate. Of all that mass of data, nothing whatever came. But of the one searching, almost childlike question about the weights that enter the construction of these simple molecules—out of that came modern atomic theory. That is the essence of science: ask an impertinent question, and you are on the way to the pertinent answer.

In this chapter, we will explore the benefits of asking and then answering questions that lead us to discover how processes work. While the questions themselves may seem simple, remember the Bronowski dictum that people of genius "ask transparent, innocent questions." While your question may not turn out to have what Bronowski calls the "catastrophic answers" scientific geniuses discover, the technique of questioning will help you to clarify and organize your thinking.

Often an entire writing task or a significant part of a writing task is to answer questions such as *How does X work? What steps must you take to accomplish X?* Because scientific writing often involves explaining such processes, this chapter will use examples from science to explore and illustrate the most effective ways to find and then to communicate the answers to these questions.

Scientists use three primary methods to identify research questions and to generate answers to such questions—methods that can also prove very valuable to you when you write:

1. **Use your creative thought processes to explore what you already know about your subject.** Recall from Chapter 1 how Einstein and Kekule did this. Clustering, brainstorming, and freewriting are effective methods to use in this exploration.

2. **Use your creative thought processes to generate questions and other ideas that will direct your research and writing.** Both brainstorming and freewriting are effective methods to generate such questions and ideas.

3. **Research the answers to your questions in the library, in dialogues with others, in interviews with authorities, and in observations of activities relevant to your questions.** This step goes back and forth. Reading background information may help you generate ideas for research questions. Then you may interview an expert or observe a relevant activity before returning to the library. Discussions with peer groups or with family and

158

DISCOVERING
IDEAS
THROUGH
QUESTIONS:
WRITING
ABOUT
PROCESSES

friends can also provide valuable feedback, similar to the feedback scientists get through discussions with colleagues and through having their papers reviewed by other scientists.

The best method to use to generate and organize your ideas depends upon the subject matter and upon your own psyche. A method that is especially effective for one writer might not work for another writer. A method that works well for you with one type of writing might be less effective with other writing tasks. Of course, most writing profits from use of several methods of idea-generating and idea-organizing—as you have seen in previous chapters.

While this chapter concentrates on scientific subjects, the techniques of this chapter are helpful for developing essays on a broad variety of non-scientific topics as well. Furthermore, these techniques are helpful regardless of whether the process you want to describe will provide a set of instructions for your readers to follow (for example, how to get financial aid to help pay for college) or will provide a description of how a process occurs (for example, what causes the greenhouse effect).

Your turn

To take advantage of the fact that the ideas of others help to inspire our own ideas, do this exercise in a peer group.

1. Select one of the following topics: the greenhouse effect, the ozone layer, acid rain, alternative energy, AIDS research, cancer research, genetic engineering, or an instructor-approved topic of your choice.

2. Use the three steps listed in the preceding section to create a list of questions that could lead to a thesis for an essay.

3. Substituting one of the suggested topics for X, answer one of this chapter's key questions: *How does X work? What steps must you take to accomplish X?* You may have to narrow your subject during this process. For example, cancer research could be limited to research in a particular kind of cancer such as skin cancer or breast cancer.

 ## YOUR PURPOSE, YOUR AUDIENCE, AND YOUR THESIS

As you saw in the "Your Turn" exercise above, a single broad subject area can lead people to a variety of thesis statements. As writers decide upon an approach to a subject, their interests, audience, and purpose help them discover the questions that will lead to their thesis.

The poem that follows provides an example of the problems that can arise when an author's purpose and interest conflict with those of the intended audience. If the questions the audience wants answered are ignored, that audience will often wander off mentally (and perhaps physically as well). The triangular interaction between text, writer, and reader discussed in Chapter 4 will break down. Such a breakdown is described in the following poem by nineteenth-century poet Walt Whitman.

During Whitman's life, science was making remarkable discoveries that were changing humankind's conception of the universe. Like other thoughtful people of his time and our own, Whitman was interested in and reacted to the new ideas being expounded by science. Unlike many of his contemporaries, however, Whitman was not willing simply to accept astronomy's new view of the universe as the only way of seeing reality.

Not one to unquestioningly accept another's ideas, Whitman began his career as a conventionally dressed journalist who wrote bad imitations of English poetry. He abandoned conventional dress for worker's clothes; likewise, he abandoned poetry with conventional rhyme and rhythm when he discovered that his purpose was better stated by the loose, rolling rhythm and irregular rhyme of *free verse*.

As you read the following poem, note how the audience and purpose of the "learn'd astronomer" conflict with Walt Whitman's interest and purpose.

When I Heard the Learn'd Astronomer

When I heard the learn'd astronomer,
When the proofs, the figures, were ranged in columns before me,
When I was shown the charts and diagrams, to add, divide, and measure
   them,
When I sitting heard the astronomer where he lectured with much applause
   in the lecture-room,
How soon unaccountable I became tired and sick,
Till rising and gliding out I wandered off by myself,
In the mystical moist night-air, and from time to time,
Looked up in perfect silence at the stars.

For Thought and Discussion

1. How does Whitman react to the lecture?

2. Based on Whitman's comments and reaction, describe the type of material the lecture included.

3. What kinds of concepts does the astronomer's lecture exclude that Whitman wants to be included?

4. Explain why you think that the lecturer should or should not have tailored the lecture more to Whitman's interest.

5. Why does Whitman go outside and look up "in perfect silence"?

160

DISCOVERING
IDEAS
THROUGH
QUESTIONS:
WRITING
ABOUT
PROCESSES

6. How does the central idea of this poem especially lend itself to the unstructured rhythms of free verse?

COMMUNICATING THE COMPLEX

Like many contemporary audiences of nonscientists, Whitman wanted more from a scientific lecture than statistics. However, the astronomer whose lecture Whitman attended evidently was directing his words to people similarly caught up by charts and numbers. Through his failure to consider those in the Whitman segment of the audience, the astronomer lost them.

As scientists such as Copernicus, Darwin, Curie, and Einstein have altered our view of reality, we nonscientists have struggled to keep up—to understand just what kind of a universe we inhabit. Scientists will continue turning our world upside down—both theoretically and literally—with their work, work which so far has resulted in everything from surrogate mothers to pineapples that grow to the proper size to fit into a can.

What does this mean to the average person? In a democratic society, it is vital that science communicate its complex and powerful reality in terms the average person can understand. Science by itself is neither good nor bad: It searches for vaccines for diseases like AIDS, and it provides the technology to blow civilizations apart. Alan Valentine summarizes the reason that we must understand modern science and be able to form and communicate our own views about it: "Whenever science makes a discovery, the devil grabs it while the angels are debating the best way to use it." Joseph Wood Krutch puts this idea in another way: "Though many have tried, no one has ever yet explained away the decisive fact that science, which can do so much, cannot decide what it ought to do."

Among the complex questions about what science "ought to do" are the following: Should scientists be unregulated in their experiments with creating new life forms? What if an experimental new life form escapes from the test tube and becomes a disease even more horrible than AIDS? Should strawberry growers be allowed to spray their fields with a genetically engineered bacteria that protects the plants from frost? What impact would such an alien bacteria have on the rest of the ecosystem? Should scientists be allowed to experiment with human embryos? Should they create life in a test tube? Should a test tube baby be raised in an artificial environment to see what will happen to it as it grows up?

We already know that some genetic diseases single out specific ethnic groups—Tay-Sachs syndrome and sickle-cell anemia, for example. What if a modern-day Hitler or a real Dr. Strangelove decided to use genetic research to eliminate a group he felt to be inferior—for example, people of white, Anglo-Saxon background? Or Hispanics? Or Asians?

"Science cannot stop while ethics catches up," Elvin Stackman contends, "and nobody should expect scientists to do all the thinking for the country." If we want to live in a reasonable, rational, humane world, if we do indeed believe in the democratic process, we need to keep an eye on science. We need a basic understanding of what scientists are doing to our universe.

"Sure," some say. "But science is complicated. Obscure. I can't understand all that mumbo-jumbo. And to make matters worse, if ordinary people start catching on to their words, scientists switch to numbers. They write things like $E = mc^2$." The point is that complex processes are far easier to understand when they are explained properly. One of the most important communications skills we can develop in our complex world is the ability to explain a complex process to an audience of nonexperts in terms they can understand. Writing helps us to understand complex processes ourselves and then to formulate and communicate our ideas about these processes.

For Thought and Discussion

1. Look at the cartoon on page 162. Why does some modern technology inspire the feeling expressed in this cartoon?

2. List an example of one scientific discovery you consider good and one you consider either bad or dangerous.

3. Give an example of a scientific process you find difficult to understand. If you understand a process that a classmate finds mystifying, explain the process to that person. Suggestions: $E = mc^2$, fusion and fission, cold fission, how vaccines work, how the ozone layer is being destroyed by chemicals, genetic engineering.

SELECTING AND LIMITING YOUR SUBJECT

The principles we have studied in the first four chapters of this text will be useful in writing essays that describe processes—whether they are the processes of science and technology such as genetic engineering or personal or social processes such as how to survive a divorce or create housing for the homeless.

You can use any of the idea-generating methods to help you select a subject for your process essay. A good sequence is to get background information by reading an article, watching a documentary, or talking with an authority. Then survey your knowledge and discover what you want to say by brainstorming, clustering, freewriting, questioning, or a combination of these methods.

162

**DISCOVERING
IDEAS
THROUGH
QUESTIONS:
WRITING
ABOUT
PROCESSES**

In Chapters 2 and 3, we discussed the importance of limiting your subject. Such limiting is vital when explaining most processes because there are usually many potential subjects in any process. In a process essay about gardening, for example, you could write lengthy papers about controlling garden pests, determining soil type, or selecting appropriate plants. Or you could focus on the process of selecting plants for your climate. While your initial prewriting may suggest a method of limiting your subject, you may want to alter your thesis after your initial prewriting. Often you will further limit your subject as you learn more about it.

LEARNING ABOUT YOUR TOPIC

In writing, it is not enough to be organized and to have no mechanical errors. You must also have something worthwhile to write about. If you are a walking encyclopedia about a topic, you may be ready to begin writing. However, most people need a little of what rocket engineer Werner von Braun called "basic research." Von Braun wrote, "Basic research is when

I'm doing what I don't know what I'm doing." To find out what you should be writing about in an essay, you usually will benefit from examining the ideas of others.

163

DISCOVERING
IDEAS
THROUGH
QUESTIONS:
WRITING
ABOUT
PROCESSES

In an essay about how to get gophers out of a garden, for example, you might have to learn more about the effects of poison on gophers. You may know that there is more than one type of gopher poison and that the poison comes in several forms, but you may not know about how these poisons work. If you have pets you are probably concerned about the danger of poison to them. Furthermore, you do not want the gophers to suffer; you just want them to die. Or go away.

Personnel in a garden-supply store would be a good source of information about getting rid of gophers. Libraries have periodicals with articles on everything from aardvarks to zebras. They could help as well. If your library skills are rusty, check back in Chapter 5 for specific suggestions for researching.

In addition, you can draw upon the knowledge of an authority to help you with your research. Do some basic research before turning to authorities, however. The authorities will be more helpful if you do not waste their time with questions answered in generally available articles.

Where do you look for these authorities? Finding such an authority may take a little thinking and exploration. One of your professors might be an authority on a subject you are researching. For example, a botany or horticulture instructor may be able to help with a gardening article. Institutional grounds keepers have a great deal of practical knowledge about gardening—and perhaps about combating gophers.

In researching an article about gophers, you could check with a veterinarian about the use of cats against a gopher invasion. All cats are not created equal. Some cats are master gopher getters. Others are master sleepers. A veterinarian could tell you if there is any way to determine the hunting prowess of a cat—other than trial and error. For example, are female cats better hunters than males? Are some breeds better hunters than other breeds?

An additional benefit of conducting an interview is that an authority will often suggest others who can give you yet more information. Don't be afraid to seek expert help in your research. Most people will be very sympathetic with you because they too were once students. If the authority is too busy to help, you have lost only the few minutes required for a phone call.

The point is, unless you are already an expert on the process you choose to describe, you will have to "go-fer" to ferret out additional information. You will want to do some of this ferreting before you write a thesis if you do not already know a good deal about your subject. Begin by listing questions about your area of interest. The answer to one of these questions often will make an excellent thesis.

164

DISCOVERING
IDEAS
THROUGH
QUESTIONS:
WRITING
ABOUT
PROCESSES

For Thought and Discussion

Form a peer group and select a subject from the following list:

Getting rid of fleas
How acid rain is caused
How to stop acid rain
How to decrease, through diet, the chances of getting cancer
How to avoid a particular kind of cancer
How the greenhouse effect is caused
How the ozone hole is caused
How to attack the ozone hole problem
How to help remedy the garbage crisis in this country
How to start a successful business
How to grow a healthy garden
An instructor-approved topic of your choice

1. Make a list of questions that will help you *limit* the topic, so you can adequately develop it in about 500 words.

2. Make a list of sources to research the topic. Each student in the peer group should research one source before the next class.

3. Share your information. Then cluster, brainstorm, or list questions to help find a thesis.

4. Make a list of information you need to develop your thesis.

 ## ORGANIZING AND PRESENTING YOUR IDEAS

An essay in which you explain how to perform a process has some natural organizational advantages. In many processes you must complete one step before going on to the next; for example, the first step in "How to Grow a Healthy Garden" is to determine what type of garden you want—an ornamental garden, a food-producing garden, or a combination of these.

Of course, you don't have to worry about the order of the steps in your initial prewriting. Simply brainstorm a list. Then arrange the list in an effective order. For instance, in growing a garden, you must:

1. Get rid of the weeds on the chosen plot.

2. Cultivate the soil.

3. Determine your soil type.

4. Decide what types of plants will grow best in your climate, soil conditions, and amount of sunlight.

5. Add proper nutrients.

6. Plant the garden.

7. Weed and water the garden.
8. Control insects and other pests such as gophers.

165

DISCOVERING
IDEAS
THROUGH
QUESTIONS:
WRITING
ABOUT
PROCESSES

When you are generating ideas for an essay, you will find the ideas do not arrive neatly packaged in the proper order. Don't worry. You can go back and rearrange them before you begin to write the essay.

In addition, processes often have categories of information to explain. For example, in an essay about how to rid your garden of gophers, you might brainstorm to discover categories of the various methods of control:

1. Hire a cat.
2. Adopt a gopher snake.
3. Paralyze gophers with poison.
4. Trap the varmints.
5. Scare gophers away.

Transition Time

Be sure to signal to your reader where you are in your description of a process. Transitional words like the following that signal sequence will be especially helpful: *to begin, starting with, initially, first, second, third, then, next, from this point, after that, finally.*

You should also consider using transitional words like the following to signal cause and effect: *as a result, because, consequently, for, since, so, therefore.*

Remember that sometimes a single transitional word or phrase is inadequate. Sometimes you need a sentence or more to ensure that your reader follows your thinking; for example, *This step is very important because . . . .*

Figurative Language Revisited

Figurative language is a powerful means for making concrete and thus better communicating complex, often abstract processes. In *Physics as Metaphor,* University of Minnesota physicist Roger James points out that "in metaphorical comparison, a new quality or connection is disclosed in the thing compared that was not previously apparent."

James says that using figurative language helps scientists understand and communicate such concepts as a "black hole" in space, a bottomless well from which nothing—not even light—can escape. For Kekule, the metaphor of the snakes biting their tails became a key to help him understand the chemical structure of the benzene molecule. Similarly, the "greenhouse effect" is figurative language that helps scientists and nonscientists alike understand the heating up of the earth's atmosphere; this warming

166

DISCOVERING
IDEAS
THROUGH
QUESTIONS:
WRITING
ABOUT
PROCESSES

occurs due to a buildup of gases that prevent the sun's heat from escaping—much as the glass of a greenhouse traps the sun's heat. When a writer or a scientist plays with an idea, such illuminating figurative language can spring from the creative thought process because we tend to think in such concrete images and comparisons.

The Analogy: Figurative Language Expanded

The more abstract and complex the process that needs to be communicated, the better served are the writer and the audience by the use of figurative language. When figurative language is extended for several sentences, it becomes an *analogy*. Like other figurative language, analogies illustrate similarities between things that—except for these similarities—are very different.

Physicist James Trefil uses *analogy* to help his readers understand a complex process in the following excerpt from "Quantum Physics' World: Now You See It, Now You Don't" from *Smithsonian*. In this article, Trefil answers these questions: *How does quantum physics work? How do physicists measure and describe electron activity?*

As you read, note how the use of analogy and other figurative language helps to make difficult and abstract concepts more understandable.

Quantum Physics

1   The first great difference between the familiar world and the quantum world—the world of the atom—is that we do not "see" things in the same way in the two worlds. This difference leads to results that defy our understanding, such as an electron going through a wall without leaving a hole behind it. The electron, in effect, disappears from one side of the wall and reappears on the other. Nothing in our everyday life prepares us for this.

2   You probably never thought about it, but when you look at something, you're detecting light that has come from some source, bounced off the object and then come to your eye. The reason we normally don't think about seeing in this way is that in our everyday world we can safely assume that bouncing light off a magazine doesn't change the magazine in any way that matters. The light from a lamp does not push the magazine away.

3   When we get to the quantum world, however, comfortable assumption no longer works. If you want to see that bundle of matter we call an electron, you have to bounce another bundle off it. In the process, the electron is bound to be changed.

4   A simple analogy can help with this point. Suppose you wanted to find out if there was a car in a long tunnel, and suppose that the only way you could do this was to send another car into the tunnel and listen for a crash. It's obvious that you could detect the original car in this way, but it's also obvious that after your detection experiment that car wouldn't be the same as it was before. In the quantum world this is the *only* sort of experiment you can do.

Therefore the first great rule of quantum mechanics is: *You cannot observe something without changing it in the process.* This is the basis of what is called the Uncertainty Principle: When you choose to observe one thing (e.g., the location of the car in the tunnel) you must forever be uncertain about something else (e.g., how fast the car was moving before the collision).

5   The inability to observe things in the subatomic world without at the same time disturbing them brings some surprising consequences when you start to think about the way that particles move from one point to another. Let's use another automotive analogy. Suppose I asked you to tell me where a particular car will be tomorrow. Ordinarily, you would look to see where the car is, look again to see which way it is going, and look again to see how fast. After a moment with your calculator, you would come back with a definite answer. If the car is like an electron, however, you can't look at it more than once—the first look changes everything. You cannot know with precision both where it is and how fast it is going; the best you can do is to play off the uncertainties. You might, for example, be able to say that the car is somewhere in the Chicago area and heading in a generally eastward direction at roughly 40 to 60 miles per hour. You can't be more precise than that without more measurements, and more measurements would only change the car's location or velocity and therefore increase your uncertainty.

For Thought and Discussion

1. List the examples of analogies and other figurative language in this excerpt.

2. Explain in your own words Trefil's point about the cars.

3. Use clustering or brainstorming to suggest how the following dissimilar things could be paired in an analogy:

   a. A beehive and a factory

   b. United Parcel Service (UPS) delivering a package and your body digesting food.

4. Suggest another example of using figurative language to help illuminate a process. Use either an original example or one you know about that is not mentioned thus far in this chapter.

AUDIENCE AWARENESS

As Whitman and Trefil illustrate, whenever we communicate, whether it be about quantum physics or about how to write an essay, we are most successful when we keep our audience's interests and knowledge in mind. We don't want to insult or bore our audience by overexplaining our point. On the other hand, when our message involves complex, specialized terms and ideas—as it certainly must when we write about science or any other specialized field—then we need to explain ourselves adequately. So tailoring

167

DISCOVERING
IDEAS
THROUGH
QUESTIONS:
WRITING
ABOUT
PROCESSES

168

DISCOVERING
IDEAS
THROUGH
QUESTIONS:
WRITING
ABOUT
PROCESSES

language and ideas to an audience is a balancing act between your creative brain's search for ideas and your critical brain's questioning about the impact of your words on your audience.

It is important that you assume your audience is reasonably intelligent and well-informed; it is difficult to communicate with someone you are insulting by being condescending. In addition, don't assume your audience is eager to read what you have to say. (Your audience rarely consists solely of people who know and love you.) When you write, consider the following:

- How much is your audience likely to know about your subject? What technical terms will you have to explain for them? If you are writing for an audience of astronomy buffs such as those who read *Astronomy,* you won't have to explain what you mean by the Doppler effect. For an audience with less knowledge of scientific terms, however, you will need to provide a short explanation.

- Does your audience have any specific beliefs? Most Western audiences, for example, believe in personal liberty and the value of the individual. Some audiences have more specialized beliefs and interests. For example, it is safe to assume the typical audience for *Sierra,* the Sierra Club magazine, has a set of interests and beliefs different from the audience of *Knitting Times.* Take into consideration your audience's beliefs and interests in developing your ideas.

- If your audience could respond to you, what might they ask you? What parts of your message might they find difficult to understand? Most writing in the nonacademic world is a team effort, so it is a good idea for you to try out your ideas on your peer editing group or acquaintances who are typical of your intended audience. Listen carefully to their reactions. After all, the burden of communication is primarily on the writer. While you understand your ideas perfectly, your audience may need additional clarification or explanation.

- Does your audience require a formal tone such as that used in many technical and scientific journals? Or should you use an informal tone? Do you need to gallop in verbally to capture the attention of an audience that might not otherwise be interested in your subject?

Tone, you learned in Chapter 4, is an author's attitude toward a subject as reflected in the word choice, subject, and comparisons. An author could be businesslike, using a scholarly, formal tone as Robin S. Keir does in the following introduction to "On the Late Pleistocene Ocean Geochemistry and Circulation" from *Paleoceanography.*

> During the Pleistocene Epoch, climate on the Earth's surface has been characterized by a rhythmic expansion and contraction of the polar ice sheets, with the extrema often referred to as "glacial" or "interglacial." The climate oscillation appears to be a nonlinear response to a variation of the orbital configuration of the Earth about the Sun. Analysis of the CO_2 concentration

169

DISCOVERING
IDEAS
THROUGH
QUESTIONS:
WRITING
ABOUT
PROCESSES

of air trapped in polar ice has indicated that the atmospheric CO_2 partial pressure was about 30% less during the last glacial than the preindustrial present.

On the other hand, an author may choose a chatty, informal tone as Harold Steinberg does in the following introduction to "Astronomy 101: Alone against the Universe" from *Astronomy:*

> I was too lazy to take chemistry, too uninterested to take biology, too intimidated to take physics, and too proud to take geography. So, to fulfill the science requirement during my sophomore year at Columbia University, I ended up taking astronomy.
> Professor Elmegreen began the first class with the Doppler effect, but my attention was torn between his lecture and the dark-eyed girl next to me. I was amazed by what I was learning.

Your subject may help you decide upon your tone. If you are writing about child abuse or euthanasia, for example, your tone will usually be formal and serious. In selecting his formal tone in the article from *Paleoceanography,* "On the Late Pleistocene Ocean Geochemistry and Circulation," Keir was influenced by his audience (scientists who read that journal), by the technical-scientific bias of his audience, and by his purpose (to inform). On the other hand, in the article from *Astronomy,* "Astronomy 101: Alone against the Universe," Steinberg was influenced by a different audience (largely nonscientists who read the magazine), by a broader purpose (to inform, interest, and entertain), and by the less technical inclination of his audience. If your purpose is solely to inform, your tone will be more formal. If you seek to interest and entertain as well as to inform, your tone will be less formal.

Note the interplay of your critical and creative brains as you determine your tone, consider your purpose, and analyze the needs of your audience. While your creative brain generates ideas, your critic serves as a monitor to warn you if your ideas are going astray. However, if your critical brain is especially active, you may need to ignore it as you generate ideas. Later you can bring it on stage to help you make sure that your purpose and tone are in harmony. (See page 89 in Chapter 4 to review *purpose.*)

For Thought and Discussion

1. List the words and phrases in the *Paleoceanography* article that make its tone formal. Next list the words and phrases in the *Astronomy* article that make its tone informal.

2. How does the intended audience's purpose for reading an article affect the author's choice of tone? In answering this question, think about why scientists read scientific journals as opposed to why people read scientific magazines aimed at a general audience.

170

DISCOVERING
IDEAS
THROUGH
QUESTIONS:
WRITING
ABOUT
PROCESSES

3. To further help you understand *audience,* make a list of at least ten items of common knowledge or beliefs shared by your classmates. (Examples of such knowledge and beliefs appear in the first two items of the list under "Audience Awareness.")

4. Reread the Walt Whitman poem at the beginning of this chapter. Judging from Whitman's reaction to the lecture, what tone did the "learn'd astronomer" use?

HOW TO CAPTURE YOUR READERS' ATTENTION

Process essays explain how to do something or how some process works. Many otherwise curious, intelligent people avoid reading directions or discussions of how something works because they find the writing boring or confusing. Process essays are particularly vulnerable to being dull.

To keep your readers' attention be sure to do the following:

• Motivate your readers by explaining the importance not only of your topic but of the various steps in the process you describe.

• Put yourself in your readers' shoes. Try to anticipate their questions. Clear up any misunderstandings they might have. Define any technical terms in understandable language.

• Use vivid, concrete details to *show* your readers instead of merely telling them about your topic. Good writing—even that for formal scientific journals—is vivid and concrete.

Introductory Techniques

Hook your readers' attention at the beginning of your essay. How you write this introductory hook depends upon your audience and purpose. Your audience might require a statement of your thesis, or you might begin with an introduction intended to give necessary background or pique your readers' curiosity. The following examples of techniques used by scientists to begin essays are applicable to nonscientific writing as well.

1. Begin with a statement of your thesis. Note how Ian Woodward does this in his introduction to "Plants in the Greenhouse World" from *New Scientist:*

> A world in the grip of the greenhouse effect will be a very different place from the one we know today. By the middle of the next century the climate will be much warmer, perhaps as much as 12°C warmer near the poles. Patterns of rainfall will change: some places will be wetter, others drier. The amount of carbon dioxide—one of the gases responsible for the greenhouse

effect—will continue to build up in the atmosphere. All these factors affect the way a plant draws up water through its roots. These factors therefore determine which types of plants grow in particular places. One of the most striking features of the greenhouse world will be the new look of the belts of vegetation that girdle the globe.

2. Ask a question. Questions involve readers by eliciting a response as John Polly does in the introduction to "Warning: What You Don't Know About Cholesterol Could Hurt You" from *San Francisco Focus:*

> Quick, what are your cholesterol levels? If you know the numbers, you're exceptional—the one person out of every six in the United States who does, according to a Gallup survey earlier this year. And if you know why the above question says "levels," plural, you're definitely one of the elite.

3. Use narrative techniques. People's curiosity is piqued by stories. Note how David Soren uses some of the narrative techniques of Chapter 2 in the following introduction to "The Day the World Ended at Kourion" from *National Geographic:*

> They were in their bedroom. The mother, a young woman of nineteen, still clutched her one-and-a-half-year-old baby to her breast. The child, its teeth still coming in, grasped its mother's elbow. Over them lay a man of about twenty-eight, presumably the father, who had tried to shield the pair from a deadly rain of limestone building blocks weighing as much as three hundred pounds.

4. Use concrete description to draw your reader into your essay. Show your readers your point by appealing to several of their five senses. Use imagery as K. C. Cole does in the following introduction to "A Theory of Everything," an article about quantum physics from the *New York Times Magazine:*

> Despite his thick glasses, rumpled jacket, a tie that barely reaches past his sternum and the obligatory chalk-covered pants of a professor, he cuts a handsome figure. Striding across the room in long, sure steps, he conducts his lecture like a maestro, the rat-a-tat-tat of the chalk on the board providing a counterpoint to his high, breathy, sometimes inaudible voice.

5. Use facts. Bill Vernon uses engaging factual detail in the introduction to "Probing Earth's History" from *Earth Science:*

> Drillers stopped working early one Saturday in August 1859. After months of setbacks while searching for black gold buried along the banks of Oil Creek in Titusville, Pennsylvania, the prospector had gotten used to disappointment. The drill bit had fallen into a crevice, nearly 21 meters from the surface. After pulling equipment out of the hole, the weary workers went home. No one knew they had struck oil.

6. Contrast your idea with a commonly held view. Kirk R. Smith does this effectively in the introduction to "Air Pollution" from *Environment:*

172

DISCOVERING
IDEAS
THROUGH
QUESTIONS:
WRITING
ABOUT
PROCESSES

Concern about air pollution has traditionally focused on the immediately obvious effects of local outdoor environments. We have become accustomed to thinking of air pollution in the context of such visual symbols as the industrial smokestack and the dark air layer smothering modern cities. In recent years, however, a focus on ambient (outdoor) air pollution and on the largest outdoor emission sources has diverted our attention from our principal goal of reducing the exposure of people to the health-damaging pollutants in air they actually breathe. These exposures can be caused by relatively tiny localized sources that literally are often right under our noses: cigarettes, spray cans, and dry-cleaned clothes, for example.

7. Use a quotation as a springboard for your ideas. Jon Luoma uses a quotation in the following introduction to "SO_2, UV, Vitamin D, and Calcium: The Acid Rain–Cancer Connection" from *Audubon:*

> The news item seemed, at first glance, to have come straight from a supermarket tabloid. "Two researchers have found that high cancer rates reported in Canada, Europe, and the northeastern United States are linked to acid rain," said a story on the United Press International wire.

8. Begin with a puzzling statement that you explain in your essay. Edwin Kiester does so in this introduction to "Doctors Close in on the Mechanisms Behind Headache" from *Smithsonian:* "It was a headache to make history."

9. Begin with an analogy. Wallace Broecker does this in his introduction to "Unpleasant Surprises in the Greenhouse?" from *Nature:*

> The inhabitants of planet Earth are quietly conducting a gigantic environmental experiment. So vast and so sweeping will be the consequences that, were it brought before any responsible council for approval, it would be firmly rejected. Yet it goes on with little interference from any jurisdiction or nation. The experiment in question is the release of CO_2 and other so-called "greenhouse" gases to the atmosphere. Because these releases are largely by-products of energy and food production, we have little choice but to let the experiment continue. We can perhaps slow its pace by eliminating frivolous production and by making more efficient use of energy from fossil fuels. But beyond this we can only prepare ourselves to cope with its effects.

The Model Writer

These techniques are not the only methods for capturing your readers' interest, of course. Instead the techniques are samples of a plethora of introductory methods. Do remember to think about your readers; attempt to interest them as you revise your essays. In your own reading, notice what effective introductory techniques successful authors use. Playing with ideas through brainstorming, clustering, and freewriting can help you create effective beginnings. So too can imitating writing techniques you have found effective. Imitating writing techniques, of course, is very different from using another writer's specific words or ideas; when you borrow specific words or ideas, you must credit the original source. (See the discussion of plagiarism in Chapter 5.)

173

DISCOVERING
IDEAS
THROUGH
QUESTIONS:
WRITING
ABOUT
PROCESSES

You will be asked to use one of the introductory techniques listed above in the writing assignment at the end of this chapter. When you are ready to write your introduction, reread the techniques to prime your creative thought processes. Your ability to imitate effectively is controlled by your creative rather than your critical thought process; however, the critical thought process can help analyze effective techniques, and, of course, it edits to make sure you are on the right track.

 ## FOLLOWING THE PROCESS OF WRITING A PROCESS ESSAY

To better understand how to write an essay that explains a process, let's follow the steps used by Samantha Jackson, a first-year composition student, in writing one such essay. The process essay was to be approximately 500 words long. Samantha kept a journal tracing the steps of the writing process.

Samantha's Writing Journal

Step One

We have one week to write an essay that explains a process to our classmates. My first task is to figure out what I know enough about to explain. My critical brain's immediate response to this task is, "You know nothing worth writing about." This is typically negative of my critic, and I decided to slip past its negativism by brainstorming a few minutes to generate ideas.

Brainstorming List

1. How to stop the acid rain problem
2. How to deal with an alcoholic relative
3. How to help an abused child
4. How to slow down the greenhouse effect
5. How to decrease the chances of getting cancer
6. How to help remedy the garbage crisis in this country
7. How to start a successful business
8. How to grow a healthy garden
9. How to help homeless people
10. How to build better bones: preventing osteoporosis

Step Two

Osteoporosis. My aunt is being increasingly crippled by osteoporosis. This is a topic I'd like to explore. I keep reading about it, and I certainly see evidence of it almost every day in my aunt and in others.

Once I decided to investigate osteoporosis, I then further explored my

174

DISCOVERING
IDEAS
THROUGH
QUESTIONS:
WRITING
ABOUT
PROCESSES

knowledge of and questions about this disease through clustering. [See Figure 6-1.]

Step Three

Like most topics, osteoporosis is very broad. Books have been written about it. So I was "listening" to my right brain as I clustered. When I got to the "Prevention" bubble, a light turned on in my brain. This was obviously the direction I wanted to take. I plugged my interest in osteoporosis prevention into the question model: How does osteoporosis occur? What steps must one take to avoid osteoporosis?

I decided to target as my audience average people who are willing to take responsibility to help themselves live long, healthy lives. My subject will be limited to measures my audience can take to help avoid osteoporosis.

After looking at my clustering, it is obvious I already knew quite a bit about osteoporosis. Every female over age nine should. And of course males have mothers, sisters, wives, and friends who are at risk for osteoporosis; also men who smoke have more trouble with osteoporosis. In addition those men who plan to live a long time need to protect their own bones because everyone's bones decalcify.

Step Four

While I knew quite a bit about my subject, I did not know enough to fill in exact details for an essay, so my next steps were to the library to look up "Osteoporosis" in *Reader's Guide to Periodical Literature.*

I found two general articles and photocopied them. Then I skimmed them with a highlighter in hand to mark sections that fit my focus. Since the articles were relatively short and this was not a research paper, I did not need a more elaborate note-taking system.

Since my paper was to be about 500 words long, I would obviously need to

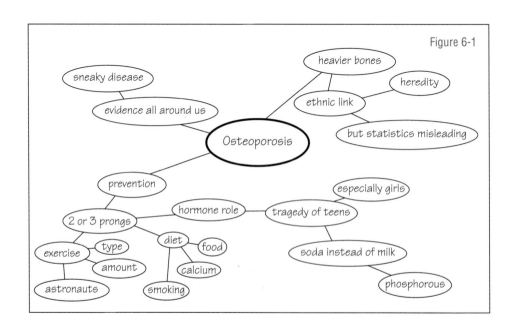

Figure 6-1

limit my subject. Since I had decided to target the average person, I would omit specialized problems involved with such issues as hereditary bone structure and hormone replacement therapy. I would not go into detail about why substances like alcohol and tobacco can cause bones to decalcify. As I began to write, I also decided to eliminate a thorough discussion of which calcium supplements are best. That subject alone could gobble up several hundred words.

Step Five

After skimming two general articles, I brainstormed and freewrote to create the following list:

Introduction
  Definition
  Motivation of audience

Two-pronged approach: diet & exercise
  Diet
    Food and supplements: Give lists?
    Ask about in Dr. Raisz interview:
      1. Are soft drinks harmful themselves or because they are substitutes?
      2. Is caffeine bad? If so, why?
      3. Are calcium supplements less effective than food?
  Exercise
    1. How much daily?
    2. Can exercise time be averaged weekly?
    3. What kinds of exercise?
    4. Why exercise?

Of course, most metropolitan communities have people who know about osteoporosis. We have a local osteoporosis clinic I could have called for additional information. Our college health clinic was another possible information source. I know someone who is an expert on osteoporosis, so I phoned him (Dr. Lawrence Raisz). Most family physicians have pamphlets on important health topics. Some physicians are happy to talk with students; after all, they were once students themselves.

Step Six

When I brainstormed, I jotted down issues that weren't clear to me as I read the articles, so I would remember what to ask Dr. Raisz. I needed to do enough research before interviewing my authority to have a general understanding of the subject. With enough background information, I wouldn't waste his time. And I jotted down questions ahead to make the most efficient use of this interview opportunity.

If I hadn't found an authority to interview, I would still need this list of unclear issues, so I could research them in the library.

Step Seven

Because my thesis was so clearly focused after my initial brainstorming, it was easy to make a rough, informal outline. I was lucky because sometimes subjects do not organize themselves quite so effectively and efficiently in the

176

DISCOVERING
IDEAS
THROUGH
QUESTIONS:
WRITING
ABOUT
PROCESSES

first prewriting exercise. In such cases, I help my brain to focus and organize by clustering and/or brainstorming after I finish my research.

I have discovered that my brain works most effectively with a simple outline that I generate from my prewriting. I use this simple outline as a guide when I write. My final brainstorming above was a huge help in making an informal outline.

My Informal Outline

Introduction
    Specific victim: describe
    Statistics
        500,000 women break bones per year!
        195,000 break hips
         30,000 related deaths
Emphasize 2-pronged defense against osteoporosis
    1. Diet
      List (blue highlighter)
      List do not's (green highlighter)
    2. Exercise
      30 minutes per day
        weight-bearing
        e.g. astronauts
Conclusion
    All measures for good health in general

Step Eight

I wrote my first draft the day after the interview. At first I was nervous getting started, but once I began to freewrite about the first topic on my rough outline, the words began to flow. I allowed the words to flow onto my computer screen without any action from my critical brain.

Step Nine

I put my first draft away for two days. This break helped me gain objectivity. When I came back to my essay draft, it was far easier to do the necessary revisions than it would have been immediately after I wrote the draft. Previously it was very hard for me to cut material from an essay, but this time, I discovered that my two-day break helped me recognize and get rid of irrelevant chunks of information about osteoporosis. The break also helped me identify sections that needed clearer transitions. In addition, it was easier to spot mechanical errors.

Step Ten

Once my essay was revised I read it aloud to my peer editing group. This helped me discover a couple of places in which my wording was awkward and unclear. My group's questions and comments helped me a great deal in my revision and proofreading process. Because spelling is a problem for me, I asked my group to read especially carefully for misspelled words. My computer spell-checker skips over misspellings that are actually other words (for example *their, there, they're*). I added words I had misspelled to a list I keep in my notebook where I jot down words my spell-checker calls up.

177

DISCOVERING
IDEAS
THROUGH
QUESTIONS:
WRITING
ABOUT
PROCESSES

A Quick Review

1. I brainstormed to select a subject.
2. I clustered to explore my knowledge of and questions about osteoporosis.
3. I clustered and questioned to limit and focus my subject. When I don't know a good deal about a subject before I begin to work on it, I often modify my thesis further after my research. (See the next step.)
4. I researched to learn more about osteoporosis. The questions I devised in Step Three were a big help in deciding what I needed to learn through research. (When necessary, I modify my thesis after my research.)
5. I brainstormed a list of subtopics. (When I am still having trouble limiting my thesis, I cluster again at this point.)
6. I researched to answer questions that had popped into my mind during this brainstorming process.
7. I made an informal outline derived from my questions in Step Three.
8. I wrote a preliminary draft.
9. I revised my essay.
10. My peer group and I evaluated my essay for content, development, organization, and mechanical errors.

Building Better Bones: The Final Draft

1   When Fran Johnson fell, she was simply walking up a ramp into a restaurant. Even before she hit the ground, she heard a crunch and a blinding pain shot through her body. She had become a tragic statistic—one of the 500,000 American women who will break bones this year and one of the 195,000 who will fracture their hips. Of these women, 30,000 will die from complications caused by the broken hip, and many of the rest will live out their years crippled and in pain.

2   The villain in the vast majority of these fractures? Osteoporosis, a disease doctors once believed was a worry only for older women. But new research shows osteoporosis should be a concern for people of all ages, especially for young and middle-aged women and for men who smoke or who are heavy drinkers of alcohol. According to University of Connecticut Professor of Medicine and leading authority on osteoporosis Dr. Lawrence Raisz, people must begin to prevent the ravages of this disease decades before it cripples them. Although they will have no bad effects from osteoporosis until they near retirement age, the earlier people begin to fight this disease, the more likely they are to escape its scourge.

3   When people reach their early twenties their bones cease to grow, and in fact begin to shrink at about one percent per year—a loss that eventually causes nearly one quarter of all American women to break a bone by age sixty-five. In fact, everyone's bones decalcify with age, but since males usually start out with heavier bones, osteoporosis is less of a scourge for them. Thus—in addition to men who smoke or drink heavily—the only men who need to worry about osteoporosis are ones who plan to live to a healthy old age.

4   Just what is osteoporosis and what are the safe, simple practices that may

178

DISCOVERING
IDEAS
THROUGH
QUESTIONS:
WRITING
ABOUT
PROCESSES

prevent this scourge? Osteoporosis is a disease that causes the bones to shrink and become porous and fragile because the body needs more calcium than the victim is getting, or because the body can't use calcium efficiently. Used to control nerve impulses, muscle contractions, heart rhythms, and blood coagulation, calcium is stored in the bones and teeth, so it is to them the body goes when it needs more calcium.

5   The prevention methods recommended by experts like Dr. Raisz include a two-pronged diet and exercise program. Before menopause, women need about 1,000 milligrams of calcium daily—though the average American woman gets only about 450 milligrams. The calcium drain is exacerbated by pregnancy as the fetus absorbs about 400 milligrams of calcium per day while a nursing baby consumes about 300 milligrams. After menopause, the body uses calcium less efficiently, so women then need 1,500 milligrams each day.

6   Dairy products are an excellent source of calcium. For calorie-counters, broccoli is a good, low-calorie reservoir of usable calcium.

Calcium Rich Foods

	MILLIGRAMS OF CALCIUM	CALORIES
1 cup of low-fat milk	297	121
1 cup of low-fat yogurt		
plain	415	144
fruited	314	225
1 cup of low-fat cottage cheese	138	164
1 ounce of Swiss cheese	272	107
1 ounce of American cheese	174	106
1 cup of ice cream	176	296
3 ounces of salmon	285	188
1 cup of broccoli	136	40

7   What do the doctors recommend if you are unwilling to consume adequate amounts of calcium-rich foods—and the calories such foods contain? First, keep track of your eating habits to determine how much calcium you usually consume, and then take a calcium supplement to provide the rest—though doctors stress that the most usable form of calcium is that found in foods, not in supplemental pills.

8   But bones do not thrive by calcium alone. Exercise is a vital ingredient in an osteoporosis prevention program. "Use it or lose it" is the motto for protecting bones. Putting weight on a bone causes a little electrical impulse to shoot through the bone strengthening it. People with sedentary lives thus increase their risk of osteoporosis. For example, while in space, both male and female astronauts have a serious problem with calcium loss; without gravity, they cannot put weight on their bones. Hence researchers are striving to devise corrective exercises for astronauts. Back on earth, of course, we have gravity working for us in exercises like walking, running, dancing, playing tennis—or any other bone-jiggling exercise. To help prevent osteoporosis, we should do such exercises for thirty minutes a day.

9   Avoid smoking and heavy alcohol drinking (more than two drinks a day).

179

DISCOVERING
IDEAS
THROUGH
QUESTIONS:
WRITING
ABOUT
PROCESSES

Both smoking and heavy drinking are associated with poor calcium absorption in both men and women. Such people are at high risk for osteoporosis.

10   Avoid excess phosphorous such as that found in red meats and carbonated soft drinks. Consume these in small to moderate amounts.

11   Avoid excess salt as it causes calcium loss.

12   While osteoporosis is a serious problem, the good news is that the measures recommended to prevent it are sensible measures for health in general. With proper care now, you can build better bones—and avoid becoming an osteoporosis victim in later life.

For Thought and Discussion

1. With what introductory technique does the essay begin? Explain why this introductory technique is or is not effective for the targeted audience (average people who are willing to take responsibility to help themselves live long, healthy lives).

2. List the techniques the author used to generate, organize, and develop ideas for this essay.

3. What concrete evidence does the essay give to motivate the reader to follow its advice?

4. How does the essay give credibility to its ideas about osteoporosis prevention?

5. What information does the article include for its general audience that it would not have included for an audience of physicians?

6. Cite any figurative language contained in this essay.

7. List the transitions that help tie this essay together.

A PROFESSIONAL WRITER AT WORK

One of the best ways to learn to explain a process to a broad, nonexpert audience is to examine how such explanations are made by masters such as Carl Sagan. Sagan, who is director of the Laboratory for Planetary Studies at Cornell University, played a leading role in the *Mariner, Viking,* and *Voyager* expeditions to the planets. A scientist keenly aware of nonscientific audiences, Sagan has published more than 400 scientific and popular articles. In addition, he has written more than a dozen books. In 1978, Sagan was awarded the Pulitzer prize for literature. In the following excerpt from his book *Cosmos,* Sagan describes how a resourceful scientist measured the Earth's circumference aided only by an active mind and a pair of sticks.

Measuring the Earth

1   The discovery that the Earth is a *little* world was made in the ancient Near East, in a time some humans call the third century B.C., in the greatest metropolis of the age, the Egyptian city of Alexandria. Here lived a man

180

DISCOVERING
IDEAS
THROUGH
QUESTIONS:
WRITING
ABOUT
PROCESSES

named Eratosthenes. He was an astronomer, historian, geographer, philosopher, poet, theater critic and mathematician. The titles of the books he wrote range from *Astronomy* to *On Freedom from Pain*. He was also the director of the great library of Alexandria, where one day he read in a papyrus book that in the southern frontier outpost of Syene, near the first cataract of the Nile, at noon on June 21 vertical sticks cast no shadows. On the summer solstice, the longest day of the year, as the hours crept toward midday, the shadows of temple columns grew shorter. At noon, they were gone. A reflection of the Sun could then be seen in the water at the bottom of a deep well. The Sun was directly overhead. It was an observation that someone else might easily have ignored.

2   Eratosthenes was a scientist, and his musings on these commonplaces changed the world; in a way, they made the world. Eratosthenes had the presence of mind to do an experiment, actually to observe whether in Alexandria vertical sticks cast shadows near noon on June 21. And, he discovered, sticks do.

3   Eratosthenes asked himself how, at the same moment, a stick in Syene could cast no shadow and a stick in Alexandria, far to the north, could cast a pronounced shadow. Consider a map of ancient Egypt with two vertical sticks of equal length, one stuck in Alexandria, the other in Syene. Suppose that, at a certain moment, each stick casts no shadow at all. This is perfectly easy to understand—provided the Earth is flat. The Sun would then be directly overhead. If the two sticks cast shadows of equal length, that also would make sense on a flat Earth: the Sun's rays would then be inclined at the same angle to the two sticks. But how could it be that at the same instant there was no shadow at Syene and a substantial shadow at Alexandria?

4   The only possible answer, he saw, was that the surface of the Earth is curved. Not only that: the greater the curvature, the greater the difference in the shadow lengths. The Sun is so far away that its rays are parallel when they reach the Earth. Sticks placed at different angles to the Sun's rays cast shadows of different lengths. For the observed difference in the shadow lengths, the distance between Alexandria and Syene had to be about seven degrees along the surface of the Earth; that is, if you imagine the sticks extending down to the center of the Earth, they would there intersect at an angle of seven degrees. Seven degrees is something like one-fiftieth of three hundred and sixty degrees, the full circumference of the Earth. Eratosthenes knew that the distance between Alexandria and Syene was approximately 800 kilometers, because he hired a man to pace it out. Eight hundred kilometers times 50 is 40,000 kilometers: so that must be the circumference of the Earth.

5   This is the right answer. Eratosthenes' only tools were sticks, eyes, feet, and brains, plus a taste for experiment. With them he deduced the circumference of the Earth with an error of only a few percent, a remarkable achievement for 2,200 years ago. He was the first person accurately to measure the size of a planet.

For Thought and Discussion

1. In this essay how does Sagan attempt to interest his audience of nonscientists?

181

DISCOVERING
IDEAS
THROUGH
QUESTIONS:
WRITING
ABOUT
PROCESSES

2. What central point about science and scientific thinking does this story about Eratosthenes illustrate? How is this point related to writing?

3. What processes did Eratosthenes use to generate the idea for measuring the earth? Review the steps beginning on page 157 of this chapter before answering this question.

4. Trace the steps in Eratosthenes' process of measuring the Earth.

5. What transitions help you to follow Sagan's point?

 WRITING ASSIGNMENT

Write an essay of at least 500 words in which you explain a process to a general audience that is intelligent but not especially well informed about your subject.

While we have concentrated on scientific subjects, the techniques of this chapter are helpful for developing essays on a broad variety of nonscientific topics as well. Furthermore, these techniques are helpful regardless of whether the process you want to describe will provide a set of instructions for your readers to follow or will provide a description of how a process occurs.

Remember to do the following:

1. Interest your audience as you educate them. Begin with an introduction intended to hook your audience into reading.

2. Define technical terms.

3. Limit your subject so it is not too complex to explain in about 500 words.

4. Be well informed about your subject. Make sure your information is fresh and worthwhile for your readers.

5. Use analogy and other figurative language when it will help to clarify your point.

6. Review and follow the steps Samantha Jackson used in her journal for the osteoporosis paper (see page 177).

Suggestions for Topics

How to get rid of fleas safely
How acid rain is caused
How to stop acid rain
How to decrease, through diet, your chances of getting cancer
How the greenhouse effect is caused
How the ozone hole is caused
How to attack the ozone hole problem

182

DISCOVERING
IDEAS
THROUGH
QUESTIONS:
WRITING
ABOUT
PROCESSES

How to help remedy the garbage crisis in this country
How to start a successful business
How to grow a healthy garden
How to stop smoking
How to get "unhooked" from drugs, or alcohol, food, or gambling
How to survive a divorce
How to survive the death of a loved one
How to prevent heart disease
How to deal safely and effectively with a mugger
How to obedience-train a dog
How to improve your vocabulary, spelling, or writing
How to manage your money
How to survive life with a snorer
How to cope with stress
An instructor-approved topic of your choice

Peer Editing Checklist

After you have completed the prewriting and the first draft of your essay, meet with a peer editing group so that you can assess the reaction of an audience to your writing. Make enough copies of your essay for each member of your peer editing group.

As you discuss your writing in your peer group, remember the comment of chemist and physicist Sir Humphrey Davy: "The most important of my discoveries have been suggested to me by my failures." Begin by discussing how Davy's comment could apply to your writing. Next have a peer group member read a paper aloud as the rest of the group follows with a photocopied version.

1. Point out the positive qualities of the paper such as effective words, phrases, figurative language, allusions, alliteration, the essay title, or the subject of the essay. Positive reinforcement is a powerful tool.

2. Tell the writer what you think the thesis is. (If you are not sure what the thesis is, indicate this.)

3. What is your reaction to the essay's introduction? Does the introduction help you better understand the author's point or pique your interest in reading the essay?

4. List the technical terms the paper uses. Circle any terms that need further explanation.

5. List information that would be obvious to the intended audience before they read the paper.

6. Which steps or explanations need further clarification? Suggest places where figurative language would help clarify the point.

7. Point out any details or passages that do not seem relevant to the author's point. The author can then decide whether a transition could clarify the connection with the thesis or if the point is truly irrelevant.

8. What is your reaction to the essay's title? Does the title help you better understand the author's point, or does the title pique your interest in reading the essay?

183

DISCOVERING
IDEAS
THROUGH
QUESTIONS:
WRITING
ABOUT
PROCESSES

When writers have revised the content of their essay to their satisfaction and are ready for feedback about mechanics, point out but do not correct any problems you suspect with spelling, grammar, and punctuation. It is the writer's responsibility to make such corrections.

Help! For Further Work

The following essay is an early draft. Read it and then evaluate it using the peer editing checklist as your guide.

Fleeing Fleas

1   Boy did I have an embarrassing problem! One I really don't especially feel really comfortable talking or writing about publicly. I have fleas. Not just me personally. My pets actually harbor them. But they take me out for lunch too. And breakfast and dinner.

2   Sick of itchy, red bumps all over my body—especially around my ankles and lower legs, but elsewhere also, I decided to do something about my problem. I decided to deflea me, my pets, and my apartment.

3   Of course I didn't want to die twenty years later or even five or ten years later for that matter because the pesticide I used was carcinogenic. So I found a really safe pesticide. Did you know there are currently chemicals on the market that don't harm humans, but prevent a juvenile flea from molting. So unless you are planning to molt, these are great, safe ideas to help you rid yourself and your environment of fleas.

4   However, such chemicals are not enough. You have to attack adult fleas as well. You can't believe how prolific an adult flea is. "X" rated movies have nothing on the sex life of adult fleas. And they don't use birth control ever. So you have to help them by vacuuming your carpets often and by spraying frequently. Also shampooing your pets is a good idea too. In fact, cleanliness is always a good idea even when fleas aren't a problem. So clean up your own act as well as your environment.

5   Which reminds me, my vet told me about a wonderful new product that comes in a small plastic tube. You squeeze it on your dog's back and any flea that bites it for the next two weeks: BINGO—its bye bye world. However, a friend of mine told me this product may decrease the length of your dog's life of course I would rather live a shorter time and not have raw, itchy skin. And you can't use this product on cats. Cats are actually very sensitive animals. My vet says they are tricky to anesthetize as well. You have to get this flea product from a vet. He or she will prescribe it if your dog is healthy enough. Also the dose varies according to your dog's weight.

6   There are other ways to fight fleas of course. I have a friend who hand-picks fleas off her dog every night. However the dog still gets flea rashes, so that doesn't work perfectly. I mean, the dog goes outside and ZAP another flea zooms in on it. And the flea may be pregnant, and three days later the place is crawling with flea embryos.

7   Which reminds me of another important tactic in the Flea War. Spray your carpet with one of those wonderful 120 day carpet sprays. They contain a chemical to keep juvenile fleas from molting and they also contain a chemical that will zap adult fleas for up to ten days. Unfortunately this chemical breaks down in sunlight.

8   If you have a really serious flea problem, you might have to spray your yard if you have a yard. Otherwise your animals will pick up fleas there. And don't forget your car. No one wants to do battle with a flea while battling traffic. That's more dangerous than fleas. And fleas, by the way, can be dangerous. Did you know that fleas cause bubonic plague? Rat fleas carrying the plague virus bite people and they died after suffering a good deal first. In fact, medical science still isn't very effective against this disease. Ground squirrels in my home area have been found with these fleas.

9   So ridding yourself your pets and your home environment of fleas is more than just a comfort measure. It may save your life—or the lives of your loved ones.

STUDENT STARS

While the examples thus far in this chapter have centered around science, the methods discussed in this chapter apply to many other subjects. Therefore, the student star essays are on a variety of topics.

Note how the authors of the following essays use the process technique described in this chapter to develop their points. Also note the introductory techniques they use to interest their audience.

The students who wrote these essays did the following:

1. Prewriting

2. Writing

3. Revision of content

4. Proofreading and revision of mechanics.

How to Complain

1   I have spent countless hours sitting in waiting rooms in garages after being told that my car would be ready "soon." I have suffered through appliances that broke right after the warranty expired. I have wandered around stores that seemed devoid of human help. I have sat silently behind a couple in a movie who thought their own chatter was more interesting than that of Meryl Streep or Robert Redford. What I did not do in these cases was *complain*.

2   In the past I let these annoyances slide. I let off steam by slamming doors,

185

**DISCOVERING
IDEAS
THROUGH
QUESTIONS:
WRITING
ABOUT
PROCESSES**

kicking dogs, or yelling at my kid. Or I held in my frustration until I exploded in useless anger at some hapless bystander. Maybe I thought my complaining would be to no avail. Maybe I was shy. What I was *not* was properly assertive. Until recently I had difficulty standing up for my rights, even when I was sure I was right.

3   But I have learned. I know now that the only way to get what I want is to be properly assertive. Done properly, it really helps to complain. As a result of a class I took two years ago, some reading I have done, and lots of personal experience, I have compiled some basic rules to follow when complaining. The next time you are the victim of an injustice, try my personally-tested rules for the redress of your grievances.

4   The first rule is *keep your cool.* Don't start yelling at the person assigned to deal with your complaining; chances are she is not responsible for the problem, so don't vent your anger on her. You might even be able to enlist her help to solve your problem.

5   Once you have someone's attention, *make your point quickly.* If you ramble on with a long explanation about what was wrong, you will see your audience's eyes—or at least your audience's attention—glaze over. For example, if you brought your car in because the new brake pads screech, say so. You don't have to explain you were showing your ex-mother-in-law the town and wanted to impress her with a car that kept screaming like a banshee every time you touched the brake.

6   Next, try to *gain the upper hand.* Don't let yourself be at the mercy of the offender. For example, I once took my car in three times for service. The brakes still screamed at me every time I slowed down. I began by telling the service manager that I had brought my cars in before and hoped I could continue to do so. I then recounted my instructions on my first two visits for the screaming brakes. I declared that I had been put off enough and expected the repair to be done correctly this time. I made *eye contact* with him and appeared strong. My knees knocked and my stomach flip-flopped, but—locked in my iron eye-contact—the service manager saw only my strength.

7   Sometimes a local representative mumbles that there is nothing his outlet can do. Then *take your complaint to headquarters.* Do not give up until you reach satisfaction—or the boss. A few years ago, IBM Chairman Thomas Watson called a meeting about a top priority problem. An employee with an unresolved complaint had written about it to Watson's mother. Remember this the next time you are told, "We can do nothing about your complaint." Ask for the name, phone number and address of the appropriate executive (or mother!). I recently got a letter—with coupons worth over a hundred dollars—when I complained to the president of Hertz about my treatment at this We Didn't Try Harder agency. I didn't threaten. I didn't get hysterical. I simply explained with exact times, dates, locations, names, and receipts what my problem had been. The whole complaint took me twenty-five minutes. Not bad for a hundred dollars.

8   When voice-contact and eye-contact fail, it is time for ink-contact. As you climb the ladder of complaint, you will eventually find you must put your complaint in writing—as I did with Hertz. Keep your letter concise, but include all necessary information. Enclose copies of receipts and warranty. Be

186

DISCOVERING
IDEAS
THROUGH
QUESTIONS:
WRITING
ABOUT
PROCESSES

specific—and be realistic about the remedy you seek. You won't get a new Rolls Royce, but you should get new brake pads that don't scream at you. Keep a copy of all correspondence. If you need proof of receipt, send a registered letter.

9   Finally, know when to give up—or sue. Life would be even more stressful than it is if we insisted on exhausting every possible avenue for redressing every grievance. When the above steps have failed (and they rarely do) ask yourself if it is worthwhile to pursue your complaint through a ponderous governmental regulatory agency or through the courts. If your answer is "yes," good luck. If not, save your time and energy for the next battle on the consumer front. The next battle will indeed come. And this time you will probably be successful. And remember, even when you appear to have lost, you have won at least part of the battle when you make your complaint known. Also remember: with my method of complaining, so far I have never lost.

—Emlee Gilman

Waste Not, Want Not

1   When old Mr. Michaels hired young Joey to clean out his garage, he simply told Joey to throw everything in the dumpster. When Joey came across a shelf of old dusty brown bottles half filled with some mysterious liquid, he didn't think of the consequences as he threw them in with all the other junk. What Joey didn't know was that those bottles contained toxic chemicals, chemicals such as pesticides and herbicides.

2   Improper disposal of residential toxic waste is a problem that affects us all, both directly and indirectly. Let's look at the process of improper residential toxic waste disposal and then at the proper procedure for its safe disposal.

3   First, we need to better acquaint ourselves with the subject of toxic waste disposal. The Environmental Protection Agency defines residential toxic waste as "any substance bought for private use with a volatile or toxic nature." This includes many common household chemicals such as paint thinner, weed killer, and metal and asphalt cleaners.

4   When Joey threw the bottles of toxic waste into the dumpster, he unknowingly started a chain of events with many variables. The bottles could have broken in the dumpster and affected anything that got close to it. The bottles could have survived to the dump unaltered only to break there and spill onto a half-eaten Big Mac that a seagull or other scavenger might consume. The bottle could have survived unaltered to the burying stage only to be broken by an old box spring; once broken, the toxic contents could seep into the water table that is the supply for the water we all, man and beast, drink and bathe in. As you can see, there are many things that can go wrong when residential toxic waste is disposed of improperly.

5   The Environmental Protection Agency and the Monterey County Health Department's Office of Environmental Health stated in a recent report that 60 to 80 percent of all residential toxic waste is disposed of improperly. Most of this improper and illegal dumping is done by unknowing people like Joey. Who hasn't cleaned out a paint brush with paint thinner and then just dumped it on the ground? In addition, EPA states that from 10 to 20 percent of all improper residential toxic waste dumping is done intentionally. This out-of-sight, out-of-mind mentality must stop.

187

DISCOVERING
IDEAS
THROUGH
QUESTIONS:
WRITING
ABOUT
PROCESSES

6   With the staggering statistics facing them, the EPA and the Environmental Health Office along with local landfill companies have started a program to make it easier for citizens to dispose of their accumulated toxic waste safely. This program has specifications and locations for people to bring in their waste up to five gallons for disposal. What process does the local landfill company follow once they receive these wastes?

7   Marina Landfill is typical of those across the country that properly dispose of toxic waste. Marina Landfill accepts up to five gallons by appointment only. When they receive the waste, they go through a carefully regulated procedure for disposal. First the chemicals are sorted into groups of chemicals that won't react when mixed together. Then the chemicals are poured into metal containers filled with vermiculite, an inert substance that absorbs many times its weight. When their fifty-gallon metal containers are filled, Marina Landfill has a licensed toxic waste transportation company transport the containers to a Class A dumpsite. A Class A dumpsite is licensed and regulated by local, state, and federal agencies. At these dumpsites, the containers are safely buried.

8   Unregulated illegal dumping is chancy at best. We must stop the improper dumping of residential toxic waste. When dumped improperly, toxins enter the environment and affect us all. Think about that the next time you turn on your kitchen faucet or the next time you hire Joey to clean out your garage.

—Fritz Nolan

I'm Sorry

1   Johnny jumped up and down with excitement while he watched his mother prepare his bath. Tomorrow was Johnny's first day of school, but Johnny was not an ordinary seven-year-old; he was homeless. His mother did not run warm water into a tub but heated it over an open fire.

2   For the past half hour, his mother had carried buckets of water for his bath. The water was located at the gas station, down the alley, a half block away. She brought back a bucket of cold water and poured it into the big, black, round kettle that sat in the open fire. Then she went back for more. After several trips she had enough water. Once the water was warm enough, she had Johnny take off all his clothes. She poured some warm water into the bucket and had Johnny stick his head into the water. Johnny's mother took an empty shampoo bottle out of her bag; she had found the bottle in the trash the day before. She put a little water inside the bottle and shook the bottle around. She then poured the diluted shampoo over Johnny's head and lathered his hair. She took more warm water from the big, black kettle and rinsed Johnny's head. Then she washed his body down with an old rag and the sudsy shampoo water. Finally, she was done with the bath and Johnny dried himself off with paper towels from the gas station and put his clothes back on. Off to the old, broken-down shed he went. This was his home. He lay down on the shabby, torn mattress on the floor in one corner. Sleep was impossible; tomorrow he was off to school for the first time.

3   The next morning Johnny woke up early and shook his mother, who was sleeping next to him. He wanted to get up and get ready for school. Johnny dressed in his best clothes. His blue pants were old and faded, and they ended two inches above his ankles; his red shirt had a button missing in the middle

188

DISCOVERING
IDEAS
THROUGH
QUESTIONS:
WRITING
ABOUT
PROCESSES

of his chest. His old tennis shoes had two different colored shoe strings—one blue and one orange and black striped. Johnny thought he looked great; he couldn't wait to leave for school.

4   The school was eight blocks from their home. As they got closer to the school, Johnny's mother noticed some of the other children. Dressed in their new clothes, they carried new book bags and shiny new lunch pails. Some of the other children noticed Johnny and snickered. Johnny didn't notice; he was going to school.

5   Once inside the building, Johnny and his mother headed for the main office. Behind the counter was a gray-haired lady with glasses resting half way down her nose. She looked up and said, "May I help you?"

6   Johnny's mother began to wonder if she had made the right decision, but she knew how important this was to Johnny so she said, "I'm here to put my son in school."

7   "Do you have the required papers?" the lady asked.

8   Johnny's mother had no idea what "required papers" she needed, so she asked, "What papers?"

9   The gray-haired lady explained that before children could enroll in school, they needed a birth certificate, a shot record, and a health report. The mother also needed to fill out a form with her home address, phone number, emergency contact, place of employment, name of doctor, and any health problems Johnny had. Johnny's mother realized she was unable to produce a birth certificate or shot record, that she had no money for a physical examination and the only information she could fill out on the form was her name and Johnny's. She tried to explain this to the lady behind the counter. The lady looked at Johnny's mother and said, "I'm sorry, but you need to have all the proper paper work before you can enroll your son in school. Next, please."

10   With the form crumpled in her hand, Johnny's mother took him by the hand and walked out of the building. She felt defeated, confused, and angry. All she wanted to do was enroll her son in school, to give him a chance for a better life. But nothing is that simple. That day, there were no answers; there was no help for her and Johnny.

—Joyce McGowan

7

DISCOVERING AND ORGANIZING IDEAS THROUGH DIVISION-CLASSIFICATION

CONCEPTS TO LEARN

Discovering and organizing ideas about subjects by asking these key questions:

What are the types, classes, or categories into which X can be divided?

How do the classes differ?

Concluding techniques

Part of the difficulty with generating and then organizing essay ideas is that many topics are so complex writers feel overwhelmed. However, the approaches we have examined thus far in this text are tools to help writers sort out the complexities of such topics. This chapter will use the broad topic of education to demonstrate yet another tool to help you negotiate the jungle of facts, ideas, and theories that many topics involve. We will demonstrate how to ask key questions that help you divide a topic into parts and explore why the parts fit into a particular class.

According to French writer-editor Raymond Queneau:

> Learning to learn is to know how to navigate in a forest of facts, ideas and theories, a proliferation of constantly changing items of knowledge. Learning to learn is to know what to ignore but at the same time not reject innovation and research.

Just as the learner must navigate through a forest of facts and ideas, so too the writer must explore a multitude of facts and ideas to discover and develop a point about a particular topic. Should you need to write about a complex topic such as education, you may feel overwhelmed by all the directions your essay could take. In such situations, the techniques developed thus far in this text are tools to help you. Using the approach of Chapter 2, you could narrate a story that makes a point about education.

189

190

DISCOVERING
AND
ORGANIZING
IDEAS
THROUGH
DIVISION-
CLASSIFI-
CATION

Using Chapter 3's approach, you might choose to illustrate your point about education by describing a good or a bad teacher in action. Using Chapter 5's research techniques, you might make a point about the effectiveness or ineffectiveness of a particular educational process. Or you might use a combination of these techniques to develop a thesis.

In this chapter you will investigate generating and organizing ideas by analyzing the categories into which a subject can be divided. We employ such a divide-and-conquer technique in a myriad of situations in life. A multipurpose drugstore, for example, is divided into sections, each of which contains a particular class of products. Instead of showing its wares in a hodgepodge, the store helps us retrieve products by organizing them for us into sections ranging from painkillers and laxatives to dog food and cosmetics.

We use this analytical method of classification automatically every day for both simple and complex subjects. When we buy dog biscuits, we see they come in three sizes: small for dogs under twenty pounds, medium for dogs under thirty-five pounds, and large for the canine heavyweights. We similarly put religions, universities, friends, relatives, politicians, career opportunities, and a plethora of other subjects into classes that we distinguish from members of other classes. When we are exploring a topic that might benefit from dividing it into classes, such division can help us better understand and evaluate both individual classes and the similarities and differences between the classes; thus we can help ourselves understand a topic and then organize and communicate our ideas to others.

Answering one or both of the following questions helps us to explore ideas, find a focus, and generate and organize support for that focus: *What are the types, classes, or categories into which X can be divided? How do the classes differ?* These questions will help us analyze a topic by helping us to divide that topic into its parts, to clarify why particular items belong in a particular category, or to analyze the interrelationship among the parts. For instance, a kindergarten-through-high-school education is commonly divided into three parts: elementary school, middle school, and high school. Using classification as a tool for generating ideas and organizing them, we could zero in on one of these parts and analyze what type of skills students should acquire at that level. Or we could classify the kinds of skills students should acquire during their entire kindergarten-through-high-school education (as does the author of this chapter's professional essay). Then we could explore ways of dividing this learning into classes based on age or on some other criteria.

DIVISION-CLASSIFICATION: A MAP THROUGH A FOREST OF FACTS

Many subjects can be classified in several different ways. For example, writers can be classified by the time in which they wrote: Toni Morrison writes in the twentieth century while Emily Dickinson wrote in the nineteenth century. Writers can also be classified by genre: Morrison is a novelist while Dickinson was a poet. The poet classification could be narrowed further to nineteenth- or twentieth-century African-American women poets or women poets of New England.

In our highly specialized era, every field of study is subdivided. People do not get graduate degrees in oceanography, for example; they get degrees in biological oceanography, chemical oceanography, geological oceanography, or physical oceanography.

191

DISCOVERING
AND
ORGANIZING
IDEAS
THROUGH
DIVISION-
CLASSIFI-
CATION

Why Use Classification?

How does this division of a topic into classes help you generate and organize ideas? You could select one division and explore what is unique to that class. You could compare classes. Or you could develop the thesis that the usual classification for your subject is variously misleading, helpful, inaccurate, or a key to understanding a larger principle. For example, is chronological age really an effective guide for dividing learning skills? Trying to divide learning by age can give you insight into the answer. Through dividing a topic into classes and determining which part of a topic belongs in which class, you might gain some insight into a topic.

For example, in examining the writing of oppressed groups early in our history, you might discover that Caucasian women and slaves of both sexes wrote autobiography. This classifying principle could lead you beyond classification to ask why such people wrote autobiography. The answer to that question could lead to yet further insights. The point is that dividing a topic into classes and determining what criteria each class is based on can help you focus and clarify your thinking so you can more easily explore and discover a thesis. While division-classification *can* be an end in itself, often it is *not* an end in itself but rather a valuable tool to help you gain insight into a topic.

Avoiding Pitfalls When Classifying

When placing something in a class, be sure to do the following:

1. Use logical criteria
2. Include all important subdivisions of your subject
3. Be sure the subdivisions are distinct from each other.

What are logical criteria? Criteria that are consistent are logical criteria. For example, college textbooks can be classified by subject, price, clarity, and interest level. However, if you decide to classify textbooks solely by subject matter, you cannot logically interject comments about the interest

192

DISCOVERING
AND
ORGANIZING
IDEAS
THROUGH
DIVISION-
CLASSIFI-
CATION

level or price of the textbooks. Nor can you mention an aspect such as price for some but not for others.

Furthermore, you cannot logically ignore a major category of your topic. If you classify textbooks by price, you cannot ignore a major price category; if 25 percent of all textbooks fall into a $35 to $55 category, you cannot ignore that category. Similarly, if you are classifying the threats to Earth's climate caused by humans, you cannot exclude a major category of such threats—for example, the greenhouse effect, acid rain, or ozone depletion. Certainly you could choose to write only about acid rain or the greenhouse effect or the deterioration of the ozone layer. But if you are going to classify the major threats, you must include all major threats or you must logically explain why you have left out a major subdivision of your class.

In addition, when you generate and organize ideas using the principle of classification, you must make it clear how the subclasses are distinct from each other. How, for example, does the threat caused by the hole in our ozone layer differ from the threat caused by the greenhouse effect? Certainly some greenhouse gases also affect the ozone layer, but the threats to our planet resulting from these phenomena are different—as are the causes.

Division-Classification in Action

When we divide and classify a topic, we are making use of both our critical and our creative brain. Some of us work best when we give our creative selves rather free rein. Others work most effectively in a somewhat more structured frame. When we explore an organizational pattern such as division-classification, we can loop back and forth between that part of us that likes to look at smaller components of a topic (our critical brain) and that part of us that likes to look at an entire picture without paying special attention to its parts (our creative brain).

To see this interplay of the creative and critical brains in action, let's examine the process by which Bob Higashi used classification to help him explore the decision about where to go to college. Notice that Bob looped back and forth between his critical and his creative brain as he explored his topic. Since Bob's purpose was to generate ideas, he was not a slave to a strict brainstorming format. He freewrote notes to himself as ideas occurred to him.

Bob's first step was to ask himself the key questions: What are the types, classes, or categories into which X can be divided? How do the classes differ? He then answered the questions as shown.

Bob's Brainstorming

Into what classes or categories can I divide the criteria to help me decide where I want to go to college when I finish my work at Monterey Peninsula College [a community college]?

Cost: Living Expenses
    Some areas cost more than other areas.
        Can I get any specific data on this?
        Check in the library.
        Check financial aid office at MPC.
    (I'd better limit this to certain campuses.)
Cost: Tuition
    How much does this vary between the University of California, California State University, and the small, liberal arts college I'd like to attend?
Cost: Transportation
Cost: Miscellaneous

Educational Opportunities

This is a tough category because I'm not sure what I want to major in just yet. I'm thinking about psychology—maybe industrial relations. But I'm not sure. Anyway, I'll probably have to go to graduate school, so as long as I get a good general education, I don't have to be superconcerned about this category. I'm trying to decide between several campuses of Cal State (California State University) and UC (University of California) and Colby where my dad went to college. These schools all have good reputations as far as their undergraduate degrees go.

Location

Since this is related to cost, should it go under "cost"? Maybe not as I have other criteria than just travel expenses in mind. In fact, it suddenly occurred to me that I can subdivide the whole issue of location into categories, for example:

How near home should I be? Will I get homesick if I go to the East Coast? I'm a California coastal kid, after all. On the other hand, it would broaden my perspective if I went to a different section of the country—or even of the state.

Can I learn by the experience of living in a different area? Everyone is always saying that much of what you learn in college occurs outside the classroom. The campus environment itself could be a learning experience for me. It seems to me that selecting an environment quite different from the one in which I have lived all my life would be a learning experience. If this is a really important criteria, then I should head to the East where I won't be surrounded by California people.

If I went to an inland school such as Sac State [California State University at Sacramento] or UC Davis I would experience a different weather climate and even a different social climate from the one I grew up with in Monterey.

Do I want a sophisticated big-city adventure? If so, I should go to a CSU or a UC campus in San Francisco or Los Angeles. If I do want a big city, Colby would be out because Waterville, Maine, is a small town type of environment.

194

DISCOVERING
AND
ORGANIZING
IDEAS
THROUGH
DIVISION-
CLASSIFI-
CATION

Am I a country boy at heart? Maybe I want a small town environment. If so, my list of choices would include campuses like CSU Humboldt, Sonoma, or Chico. Santa Cruz is a medium size town so UCSC would be on my list. Davis, of course, is a small town, so UC Davis would be a possibility.

What about my love-affair with the salty blue? I'm very sensitive to the environment. I love to surf. And I can't remember a single day of my entire life when I haven't seen the ocean. I'd really miss the ocean. Maybe I should look for a campus on the coast—for example San Francisco State, Cal State Long Beach—I just got an idea. I'd better stop by the counseling office for a map of UC and Cal State campuses.

On the other hand, I should experience a different environment. This section probably belongs with my discussion of whether or not I should choose an area different from home.

At this point in my brainstorming-freewriting session, my critic brain has zoomed into action. It's telling me that I might have enough material for a five-hundred-word essay by simply classifying the issues involved with location. I certainly need to limit my topic. Classifying the issues involved with the location of a college would help do that without illogically eliminating categories.

On the other hand, something (probably my critic brain) is telling me that location is a pretty superficial reason for selecting a college. But location is certainly a major factor I need to consider. Even if I don't ultimately choose to write on this, I'll learn something of importance to me by exploring just what I want in terms of location. Certainly location is a factor that I will weigh along with some of the other factors I've listed like cost, educational opportunities/academic program, and social climate.

I just asked my computer for a word count. So far, in just a few minutes I've written 557 words. I'll play with limiting my topic to location and see what happens.

The following is Bob's journal entry.

Education and Location: The Determination

1   My mother is one of those people who latches on to quotes and hangs them on the refrigerator along with postcards, memos, and coupons. Generally I'm able to raid the fridge without too many of these missives raining to the floor. Yesterday, however, a serendipitous event occurred. A quote caught my eye and leaked into my brain before I could scrape it off the floor and return it to its home on the fridge. The quote was for me an epiphany. It captured my thoughts about where I want to transfer when I finish my work here at Monterey Peninsula College. It was, classily enough, Milton who captured my sentiments exactly in these lines from *Paradise Lost:* "Chaos umpire sits,/And by decision more embroils the fray/By which he reigns: next him high arbiter/Chance governs all."

2   Chaos has certainly called the shots so far as I struggle to decide where to go when I transfer to a four-year college. I have made lengthy lists of the pros and cons of various campuses where I might earn my cherished baccalaureate degree. But, alas, the more I think about the decision, the more "Chaos

umpire sits'' and "embroils the fray." There are so many factors to consider that even thinking about where I should go makes my brain feel like it was caught in a Cuisinart. Is a private college worth the cost? Would I be better off escaping from the small town atmosphere of the Monterey Peninsula and going to a sophisticated, big campus? Would I become an anonymous number at such a campus? Would I learn more if I picked a campus far removed in time, space, weather, and custom from my home on the central coast of California?

195

DISCOVERING
AND
ORGANIZING
IDEAS
THROUGH
DIVISION-
CLASSIFI-
CATION

3 Milton's chaos comment got me to thinking. What I need to do is to organize, to divide the decision into logical components; that way I can analyze each component carefully. Of great importance to me among the several factors that I need to analyze is the location of a campus. To help me decide about that location, I've come up with a number of questions:

4 How near home should I be? My grandmother claims that my father's first word was *home*. She said he learned to spell it when he was still toddling about. "I want to go h-o-m-e," my grandmother says Dad would say. I inherited the home gene. How far from home do I really want to be? Will I be able to concentrate if I am far from my beloved home, my dog, my cats, my surfboard? Kipling wrote: "God gives men all earth to love,/But since our hearts are small,/Ordained for each one spot should prove/Beloved over all."

5 On the other hand, even Kipling ventured out and tried the world on for size. I do not want to remain an unsophisticated, backwoods type. The philosopher George Santayana wrote: "A child educated only at school is an uneducated child." Perhaps I should select a campus in an area that challenges me with the unfamiliar. My mother grew up in Michigan while my father grew up in Connecticut. It takes about five seconds in each state to see that in many ways there are still regional differences in the cultures of different sections of the country.

6 Take attitude toward food, as just one small example. The restaurants where I've gone in Michigan are still not health food oriented. Finding a vegetarian entry in the rural area where my mother grew up is a little like searching for a snowball in the Sahara. Finding a cup of cappuccino is as tough. The Connecticut restaurants I've visited are more likely to have a nodding acquaintance with healthy food and good coffees, but in neither state, have I found the lean-green attitude toward eating that is common in restaurants at home.

7 Similarly, it seems to me that people in grocery stores or gas stations are a lot more friendly and outgoing in California than they are in Connecticut. Michigan people are more friendly than those in Connecticut but less friendly than people at home. Even the cars people drive seem different in different areas. I haven't done a scientific survey, but I see a lot more foreign cars in California than I see in Michigan. I wonder if my limited experience in these areas is a true reflection of what they are like. The only way I can find out is to live there. The fact that state laws vary so much on issues like capital punishment and abortion is an indication that there are regional differences in attitudes.

8 I know I should push myself. Since much of what I learn in college can take place outside the classroom, I am not doing my intellect or my sophisti-

196

DISCOVERING
AND
ORGANIZING
IDEAS
THROUGH
DIVISION-
CLASSIFI-
CATION

cation any good by simply immersing myself in the familiar. To grow intellectually and spiritually, I need to challenge myself.

9   But it is not just the section of the country I should go to that is at issue.
Do I want a sophisticated big-city campus, or am I a country boy at heart? I
am used to open spaces. When I'm in a big city very long, I begin to feel like
I can't breathe. Of course the air quality may make this literally true, but I
also feel too closed in—too claustrophobic. Yet the big cities offer unparal-
leled concerts, plays, and museums to help further my education.

10   Another location-related factor that I have to come to terms with is my love
for the salty blue. When the world is crashing down around my ears, the best
way to mellow out my mind is to immerse myself in the din of crashing waves.
The East Coast is not noted for its swarm of surfing beaches—nor is inland
California. Of all the mind-altering drugs available to help relieve the tensions
of living, surfing seems to me to be the most healthy. In addition, if I chose
a California campus, I can come home from time to time. Maybe I could
expand my brain and reduce my tension by doing what the locals do at
whatever campus I select. For example, I could jog, hang glide, or ski.

11   Clearly Chaos is reigning in my brain when it comes to selecting the location of a campus, but by analyzing the factors involved in the decision about
location, it seems clearer to me what my options are. It also seems clearer to
me that I am clinging to the comfortable rather than accepting the challenge
of a different world. Chaos is in a little less control now as my thinking is
clearer to me.

Will Division-Classification Work with Your Topic?

Through brainstorming and freewriting about this chapter's key questions,
Bob has been able to limit his topic and then explore his thinking about a
particular aspect of that topic. Bob has not only gained valuable insight into
his own thinking, he has generated a rough draft that will make writing his
essay a great deal faster and easier.

For Thought and Discussion

1. Into what categories has Bob divided the issues involved in selecting
a college? What additional categories would you include?

2. Point out sections of Bob's journal entry that he will have to research
if he is to include them in a formal essay.

3. Indicate any sections you would consider modifying or excluding
from a formal essay.

Exploring Classification with Your Own Topic

How do you know if you can gain insight into a subject by using questions
that divide it into classes or categories? Try brainstorming a list of questions

based on this chapter's key questions: *What are the types, classes, or categories into which X can be divided? How do the classes differ?* To see how this is done with a broad topic such as education, work with your peer group to read and answer the following "For Thought and Discussion" questions.

197

DISCOVERING
AND
ORGANIZING
IDEAS
THROUGH
DIVISION-
CLASSIFI-
CATION

For Thought and Discussion

1. What are the types, classes, or categories into which our schools are divided (or should be divided)? How do these classes differ?

2. What are the types, classes, or categories into which effective teachers can be divided? What are the types, classes, or categories into which ineffective teachers can be divided? How do these classes differ?

3. What are the types, classes, or categories of information and skills every student should learn by high school graduation? How do these differ?

4. What are the types, classes, or categories of changes that would make education more effective in this country?

5. What are the types, classes, or categories of goals that education should have?

6. Using this question pattern, suggest another way of analyzing the subject of education.

Transition Time

Help your readers follow your point by giving them adequate transitional signals. The following transitions are especially helpful in essays using a classification organizational pattern: *another group (type, class), first, second, third, last, the first (second, third) type, in this class (type, group, category), another common trait, to distinguish from.*

 YOUR PURPOSE, YOUR AUDIENCE, AND YOUR FOCUS

As with other writing, when you use division-classification as an idea-generating and organizational tool, you need to switch to your critical brain to ask yourself for whom you are writing and why you are writing.

Is yours a captive audience who must read your report or memo because they need *to be informed* about your topic? Is yours an audience you must *entertain* to capture and maintain their attention? What will your audience already know about your subject? What information will you need to give them so they can follow your thinking?

Is your purpose simply to *explain* why something fits into one category rather than another? Or is your purpose to *persuade*? Of course, it is always possible that your audience is yourself, as it was with Bob Higashi's decision

198

DISCOVERING
AND
ORGANIZING
IDEAS
THROUGH
DIVISION-
CLASSIFI-
CATION

about where to transfer: in this case you are using classification to *explore* and *discover* what it is you think about a particular topic.

When you are assigned an essay, often your initial purpose is simply to finish the assignment. However, if you take time to identify a purpose (other than merely completing the assignment) and an audience, you will find your writing is more consistent and thus more effective.

How narrowly you focus (or limit) your subject depends upon your purpose, the point you wish to make, and the length of your intended essay. Classifying a subject is rarely an end in itself. Rather, classifying helps writers to support and develop their point and thus to accomplish their purpose. For example, if your purpose is to convince your reader that students should have a basic knowledge of biology, you could divide biology into classes of information and explain the value of knowing about each class. If your purpose is to argue either for or against more military spending on high-tech weapons, you could classify these weapons and explain their strengths and weaknesses.

For Thought and Discussion

1. Look at the accompanying cartoon. What two methods of classifying are implied in this cartoon?

THE FAR SIDE   By GARY LARSON

"Well, I've got your final grades ready, although I'm afraid not everyone here will be moving up."

2. How do we subdivide knowledge in most educational institutions?

3. What types of benefits do societies achieve by supporting educational institutions?

4. List the major problems that would arise in our society if it stopped educating its members.

5. What types of information should our society teach its members? Defend your answer.

Your turn

1. Working in peer groups, answer the question *What are the types, classes, or categories into which X can be divided?* for the following:
   a. Literature
   b. Science
   c. Religion
   d. Colleges.

2. Select one of the subcategories from number 1 and again answer the question posed there. For example, what categories of information might you study in astronomy?

3. Brainstorm a list of the criteria that place something in a class; include the important subdivisions of that class. Be sure the criteria for each subdivision clearly distinguish it from other subdivisions.

4. Select two of the subjects from number 1. Use the key questions from this chapter to generate ideas. Then write a thesis for each of the two subjects. Next explain the purpose you would use in developing each thesis.

SOMETHING WORTH SAYING: ANOTHER OPPORTUNITY TO GROW

As we have noted, classification is a tool to help writers discover and express a point they would like to demonstrate to their readers. When searching for ideas, it is important to find something that will inspire your reader to see your subject in a new light. In other words, you need to find something worth saying. To say that American public school districts are generally divided into elementary school, middle school, and high school is a fact that American audiences know. Such a classification lacks the argumentative angle of a good thesis, and it bores its readers by telling them something they already know. However, you might decide that this division of schooling is especially effective or especially ineffective; supporting either point could provide both you and your reader with the opportunity to explore new, worthwhile ideas.

200

DISCOVERING
AND
ORGANIZING
IDEAS
THROUGH
DIVISION-
CLASSIFI-
CATION

How would classification help support the idea that the current division of schools is ineffective? First ask the key questions: What are the categories into which most public schools are currently divided? How do the categories differ?

As you develop each category, you might further explore by asking the following questions for each category: Do the categories function effectively? For example, do students in grades 6 through 8 benefit from being separated from other grade levels? Why were students originally separated into these groupings? Has the original rationale for such separation proved valid? The answers to these questions provide a framework for focusing and understanding your subject and for finding a fresh insight into that subject.

Before you write an essay in which you explore your ideas through classification, you need to understand your subject on more than a superficial level. Your general impression will not be riveting—or even interesting—to your reader unless you have something worthwhile to say. Therefore, unless you select a subject about which you are an expert, you will have to do some research to find out about your subject.

On your way to the library, you will be immensely cheered by contemplating a statement by Irish poet William Butler Yeats: "Education is not the filling of a pail but the lighting of a fire." The ability and desire to learn new information is a truer test of your education than writing about something you already know thoroughly.

See Chapter 5 if your research skills are not burning brightly enough to light your path. The *Reader's Guide to Periodical Literature* or its computerized equivalent will be especially helpful in finding the magazine articles you need to become better informed.

While you may know enough about a subject to write a fascinating and informative essay about it, almost everyone benefits from the point of view of others. In addition to reading about your subject, try talking to knowledgeable people about it. For a thesis involving education, you could interview a professor of education, a teacher, or an administrator such as a dean or a principal.

For Thought and Discussion

Working in a peer group, examine the answers to question 4 in the previous "For Thought and Discussion" questions. List the major problems that would arise in our society if it stopped educating its members. From your answers, select one topic and do the following:

1. Make a list of thesis statements that furnish a fresh insight.
2. Suggest relevant reference sources in the library.
3. Suggest people who could be interviewed about the topics.

Let's now look at how classification works as one of the tools to help develop an idea. In this chapter's opening quotation, Raymond Queneau points out that in our rapidly changing society, specific information often is outdated rather quickly. In such a society, the goal of education should not be just to impart specific information; instead education must also equip and inspire people to seek further learning. The goal of education then should be "the lighting of a fire" that will continue to provide energy rather than a one-time "filling of a pail" with information that may be quickly outdated.

Robert Francis, the author of the following poem, has spent his life keeping his learning fire burning by continuing to educate himself about the world around him and teaching others through his workshops and his poetry. For Francis, three categories of activities—learning, reflecting, artistic expression such as writing—are so important that he organizes his life to ensure he has enough time for these activities. According to Francis:

> Except for summer teaching and brief visits to universities, I live the year-round in my one-man house, Fort Juniper, in a wooded area on the outskirts of Amherst, Massachusetts. By reducing my needs and doing all my own work, I am able to live on a very small income and to have most of my time free for writing, reading, music, and gardening.

In the following poem, Francis asks to be kept awake—or if that fails, to be awakened so he can continue to learn about his world.

Summons

Keep me from going to sleep too soon
Or if I go to sleep too soon
Come wake me up. Come any hour
Of night. Come whistling up the road

Stomp on the porch. Bang on the door.   5
Make me get out of bed and come
And let you in and light a light.
Tell me the northern lights are on
And make me look. Or tell me the clouds

Are doing something to the moon   10
They never did before, and show me.
See that I see. Talk to me till
I'm half as wide awake as you
And start to dress wondering why

I ever went to bed at all.   15
Tell me the waking is superb

202

DISCOVERING
AND
ORGANIZING
IDEAS
THROUGH
DIVISION-
CLASSIFI-
CATION

Not only tell me but persuade me.
You know I'm not too hard persuaded.

—Robert Francis

For Thought and Discussion

1. Explain the similarity between this poem and the William Butler Yeats quotation that education should light a fire.

2. According to the Francis quotation preceding the poem, into what types of activities does Francis divide his life? Into what categories of activities could you divide your own life?

3. Francis is using the concepts of waking and sleeping metaphorically. What is he literally asking for?

4. What types of things does Francis ask be done to keep him awake? Give specific examples of how these "keeping awake" techniques translate literally to life.

5. How does this poem apply to education?

6. What types of learning situations help you stay interested in a subject and learn about it effectively?

7. To what kind of a person does Francis address his request? What kind of a teacher would such a person be?

8. Why does Francis want to be kept awake?

A PROFESSIONAL WRITER AT WORK

As you read the following essay, note how the author, Dr. Ernest L. Boyer, uses division-classification as a major idea-generating and organizing technique to help develop his thesis. Dr. Boyer is president of the Carnegie Foundation for the Advancement of Teaching. Previously he served as a United States commissioner of education and chancellor of the State University of New York.

From "Toward School-College Collaboration"

1   It was a dreary Monday morning and to avoid the pressures of the day I turned instinctively to the stack of third class mail that I kept on the corner of my desk. It was a typical administrative move to create the illusion that I was very, very busy. On top of the heap was the newspaper from Stanford University.

2   The headline announced that the faculty at Stanford had reintroduced a required course in Western Civilization. The students were offended. And in a front page editorial they declared that a required course is "an illiberal

act." The editors concluded with this blockbuster question: How dare they impose uniform standards on nonuniform people?

3   At first I was slightly amused and then deeply troubled by this statement. I recognized that frequently Western Civilization courses neglected other cultures and the role of minorities and women. Still, I was troubled that some of America's most gifted students, after fourteen years or more of formal education, still had not learned that while we are not uniform we still have much in common. They had not discovered that while we are all autonomous human beings with our own aptitudes and interests we still are deeply dependent on each other.

4   This experience led me to conclude that education has two essential goals. The first goal is to help students become personally empowered and discover their own aptitudes and interests. Indeed, one of the distinctive features of American education is diversity. This must remain a centerpiece of our works so that we do not drive students toward a false conformity. Individuality is central to our quest.

5   At the same time, there is another purpose to be pursued. The second goal of education is to help students go beyond their private interests and put their own lives in historical, social, and ethical perspective. Individuality *and* community remain the tension points of education just as, inevitably, they remain the tension points of life. Is our separation so great that we have lost sight of the agenda to be commonly pursued?

6   At one level, we're all divided, but at another level we must search for our connections. Let me cite four examples to illustrate the point.

7   *First, we must help students understand that we are all connected through the exquisite use of symbols.* Language, the most essential human function, and our own capacity to communicate carefully with each other, sets us apart from all other forms of life. Language is not just another subject. It's the means through which all other subjects are pursued.

8   Children learn, very early, both the majesty and the weaponry of language. When I was a boy we used to say "sticks and stones may break my bones, but names will never hurt me." What nonsense! I would say those words with tears running down my cheeks, thinking all the time—for goodness sake, hit me with a rock, but stop those words that penetrate so deeply and inflict so much pain.

9   In an earlier incarnation I worked with children who were deaf. I used to watch these beautiful little people experience anguish because of their frustration at not being able to make connections through the use of symbols. Language is the key to human interaction, and the first task of formal education is to help students become empowered in the written and the spoken word.

10   This task calls for close collaboration between colleges and schools. We found during our study of colleges that one of the greatest frustrations among faculty is the inadequate preparation of the students—and most especially their lack of proficiency in language. More than half the faculty we surveyed rated the academic preparation of their students as only fair or poor. Eighty-three percent of the faculty said that today's high school students should be

204

DISCOVERING
AND
ORGANIZING
IDEAS
THROUGH
DIVISION-
CLASSIFI-
CATION

academically better prepared, and two-thirds agreed that their institutions spend too much time teaching students what they should have already learned in high school.

11   I'm suggesting that language is the centerpiece of learning, and in our report *High School*, we stressed writing because through clear writing clear thinking can be taught.

12   Lewis Thomas said that "childhood is for language," and in our dangerous and interdependent world, with its bellicose language of political confrontation, in such a climate it's urgently important that we teach students not just the parts of speech but also the need to speak and listen carefully to each other—and communicate with *integrity* as well.

13   Several centuries ago the Quakers would risk imprisonment and even death because in court they would not swear to "tell the truth, the whole truth and nothing but the truth, so help me God." The problem was not that they were against swearing. The larger problem was their unwillingness to swear that they would tell the truth *in court,* suggesting that outside it might be an option. After all, wasn't truth something that one should just assume, not something that one would swear to do only under oath? So the Quakers would respond by saying, "Your Honor, I speak truth."

14   Well, that is perhaps an exotic point to make, especially when your head is on the block, but the larger point should not be denied. When we teach language, we are not teaching parts of speech. We're teaching the most elegant obligation of the human experience, to handle reverentially and respectfully the messages we send. Integrity is the key.

15   *This leads to a second priority for education. I suggest that all students should, through science, begin to understand the eloquent underlying patterns of the natural world and learn that we are connected through the ecology of the planet.* I find it significant that, during 1983, in addition to the National Commission report on education, three other major reports were released. These studies did not receive as much notoriety, but, in my view, they were also reports on education.

16   One, by the National Academy of Sciences, warned about the so-called greenhouse effect, the gradual warming of the earth's atmosphere by excessive carbon dioxide in the air. Another report by a group of equally distinguished scholars predicted that a nuclear holocaust could leave half the earth in frozen darkness. Finally, a group of outstanding biologists reported that the tropical rain forests, which harbor at least two-thirds of all the earth's animals and plants, are being destroyed at the rate of about 100,000 square kilometers every year—an area about the size of the state of Missouri.

17   The simple truth is that all forms of life are interlocked, yet students remain woefully ignorant about the natural world in which we all are embedded as working parts. When researchers [doing background work for *3-2-1 Contact*] asked junior high school students, "Where does water come from?" a significant percentage of students said, "the faucet." When they were asked, "Where does light come from?" they said "the switch." And when they were asked, "Where does garbage go?" "down the chute," they said.

18   Are we raising a generation of students who see no connectedness beyond the things that they can feel and touch, students who do not understand their

interdependent relationship with energy, with ecology, and with other forms of life?

19   Lewis Thomas, in his Phi Beta Kappa oration at Harvard, spoke eloquently about our interdependent world when he observed that "there are no solitary, free-living creatures. Every form of life is dependent on all other forms, and we should go warily into the future watching our step and having an eye out for our partners, wherever they may be." Through the study of science, students must learn about the elegant underlying patterns of the natural world. They must discover the connections.

20   *This brings me to priority number three. It's urgently important that all students also learn about our social and civic institutions and become familiar with cultures other than their own.* As far as we know, the human species is the only form of life that has the unique capacity to recall the past and anticipate the future. And in an age when planned obsolescence makes everything but the moment seem irrelevant, it is exceedingly important that students put the human story in perspective.

21   During the past five years, we at the Carnegie Foundation have been studying colleges and schools. And the signs of isolation are to me enormously discouraging. We found, for example, that a large group of community college students could not locate either Iran or El Salvador on a map. And in a survey of 5,000 college students, 30 percent said they had nothing in common with people from underdeveloped countries. Nothing in common with those less fortunate than themselves?

22   The University of Notre Dame campus minister William Toohey wrote that the trouble with many colleges is that they encourage the nesting instinct by building protective little communities inside their great and learned walls. I'm convinced that one of our most urgent obligations is to help students become less parochial and develop a perspective that is not just national, but global.

23   Henry Steele Commager recently described the 18th century as an era that was, in some respects, more enlightened than our own. Commager said that the 18th century was an age when the United States and France could decree immunity for Captain Cook and his men during wartime because "they were common friends of mankind." It was a time when Rousseau could pay tribute to those great political cosmopolitan minds who "embrace all mankind within the scope of their benevolence." It was a time when Tom Paine declared himself "a citizen of the world."

24   Today the world's more than 160 independent nations and 60-odd political units are inextricably interlocked. Interest rates in the United States impact Common Market countries; bad harvests in the [former] Soviet Union help farmers on the Western plains; Middle Eastern oil gluts produce recessions in Oklahoma; unemployment in Germany sends ripples to Spain; and a robotics breakthrough in Tokyo makes a dramatic difference in Detroit. The world may not be a global village, but surely our sense of neighborhood must include more people and more cultures than our own.

25   One further concern about the undergraduate experience. *As we prepare students for the world, it is also important that we build connections between general and specialized education.* We now typically require two years of general edu-

206

DISCOVERING
AND
ORGANIZING
IDEAS
THROUGH
DIVISION-
CLASSIFI-
CATION

cation that students say they want to "get out of the way" so they can move on to their specialization. And while we want students to be competent, we are not asking the essential question: Competence to what end?

26   During my days in Washington, I'd often be seated at a table where experts would try to prove how technically "competent" they were. But almost all of the really tough questions we encountered had less to do with specialized knowledge than with insights, wisdom, even compassion. What we worried about were such questions as these: Should HEW fund gene-splicing research that might introduce mutations on the planet earth? How can we keep human subjects from being harmed during experiments in the lab? How can the city of Chicago desegregate its schools in a way that serves all children and avoids white flight to the suburbs? On topics such as these there are no experts, there are only human beings trying to solve new and complicated problems.

27   In the Carnegie book titled *College,* we propose something called the "Enriched Major." Instead of assuming that general education is something for a student to "get out of the way," why not extend it from the freshman to the senior year and build it into the major so that the student's special field of study is put into a historical, social, and ethical perspective. We say that general and specialized education should be blended during college just as, inevitably, they must be blended during life. If a college cannot blend the liberal and the useful arts, why not turn the effort over to a proprietary school or a corporate classroom where students can get on with technical competence unhindered by the burden of collegiate education?

28   Eric Sakby, a noted British educator, wrote that the path to culture should be through a man's and woman's specialization, not by bypassing it. He said, "A student who can weave his technology into the fabric of society can claim to have a liberal education; a student who cannot weave his technology into the fabric of society cannot claim even to be a good technologist."

29   I have one final observation. *In the end, the discovery of connections is not only accomplished through a good curriculum, but through the teacher in the classroom.* It's the teacher who helps students gain insights, and I'm convinced that if this nation is to achieve better education we must find ways to give greater status to our teachers.

30   Perhaps the key to Japanese education is the status of *teacher.* The word *sensai* carries with it a position of great honor. To be a *sensai* is to be revered. The teacher is viewed as one who shapes the coming generation and is looked to with high regard, even reverence, by students and their families.

31   In this country, we say, "Oh, he or she is just a teacher." If you look at *sensai* in Japan and just-a-teacher here at home, you begin to understand the central issue of the differences in our systems.

32   Several years ago I couldn't sleep, and instead of counting sheep, I counted all the teachers I had. I remembered rather vividly 15 or more. There were a few nightmares in the bunch. But then I remembered several outstanding teachers who truly changed my life.

33   I then wondered to myself, what made these teachers truly great? Why did they stand out from all the rest? I thought of three characteristics that were the centerpiece of outstanding teaching. First they all had knowledge to convey—there was something there to teach.

34   Knowledge, however, is not enough. The great teacher also communicates at a level students understand. During our high school study, I moved unannounced into a sixth grade classroom in New Haven. I saw a teacher who was being pressed against a wall, or so it seemed, as 30 or 40 sixth graders crowded around the desk. At first I worried that they were denying him oxygen, but I stayed and discovered they were reading Charles Dickens' *Oliver Twist*. The language is 19th century English, but even so I discovered a miracle had occurred. The students were debating whether Oliver Twist could survive in New Haven. They knew the good guys and the bad guys. It was not 19th century literature they were reading, but 20th century urban life, and they were cheering for little Oliver because it was a life they lived every day. This teacher had the brilliance to connect great literature with their lives.

35   The third characteristic of good teaching is more elusive. The great teachers I had were not only well-informed, not only able to communicate with students, but they were authentic, believable human beings. They were three-dimensional and were competent enough to be vulnerable as well.

36   I am convinced that values are taught by teachers every single day in the integrity of their language and the quality of their lives. I'm suggesting that the values taught in school are the ones found intuitively and sometimes explicitly in the judgments of professors and teachers, who not only give knowledge but help students shape conclusions.

37   I worry that through intimidation or the threat of censorship we may impose upon the classroom a timidity and fear so that the creative act of exploring alternatives will be rejected. If we do not trust our teachers, and if we deny children the opportunity to move from absorbing information to the actual application of what they learn, we will have a generation that remains ignorant and unable to meet its social and civic obligations.

38   Our students increasingly are going to discover that they live in a world that is economically, politically, and ecologically connected. This must be reflected in the curriculum we provide, in the sense of community we build, and in the quality of teaching that helps students become not only well-informed but wise and compassionate as well.

39   The connectedness to things is what the educator contemplates to the limit of his capacity. No human capacity is great enough to permit a vision of the world as simple, but if the educator does not aim at the vision no one else will, and the consequences are dire when no one does. The student who can begin early in life to think of things as connected, even if he revises his view with every succeeding year, has begun the life of learning.

For Thought and Discussion

1. Restate the central point of Dr. Boyer's essay in your own words. How does this point emphasize the importance of remembering the whole and not just dividing things into parts?

2. What is the author's purpose in this essay?

3. Explain why you agree or disagree with the author's point. Support your point of view.

208

**DISCOVERING
AND
ORGANIZING
IDEAS
THROUGH
DIVISION-
CLASSIFI-
CATION**

4. If the suggested changes came about, how would they impact your education?

5. Explain how a classification pattern helped the author generate and organize his ideas. Refer to specific examples from the essay to illustrate your points.

6. Find the topic sentence for one of the categories identified in number 5. Then list the kinds of support and development used for that sentence.

7. What development techniques in addition to classification does the author use?

8. Point out four examples of transitions in this essay. Select at least one transition requiring more than three words.

9. Describe the audience for which you think this essay was intended. Explain how you arrived at your conclusion.

10. Identify the technique the author uses in his introduction to make it interesting to his readers.

IN CONCLUSION: ENDING TECHNIQUES

Once you have generated and organized the ideas for your essays, it is time to consider how to conclude effectively. The following are examples of techniques to help you do so:

1. **You can summarize your major points.** Ernest Boyer in the preceding essay summarized in his conclusion, as does Richard P. Keeling in the following conclusion to an article from *The NEA Higher Educational Journal* about how college teachers should deal with the issue of AIDS:

> Perhaps most important of all is the perspective each faculty member can provide in hundreds of informal contacts with students and colleagues: a perspective that HIV infection is a real problem, that it can happen here, that it is largely preventable, that good decisions are important, that infected persons will not transmit the virus in casual contacts, that clear, explicit, direct information is important, and that people in the community who are worried, seropositive, or ill need compassion and support, not discrimination and prejudice.

2. **You can draw a conclusion supported by your development.** Sylvia Charp uses this technique in the following conclusion to an editorial from *T.H.E. Journal: Technological Horizons in Education* about the impact of technology on education:

We must not be lulled into believing that the extended use of technology will, per se, develop exploring minds or prepare individuals to be capable of thinking creatively and making critical decisions. Revolutionary tools are being offered for use in all activities and fields of endeavor. These should serve our human values and conditions, not rule them.

3. You can narrate an anecdote relevant to your central point. Edward P. J. Corbett does this in the following conclusion to an article in *College Composition and Communication* about teaching college composition (despite his comments, Corbett is a noted authority on the teaching of composition):

> One morning recently while I was shaving—probably after a period of being conscience-stricken about my repeated failures as a teacher of writing—I stuck this big nose of mine against the tip of the nose reflected in the mirror and shouted at the top of my lungs, "CORBETT, YOU FRAUD!"
>
> Maybe we all need to assess ourselves as teachers periodically. Whatever you appropriate for your teaching from the books and articles you read or from the conferences and conventions you attend, give it a fair trial in the classroom. But from time to time, pause to ask yourself, "Am I doing my students any good?" Try it. You have nothing to lose but your delusions.

4. You can conclude with a quotation that reinforces your central point. Edward B. Fiske quotes the author of this chapter's professional essay in the following conclusion to an article from *The New York Times: Education Life* about the importance America places on test scores:

> Standardized testing has a ready appeal in a pluralistic nation such as the United States. "Testing is a way to short-circuit the discussion of what we want our schools to teach," says Ernest L. Boyer, president of the Carnegie Foundation for the Advancement of Teaching. "We can agree more on our tests than on our goals."

5. You can conclude by illustrating your main ideas. Susan Tifft does so in the following conclusion to an article from *Time* about teaching as a career:

> Of course, not everyone can have the impact of math teacher Jaime Escalante, the inspiring subject of the movie *Stand and Deliver*. But in small towns and sprawling cities there surely are people like him, each a miracle worker in his or her own way. Teachers say the best of them are born, not made. Perhaps they are right. Several years ago, Patrice Bertha took a sabbatical to see whether she really wanted to spend the rest of her life in the classroom. She wound up tutoring at home instead. "I really missed it," she says. "That's when I told myself, 'You're a teacher forever.' "

6. You can conclude by answering a question asked in the development of your essay. Anne Marie and Cullen Murphy used this technique in the following conclusion to an article from *Smithsonian* about the McGuffey readers:

210

DISCOVERING
AND
ORGANIZING
IDEAS
THROUGH
DIVISION-
CLASSIFI-
CATION

Reading scores are beginning to improve. If this keeps up, Americans are likely to look beyond the "how to" and toward the "what" of reading, and to ask of readers: Do these books express our society, pass on its virtues, contain stories of substance and literary worth?

As educators, editors, publishers, parents and politicians take a hand in rebuilding our children's reading texts, they could do worse than to emulate the spirit of compromise that marked the McGuffeys from the start. It is a colorful world: bad things happen; and guidance to the young on right behavior is needed. The editors of the McGuffeys, like Old Guff himself, bore this in mind.

7. You can conclude by restating your thesis. David P. Gardner does this in the following conclusion to a section of the report of the National Commission on Excellence in Education, *A Nation at Risk:*

> We are confident that America can address this risk. If the tasks we set forth are initiated now and our recommendations are fully realized over the next several years, we can expect reform of our Nation's schools, colleges, and universities. This would also reverse the current declining trend—a trend that stems more from weakness of purpose, confusion of vision, underuse of talent, and lack of leadership, than from conditions beyond our control.

Words of Caution

Be careful that you do not introduce a new idea in your conclusion. The longer you think about a subject, the more ideas you will generate about that subject. Often, therefore, a new idea will pop into your brain when you are writing your conclusion. At this point, loop back to your critical brain to remind yourself that everything in your essay must develop your thesis. You have two choices when a new idea occurs to you while you are concluding your essay:

1. Ignore the idea.
2. Rewrite so your thesis and development include the new idea.

In addition, be careful to make sure the tone of your conclusion harmonizes with the tone of the rest of your essay.

Transitions to Signal Conclusion

The following transitions can be useful in signaling to your reader that you are about to conclude your essay: *consequently, finally, in closing, in conclusion, therefore, thus, to conclude, to sum up.*

Write an essay of 500 to 800 words. Use the classification questions to help generate and organize ideas for your essay. While we have concentrated on topics related to education in this chapter, division-classification techniques are helpful for developing essays on a broad variety of other topics as well.

Like the professional authors in this chapter, you do not have to use classification as the only means of development. Review the development techniques you have used thus far before you begin the essay. Remember to do the following:

1. Limit your subject so you can develop it adequately. Include all major categories of your subject. When placing something in a class, make sure your criteria are logical, and make sure it is clear how the classes are distinct from each other.

2. Do not merely categorize types. Like the authors in this chapter, use classification as a tool to help you explore a topic and make a point, not as an end in itself.

3. Use at least two sources in your development. These sources may be articles you have read, television programs you have seen, or people you have interviewed.

4. Use at least one prewriting technique to get started.

5. Model your conclusion on one of the concluding techniques discussed in this chapter.

Suggestions for Topics

Here are some suggestions for topics:

   Your own suggestions for educational reform
   Disposal of waste materials such as garbage
   Drugs
   Types of careers that interest you
   Reasons students drop out of school
   Reasons Japan has been so successful in the world economy
   The types of factors that cause divorce or child abuse
   The types of factors that caused a particular war
   Types of required college courses
   Television advertising
   Learning techniques
   Teaching techniques

212

DISCOVERING
AND
ORGANIZING
IDEAS
THROUGH
DIVISION-
CLASSIFI-
CATION

Types of television programs for children
Types of threats to our international security
An instructor-approved topic of your choice

Peer Editing Checklist

After you have completed the prewriting and the first draft of your essay, meet with a peer editing group so that you can assess the reaction of an audience to your writing. Photocopy enough copies of your essay for your peer editing group.

1. First read the essay through once without stopping.

2. Indicate any ideas, passages, imagery, allusions, or other aspects of this essay you found effective. Positive reinforcement is a powerful tool.

3. Underline the thesis. If you cannot identify the thesis, ask the writer to point it out or to further clarify the thesis in writing should this prove necessary. Does the thesis offer any new insight?

4. Point out any details or passages that do not seem relevant to the author's point. The author can then decide whether a transition could clarify the connection with the thesis or if the point is truly irrelevant.

5. List the categories the author uses to develop the essay.
   a. Point out any categories that seem to overlap.
   b. List any categories the author has ignored.
   c. Indicate any place where the organization seems confusing or inconsistent.

6. What sources has the author used to help support the thesis?
   a. Suggest areas where additional support would strengthen the thesis—if such areas exist.
   b. What types of specific information would better convince you of the thesis?
   c. List information that indicates the author has a good knowledge of the subject.

7. Explain what the author has done to ensure audience interest and understanding.
   a. What in the introduction "hooks" the audience?
   b. List any technical terms that should be explained.
   c. List any technical terms the author explains that you believe are understandable to a first-year college composition student without this explanation.

8. With which technique does the author conclude? Explain why you think the conclusion is or is not effective.

When writers have revised the content of the essay to their satisfaction and are ready for feedback about mechanics, point out but do not correct any problems you suspect with spelling, grammar, and punctuation. It is the writer's responsibility to make such corrections.

213

DISCOVERING
AND
ORGANIZING
IDEAS
THROUGH
DIVISION-
CLASSIFI-
CATION

Help! For Further Work

The following draft of an essay, which uses the classification questions to organize and generate ideas, needs further work. Read the essay and evaluate it using the peer editing checklist as your guide.

Because We Chose Not to Pay We Are Paying Dearly!

1   Obviously if the United States does not start taking education more seriously, we are soon going to become a fifth rate power. Already the evidence of our failure to adequately educate our young people is causing havoc. There are several categories in which this evidence is most apparent. Look at our trade imbalance for example. Almost since its founding, the United States has represented Brain Power to the rest of the world.

2   Another way in which our educational failure is showing up is our loss of the international leadership in technology. Just think of all the wonderful inventions that resulted from our status as Number One Educator of our young. While many countries educated only a select few students, the United States realized that society as a whole would benefit from educating the masses. Thus in other countries people like Thomas Edison might have been relegated to menial jobs, but in this country it didn't matter how much money his parents had; he was still able to get enough education to stand the world on its ear—technologically speaking.

3   Another way in which our failure to adequately educate our young is very obvious is in the general morale of society. Crime is up. So are drug sales, AIDS, and unemployment. Only a generation ago being an American meant you were It—a citizen of the most freethinking, caring, innovative country in the world. Life offered hope and excitement. Now for too many undereducated Americans life offers a dirty needle and temporary escape.

4   Industrial leaders of other countries such as Sony Corporation head Akio Morita say they grew up looking to the United States as a source of new, exciting, innovative ideas. What has happened in the last few decades? We now look to countries like Japan where education is taken very seriously. According to a 1980 survey, not a single state required credits in foreign language as a condition for graduation. Thirty-five states required only one year of math and 36 states required only one year of science. Sure in the past couple of years some states have tightened their requirements, but the picture has not changed.

5   Meanwhile the Japanese high school students goes to school six days a week, five of those days from 8:30 until 5 p.m. and on the sixth from 8:30 until 12:25. Furthermore, they attend school 240 days per year! The average American high school student attends school from 8 until 2 or three, five days a week, 180 days a year. No wonder Japan is the sole producer of important new inventions. Did you know that not a single VCR is American made? And Akio Morita in his book *Made in Japan* says he could not interest unimaginative

U.S. industry in inventions like compact disk players. No wonder our balance of payments is so dismal and Americans are buying increasing numbers of Toyotas and Hondas while American auto manufacturers are forced to lay off workers.

6   Once United States corporations owned land all over the world from the banana plantations of Honduras to the sugar cane fields of Indonesia. Now Japanese corporations own much of Hawaii and a big chunk of California. Corporations from foreign countries own much of our prime agricultural lands in the Midwest and the West.

7   And while very few Americans learn Japanese, English is a regular part of the curriculum for Japanese high school students. This helps the Japanese better understand foreign markets and thus helps them penetrate these markets successfully. Meanwhile Americans have been dismal failures at understanding the Japanese markets sufficiently to have a similar dramatic impact on those markets. So we have a massive trade imbalance that costs U.S. jobs and encourages U.S. citizens to have more confidence in foreign products than in their own products. In one recent survey, American consumers were asked to choose between two similar-looking unmarked, wrapped packages. All they were told was one package contained a product made in the United States and the other contained a product made in Japan. The vast majority of Americans chose the product made in Japan! That shows how little faith we have in our own technology even though less than a generation ago ''Made in Japan'' meant a junky, inferior product.

8   Education pays tremendous benefits to a society. Unfortunately, we are only now beginning to see what happens when we ignore education. Derek Bok said ''If you think education is expensive—try ignorance''; our society indeed thinks education is expensive. We are paying very dearly for the ignorance that has resulted from that belief.

9   There is hope, of course, but only if we get our act together in a hurry. You only get what you pay for, and since we haven't been paying much for our public education compared to other industrial countries, we haven't been getting as much. But just look at what happened in the fifties after the Soviets sent up the first satellite. We panicked when we learned a communist satellite was the first to orbit the earth and we plowed enormous resources into education. Within a very short time we had caught up with the Soviet space program. It is time to go and do likewise so we can compete on the world markets and return to our former place among industrial nations of the world. Doing this will be a tremendous help at home too. Homelessness and hunger would be eliminated.

STUDENT STARS

While the examples thus far in this chapter have centered around education, the methods discussed in this chapter apply to many other subjects. Therefore, the student star essays are on a variety of topics.

Note how the following student authors use classification as a tool to help generate and organize ideas about their topics.

The students who wrote these essays did the following:

1. Prewriting
2. Writing
3. Revision of content
4. Proofreading and revision of mechanics.

Why Am I Back in School?

1   I hate to feel ignorant. Yet the world is changing at a dizzying pace. The issues are becoming more complex as technology grows in sophistication more quickly than I can comprehend. I want to participate in and react to what is going on around me. Therefore, I need an accurate and up-to-date foundation in a variety of academics so I can apply the sound judgment and knowledge that will help me live with grace and pride. More education will make me a better citizen, enhance my career prospects, enable me to assist with my children's education, and allow me to be a better role model for them.

2   Where do I get this valuable foundation? The ultimate answer is in college. College will help me understand the many kinds of changes our world experiences continually.

3   When I turn on my television set to listen to the news, I am confronted with subjects such as space exploration, genetic engineering, and political upheaval. Sitting in my living room, I listen with great interest to the issues, sometimes barely understanding the discussions, other times feeling totally ignorant because I lack important basic information.

4   As I listen to today's scholars and politicians, I realize how little I know and how much influence these people are having on my world—and on my mind. I do not want their flashy expertise to brainwash me. As Dr. Ernest Boyer pointed out in a *NEA Higher Education Journal* article, on many vital issues facing our world, "There are no experts, there are only human beings trying to solve new and complicated problems." I want to evaluate for myself important research and theories. To analyze, evaluate, and decide for myself, I must continue to educate myself. The best way to do this is to go back to college.

5   My problem with keeping up in today's fast-paced world is complicated by my background. I was born and raised in Togo, so I lack some of the basic cultural knowledge that would help me understand my new country. Courses like American Government 101 are helping me acquire the knowledge I need to understand the complicated system of governmental checks and balances in the United States. Such an understanding will help me make my voice heard in this democratic society.

6   In addition to helping me understand and participate in a democratic society, education will help me get a better job. While I do not want a job until my children are older, as the wife of a career soldier I am aware I could suddenly find myself as a single parent. In my years as a U.S. citizen, I have learned that being African-American and a woman in this country too often

216

DISCOVERING
AND
ORGANIZING
IDEAS
THROUGH
DIVISION-
CLASSIFI-
CATION

means being poor and dependent. When I work, I am determined to find a challenging, fulfilling, and rewarding job. I want to learn to communicate effectively, to share my knowledge, and to succeed. Through education I can expand my mind and improve my future.

7   But improving my own mind and career prospects are not my only education goals. As the mother of two youngsters, I realize the more educated I am, the more I will be able to help my children. Through my own growth, I help them to grow and discover new things. And as an extra benefit, I can help them with homework when they become frustrated. Jerome Bruner in his book *In Search of Mind* says parents should provide a scaffold as a thinking framework for their children to borrow until their own thinking is mature. When I am studying and growing intellectually, I am improving the scaffolding I give to my children.

8   Furthermore, I motivate my children by setting an example. Seeing me studying helps them realize the importance and the benefits of education. In *Infants, Toddlers and Caregivers,* Janet Gonzalez-Mena emphasizes the impact of sharing the joy of learning with children. According to Jacqueline Pentony, my child development instructor, in general, children see their parents as all-knowing, and children model themselves after their parents; it is a powerful influence on children to see their parents valuing learning by learning themselves.

9   Education helps keep my mind young. Education helps me understand the complex society in which I live. Education helps me improve my future job prospects. Education helps me be a better mother. I can think of no other way to reap such important benefits by keeping my mind fresh, alive, and healthy.

—Janine Wilson

Why So Many Homeless?

1   Who are the homeless and why have their numbers risen so dramatically in the last couple of decades? This alarming rise results from several factors. At the same time as the legions of homeless grew, the number of mentally ill patients in our institutions dropped from 550,000 in 1955 to 125,000 in 1985.

2   The reason for this? In 1967 ex-California Governor Ronald Reagan started letting mentally ill patients out of institutions because "They impose a great financial burden on society." The number of committed patients has been decreasing ever since. This army of mentally ill people living on the streets now account for as much as half of all the homeless people. The process known as "deinstitutionalization" is what put them there.

3   In 1971 deinstitutionalization changed from a governor's policy to law as the result of the *Wyatt vs. Stickney* suit in Alabama. This suit guaranteed mental patients the right to treatment in the least restrictive setting. The result of *Wyatt vs. Stickney* was a hasty release of patients into community facilities which were not prepared to receive them. As a result of the restrictive admission standards resulting from this court decision there is a fast growing population of young, chronically mentally ill people who have never been institutionalized. Because these people cannot function in our complex society, many have no alternative but to live on the streets,

4   Of the remaining street denizens, about forty percent are alcoholics and

217

DISCOVERING
AND
ORGANIZING
IDEAS
THROUGH
DIVISION-
CLASSIFI-
CATION

other drug abusers. The exact number of homeless families headed by drug and alcohol abusers is difficult to verify, but according to *The Christian Century*, the number of such families in New York increased four-fold in the decade of the eighties. The majority of these families are single mothers with their children. Because of their addictions, they can't get or keep a job or afford housing. Neither can they get organized enough to use such services as medical help for their addictions.

5   The remaining ten percent of street people is a mixed population. Again single mothers figure prominently. According to *The Christian Century*: "A welfare mother receiving her monthly $227 rent allotment finds it impossible to rent an apartment in Manhattan for that amount and extremely difficult to rent one anyplace else."

6   Some of the remaining homeless are unemployed workers. Some are immigrants. Others are runaway children. Illegal migrants sometimes end up on the street because they come into this country with no money and often inadequate English to hold a job. Some farmers who were hard-hit by inflation and falling farm prices wound up losing their land and searching for jobs to try to feed and house their families. Displaced workers who wind up on the street have lost not only their jobs and unemployment benefits but eventually also their homes.

7   Yet another important cause of homelessness that affects all categories of the homeless according to an article published in *Science* is "decreases in the level of income maintenance support for poor families during the past two decades." The amount of money available for housing simply has not kept pace with housing costs.

8   There is little doubt that the problem of the homeless will not solve itself. We will continue to read about runaway children forced into prostitution; we will continue to read about homeless people who freeze to death on city sidewalks—unless we as a society are willing to do more than read about such people. What we need is an alliance of concerned, committed people including the courts and lawmakers as well as private and public organizations working together. What we need to do is ask not just "Why so many homeless?" but "What can we do to help this growing army of homeless?"

—Mike Evans

8

WRITING AND NEWTON'S LAWS: CAUSE AND EFFECT

CONCEPTS TO LEARN

Writing about cause-effect relationships

Post hoc fallacies: Errors in thinking about cause-effect relationships

Using transitions to show cause-effect relationships

Revising for clarity and meaning

All of life involves *cause-effect* relationships—even life in the physical universe. One of Newton's laws of motion, a fundamental law of physics, is that "for every action there is an equal and opposite reaction": action = cause; reaction = effect. Likewise, when you approach any writing project on any topic, you can be certain that there is at least one cause-effect situation within that topic—and probably several. Asking key questions can help you discover the cause-effect relationships in your topic: *What are the causes of X? What are the effects of X?*

In the following passage, Nobel prize–winning physicist Richard Feynman tells a story which illustrates more than one cause-effect situation. As you read, notice how Feynman weaves together two episodes—the women driver and the police officer, and the physicist and the protesters—which, together, create a lively anecdote.

A few years after I gave some lectures for the freshmen at Caltech, I received a long letter from a feminist group. I was accused of being anti-women because of [a story I told about] the subtleties of velocity [which] involved a woman driver being stopped by a cop. There's a discussion about how fast she was going, and I had her raise valid objections to the cop's definitions of velocity. The letter said I was making the woman look stupid.

A year or so later, the American Association of Physics Teachers awarded me a prize, and asked me to speak at their meeting in San Francisco. As soon as I got up to speak, half a dozen protesters marched down to the front of the lecture hall and paraded right below the stage, holding their picket signs high, chanting, "Feynman sexist pig! Feynman sexist pig!"

219

WRITING AND
NEWTON'S
LAWS:
CAUSE AND
EFFECT

I began my talk by telling the protesters, "It's good that you came. For women do indeed suffer from prejudice and discrimination in physics, and your presence here today serves to remind us of these difficulties and the need to remedy them."

The protesters looked at one another. Their picket signs began to come slowly down, like sails in the wind.

After my talk, some of the protesters came up to press me about the woman-driver story. "Why did it have to be a woman driver?" they said. "You are implying that all women are bad drivers.

"But the woman makes the cop look bad," I said. "Why aren't you concerned about the cop?"

"That's what you expect from cops!" one of the protesters said. "They're all pigs!"

"But you *should* be concerned," I said. "I forgot to say in the story that the cop was a woman!"

As a physicist and as an author, Richard Feynman was aware of the cause-effect elements in his work, whether he was telling an amusing story or investigating the causes of the *Challenger* explosion. Like Feynman, experienced writers realize that an examination of the reasons behind an event, or of the results of that event, will invariably generate a good many ideas. Because looking at causes and effects is one of the principal ways we analyze material in any discipline, it is important to be aware of how this method can be most effective in helping us to generate, research, and organize our ideas.

For Thought and Discussion

1. What was the cause of the protesters' anger with Feynman? What could Feynman have done in telling the original story about the woman and the police officer to prevent such a reaction?

2. Would Feynman have acknowledged the discrimination suffered by women in physics if the protesters had not challenged him?

3. What caused the protesters to say that all "cops" are "pigs"? What is the effect of such a generalization on the person who believes it?

4. Think of a cause-effect situation in your own life. Freewrite about that situation, taking time to explore *all* the effects (and the effects of the effects).

220

**WRITING AND
NEWTON'S
LAWS:
CAUSE AND
EFFECT**

GENERATING IDEAS BY EXAMINING CAUSE-EFFECT RELATIONSHIPS

We have already suggested that looking at the causes or the effects of an event will yield a good many ideas. A useful technique for discovering cause-effect relationships is to ask key questions: *What caused this circumstance? What is the effect of this circumstance?* For example, you might ask, What has caused the erosion of the beaches along the east coast of the United States? What has caused the explosion of the homeless population? What are the potential effects of a major earthquake on the midwestern United States? What are the effects of an aging population on the marketing of products?

All the questions so far begin with the word *what,* but the words *why* and *how* will help you to answer cause-effect questions as well: Why does the Earth appear to be warming? Why are Brazil's rain forests disappearing? How have the Swiss been able to maintain a stable political and economic system for so long? Why do some parents fail to immunize their children against preventable diseases? How was Napoleon able to establish his power base in France?

As always, you will benefit most in the early stages of the writing process by using the prewriting techniques you learned earlier in this text: clustering, freewriting, and brainstorming. In addition, asking key questions will help you discover and focus your thesis, while research will help you to clarify and focus your questions. In fact, you might check yourself as you write by posting a note in your work area with this reminder: **Prewrite—Key Questions—Research.**

Think Beyond the Obvious

In the cluster shown in Figure 8-1, Michele, a compositon student, has begun her prewriting by exploring many of the issues that currently affect the nation's ability to produce a work force that has the energy and education necessary to compete effectively in the world's changing economy.

Thinking beyond her first impressions of causes and effects helped Michele avoid oversimplification. In addition, she did some preliminary research about her subject by reading a background entry in an encyclopedia and one article in a magazine.

Michele was stumped, at first, about where she could find articles about her topic, but she knew that a good, up-to-date encyclopedia, such as the *Encyclopaedia Britannica* or the *Encyclopedia Americana,* would provide her with excellent background information. In addition, she remembered that she could find articles on almost any topic by consulting the library's on-line reference guide or the many volumes of the *Reader's Guide to Periodical*

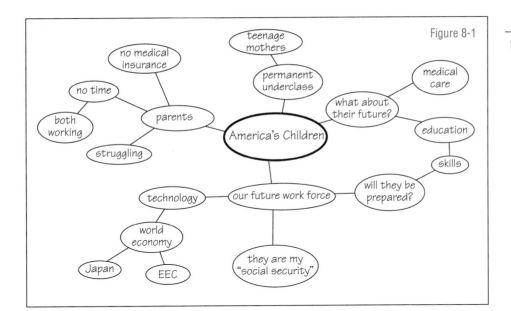

221

**WRITING AND
NEWTON'S
LAWS:
CAUSE AND
EFFECT**

Figure 8-1

Literature. Since these guides are located in the reference section of the library, Michele was able to find plenty of resource material in one quick trip.

Having informed herself about the issues, Michele found that she had trouble limiting her topic sufficiently. There were so many directions to take with the topic that she felt confused. She decided to brainstorm, listing her ideas rapidly, and as a result she discovered some key questions. Out of this she began to formulate the first draft. Since this draft is a preliminary step in the writing process, Michele felt free to ask herself questions on paper as they occurred to her: Why is an entire generation of American children threatened? What is threatening them? Why can't their parents take care of them? What is the role of the government in all of this? How will this affect the work force of the future? The answer to one of those questions might well prove to be an excellent thesis in itself.

As you can see from the initial draft, reprinted below, Michele still has a long way to go in organizing and developing her ideas, but she has provided herself with a good deal of material to work with.

> Sociologists tell us that a generation of American children is threatened. These children may become part of a permanent underclass, deprived of basic education and health needs. In fact, despite the current level of prosperity, one in five children lives in poverty, and almost the same proportion go without health insurance or proper medical care. In addition, one-quarter of the teenagers now in high school will drop out before graduation, and some 500,000 teenage girls will have become mothers by the end of the year.

What is causing this effect? Some say that it is because the escalating costs of food, shelter, and medicine are eroding families' abilities to meet their own basic needs.

Certainly these costs have risen, but is that the only or even the most important cause of this effect? What about the erosion of wages in many jobs, as well as the decline in the number of jobs for people with limited skills and training? And what effect does the increase in part-time employment have? After all, companies that hire employees for thirty hours a week or less are not obligated to provide medical insurance, and they can let employees go on short notice. Since medical insurance for a family can cost as much as a third of a worker's monthly salary, it is hardly surprising that working parents—especially those whose jobs are not secure—would take their chances and hope that no one in the family gets sick or becomes injured.

Furthermore, the government has cut back on programs that are designed to help children and their families. In the 1980s, the political atmosphere was not favorable to federal and state funding of social programs, and only recently have citizens and politicians alike realized that less money for public education translates into a future workforce that will not help America compete in the highly technological twenty-first century. Certainly our society has gone through some economic changes, but these changes seem to have affected its least vocal and most vulnerable members the most.

Avoiding Pitfalls

As Michele discovered, most cause-effect relationships are complex. In order to manage her topic effectively, she will have to be sure that she limits the amount of material; on the other hand, she must be careful not to oversimplify. In exploring her topic through her initial cluster, she identified teenage pregnancy, working parents, lack of medical insurance, and the existence of a permanent underclass as possible causes of children in crisis.

Some of these topics are causes of the problem. But some are also effects; for example, high teenage pregnancy rates do cause a further breakdown in our society's ability to handle the needs of its children. However, the high number of births to teenagers is also an effect, for teenage pregnancy rates are highest among girls whose own needs were given inadequate attention when they were young. Michele could focus her attention simply on the effects of today's teenage pregnancy upon the work force of the future; this focus would provide her with plenty of material for an essay, and plenty of cause-effect relationships to explore.

It would take a long paper indeed to adequately develop a comprehensive discussion of the problems of America's children—its future work force—but a short essay could explore in depth *one* of the problems they face. Once Michele has identified a single topic from the many she has considered, it is important that she again take the time to cluster, brainstorm, or freewrite; out of this exploration should come some new key questions. For example, What are the causes of the high rate of teenage pregnancy in the United States? What are the effects of teenage pregnancy on family life? Do the children born to teenage mothers encounter problems that other children do not have? Do these problems affect the children's ability to learn in school? What, then, are the effects of this phenomenon on our future work force?

223

WRITING AND
NEWTON'S
LAWS:
CAUSE AND
EFFECT

For Thought and Discussion

1. Remember that a question is not a thesis, but the answer to that question often is. Remember also that some questions are too broad to serve as the basis for a thesis. Read the following questions and decide which ones are too broad to be the basis for a thesis for a 500- to 800-word essay.

a. Why is the earth's atmosphere becoming warmer?

b. Why has the United States fallen behind other developed nations in educating its children?

c. How is the destruction of the earth's forests affecting the atmosphere?

d. Why have we seen a resurgence of racially motivated incidents on college campuses during the past several years?

e. How can we ensure that the United States will continue to be a wealthy nation?

f. What has led to the alarming rise in the incidence of teenage pregnancies?

g. What impact on the atmosphere does the photosynthesis of plankton have?

h. Why are some nations forging ahead of the United States economically?

i. What factors determine whether or not people comprehend what they read?

j. What are the consequences of low birth weight on children's physical and intellectual development?

2. Choose one topic suitable for a 500- to 800-word essay from the above list. Cluster, freewrite, or brainstorm around that topic; then ask the key questions, *What are the causes of X? What are the effects of X?*

3. Write a thesis statement based on your exploration, remembering that the answers to your questions can form the basis for your thesis.

Beware the *Post Hoc* Fallacy!

In Latin, *post hoc ergo propter hoc* means "after this, therefore, because of this." A *fallacy* is a false idea or notion. A person who states a *post hoc* fallacy assumes that because one event followed another, the first event caused the second. You have undoubtedly encountered this kind of fuzzy reasoning in the past.

For example:

> Larry Lanier has smoked a box of cigars every day for the past eighty years. Mr. Lanier just celebrated his hundredth birthday. Cigar smoking promotes longevity.

> Calvin Cromer dropped out of school in the eighth grade. Mr. Cromer has amassed a fortune of several million dollars. Dropping out of school early helps people become wealthy.

The *post hoc* fallacy is one of many *logical fallacies*. You will meet other examples of logical fallacies in Chapter 10.

For Thought and Discussion

1. Reread "Think Beyond the Obvious" (beginning on page 153) and suggest three ways of limiting a thesis concerning the risks to America's children. Be careful not to oversimplify in this thesis. Do not mislead your reader into thinking that the cause you select is the only cause. Language such as "one of the most significant causes" will help you to limit your subject without oversimplifying.

2. Suggest another possible cause for Larry Lanier's longevity and for Calvin Cromer's wealth.

3. Make up your own example of a *post hoc* fallacy.

Transition Time

When writing about a cause-effect issue, you can help your readers by giving them adequate transitional signals. The following transitions are especially useful in discussing cause-effect relationships:

To show cause:
> *because, due to, for, for this reason, leads to, if, in order to, since*

To show effect:
> *accordingly, and, as a result, as a consequence, consequently, eventually, for, hence, then, necessarily, of course, of necessity, resulted in, since, so, so that, then, thereby, therefore, thus.*

For Thought and Discussion

1. What are the causes of the conflict in the accompanying cartoon? What are the likely effects of this conflict?

2. Gary Larson makes a sharp point about human behavior and the nature of conflict. We all know of serious conflicts that seem trivial to

225

**WRITING AND
NEWTON'S
LAWS:
CAUSE AND
EFFECT**

One remark led to another, and the bar suddenly
polarized into two angry, confrontational factions: those
espousing the virtues of the double-humped camel on
the one side, single-humpers on the other.

outsiders. Brainstorm with your peer group a list of such conflicts that you
are aware of.

3. Since our rational, intellectual selves can see the absurdity in conflicts such as the one in the cartoon, what do you think causes human beings
to become so easily drawn into conflicts? What are the effects?

LOOK BEFORE YOU LEAP

Cause-effect relationships occur, of course, in all aspects of our lives. In the
area of human relations, the effects of a single word or action can be
devastating. More difficult, very often, is how to express in words the impact
of such carelessness or cruelty on its victim.

Countee Cullen, an African-American poet who was a leading member
of the Harlem arts community from 1926 until 1946, creates a vivid picture
of an instance of a small boy's cruelty in the following poem, and he leaves
little doubt as to its effect.

226

WRITING AND
NEWTON'S
LAWS:
CAUSE AND
EFFECT

Incident

Once riding in old Baltimore   1
    Heart-filled, head-filled with glee.
I saw a Baltimorean
    Keep looking straight at me.

Now I was eight and very small,   5
    And he was no whit bigger,
And so I smiled, but he poked out
    His tongue, and called me, "Nigger."

I saw the whole of Baltimore   9
    From May until December;
Of all the things that happened there
    That's all that I remember.

For Thought and Discussion

1. Why would this episode be the only thing the speaker remembers from his visit to Baltimore?

2. Countee Cullen has written about a painful incident that remains vivid years later. Write about an incident from your own youth the effect of which still stands out in your memory. (You may find it easier to remember the episode clearly if you cluster first.) Why do you think this incident, out of the thousands of things that have happened in your life, is so memorable?

3. Of the two children in the poem, which one was most likely to carry the deepest scars from this encounter? Explain your answer.

4. Both the cartoon and the poem deal with conflict over issues which have taken on great importance in the minds of the people involved. Why is one amusing and the other one not amusing?

A PROFESSIONAL WRITER AT WORK

The following excerpt from the book *The Content of Our Character,* by Shelby Steele, a San Jose State University English professor, was first published in *Harper's* magazine. In it Steele analyzes the problems that African-American and white college students currently face as they struggle to achieve their own identities while trying to live up to society's expectations.

Since the issues Steele raises are alive on almost every college campus in the United States, you will probably discover that you have already thought about—or dealt with—some of them. Ask yourself, as you read, what you think are the causes and effects of these problems. Your view may be very different from that expressed by Steele or by the people he quotes, but as a college student, you are well qualified to explore these questions and to arrive at conclusions of your own about this issue.

The Recoloring of Campus Life

1   In the past few years, we have witnessed what the National Institute Against Prejudice and Violence calls a "proliferation" of racial incidents on college campuses around the country. The nature of these incidents has ranged from open racial violence—most notoriously, the beating of a black student at the University of Massachusetts at Amherst after an argument about the World Series turned into a racial bashing, with a crowd of up to 3000 whites chasing twenty blacks—to the harassment of minority students, to acts of racial or ethnic insensitivity, with by far the greatest number falling in the last two categories. At Dartmouth College, three editors of the *Dartmouth Review,* the off-campus right-wing student weekly, were suspended for harassing a black professor in his lecture hall. At Yale University a swastika and the words "white power" were painted on the school's Afro-American cultural center. Racist jokes were aired on a campus radio station at the University of Michigan. And at the University of Wisconsin at Madison, pledges painted their faces black and wore Afro wigs. Two weeks after the president of Stanford University informed the incoming freshman class that "bigotry is out, and I mean it," two freshmen defaced a poster of Beethoven—gave the image thick lips—and hung it on a black student's door.

2   In response, black students around the country have rediscovered the militant protest strategies of the Sixties. At the University of Massachusetts at Amherst, Williams College, Penn State University, UC Berkeley, UCLA, Stanford, and countless other campuses, black students have sat in, marched, and rallied. But much of what they were marching and rallying about seemed less a response to specific racial incidents than a call for broader action on the part of the colleges and universities they were attending. Black students have demanded everything from more black faculty members and new courses on racism to the addition of "ethnic" foods in the cafeteria. There is the sense in these demands that racism runs deep.

3   Of course, universities are not where racial problems tend to arise. When I went to college in the mid-Sixties, colleges were oases of calm and understanding in a racially tense society; campus life—with its traditions of tolerance and fairness, its very distance from the "real" world—imposed a degree of broad-mindedness on even the most provincial students. If I met whites who were not anxious to be friends with blacks, most were at least vaguely friendly to the cause of our freedom. In any case, there was not guerilla activity against our presence, no "mine field of racism" (as one black student at Berkeley recently put it) to negotiate. I wouldn't say that the phrase "campus racism" is a contradiction in terms, but until recently it certainly seemed an incongruence.

4   But a greater incongruence is the generational timing of this new problem on the campuses. Today's undergraduates were born after the passage of the 1964 Civil Rights Act. They grew up in an age when racial equality was for the first time enforceable by law. This too was a time when blacks suddenly ap-

228

**WRITING AND
NEWTON'S
LAWS:
CAUSE AND
EFFECT**

peared on television, as mayors of big cities, as icons of popular culture, as teachers, and in some cases even as neighbors. Today's black and white college students, veterans of *Sesame Street* and often of integrated grammar and high schools, have had more opportunities to know each other—whites and blacks—than any previous generation in American history. Not enough opportunities, perhaps, but enough to make the notion of racial tension on campus something of a mystery, at least to me. To try to unravel this mystery I left my own campus where there have been few signs of racial tension, and talked with black and white students at California schools where racial incidents had occurred: Stanford, UCLA, Berkeley. I spoke with black and white students—and not with Asians and Hispanics—because, as always, blacks and whites represent the deepest lines of division, and because I hesitate to wander onto the complex territory of other minority groups. A phrase by William H. Gass—''the hidden internality of things''—describes with maybe a little too much grandeur what I hoped to find. But it is what I wanted to find, for this is the kind of problem that makes a black person nervous, which is not to say that it doesn't unnerve whites as well. Once every six months or so someone yells ''nigger'' at me from a passing car. I don't like to think that these solo artists might soon make up a chorus, or, worse, that this chorus might one day soon sing to me from the paths of my own campus.

5   I have long believed that trouble between the races is seldom what it appears to be. It was not hard to see after my first talks with students that racial tension on campus is a problem that misrepresents itself. It has the same look, the archetypal pattern, of America's timeless racial conflict—white racism and black protest. And I think part of our concern over it comes from the fact that it has the feel of relapse, illness gone and come again. But if we are seeing the same symptoms, I don't believe we are dealing with the same illness. For one thing, I think racial tension on campus is the result more of racial equality than inequality.

6   How to live with racial difference has been America's profound social problem. For the first 100 years or so following emancipation it was controlled by a legally sanctioned inequality that acted as a buffer between the races. No longer is this the case. On campuses today, as throughout society, blacks enjoy equality under the law—a profound social advancement. No student may be kept out of a class or a dormitory or an extracurricular activity because of his or her own race. But there is a paradox here: On a campus where members of all races are gathered, mixed together in the classroom as well as socially, differences are more exposed than ever. And this is where the trouble starts. For members of each race—young adults coming into their own, often away from home for the first time—bring to this site of freedom, exploration, and now, today, equality very deep fears and anxieties, inchoate feelings of racial shame, anger, and guilt. These feelings could lie dormant in the home, in familiar neighborhoods, in simpler days of childhood. But the college campus, with its structure of interaction and adult-level competition—the big exam, the dorm, the ''mixer''—is another matter. I think campus racism is born of the rub between racial difference and a setting, the campus itself, devoted to interaction and equality. On our campuses, such concentrated micro-societies, all that remains unresolved between blacks and whites, all the old wounds

and shames that have never been addressed, present themselves for attention—and present our youth with pressures they cannot always handle.

7   I have mentioned one paradox: racial fears and anxieties among blacks and whites bubbling up in an era of racial equality under the law, in settings that are among the freest and fairest in society. And there is another, related paradox, stemming from the notion of—and practice of—affirmative action. Under the provision of the Equal Employment Opportunity Act of 1972, all state governments and institutions (including universities) were forced to initiate plans to increase the proportion of minority and women employees—in the case of universities, of students too. Affirmative action plans that establish racial quotas were ruled unconstitutional more than ten years ago in *University of California Regents v. Bakke.* But quotas are only the most controversial aspect of affirmative action; the principle of affirmative action is reflected in various university programs aimed at redressing and overcoming past patterns of discrimination. Of course, to be conscious of patterns of discrimination—the fact, say, that public schools in the black inner cities are more crowded and employ fewer top-notch teachers than white suburban public schools, and that this is a factor in student performance—is only reasonable. However, in doing this we also call attention quite obviously to difference: in the case of blacks and whites, racial difference. What has emerged on campus in recent years—as a result of the new equality and affirmative action, in a sense, as a result of progress—is a *politics of difference,* a troubling, volatile politics in which each group justifies itself, its sense of worth and its pursuit of power, through difference alone.

8   I would like, first, to discuss black students, their anxieties and vulnerabilities. The accusation that black Americans have always lived with is that they are inferior—inferior simply because they are black. And this accusation has been too uniform, too ingrained in cultural imagery, too enforced by law, custom, and every form of power not to have left a mark. Black inferiority was a precept accepted by the founders of this nation; it was a principle of social organization that relegated blacks to the sidelines of American life. So when today's young black students find themselves on white campuses, surrounded by those who historically have claimed superiority, they are also surrounded by the myth of their inferiority.

9   Of course it is true that many young people come to college with some anxiety about not being good enough. But only blacks come wearing a color that is still, in the minds of some, a sign of inferiority. Poles, Jews, Hispanics, and other groups also endure degrading stereotypes. But two things make the myth of black inferiority a far heavier burden—the broadness of its scope and its incarnation in color. There are not only more stereotypes of blacks than of other groups, but these stereotypes are also more dehumanizing, more focused on the most despised of human traits—stupidity, laziness, sexual immorality, dirtiness, and so on. In America's racial and ethnic hierarchy, blacks have clearly been relegated to the lowest level—have been burdened with an ambiguous, animalistic humanity. Moreover, this is made unavoidable for blacks by the sheer visibility of black skin, a skin that evokes the myth of inferiority on sight. And today this myth is sadly reinforced for many black students by affirmative action programs, under which blacks may often enter

college with lower test scores and high-school grade point averages than whites. "They see me as an affirmative action case," one black student told me at UCLA.

10 So when a black student enters college, the myth of inferiority compounds the normal anxiousness over whether he or she will be good enough. This anxiety is not only personal but also racial. The families of these students will have pounded into them the fact that blacks are not inferior. And probably more than anything, it is this pounding that finally leaves a mark. If I am not inferior, why the need to say so?

11 This myth of inferiority constitutes a very sharp and ongoing anxiety for young blacks, the nature of which is very precise: It is the terror that somehow, through one's actions or by virtue of some "proof" (a poor grade, a flubbed response in class), one's fear of inferiority—inculcated in ways large and small by society—will be confirmed as real. On a university campus, where intelligence itself is the ultimate measure, this anxiety is bound to be triggered.

12 A black student I met at UCLA was disturbed a little when I asked him if he ever felt vulnerable—anxious about "black inferiority"—as a black student. But after a long pause, he finally said, "I think I do." The example he gave was of a large lecture class he'd taken with more than 300 students. Fifty or so black students sat in the back of the lecture hall and "acted out every stereotype in the book." They were loud, ate food, came in late—and generally got lower grades than the whites in the class. "I knew I would be seen like them, and I didn't like it. I never sat by them." Seen like what? I asked, though we both knew the answer. "As lazy, ignorant, and stupid," he said sadly.

13 Had the group at the back been white fraternity brothers, they would not have been seen as dumb *whites,* of course. And a frat brother who worried about his grades would not worry that he would be seen "like them." The terror in this situation for the student I spoke with was that his own deeply buried anxiety would be given credence, that the myth would be verified, and that he would feel shame and humiliation not because of who he was but simply because he was black. In this lecture hall his race, quite apart from his performance, might subject him to four unendurable feelings—diminishment, accountability to the preconceptions of whites, a powerlessness to change those preconceptions, and, finally, shame. These are the feelings that make up his racial anxiety, and that of all blacks on any campus. On a white campus a black is never far from these feelings, and even his unconscious knowledge that he is subject to them can undermine his self-esteem. There are blacks on every campus who are not up to doing good college-level work. Certain black students may not be happy or motivated or in the appropriate field of study—*just like whites.* Moreover, many more blacks than whites are not quite prepared for college, may have to catch up, owing to factors beyond their control: poor previous schooling, for example. But the white who has to catch up will not be anxious that his being behind is a matter of his whiteness, of his being *racially* inferior. The black student may well have such a fear.

14 This, I believe, is one reason why black colleges in America turn out 34

percent of all black college graduates, though they enroll only 17 percent of black college students. Without whites around on campus the myth of inferiority is in abeyance and, along with it, a great reservoir of culturally imposed self-doubt. On black campuses feelings of inferiority are personal; on campuses with a white majority, a black's problems have a way of becoming a "black" problem.

15   But this feeling of vulnerability a black may feel in itself is not as serious a problem as what he or she does with it. To admit that one is made anxious in integrated situations about the myth of racial inferiority is difficult for young blacks. It seems like admitting that one is racially inferior. And so, most often, the student will deny harboring those feelings. This is where some of the pangs of racial tension begin, because denial always involves distortion.

16   In order to deny a problem we must tell ourselves that the problem is something different than what it really is. A black student at Berkeley told me that he felt defensive every time he walked into a class and saw mostly white faces. When I asked why, he said, "Because I know they're all racists. They think blacks are stupid." Of course it may be true that some whites feel this way, but the singular focus on white racism allows this student to obscure his own underlying racial anxiety. He can now say that his problem—facing a class full of white faces, *fearing* that they think he is dumb—is entirely the result of certifiable white racism and has nothing to do with his own anxieties, or even that this particular academic subject may not be his best. Now all the terror of his anxiety, its powerful energy, is devoted to simply *seeing* racism. Whatever evidence of racism he finds—and looking this hard, he will no doubt find some—can be brought in to buttress his distorted view of the problem, while his actual deep-seated anxiety goes unseen.

17   This process generates an unconscious need to exaggerate the level of racism on campus—to make it a matter of the system, not just a handful of students. Racism is the avenue away from the true inner anxiety. How many students demonstrating for a black "theme house"—demonstrating in the style of the Sixties, when the battle was to win for blacks a place on campus—might be better off spending their time reading and studying? Black students have the highest dropout rate and lowest grade point average of any group in American universities. This need not be so. And it is not the result of not having black theme houses.

18   Race is, by any standard, an unprincipled source of power. And on campuses the use of racial power by one group makes racial or ethnic or gender *difference* a currency of power for all groups. When I make my difference into power, other groups must seize upon their difference to contain my power and maintain their position relative to me. Very quickly a kind of politics of difference emerges in which racial, ethnic, and gender groups are forced to assert their entitlement and vie for power based on the single quality that makes them different from one another.

19   This politics of difference makes everyone on campus a member of a minority group. It also makes racial tensions inevitable. To highlight one's difference as a source of advantage is also, indirectly, to inspire the enemies of that difference. When blackness (and femaleness) becomes power, then

232

**WRITING AND
NEWTON'S
LAWS:
CAUSE AND
EFFECT**

white maleness is also sanctioned as power. A white male student at Stanford told me, "One of my friends said the other day that we should get together and start up a white student union and come up with a list of demands."

20   It is certainly true that white maleness has long been an unfair source of power. But the sin of white male power is precisely its use of race and gender as a source of entitlement. When minorities and women use their race, ethnicity, and gender in the same way, they not only commit the same sin but also, indirectly, sanction the very form of power that oppressed them in the first place. The politics of difference is based on a tit-for-tat sort of logic in which every victory only calls one's enemies to arms.

21   This elevation of difference undermines the communal impulse by making each group foreign and inaccessible to others. When difference is celebrated rather than remarked, people must think in terms of difference, they must find meaning in difference, and this meaning comes from an endless process of contrasting one's group with other groups. Blacks use whites to define themselves as different, women use men, Hispanics use whites and blacks, and on it goes. And in the process each group mythologizes and mystifies its difference, puts it beyond the full comprehension of outsiders. Difference becomes an inaccessible preciousness toward which outsiders are expected to be simply and uncomprehendingly reverential. But beware: In this world, even the insulated world of the college campus, preciousness is a balloon asking for a needle. At Smith College, graffiti appears: "Niggers, Spics, and Chinks quit complaining or get out."

22   Most of the white students I talked with spoke as if from under a faint cloud of accusation. There was always a ring of defensiveness in their complaints about blacks. A white student I spoke with at UCLA told me: "Most white students on this campus think the black student leadership here is made up of oversensitive crybabies who spend all their time looking for things to kick up a ruckus about." A white student at Stanford said: "Blacks do nothing but complain and ask for sympathy when everyone really knows they don't do well because they don't try. If they worked harder, they could do as well as everyone else."

23   That these students felt accused was most obvious in their compulsion to assure me that they were not racists. Oblique versions of some-of-my-best-friends-are stories came ritualistically before or after critiques of black students. Some said flatly, "I am not a racist, but . . ." Of course, we all deny being racists, but we only do this compulsively, I think, when we are working against an accusation of bias. I think it was the color of my skin, itself, that accused them.

24   This was the meta-message that surrounded these conversations like an aura, and in it, I believe, is the core of the white American racial anxiety. My skin not only accused them, it judged them. And this judgment was a sad gift of history that brought them to account whether they deserved such an accounting or not. It said that wherever and whenever blacks were concerned, they had reason to feel guilt. And whether it was earned or unearned, I think it was guilt that set off the compulsion in these students to disclaim. I believe it is true that in America black people make white people feel guilty.

25   Guilt is the essence of white anxiety, just as inferiority is the essence of

black anxiety. And the terror that it carries for whites is the terror of discovering that one has reason to feel guilt where blacks are concerned—not so much because of what blacks might think but because of what guilt can say about oneself. If the darkest fear of blacks is inferiority, the darkest fear of whites is that their better lot in life is at least partially the result of their capacity for evil—their capacity to dehumanize an entire people for their own benefit, and then to be indifferent to the devastation their dehumanization has wrought on successive generations of their victims. This is the terror that whites are vulnerable to regarding blacks. And the mere fact of being white is sufficient to feel it, since even whites with hearts clean of racism benefit from being white—benefit at the expense of blacks. This is a conditional guilt having nothing to do with individual intentions or actions. And it makes for a very powerful anxiety because it threatens whites with a view of themselves as inhuman, just as inferiority threatens blacks with a similar view of themselves. At the dark core of both anxieties is a suspicion of incomplete humanity.

26   So the white students I met were not just meeting me; they were also meeting the possibility of their own inhumanity. And this, I think, is what explains how some young white college students can so frankly take part in racially insensitive and outright racist acts. They were expected to be cleaner of racism than any previous generation—they were born into the Great Society. But this expectation overlooks the fact that for them, color is still an accusation and judgment. In black faces there is a discomforting reflection of white collective shame. Blacks remind them that their racial innocence is questionable, that they are the beneficiaries of past and present racism, and that the sins of the father may well have been visited on the children.

27   The politics of difference sets up a struggle for innocence among all groups. When difference is the currency of power, each group must fight for the innocence that entitles it to power. Blacks sting whites with guilt, remind them of their racist past, accuse them of new and more subtle forms of racism. One way whites retrieve their innocence is to discredit blacks and deny their difficulties, for in this denial is the denial of their own guilt. To blacks this denial looks like racism, a racism that feeds black innocence and encourages them to throw more guilt at whites. And so the cycle continues. The politics of difference leads each group to pick at the sore spots of the other.

For Thought and Discussion

1. What is the central cause of all of the issues discussed by Shelby Steele?

2. What are the major effects of racism on black students? On white students?

3. Describe the "politics of difference." How does this manifest itself in the subgroup to which you belong? How is your group set apart from all others?

4. According to Steele, the politics of difference leads to a sense of "racial innocence" among members of all groups. What does he mean by

234

WRITING AND
NEWTON'S
LAWS:
CAUSE AND
EFFECT

this term? Give an example, either from the article or from your own experience.

5. Which of the behaviors Steele describes are, in your opinion, deliberately cruel, and which are the result simply of carelessness?

6. How is the present-day college campus different from that of the sixties in terms of race relations?

7. In what ways is your campus similar to those described by Steele? Do you have "micro-societies" which end up dividing students and creating competition? Discuss your answer.

8. Why, in Steele's opinion, do black colleges have an advantage over others in helping black students to succeed?

9. How, in your opinion, can the generation of young people now in college work toward solutions of the problems Steele describes?

 ## REVISING YOUR ESSAY FOR CLARITY AND MEANING

There is little reason to write for an audience if you do not make your meaning clear and if you do not have a fresh insight, a new perspective, or new information to offer. While this may seem obvious on the face of it, the tendency of many student writers is to consider meaning—if they consider it at all—only after they have considered such factors as spelling, grammar, and sentence structure. Yet, the best-spelled, most grammatically correct essays in the world will lie unread if they do not communicate their ideas with a sense of purpose and clarity.

After you have written the initial drafts of your essay, and after you know what you want to say and how you want to say it, you must edit your writing for clarity. Following are some of the factors you should consider during the revision process.

Be Specific

Use concrete details to avoid abstractions (see Chapter 2) whenever you write.

For example:
"There is a lot of racial tension on our campus" is an abstract statement that requires concrete support as in the following: "The racial tension on our campus is reflected in the graffiti on dorm walls, the fights that break out between groups of blacks and whites, and the inability of students to socialize with those from ethnic groups other than their own."

Be Clear

235

WRITING AND
NEWTON'S
LAWS:
CAUSE AND
EFFECT

It is often difficult to be objective about whether you have used too many, too few, or just the right number of words to express your meaning—especially after you have spent a great deal of time working on a piece of writing. This is where another reader in a peer editing session is particularly valuable. If possible, read the essay out loud to your peer editor.

For example:

Unclear: "Today's college students have had plenty of opportunity to know one another."

Corrected: "Today's black and white college students, veterans of *Sesame Street,* and often of integrated grammar and high schools, have had more opportunities to know each other—black and white—than any previous generation in American history" (Shelby Steele).

Be Concise

When you are evaluating your essay by yourself, you can read it aloud to catch *wordiness* (unnecessary repetition or the use of too many words to express an idea or to illustrate an example). In addition, you should evaluate each sentence for its ability to create a picture in the reader's mind. If you find that most of your sentences fail to be concise and clear, they are likely to be *anemic,* to lack vitality.

For example:

Wordy: "It has long been my belief that the problems and disagreements between blacks and whites in this country are radically different from what they appear to be on the surface."

Corrected: "I have long believed that trouble between the races is seldom what it appears to be" (Shelby Steele).

Use Vivid Verbs

One of the best methods for overcoming anemic writing is to add active, vivid verbs. Remember that active verbs provide the energy for your sentences and can help to keep your readers awake and involved, while dull, lifeless verbs can put them to sleep.

For example:

Look at how Shelby Steele uses vivid verbs to make a point: "Blacks sting whites with guilt, remind them of their racist past, accuse them of new

236

WRITING AND
NEWTON'S
LAWS:
CAUSE AND
EFFECT

and more subtle forms of racism." The words *sting* and *accuse* move the readers, however they feel about the issue Steele discusses. If Steele had simply said, "Blacks make whites feel guilty about their racism, past and present," the passage would not carry the same impact.

Use Simple, Direct Verbs

Verbs do not need to be complicated. Use the simplest forms possible, for example, *sting* instead of *had been stinging.* All of those special tenses with their shades of meaning are just that—special. Save them for special occasions.

Also remember to pay attention to which tense you are using, and be consistent. Many students forget to notice verb tenses, and will switch from past to present to conditional without realizing it.

For example:

In the example from Shelby Steele in the preceding section, notice that all three of the verbs—*sting, remind,* and *accuse*—are in the present tense, and that part of their power lies in the implication that the action is taking place *now.*

Use Active Verbs

Whenever you use verbs accompanied by *would* and *could,* you are slowing down the action of your sentence. Ask yourself if this is the effect you want to create. Use the simple present and past tenses, as Steele does in the following passages.

For example:

> If the darkest fear of blacks is inferiority, the darkest fear of whites is that their better lot in life is at least partially the result of their capacity for evil— their capacity to dehumanize an entire people for their own benefit, and then to be indifferent to the devastation their dehumanization has wrought on successive generations of their victims.

This is a bold statement, and if he had been less courageous, Steele might have tried to hide behind his verbs and tone down its impact by using less active verbs, as in the following revision:

> The darkest fear of blacks could be inferiority, and the darkest fear of whites could be that their better lot in life might be at least partially the result of their capacity for evil.

Use the Passive Voice Appropriately

237

**WRITING AND
NEWTON'S
LAWS:
CAUSE AND
EFFECT**

The passive voice avoids making anyone or anything responsible for the action in the sentence. Sometimes this is the effect you want to create in an essay, but many times it is not.

> *For example:*
> "At Yale University a swastika and the words 'white power' were painted on the school's Afro-American cultural center" uses the passive voice appropriately because neither Steele nor his sources know who committed that act.

In most of your writing, the subject should be the primary focus of a sentence because the passive voice can cause unnecessary drag on your message. When Shelby Steele says, "Blacks use whites to define themselves as different, women use men, Hispanics use whites and blacks, and on it goes," he is providing energy and economy to the sentence. If Steele had used the passive voice, he would have distanced the actions from the actors, and the sentence might have read, "Whites are used by blacks to define themselves as different, men are used by women, whites and blacks are used by Hispanics, and so on." Such use of the passive voice bores your readers.

However, if you are writing for a technical, scientific, or social science class, you may be instructed to use the passive voice, as in the following from a manual on wildlife restraint: "The decision whether to use chemical or physical restraint is based on the skill of the handlers, facilities available, and the psychological and physical needs of the species to be restrained. No formula can be given." *Who* makes the decision or *who* gives the formula is not important; rather, the factors leading to those decisions are of primary importance.

Use Adjectives and Adverbs with Care

Adjectives and adverbs are wonderful when they help you describe, but they lead to wordiness and slow down the action when they are overused.

> *For example:*
> Shelby Steele uses two powerful adjectives effectively when he writes, "In America's racial and ethnic hierarchy, blacks have clearly been relegated to the lowest level—have been burdened with an ambiguous, animalistic humanity." Would the sentence have been as effective without "*ambiguous, animalistic* humanity"? Not only are these adjectives alliterative, but the words themselves speak to the terrible dilemma of blacks who find themselves the objects of racist literature on the one hand and the symbols of America's success in integrating its universities on the other. Additional

adjectives would have diluted the impact of those two carefully chosen words.

Vary Your Sentences

Your sentences should provide variety, both in rhythm and length. Combine some sentences, using parallelism to blend ideas, as Shelby Steele does in the following sentence: "In this context, racial, ethnic, and gender differences become forms of sovereignty, campuses become balkanized, and each group fights with whatever means are available."

For contrast, find some sentences that you can make short and dramatic, as Steele does when he follows a long discussion of stereotypes of black and white students with "The black student may well have such a fear." This kind of variation will keep your reader awake, curious, and interested.

For example:

In the following paragraph taken from Shelby Steele's essay, notice the way in which he has varied sentence length in order to emphasize his point that students who demonstrate for theme houses may be missing what is truly important for their own progress:

> This process generates an unconscious need to exaggerate the level of racism on campus—to make it a matter of the system, not just a handful of students. Racism is the avenue away from the true inner anxiety. How many students demonstrating for a black "theme house"—demonstrating in the style of the Sixties, when the battle was to win for blacks a place on campus—might be better off spending their time reading and studying? Black students have the highest dropout rate and lowest grade point average of any group in American universities. This need not be so.

Your turn

Using an essay you have written for a previous assignment, find an example of one of the following problems requiring editing. Revise the passage, paying close attention to the guidelines given above:

1. For a passage that is too abstract: Rewrite it, adding details that will make it more concrete.

2. For a sentence or a passage that is wordy: Make it concise.

3. For a description that lacks vitality and that fails to create a mental picture for the reader: Revise it, providing active, vivid verbs and descriptive adjectives.

4. For a paragraph in which the sentences tend to be of the same length: Rewrite it, combining some sentences, and see if you can add one sentence that is very short to create a dramatic impact.

Choose a topic from the following suggestions and begin by clustering, freewriting, and brainstorming about that topic. Use key questions to help discover the cause-effect relationships, limit your topic, and generate and organize your ideas. Then read at least two articles in a periodical about the issue you have chosen (remember to use the *Reader's Guide* or the on-line data base in the library to locate your articles). Be careful to avoid using *post hoc* fallacies, and remember to limit your subject adequately so that you can develop your thesis with specific examples.

Write an essay of at least 600 to 800 words in which you answer the following key questions: What caused this circumstance? What is the effect of this circumstance?

Suggestions for Topics

Here are some suggestions for topics:

Racism on campus
Campus microsocieties
Homelessness in America
Child abuse
Environmental degradation
Decline of U.S. social services
Alcohol and drug abuse
School dropout incidence
Prejudice of one ethnic group toward another

Peer Editing Checklist

After your peer editing group has practiced peer editing on "Crybabies" (reprinted in the following section), it should go to work with the papers written by group members. Make enough photocopies of your essay for your peer editing group.

1. Indicate any ideas, passages, imagery, allusions, or other aspects of this essay you found effective. Positive reinforcement is a powerful tool.

2. What is the central point this essay illustrates? What is the cause-effect relationship?

3. List the concrete details that develop the central point.

4. Point out any places where you do not understand how the essay illustrates the central point.

240

**WRITING AND
NEWTON'S
LAWS:
CAUSE AND
EFFECT**

5. Ask the author about any concrete details you would like to know to strengthen or clarify the central point.

6. Examine the cause-effect relationship in the essay, making sure that it is clearly identified and fully explained.

7. Point out any verbs that need to be simpler, livelier, or more vivid.

8. Indicate whether the writer has varied the sentences. If all of the sentences in the essay are approximately the same length, encourage the writer to revise for variety.

9. What is your reaction to the essay's title? Does the title help you better understand the author's point, or does the title pique your interest in reading the essay?

When writers have revised the content of the essay to their satisfaction and are ready for feedback about mechanics, point out but do not correct any problems you suspect with spelling, grammar, and punctuation. It is the writer's responsibility to make such corrections.

Help! For Further Work

Read the following student draft as if you were its peer editor. Then respond to the points in the peer editing checklist.

Crybabies

1   Americans, living under better conditions than those of any other society in history, often find themselves unhappy over very minor annoyances. Under analysis, the main scource of this unhappiness is created, first, by our tendency to demand too much out of life, and, second, from emotional softness.

2   According to Dr. James Dobson, a child psychologist, Americans' emotional stability is based directly on what we expect out of life. For instance, Americans find themselves upset over cloudy days, cold weather, imperfect fruit, and waiting in heavy traffic. When one goes to the store for apples, building up an expectation for shiny, firm, bright, red apples, but finds only those that are bruised and imperfect, he will likely reject them. For some people, the disappointment in not being able to bring home perfect apples, as planned, creates unhappiness, despite the fact that there is really nothing "wrong" in the person's life.

3   Such disappointments can apply to emotions, as well. For example, women's magazines will feature beautiful models who have spent hours preparing for each photograph. Young women will buy the magazines, hoping that the articles inside will help them to improve their own looks. They expect that, magically, they will be able to look just like the model in the picture. John Ciardi, in an article in *The Saturday Review* calls advertising such as this "the dream of perfect beauty." Staring into the mirror with a brush and a tube of lipstick, girls will become very emotionally upset when they fail.

4   Emotional softness also plays a major role in the depression of Americans.

241

WRITING AND
NEWTON'S
LAWS:
CAUSE AND
EFFECT

By being prosperous, Americans have become soft to simple dilemmas, whereas adversity would breed toughness. For instance, the necessity to wait in line for something we need or want. During the gasoline shortage of the 1970's, long lines would form at the gas stations and the people who were waiting became tremendously agitated and upset with one another. It was not uncommon for those who were waiting to verbally abuse or physically assault someone who cut in line; one man was shot for cutting ahead of someone in Southern California. But even Santa Claus can bring out the worst in people. There was a case in Ohio where people were waiting in line to have their children's pictures taken on Santa's lap and the father of one child was shot in a dispute about his place in line. The extra few minutes' waiting caused by someone else's selfishness is intolerable to many Americans, because we have been conditioned to expect to get what we want when we want it. We are soft because of our prosperity as we can't stand to wait five minutes in a fast food store or work ten minutes overtime, etc.

5   Unhappiness has arisen from high expectations and emotional softness, but with some effort, Americans, like people in other countries, can learn to overcome this impatience and the ensuing sense of frustration and depression. An effort can be seen in this quote from Dr. Dobson about the British in World War II. "At England's darkest moment in history, when it looked as if she would fall that night to the Germans, someone wrote the song, 'There'll be blue birds over the White Cliffs of Dover tomorrow—just you wait and see.' " This person had a very good reason to be unhappy, but even at one of the bleakest moments this person had probably ever known, hope was found. It sounds corny to us now, but in desperate times, such slogans as these were enough to give people the patience and courage to continue their efforts against the Germans. When I find myself frustrated over a simple dilemma, I think of what all I have to be thankful for. Americans have so much to be thankful for, but yet they often focus on the unimportant details of life and become depressed over them.

6   Americans demand so much out of life, and combined with their already prosperous life styles, they still find themselves depressed much of the time. Our tendency to become depressed often has its roots in the truly insignificant "problems" that arise and the unrealistic expectations we have about their solutions. Hopefully, as we become more mature as a nation, we will learn to accept the fact that adversity is a normal and predictable part of life, and that there is always a positive way to deal with any situation. For instance, when I know I'm going to be in a long line, I put a book in my pocket. I can put in a lot of study time while I'm waiting!

STUDENT STARS

The students who wrote these essays did the following:

1. Prewriting
2. Writing

3. Revision of content

4. Proofreading and revision of mechanics

Save the Whales

1   Increasingly, man is becoming aware that seemingly insignificant actions by individuals can have cumulative effects that impact the entire planet. One example is that of the gray whales which can be seen off the California coast every year on their long migrations between Baja California and their summer feeding grounds in the Arctic. While scientists and laymen alike have been observing the whales for decades, marveling at their size, grace, and power, only now are we beginning to understand what it is in the Arctic that attracts them and inspires their great journey.

2   As the grays start to travel from Baja, the long, Arctic winter comes to an end. During the winter a remarkable process took place that will provide food for the whales and their young all summer long. As the sea water began to freeze and ice crystals formed, sea salt was forced from the ice into the surrounding unfrozen water. The crystals connected and eventually closed off pockets of salty water which become even smaller and more saline. Because of its increased salinity in these pockets, the water did not freeze, even when the temperature dropped below twenty-eight degrees. Although it had long been thought that nothing could live in such a brine, a recent study has disproved this.

3   By the end of winter, when the whales start to arrive, these very salty, cold pockets in the ice are teeming with microorganisms. As summer approaches, the packed ice begins to melt and the small pockets join those nearby to form larger pools which eventually dump into the ocean, dispersing their bounty and providing the small, shrimplike Arctic krill—the whales' main summer food source—with more than enough to eat. In turn, the result is a krill population explosion that peaks at just about the time the whales arrive from the south, supplying the whales and their offspring with abundant food during the calving season and in preparation for the return trip south.

4   This is a delicate and intricate system of coexistence that has developed over thousands of years. This precious balance and hold on life could easily be upset by man. Acid rain can pollute the pack ice and interrupt the little-understood life cycle of the brine pockets. An oil spill could wipe out the entire system and endanger the whales more than the whaling industry ever did.

5   The point is not so much that we "save the whales" or abide by any of the other trite sayings that we see on bumper stickers, but that we realize the long-term and global effects of our actions. This is only one example of an ecosystem that is endangered by man's ignorance and inaction. We have to understand that every time we start our cars, or vote (or don't vote) there are consequences. Until we realize this and begin to make some changes, the whales and every other living thing, including humans, are endangered.

—Daniel M. Swain

Life in the Slow Lane

1   It is 6:30 p.m. on Friday night, and here I sit with my life at a complete standstill. I am not going anywhere—literally—as I am stuck in rush-hour

traffic in San Jose. The mass of cars lined bumper-to-bumper and side-to-side across the freeway for as far as I can see—with everyone trying to go someplace in the fastest time—inches along, unable to get anyone anywhere in a hurry, and giving me plenty of time to sulk about living in a society with such a dysfunctional transportation system.

2   I ponder the acres of gleaming metal around me, wondering what has caused this dysfunction. I can't believe that we, so wealthy and technologically advanced, are unable to get ourselves from Point A to Point B without a major hassle. My mind runs over the genesis of this problem, back to the 1950s when the United States, instead of investing money in the kind of effective rail system that Europe has used for so many years, put its money and manpower into a massive highway construction program with the intention of providing Americans with a convenient mode of transportation that was thought to be superior to that of European countries.

3   This system harnessed the nation to the automobile and oil industries, but nobody minded because gasoline was cheap and cars provided a lot more than simple transportation. They symbolized status, freedom, and the kind of absolute individuality that our pioneer ancestors cherished. In addition, the highway-auto system promoted the growth of suburbs because of the ease and speed with which we could get from place to place. Our transportation system worked well for a while, as population pressures were not a problem in most areas, but when the massive increase in drivers began to crowd the highways and gasoline became scarce and expensive, the bottom fell out of our modern transportation network and the system began to fall apart. Now, of course, the large number of cars is a major contributor to air pollution, and the cost of maintaining the large network of highways is an enormous burden on the taxpayer.

4   It wasn't until I traveled throughout Europe on the rail system that I experienced the wonderful alternative to our foolish and extravagant highway system. I was able to ride the train from city to city, and when I arrived at my destinations, I found that the train stations were always in the center of the city; often, I could walk to my hotel and to the major sightseeing attractions. If I had to travel more than a few blocks to my destination, I could catch a bus or a subway car right at the train station and get door-to-door service to my destination.

5   After being exposed to such a convenient and effective system of transportation, I realized how much the people of the United States have been fooled into thinking that our dysfunctional automobile-highway system is functional. Now, as I sit here surrounded by other victims of the system, having moved perhaps ten feet in the last two or three minutes, I wonder how we can get out of this bind and create for ourselves a transportation system that works.

—Jane O'Loughlin Uribe

9 DISCOVERING IDEAS BY COMPARING AND CONTRASTING ALTERNATIVES

CONCEPTS TO LEARN

Discovering and organizing ideas by asking these key questions:

How is X like Y?

How is X different from Y?

For many subjects, an effective method of discovering a point and organizing your development of that point is to compare two alternatives using these key questions: *How is X like Y? How is X different from Y?*

Frequently the ideas generated by such questions go far beyond the two alternatives being compared. For example, consider Thomas Jefferson's statement: "Were it left to me to decide whether we should have a government without newspapers, or newspapers without a government, I should not hesitate a moment to prefer the latter."

In view of his political activity, Jefferson's statement seems surprising. Certainly he was a strong supporter of the United States government. After all, he had a key role in the formulation of that government as the author of the Declaration of Independence; furthermore, he filled numerous important offices ranging from governor of Virginia to third president of the United States. Let's examine Jefferson's statement using this chapter's key questions as a guide: How is government like the media (in Jefferson's case, newspapers)? How is government different from the media? Using directed freewriting we can further explore the answers to these questions.

Clearly the media is an important force in informing citizens; in a democracy the media controls most of the information the citizens get. Those who control information clearly hold the key to determining opinions, and hence ultimately they control action. In a war, if all citizens hear is how glorious the victories are and how evil the enemy is, few of those citizens will oppose the war. On the other hand, if the citizens come to believe that the war is exacting a terrible price in human suffering and the enemy is after all quite human, then citizen support for the war will erode. During the Vietnam era, for example, the media carried photographs and videotape of children seared with napalm, and Americans saw dead and wounded soldiers. Many historians suggest that such media coverage ultimately inflamed public opposition to the war and forced the government to withdraw from Vietnam.

For Thought and Discussion

1. If Jefferson had known about television, do you think he would have extended his statement to include it? Support your answer by considering the impact that television news has on public opinion.

2. Working in peer groups, use any or all of the idea-generating and organizing techniques covered thus far in this text to respond to the following:

a. List the kinds of media that help create public opinion in our society.

b. How would the lack of a free media affect an otherwise democratic government?

c. What kinds of changes can a free media help to bring about in a democratic society? Give historic or contemporary examples of how public opinion changed in our laws or governmental policies.

d. What problems does a free media create?

e. Select the two media types you think have the greatest influence on public opinion. What is the difference in their impact?

 COMPARISON AND CONTRAST: YOUR PURPOSE AND YOUR POINT

Comparing and contrasting is not just an academic exercise. We use this technique frequently in our personal lives, and we often must make comparisons at work and at school. Which television program should we watch? Which job should we take? Which person should we hire? We frequently choose and urge others to choose between two alternatives.

One of the ways we measure the quality of things—whether they be television shows or aardvarks—is by comparing and contrasting them to other similar things. Through such analysis, we can better understand both alternatives. If, for example, you want to know how effective aardvarks are at eliminating termites, you have to compare aardvarks with another method of eliminating termites, for example, a pest-exterminating company. Among

246

**DISCOVERING
IDEAS BY
COMPARING
AND
CONTRASTING
ALTERNATIVES**

the issues such a comparison would help to clarify are the following: What are the advantages and disadvantages of each method? Which method will have the best long-term result? Which method will wreak the least harm on the environment?

While exploring your ideas in a comparison-contrast framework, you might decide to compare and contrast the effects of two types of television programs. Your purpose might go far beyond merely comparing and contrasting the differences in the programs. Your purpose might be to persuade your audience of the superiority of a particular program or type of program. In your prewriting exploration it might occur to you that while some programs provide escape from reality, others help audiences better understand and deal with reality.

Or you might seek to explore the different impact of news coverage on television and in newspapers; such exploration might help you to discover a point about that difference. Because of your purpose, you might want to modify the key questions somewhat to read: What are the advantages and disadvantages of television news coverage? What are the advantages and disadvantages of newspaper news coverage?

Asking the key questions *How is X like Y? How is X different from Y?* can help you generate, understand, and organize your ideas. In addition, comparison and contrast are useful organizational patterns in an essay whose purpose is to persuade. You might, for example, compare and contrast opposing political candidates or the pros and cons of such issues as capital punishment, abortion, or U.S. military intervention in the Middle East or in Latin America. Or you might compare the results of two separate incidents involving U.S. military intervention.

Essay exams often ask students to compare and contrast such issues as the leadership styles of General Grant and General Lee during the Civil War, the impact of using biological controls against insect pests and the impact of using chemical pesticides, or the decision-making processes of President Bush and President Reagan.

Certainly the comparison-contrast questions are not the only tool you might use in focusing your thesis and generating and organizing ideas, but this chapter's key questions can be important allies in your battle to clarify your thinking and your writing. Like the answers to the key questions in previous chapters, then, the answers to these comparison-contrast questions are seldom goals in themselves. Rather, the questions provide a framework to help you generate ideas and organize your thinking.

Audience Awareness

A method we frequently use to tell people about the unfamiliar is to compare it to something with which they are familiar. In doing this—as in all writing—we must keep in mind our audience's interests and knowledge.

For example, if asked to describe a papaya to someone who had never seen or eaten one, we could say that it is shaped like a pear, but that the average papaya is twice as big as the average pear. The papaya tastes like a three-way cross between a cantaloupe, a peach, and an orange. Its texture is soft and slippery like a peach; however, a papaya is melonlike in that its skin is inedible.

So far we are using safe comparisons for the average audience. But what about the papaya seeds? They look like caviar, but they are larger than caviar—almost the size of small peas. While peas are a safe comparison, we must consider whether or not our audience will be familiar with the size of caviar. By considering what our audience knows and by using specific details of the known, we can introduce them to the unfamiliar.

Your turn

Make a list of comparison-contrast decisions you have have made—or might make—in your (1) personal life, (2) professional life, and (3) academic life.

For Thought and Discussion

Look at the accompanying cartoon, and then respond to the following:

1. Why does the bartender's expression differ from those of the four patrons? In what way does he represent a different type of audience for the speaker than for the patrons?

247

DISCOVERING
IDEAS BY
COMPARING
AND
CONTRASTING
ALTERNATIVES

"May I suggest, bartender, that instead of watching this silly sporting event we switch over to a rather important documentary now on Channel 13?"

248

**DISCOVERING
IDEAS BY
COMPARING
AND
CONTRASTING
ALTERNATIVES**

2. Contrast the speaker's purpose for viewing television with the purpose of the four other patrons.

News of the Past

Many bars and restaurants keep a television set in action to entertain patrons. And, as in the cartoon bar, sporting events often play on such television sets. After all, the purpose for which most people frequent bars and restaurants is entertainment, not education. However, like the best writing, the best educational programs often entertain while they educate.

Using comparison and contrast in "Newsreel," poet C. Day Lewis makes a powerful point about what happens when a society seeks only entertainment, only escape from reality, instead of information about reality. Before the advent of television news programs, newsreels—documentary-type news features—were common in movie theaters. Along with their main features, theaters ran their own version of the evening news. As you read "Newsreel," note the comparison and contrast between the society's view of the world and real events in that world.

Newsreel

Enter the dream-house, brothers and sisters, leaving
Your debts asleep, your history at the door:
This is the home for heroes, and this loving
Darkness a fur you can afford.   4

Fish in their tank electrically heated
Nose without envy the glass wall: for them
Clerk, spy, nurse, killer, prince, the great and the defeated,
Move in a mute day-dream.   8

Bathed in this common source, you gape incurious
At what your active hours have willed—
Sleep-walking on that silver wall, the furious
Sick shapes and pregnant fancies of your world.   12

There is the mayor opening the oyster season:
A society wedding: the autumn hats look swell:
An old crock's race, and a politician
In fishing waders to prove that all is well.   16

Oh, look at the warplanes! Screaming hysteric treble
In the long power-dive, like gannets they fall steep.
But what are they to trouble—
These silver shadows to trouble your watery, womb-deep sleep?   20

See the big guns, rising, groping, erected
To plant death in your world's soft womb.
Fire-bud, smoke-blossom, iron seed projected—
Are these exotics? They will grow nearer home: 24

Grow nearer home—and out of the dream-house stumbling
One night into a strangling air and the flung
Rags of children and thunder of stone niagaras tumbling,
You'll know you slept too long.

—C. Day Lewis

249

DISCOVERING
IDEAS BY
COMPARING
AND
CONTRASTING
ALTERNATIVES

For Thought and Discussion

1. In the first stanza, what attitude toward news does Day Lewis assume his audience has? What is the audience's purpose for watching the news?

2. What happens to the world during this newsreel? Why does it happen?

3. Explain the last line of the poem.

4. How does the world at the poem's end contrast with the world at the beginning?

5. Day Lewis does not actually state a thesis. If you were going to write an essay that tried to make a similar point to his, how would you state the thesis?

6. Drawing examples from contemporary events and television programing, cite support for your thesis from question 5.

7. Watch a television newscast. Give a specific example of the news program's effort to entertain as well as to educate its audience.

EXPLORING AND DEVELOPING IDEAS USING COMPARISON AND CONTRAST

If you want to know how effective a particular alternative is, you can explore your thoughts by comparing it with another alternative and asking the key comparison-contrast questions. With a basis for comparison, it is easier to judge and to communicate that judgment whether the subject be newspapers, television shows, instructors, careers, energy sources, or aardvarks.

If your *purpose* is to persuade your readers that a particular newspaper, instructor, career, energy source, or aardvark is superior to another, again, a comparison-contrast pattern will help you explore and organize your thinking.

Prewriting Techniques with Comparison and Contrast

Brainstorming in combination with the key questions is an effective tool for generating ideas in a comparison-contrast format. Let's look at how student Max Nguyen used comparison-contrast questions to help him generate, explore, and organize his ideas for an essay comparing two British newspapers: the *Sun* and the *Times of London*.

250

**DISCOVERING
IDEAS BY
COMPARING
AND
CONTRASTING
ALTERNATIVES**

As you read the following, notice that Max used comparison and contrast as both a creative brain method of generating ideas and a critical brain method of organizing ideas. Using the key questions, he brainstormed a list of categories to compare and contrast. Using his critical brain, he checked to make sure his ideas were balanced.

Inexperienced writers with sluggish critical or creative brains need to pay special attention to the role of each. However, as writers become more comfortable with the writing process, they move back and forth without really thinking about being in a critical or a creative mode. Note that as Max moved between his critical and creative brains, warning bells did not sound, red flags did not pop up. Instead he made the transition naturally and almost unconsciously.

How is the *Sun* like the *Times?*
   Both English newspapers
   Both therefore written for an English audience
   Both daily
   Both large circulation

How is the *Sun* different from the *Times?*

The *Times:*
   Formal
   Quality
   Reserved
   Accurate reporting important; just the facts folks
   Conventional, old-line quality—like *NY Times*
   Normal size, conventional photographs
   Discreet
   A 20th century Queen Victoria would basically approve
   The dignity of the Empire but realistic

The *Sun:*
   Sensational
   Topless photograph!
   Sensational headlines—Rudolph-found-in-meat-locker type
   Less serious, gossip stories; they must make these up—at least some of
      them
   Gullible, less educated audience
   The soap opera of the newspaper world
   Lots of pictures
   Larger type, far fewer words

Research Revisited

Max knew he must be familiar with both papers before making these lists. Nevertheless, as he brainstormed, he discovered he needed to check some additional information. He knew he should not interrupt his initial brainstorming process to find this information. Instead, he made a list as these "need-to-check" items occurred to him. For example:

251

DISCOVERING
IDEAS BY
COMPARING
AND
CONTRASTING
ALTERNATIVES

Check type size and style
Check advertising of products for different audiences
Check for other examples of slant to different audiences
Check vocabulary

The Teeter-Totter of Composition: Balance

Once Max had a list of similarities and differences, his critical brain could swing into action. As he wrote, he discovered his *purpose*. Clearly Thomas Jefferson was not referring to newspapers like the *Sun* when he said he would prefer to have newspapers rather than a government were he forced into such a choice. Max reflected that newspapers have a responsibility to do more than merely entertain their readers; yet it seemed that the *Sun* focused the bulk of its energy—and its print—on entertainment, whereas the *Times* helped inform its readers about the important issues facing their nation.

Max knew he would have to come up with concrete examples to convince his readers of his point about the two papers. In doing so, he needed to be careful to ensure that if he mentioned an aspect of one, he mentioned that same aspect of the other; after all, his purpose was to persuade his readers about the relative merits of a pair, so his development for such a purpose must have *balance*.

This balance applies whenever you use a comparison-contrast format. For example, in an essay comparing and contrasting television news commentators, if you mention the time the one spends reporting on human interest stories, you must mention the time the other spends on these stories. In an essay comparing the Volga and Thames rivers, if you mention how wide the Volga River is, you must give the same information for the Thames.

Let's return to Max's writing process. Each session of brainstorming took him less than twenty minutes. When the prewriting was finished, writing the paper's first draft was a fast, efficient process.

The Second Time Around

Once Max had recorded his initial impressions and had discovered the direction for this essay, he again brainstormed using the key questions. Although this time he let his critic get into the act a little, he still did not worry about spelling, punctuation, or other mechanics. He merely checked for balance. As he did this brainstorming, he occasionally referred to the two newspapers for ideas and examples. Also, he recorded new ideas—very

252

**DISCOVERING
IDEAS BY
COMPARING
AND
CONTRASTING
ALTERNATIVES**

informally—and discarded a few of the original ideas. Even after Max began to write, writing continued to be a process of discovery for him.

Notice his audience awareness as he clarified his *Sun-Times* comparison by further comparisons with papers he is sure his American audience would be familiar with. Thus he has a comparison within a comparison:

Size

Times: Like conventional U.S. daily (e.g., *N.Y. Times*)
Sun: Supermarket tabloid size (check spelling—*Enquirer* or *Inquirer?*)

Photos

Times: Fewer, smaller pictures; dignified photos
Sun: Wow! topless. Can you imagine that in your hometown U.S. daily? Who said the English were stuffy?

Style

Times: More serious, thoughtful style, important stories (find examples).
Sun: Sensational: sell those newspapers! "Two-headed-alien-fathers-royal-child" type—the *Sun* would love it.

Headlines

Times: Very British, reserved headlines
Sun: Slang, sensational headlines

Conclusion

End with thesis: what is appropriate audience for each?
Times: Educated, thoughtful.
Sun: Gossip, people not too concerned with truth—gullible.

Newspapers have a responsibility to do more than merely entertain. The *Sun* focuses the bulk of its energy—and its print—on entertainment.

The *Times* helps inform its readers about the important issues facing their nation.

PATTERNS OF ORGANIZATION

There are three formal ways of organizing the development of a comparison-contrast theme. Once you understand the logic of these three idea-generating and organizing patterns, you will see how the patterns were modified as they were used by contemporary professional writers.

Method 1: The Seesaw Approach to Organization

Develop one aspect of one of the pair you are comparing (for example, *size* with the newspapers), and then develop that aspect of the other. Next introduce the second aspect of one (for example, *style*), and then develop that aspect for the other.

For example

Introduction: The *Sun* and the *Times* are two of England's largest newspapers.

1. The first aspect: Size
   a. The *Times*
   b. The *Sun*
2. The second aspect: Front page
   a. The *Times*
   b. The *Sun*
3. The third aspect: The inside
   a. The *Times*
   b. The *Sun*
4. The fourth aspect: Language
   a. The *Times*
   b. The *Sun*
5. The fifth aspect: Audience
   a. The *Times*
   b. The *Sun*

The conclusion (which in this case contains the thesis): For sensation and gossip, choose the *Sun*. For accurate information about world events, choose the *Times*.

Method 2: First One and Then the Other

Develop all your points about one subject (for example, *size, style, audience*) and then develop all your points about the other.

For example

Introduction: The *Sun* and the *Times* are two of England's largest newspapers.

The *Times*

1. Size
2. Front page
3. Inside
4. Language
5. Audience

The *Sun*

1. Size
2. Front page
3. Inside
4. Language
5. Audience

The conclusion (containing the thesis): For sensation and gossip, choose the *Sun*. For accurate information about world events, choose the *Times*.

Method 3: Organizing by Similarities and Differences

Develop the similarities, and then develop the differences, or the differences and then the similarities. Remember that what you place last will receive the most emphasis. Therefore, if you want to emphasize the differences, the differences will come last.

For example

Introduction: The *Sun* and the *Times* are two of England's largest newspapers.

The similarities:

1. Both are newspapers.
2. Both are English.
3. Both have a large circulation.
4. Both are daily papers.

The differences:

1. Size
2. Front page
3. Inside content
4. Language
5. Audience

The conclusion (containing the thesis): For sensation and gossip, choose the *Sun*. For accurate information about world events, choose the *Times*.

Transition Time in Comparison-Contrast Essays

Where necessary, use transitions to help your reader follow your ideas. These transitions signal that a similar idea will follow: *also, further, in addition, in the same way, likewise, similarly.* These transitions signal that a differing idea will follow: *although, but, conversely, even so, however, in contrast, in spite of, moreover, nevertheless, nonetheless, on the other hand, still, though, yet.*

Remember that sometimes a transition will require more than a single word or phrase. Sometimes you will need to use a sentence or two of transition.

All Together Now

Once you have generated ideas using one of the organizational patterns as a framework to inspire and guide your thinking, you can use the informal outline you have created to prompt ideas for the first draft of your essay. With the idea-generating and organizing help you got from the comparison-contrast framework, the actual writing comes much faster and easier. Read Max's essay about the *Sun* and the *Times* to see how the comparison-contrast framework facilitates writing the essay.

The *Sun* and the *Times*

1   The *Sun* and the *Times of London,* two of England's largest selling newspapers, are as different as Scotch and tea. This difference is apparent at a glance, as the *Times* is the size of a conventional U.S. newspaper such as the *New York Times,* while the *Sun* is the size of a supermarket tabloid such as the *National Enquirer.*

2   The front pages of these papers reveal further differences. On its front page the *Times* carries half a dozen stories of national and international importance—stories, for example, about race relations in South Africa and a parliamentary vote to ban spankings in British schools. These stories are developed in detail with several columns given to the more important stories. The *Sun,* on the other hand, has little room for stories after its huge headlines and photographs. The stories it does contain are often sensational; for example, a typical front page has stories about a friend of the Duchess of York (referred to by the *Sun* as ''Fergie'') being arrested on drug charges and the battered body of a missing woman being found.

3   A peek inside these papers confirms their differences. The *Times* continues to use fewer and smaller headlines and pictures. The *Times* pictures are mostly of people from the shoulders up. When any other part of a person is shown, the person is clothed. The *Sun,* on the other hand, is infamous for topless photos. While its other pictures are more sedate, nearly half of each page is taken up with photographs—many of which are full-length portraits.

4   In its stories, the *Times* uses a formal style; its headlines reflect this with language like ''U.S. President Refuses to Back Sanctions'' and ''Radiation Levels Higher than First Thought.'' In contrast, the *Sun* uses informal language which sometimes dips into slang. Typical of its style are headlines that read ''Pal Admits Drug Charge'' and ''Queen Must Sack Palace Mole.''

5   Certainly many of us find gossip diverting. For those seeking sensational stories, the *Sun* is the right choice. However for people who wish to be well-informed about world events, the *Times* is the proper cup of tea.

256

DISCOVERING
IDEAS BY
COMPARING
AND
CONTRASTING
ALTERNATIVES

6   Is one newspaper preferable to the other? The answer to this question depends upon what the function of a newspaper should be. Thomas Jefferson wrote: "Were it left to me to decide whether we should have a government without newspapers, or newspapers without a government, I should not hesitate a moment to prefer the latter."

7   In a democracy, newspapers have a responsibility to do more than merely entertain their readers; citizens cannot act wisely without being adequately informed. Yet the *Sun* focuses the vast majority of its energy—and its print— on entertainment, while the *Times* helps inform its readers about the important issues facing their nation.

For Thought and Discussion

1. Where does this essay's thesis appear?

2. What concrete examples develop this thesis?

3. Which of the comparison-contrast organizational patterns is used?

4. List the characteristics of the audience to which each newspaper would appeal.

5. Suggest other organizational patterns you might use to develop the following thesis: Some newspapers primarily offer escape to their readers, while others help their readers understand the important issues of the day.

6. Working with a partner, examine two daily newspapers that circulate in your area. (This includes not just local newspapers but those with national circulation such as the *Christian Science Monitor, USA Today,* and the *Wall Street Journal*). Determine how much space is devoted to the following:
    a. Stories you should know about to function as a citizen in a democratic society
    b. Human interest stories
    c. Sensational stories whose primary purpose is to sell newspapers.

7. List the characteristics of the audience to which each newspaper would appeal.

PROFESSIONAL WRITERS AT WORK

The controversy about what our newspapers and television and radio stations say—and how we respond to those messages—is hardly a new one. Before the advent of the electronic media—and long before the printing press—people argued politics, religion, and philosophy through the media of their day. This media had a great deal more to do with vocal cords than electrical ones.

Socrates, a Greek teacher-philosopher who lived 2,400 years ago, believed that all wickedness is due to ignorance and that knowledge is virtue;

257

DISCOVERING
IDEAS BY
COMPARING
AND
CONTRASTING
ALTERNATIVES

these ideas are still popular with many twentieth-century teachers and journalists.

However, Socrates wasn't one who believed wisdom could be handed out on a silver platter; his method of teaching relied on asking key questions to inspire his students to think—to wake them up before they "slept too long." As you know, thinking is a painful, often unpopular, and certainly dangerous pastime—and the freedoms protected under our First Amendment were not the law of the land in Socrates' Athens. In 399 B.C., Socrates was sentenced to death for his teachings.

Gilbert Highet, author of the following paragraph about Socrates, was a Scottish-born classicist who taught in the United States for many years. In his books such as *The Classical Tradition,* published in 1949, Highet makes complex philosophical ideas concrete and thus more understandable.

As you read the following professional essays, note how their authors use comparison and contrast, not as goals in themselves, but as a framework to help organize and develop their larger point.

Socrates

To some of his contemporaries Socrates looked like a Sophist.[1] But he distrusted and opposed the Sophists wherever possible. They toured the whole Greek world; Socrates stayed in Athens, talking to his fellow citizens. They made carefully prepared continuous speeches; he only asked questions. They took rich fees for their teaching; he refused regular payment, living and dying poor. They were elegantly dressed, turned out like filmstars on a personal-appearance tour, with secretaries and personal servants and elaborate advertising. Socrates wore the workingman's clothes, bare feet and a smock. They spoke in specially prepared lecture-halls; he talked to people at street-corners and in the gymnasium where every afternoon the young men exercised, and the old men talked, while they all sunbathed. He fitted in so well there that he sometimes compared himself to the athletic coach, who does not run or wrestle, but teaches others how to run and wrestle better: Socrates said he trained people to think. Lastly, the Sophists said they knew everything and were ready to explain it. Socrates said he knew nothing and was trying to find out.

For Thought and Discussion

1. In what ways did Socrates differ from the Sophists?

2. What modern word has its origin in *sophist*? How is the connotation of this word influenced by the kind of people the Sophists were?

3. What is the thesis of this essay?

---

[1] Sophist: A teacher of rhetoric and philosophy in ancient Greece; a clever but misleading reasoner.

258

**DISCOVERING
IDEAS BY
COMPARING
AND
CONTRASTING
ALTERNATIVES**

4. How does author Gilbert Highet organize the support for his thesis? Make a brief informal outline so you can more clearly see the organization of the essay.

5. How do the details of Socrates' appearance and personality reinforce the thesis of the essay?

6. How do you think Socrates would have been treated by our world? Would he have been electable to high public office? How would he have come across on television? Support your answer.

Marie Winn, the author of eleven books for parents and children, is a regular contributor to the *New York Times Magazine.* Winn's interest in the electronic media is reflected in such books as *The Plug-in Drug,* a book about the impact of television on our culture. Called "thoughtful and lucid" by *The New Yorker,* Winn's book was billed as "extremely important" by the *Los Angeles Times.* In the following excerpt from *Children Without Childhood,* Winn uses a comparison-contrast organizational pattern to discuss the impact of another form of media on children: video games.

Video Games versus Marbles

1   Is there really any great difference between that gang of kids playing video games by the hour at their local candy store these days and those small fry who used to hang around together spending equal amounts of time playing marbles? It is easy to see a similarity between the two activities: each requires a certain amount of manual dexterity, each is almost as much fun to watch as to play, each is simple and yet challenging enough for that middle-childhood group for whom time can be so oppressive if unfilled.

2   One significant difference between the modern pre-teen fad of video games and the once popular but now almost extinct pastime of marbles is economic: playing video games costs twenty-five cents for approximately three minutes of play; playing marbles, after a small initial investment, is free. The children who frequent video-game machines require a considerable outlay of quarters to subsidize their fun; two, three, or four dollars is not an unusual expenditure for an eight- or nine-year-old spending an hour or two with his friends playing Asteroids or Pac-Man or Space Invaders. For most of the children the money comes from their weekly allowance. Some augment this amount by enterprising commercial ventures—trading and selling comic books, or doing chores around the house for extra money.

3   But what difference does it make *where* the money comes from? Why should that make video games any less satisfactory as an amusement for children? In fact, having to pay for the entertainment, whatever the source of the money, and having its duration limited by one's financial resources changes the nature of the game, in a subtle way diminishing the satisfactions it offers. Money and time become intertwined, as they so often do in the adult world and as, in the past, they almost never were in the child's world. For the child playing marbles, meanwhile, time has a far more carefree quality, bounded only by the requirements to be home by suppertime or by dark.

259

DISCOVERING
IDEAS BY
COMPARING
AND
CONTRASTING
ALTERNATIVES

4   But the video-game-playing child has an additional burden—a burden of choice, of knowing that the money used for playing Pac-Man could have been saved for Christmas, could have been used to buy something tangible, perhaps something "worthwhile," as his parents might say, rather than being "wasted" on video games. There is a certain sense of adultness that spending money imparts, a feeling of being a consumer, which distinguishes a game with a price from its counterparts among the traditional childhood games children once played at no cost.

5   There are other differences as well. Unlike child-initiated and child-organized games such as marbles, video games are adult-created mechanisms not entirely within the child's control, and thus less likely to impart a sense of mastery and fulfillment: the coin may get jammed, the machine may go haywire, the little blobs may stop eating the funny little dots. Then the child must go to the storekeeper to complain, to get his money back. He may be "ripped off" and simply lose his quarter. This possibility of disaster gives the child's play a certain weight that marbles never imposed on its light-hearted players.

6   Even if a child has a video game at home requiring no coin outlay, the play it provides is less than optimal. The noise level of the machine is high—too high, usually, for the child to conduct a conversation easily with another child. And yet, according to its enthusiasts, this very noisiness is a part of the game's attraction. The loud whizzes, crashes, and whirrs of the video-game machine "blow the mind" and create an excitement that is quite apart from the excitement generated simply by trying to win a game. A traditional childhood game such as marbles, on the other hand, has little built-in stimulation; the excitement of playing is generated entirely by the players' own actions. And while the pace of a game of marbles is close to the child's natural physiological rhythms, the frenzied activities of video games serve to "rev up" the child in an artificial way, almost in the way a stimulant or an amphetamine might. Meanwhile the perceptual impact of a video game is similar to that of watching television—the action, after all, takes place on a television screen—causing the eye to defocus slightly and creating a certain alteration in the child's natural state of consciousness.

7   Parents' instinctive reaction to their children's involvement with video games provides another clue to the difference between this contemporary form of play and the more traditional pastimes such as marbles. While parents, indeed most adults, derive open pleasure from watching children at play, most parents today are not delighted to watch their kids flicking away at the Pac-Man machine. This does not seem to them to be real play. As a mother of two school-age children anxiously explains, "We used to do real childhood sorts of things when I was a kid. We'd build forts and put on crazy plays and make up new languages, and just generally we *played*. But today my kids don't play that way at all. They like video games. . . . But they don't seem to really *play*."

8   Some of this feeling may represent a certain nostalgia for the past and the old generation's resistance to the different ways of the new. But it is more likely that most adults have an instinctive understanding of the importance of play in their own childhood. This feeling stokes their fears that their

260

DISCOVERING
IDEAS BY
COMPARING
AND
CONTRASTING
ALTERNATIVES

children are being deprived of something irreplaceable when they flip the levers on the video machines to manipulate the electronic images rather than flick their fingers to send a marble shooting towards another marble.

For Thought and Discussion

1. What is Winn's purpose in writing on this topic?

2. What is Winn's thesis in this excerpt?

3. Make an informal outline of the points Winn makes to support her thesis. How does she organize her material?

4. Point out transitions that help Winn tie her ideas together.

5. Indicate any points you think lack convincing support.

6. With which points do you agree? With which do you disagree? Why?

7. Explain why you agree or disagree with the idea that it is important for children to engage in free play, undirected by the media. Support your answer.

8. Explain what clues indicate the type of audience for which Winn was writing. Consider vocabulary, subject matter, and point of view.

Ella Taylor, who wrote the following essay for the *Boston Review,* teaches communications and popular culture at the University of Washington. The author of *All in the Work-Family: Family and Workplace Imagery in Television* and numerous journal articles, Taylor uses comparison and contrast as a development technique to support her thesis.

Because communicating an important idea rather than writing a comparison-contrast essay is her ultimate goal, Taylor does not adhere strictly to one of the three comparison-contrast types discussed earlier in this chapter. Instead she introduces comparison or contrast when it helps her make or clarify a point.

TV Families: Packaged Dreams

1   In 1970 a decisive shift in network ratings policy reshaped the television industry's perceptions of its audience and created conditions more hospitable to the emergence of new kinds of family-oriented shows. Bob Wood, the incoming president of "top network" CBS, quickly realized that the network's most successful shows (*Gunsmoke, The Beverly Hillbillies,* and *Hee Haw*) appealed to older, rural viewers and did less well in the big cities. Wood also saw that from the advertising sponsors' point of view, what mattered was less how many people tuned in than how much they earned and spent. So he turned his attention to the political attitudes of the younger, better educated, and more affluent urban viewers between the ages of eighteen and thirty-four who, at least in the eyes of the media, were fast becoming cultural leaders. The news ratings game of "demographics" would break down the mass audience by age, gender, income, and other variables to isolate the most profitable markets for TV entertainment. Accordingly, scheduling became an elaborate strategic

261

**DISCOVERING
IDEAS BY
COMPARING
AND
CONTRASTING
ALTERNATIVES**

exercise whose purpose was no longer merely to reach the widest possible audience with any given show, but to group programs and commercials in time slots by the type of audience most likely to watch—and spend. The mass audience became a collection of specific "target" audiences.

2   It was, then, largely as a marketing device that the turbulence of the middle to late sixties, and the lively adversarial spirit and liberal politics of the generation coming of age during this period, found their way into television entertainment. The "age of relevance," as it's often called in TV histories, was ushered in by Norman Lear's *All in the Family*, which after a rocky start on CBS shot to number one in the ratings and reigned over the top three positions for much of the decade, spawning spinoffs and clones on all three networks as it went. The Bunkers (and in their wake, the George Jeffersons and Maude Findlays and the Ann Romanos of *One Day at a Time*) quarreled and stormed and suffered their way through the 1970s, blazing a trail for the vast array of social problems that have since become the standard fare of television families.

3   In their early years the Bunkers remained resolutely intact as a family unit, confining their squabbles to highly formalized public issues of race, class, gender, and government corruption. But as the decade went on, the problems that plagued those close to them—menopause, infidelity, divorce, alcoholism, impotence, depression—became steadily more private in nature and drew closer to the Bunkers themselves. Family-show comedy was mixed more and more with drama as the issue became the painful fragility of marriage and the family unit; many episodes were barely identifiable as comedies. Finally Gloria and Meathead, true to their generation, moved to California and divorced, and with Edith's death both Archie and Gloria were left free to negotiate the vicissitudes of life after nuclear family, on their own spinoff shows. . . .

4   Like *All in the Family, The Cosby Show* has attracted an enormous amount of attention from critics and public interest groups, as well as a huge and devoted audience, but there the similarity ends. The robustly working-class Bunker household was never a model of consumer vitality, nor did it aspire to be. If Archie was dragged, kicking and screaming, into the seventies, the Huxtables embrace modernity with gusto. From grandparents to the disarmingly cute Rudy, this family is sexy and glamorous. Surrounded by the material evidence of their success, the Huxtables radiate wealth, health, energy, and up-to-the-minute style. *The Cosby Show* offers the same pleasures as a commercial, a parade of gleaming commodities and expensive designer clothing, unabashedly enjoyed by successful people. And Cosby himself is a talented promoter of the goods and services, from Jell-O to E. F. Hutton, that finance his series.

5   Given the troubled condition of many American families in the eighties, "Cosby" must be palpably compensatory for many of its fans. Week after week, the show offers what family comedy in the fifties offered, and what most of us don't have, the continuity of orderly lives lived without major trauma or disturbance, stretching back into an identical past and reaching confidently forward into an identical future. Two generations of Huxtable men attended "Hillman College" and met their wives there, and although Cliff's eldest daughter chooses Princeton, the next goes for Hillman too.

262

**DISCOVERING
IDEAS BY
COMPARING
AND
CONTRASTING
ALTERNATIVES**

6   But where the TV families of the fifties casually took harmony and order for granted, the Huxtables work strenuously and self-consciously at showing us how well they get along. Not that much happens on "Cosby." It's a virtually plotless chronicle of the small, quotidian details of family life, at the heart of which lies a moral etiquette of parenting and a developmental psychology of growing up. Every week provides family members, and us, with a Learning Experience and a lesson in social adjustment. Rudy's terrified playmate learns to love going to the dentist. Rudy learns to stop bossing her friends around. Theo learns not to embark on expensive projects he won't complete. Sondra and her boy friend learn to arbitrate their bickering over sex roles. Denise learns to cope with bad grades in college. Even Cliff and Clair, who despite high-powered careers as physician and lawyer respectively, have all the leisure in the world to spend "quality time" with their kids, teach each other parenting by discussions as well as by example. The show's endless rehearsal of mild domestic disorder and its resolution suggests a perfect family that works. The family that plays, sings, dances, and, above all, communicates together, stays together.

7   Didacticism is nothing new in television entertainment. *All in the Family* was stuffed with messages of all kinds, but on *Cosby,* moral and psychological instruction are rendered monolithic and indisputable. Unlike the Bunkers, for whom every problem became the occasion for an all-out war of ideas, no one ever screams at Huxtable Manor. True, beneath their beguiling mildness there lurks a casual hostility, in which everyone, Clair and Cliff included, trades insults and makes fun of everyone else. But there's no dissent, no real difference of opinion or belief, only vaguely malicious banter that quickly dissolves into sweet agreement, all part of the busy daily manufacture of consensus.

8   Undercutting the warm color and light, the jokey good humor and the impeccable salutes of feminism, is a persistent authoritarianism. The tone is set by Cosby himself, whose prodigious charm overlays a subtle menace. If the pint-sized Rudy gets her laughs by aping the speech and manners of adults, Cliff gets his laughs—and his way—by turning into a giant child, and then slipping his kids or his wife their moral or psychological pills with a wordless, grimacing comic caper. A captivating child, undoubtedly, with his little vanities and his competitiveness, but he's also quietly coercive: Father knows best, or else. The cuddly, overgrown schoolboy becomes the amused onlooker and then the oracle, master of the strategic silence or the innocent question that lets one of his kids know they've said or done something dumb, or gives his wife to understand that her independence is slipping into bossiness. In Huxtable-speak, this is called "communicating." Cliff practices a thoroughly contemporary politics of strong leadership, managing potential conflicts with all the skill of a well-socialized corporate executive.

9   There's none of the generational warfare that rocked the Bunker household every week. And this family doesn't *need* the openly authoritarian "tough love" that's cropping up more and more in recent TV movies, because parental authority has already been internalized.

10   The Huxtables have friends but no discernible neighborhood community,

263

**DISCOVERING
IDEAS BY
COMPARING
AND
CONTRASTING
ALTERNATIVES**

indeed no public life to speak of aside from their jobs, which seem to run on automatic pilot. They inhabit a visibly black world, whose blackness is hardly ever alluded to. "I'm not going to talk about social justice or racial harmony or peace, because you all know how I feel about them," intones the retiring president of Cliff's alma mater, and delivers a limp homily exhorting old alumni to invite young alumni to dinner, which earns him a standing ovation from old and young alike—all black. No wonder *The Cosby Show* is number one in South African ratings. It is, as a Johannesburg television executive remarked complacently on the nightly Hollywood chat show *Entertainment Tonight* last year, not a show about race, but about "family values. . . ."

11   In each successive television era, a particular congruence of marketing exigencies and cultural trends has produced different portraits of the American family. In television, genre is always about 80 percent commerce. But in the 1970s, commerce made room for lively, innovative programming that interrupted the hitherto bland conventions of the TV family, giving us programming that above all didn't condescend to its audiences. The Bunkers were never a restful or reassuring family, but their battles, however strident, raised the possibility that there might be, might *have* to be more ways than one to conduct family life, that blood ties are not the only bonds of community, that divorce is a feature of modern life to be confronted, that women and men must find new ways of living together and raising children.

12   Today, the generous space that was opened up then for public discussion is once again being narrowed. With their eyes firmly fixed on the new mass audience, *The Cosby Show* and its clones are short-circuiting the quarrelsome gutsiness of seventies TV by burying their heads in the nostalgic sands of "traditional values" that never were. Public interest groups may be all smiles at the jolly harmony of these shows. But their obsession with engineering a spurious consensus returns us the dullest kind of television, with its twin besetting sins, sentimentality and a profound horror of argument.

For Thought and Discussion

1. What is Ella Taylor's purpose in writing this essay?

2. What is the thesis of "TV Families: Packaged Dreams"?

3. Point out the sections of this essay that use comparison-contrast development.

4. What similarities and differences between *All in the Family* and *The Cosby Show* does Taylor discuss?

5. What kinds of topics does Taylor deal with for *The Cosby Show* but not for *All in the Family*? Do these omissions interfere with the support of the thesis? Why?

6. Does Taylor prefer *All in the Family* or *The Cosby Show*? Why?

7. In addition to comparison and contrast, what techniques does Taylor use to develop her point?

264

DISCOVERING
IDEAS BY
COMPARING
AND
CONTRASTING
ALTERNATIVES

WRITING ASSIGNMENT

Write an essay 500 to 850 words in length using comparison-contrast techniques for at least part of your development. While we have concentrated on topics related to the media in this chapter, comparison-contrast techniques are helpful for generating, developing, and organizing ideas for essays on a broad variety of other topics as well.

In your essay be sure to do the following:

1. Begin with an introduction designed to interest your reader.

2. Limit your subject. You cannot adequately compare all aspects of baseball and football, for example, but you might be able to compare typical injuries or training techniques.

3. Decide which comparison-contrast organizational pattern would be most effective for presenting your ideas.

4. Use transitions to help your reader follow your ideas.

5. Be sure to support your thesis with good, concrete details. If you don't have enough evidence to support your thesis, go to the library and read about your subject and/or interview an expert on your subject.

6. Think beyond the obvious. If you are contrasting dogs and cats as pets, do not simply tell us that cats are independent while dogs are friendly. By using specific, concrete details, show your reader the differences between these two pets, and *avoid the obvious*. Your audience does not want to waste time reading what they already know.

7. Write a conclusion that uses one of the concluding techniques from Chapter 6.

Suggestions for Topics

Here are some topics that lend themselves to comparison-contrast techniques:

Two newspapers, two news shows, or two newsmagazines
A major event as covered by two of the following: newspapers, television, or newsmagazines
Two family sitcoms
A specific sitcom and a real-life situation
A media-related topic of your choice (check with your instructor to get approval for your topic)
An instructor-approved topic of your choice

DISCOVERING
IDEAS BY
COMPARING
AND
CONTRASTING
ALTERNATIVES

After you have completed the prewriting and the first draft of your essay, meet with a peer editing group so that you can assess the reaction of an audience to your writing. Make enough photocopies of your essay for your peer editing group.

1. First read the essay through once without stopping.

2. Indicate any ideas, passages, imagery, allusions, or other aspects of this essay you found effective. Positive reinforcement is a powerful tool.

3. Underline the thesis. If you cannot identify the thesis, ask the writer to point it out or to further clarify the thesis in writing should this prove necessary.

4. Point out any details or passages that do not seem relevant to the author's point. The author can then decide whether a transition could clarify the connection with the thesis or if the point is truly irrelevant.

5. List the aspects of the subjects that are being compared. Note whether or not the essay achieved balance: If a quality was mentioned for one of the comparison-contrast pair, was it mentioned for the other? If this balance was not maintained, was there a compelling reason for not maintaining it?

6. List the specific examples that illustrate the aspects that are being compared. Indicate any abstract ideas that need further concrete development. Ask the author any questions you would like to have answered to better understand the essay's points.

7. Which comparison-contrast organization has the author used?

8. In the introduction to the essay, how has the author attempted to interest the audience?

9. What technique does the essay employ in its conclusion?

10. What seems to be the author's purpose in writing the essay? Was this purpose accomplished in your own response to the essay? Why or why not?

When writers have revised the content of the essay to their satisfaction and are ready for feedback about mechanics, point out but do not correct any problems you suspect exist with spelling, grammar, and punctuation. It is the writer's responsibility to make such corrections.

Help! For Further Work

The following student draft uses the comparison-contrast key questions to generate and organize ideas. Read it as if you were its peer editor. Then answer the questions in the peer editing checklist.

**DISCOVERING
IDEAS BY
COMPARING
AND
CONTRASTING
ALTERNATIVES**

1   Television game shows are more popular than ever. There are countless game shows on television which are watched by countless people who like game shows or have nothing else to do except watch them. But all people who watch game shows are not alike. Some game shows are actually informative, challenging programs that help educate their audiences.

2   For example *Jeopardy* is a thought-provoking television game show that challenges its audience. I watch this show regularly even though I often come out on the short end after matching wits with their contestants. Where do they find these people, they know the most amazingly obscure bits of information. I can't think of an example just now, but you would be astounded by what these people know. Of course sometimes a contestant will be a flop. I am embarrassed for these people, but that is the risk they take when they go on the show. This show has numerous categories of information that change frequently. The only suggestion I have for improving the show is to be more careful with the questions. Occasionally they are tricky or obscure, and don't really teach anything. Also they should figure out a way to smooth over the embarrassment of the contestant who has to drop out before the end because they have a minus score.

3   While shows like *The Price is Right* appeal to an unthoughtful audience that doesn't learn much of value from the program except how much a jar of peanut butter costs. And some of the prizes are relatively specialized. I certainly would not want them. You would have to have a special place to put some of them. I suppose this is better than watching sex and violence, but you don't really learn very much.

4   On the other hand, Jeopardy's categories such as "Science," "History," "Politics," and yes, even "Spelling," provide useful information for citizens of a fast-paced world where the more you know, the more you are. What is really interesting, however, is that Merv Griffin sold *Jeopardy* for something like 3 billion dollars to Coke.

STUDENT STARS

While the examples thus far in this chapter have centered around the media, the methods discussed in this chapter apply to many other subjects. Therefore, the student star essays are on a variety of topics.

    The authors of the following essays have done the following:

1. Prewriting
2. Writing
3. Revision
4. Correction of mechanical errors.

1   What's the difference between nuclear fusion and nuclear fission? Fission, developed in 1927, is the separation of atoms into smaller atoms. Think of the relationship of typical humans and their food. If the humans and the food are together, there is no problem. However, no energy is produced trying to get them together either. Take the humans away from the food and Bang! Instant energy as the humans go into a frenzy of activity to get the food. This is basically the concept of fission: one atom is separated from the other to produce energy. This process is beneficial because it produces energy, but it is also dangerous in both the short and long run.

2   To produce energy using fission, atoms must be split in a complicated and costly process—a process that is a little like trying to slice a sandwich blindfolded. Sometimes you get a perfect cut, but mostly you get a rather large slice and a piece with little more than crust. In the case of atoms, sadly, even a perfect cut produces harmful side effects. Since the fission process can split atoms into different size particles, the waste produced from this process is not totally predictable. Furthermore, the waste is highly radioactive and therefore dangerous to all living things for tens of thousands of years.

3   Uranium 235, a rare element making up only one percent of the total uranium deposits, is the primary atom used in fission. The earth's supply of Uranium 235 is limited. In addition, Uranium 235 is radioactive to begin with, and then it is split into another element even more radioactive—and therefore more dangerous.

4   On the other hand, fusion is quite a different process from fission. Instead of the atom-splitting of fission, fusion is the combining of two atoms. Power created by this combination is many times that of fission. Specifically, in the fusion process energy amounting to 10^{16} watts per cubic centimeter per reaction is created. This is equivalent to running a hundred light bulbs of one hundred watts each since approximately the year 2000 B.C. nonstop. Many reactions per minute can be produced amounting to almost limitless amounts of energy. Amazingly enough, fusion produces no waste, in contrast to the dangerous waste of the fission process. Furthermore, fusion has no other negative side effects.

5   So what's the reason we don't have a fusion plant in our cars and in our home? The reasons are two-fold: first we must compress the atom to 10^{12} atm (an atm is equal to one earth atmosphere). This is equivalent to ten times the pressure at the center of the sun. Even with the recent evolution of lasers, producing such pressure is very touch and go. Secondly, the abundance of energy in such concentrated amounts melts anything near it. So the only "practical" application of fusion thus far is in the hydrogen bomb—if you call massive destruction "practical." Scientists have trouble finding ways to contain the massive energy produced by fusion. You can't just pop the sun into a bottle.

6   We must continue to research the field of fusion. Fission produces dangerous waste and uses up the earth's limited supply of Uranium 235. With fusion lies the promise of an almost unlimited, safe supply of energy for the future.   —Brad Schef

DISCOVERING IDEAS BY COMPARING AND CONTRASTING ALTERNATIVES

1   The temperature is finally starting to go down. It's been hot! The needle on the thermometer has hovered around the 100 degree mark all day. I'm in a dry creek bed on hands and knees slowly moving into range of the biggest black tail deer I've seen in four years. The sweat trickles down my back as I put the final few yards on what has been a two-hour grueling stalk, most of it on hands and knees. I can sense victory as I ease back my bow at a distance of only thirty yards from my quarry. It doesn't even see me. As I am about to release my arrow, a deafening bang breaks the silence and echoes through the canyon. I am dumbfounded as I see my trophy buck take three steps and collapse in a pool of blood. Still in a state of shock I watch a four wheel drive jeep loaded with hunters racing toward me. From where they are I can see that they shot my deer from a distance of about 600 yards. This killing and my frustration are typical of the problems caused when bow hunters and gun hunters have to hunt during the same season. Bow hunters and gun hunters should have their own separate seasons.

2   Bow hunting is an art, a skill learned only through many hours in the field. To kill a deer with a bow you must be patient and face many disappointments along the way. When I first started bow hunting I thought it would be easy. I didn't know two years would pass before I bagged my first deer. To be a successful bow hunter there are several skills you must learn. First, you must be able to move through the woods as silently as possible. Second, you must know how to get close to a wild animal without it knowing you are there. Third, you must understand about scents, musks, and wind eddies. Fourth, you must be able to read signs such as tracks and deer scat. Fifth, you must know your equipment well. Last, you must be able to put an arrow into a ten-inch area at a distance of up to seventy yards, a skill gained only after many hours of practice. As you can see, it takes dedication to be a bow hunter. According to the California Department of Fish and Game, only 2% of licensed bow hunters bag their deer, a percent similar to that of other states.

3   On the other hand, gun hunting for deer takes much less knowledge, time, dedication and skill than bow hunting takes. The first time I went deer hunting with a gun I got a nice buck. The kill took little skill on my part. My friends and I were driving through the hills on public land when the noise from our truck spooked a small buck out of deep cover. The deer was running to the top of a hill when my hunting companion whistled loudly. This stopped the curious buck right before he went over the hill. I looked through the magnifying scope on the borrowed rifle, and, for the first time ever, I pulled the trigger on that gun.

4   My friends congratulated me on a great shot and a good hunt, but I couldn't help thinking that there was something missing in my triumph. I felt empty. The deer didn't have a chance. Although this was only my first experience with gun hunting, subsequent experiences showed its validity.

5   When gun hunting for deer, you don't have to creep silently along. In fact, most people scare the deer out of the brush and then shoot them while they are running away. In addition, you don't have to get close to a deer to shoot it with a gun; three hundred yards is about average. At that distance you don't

have to worry about it smelling you. And since you can rely on simply scaring the deer out into the open, you don't have to know about tracks, scat and other deer signs. Last, it takes little skill to learn how to effectively aim and shoot a gun. A few practice sessions at a gun range will make you an adequate marksman.

6 Bow hunting and gun hunting are as different as riding a bike and driving a car. Both have their advantages, but one takes a great deal more skill and stamina. If bow hunters and gun hunters had their own seasons, they would not interfere with each other's techniques. After all, you wouldn't put a bicyclist in a race at Indianapolis would you? Similarly you shouldn't put a bow hunter in competition with a hunter using a complex rifle.

—Fritz Nolan

McDrugs?

1 A young man and his wife enter a drug store. The wife asks the man behind the counter, ''Can I have one hit of acid?'' The husband asks confidently, ''May I have a pack of High Time joints?'' The pharmacist rings up the couple's order. Are you waiting for the punchline? This scenario is not a joke. If drugs like heroine, cocaine, LSD, and marijuana are legalized such transactions could become commonplace.

2 In a recent *New York Times*–CBS News survey, 16 percent of those questioned called drugs the nation's number one problem. Many believe drug legalization is the answer to the problem. If drugs were legal, the government could regulate their sale and set a much lower price than current drug dealers charge. Drug addicts could support their habits without stealing. The lack of profit for drug dealers could diminish the growing ranks of criminals. The drug dealing gangs would disappear just as the boot-leggers did after the repeal of Prohibition. Drug dealing wouldn't tempt underclass youths to turn to crime to make money and thus get out of the ghetto. Many believe that drug-related crimes are far more destructive to society than drug use itself.

3 In addition, drug legalization would make both foreign and domestic drug trafficking a thing of the past thereby helping U.S. foreign policy. The current effort to stop drug smuggling has jeopardized our relationship with many friendly Latin American nations such as Columbia and Mexico.

4 Moreover, drug legalization would save our nation enormous amounts of money spent on drug enforcement. Currently we spend about eight billion dollars a year on this enforcement. Billions more are spent on indirect costs such as caring for imprisoned drug dealers. Furthermore, the tax on the sale of legalized drugs would bring in billions in new revenues—money that could be spent on drug education and the rehabilitation of drug addicts.

5 But there are also convincing arguments on the other side of the drug legalization problem. Legalization could increase the number of addicts because drugs would be cheaper and more readily available. Removing legal disapproval could also make drugs more socially acceptable. More people could come to believe that drugs are all right. The estimated cost of medical care necessitated by drug abuse is sixty million dollars. That could skyrocket still more with legalization. In addition, because drugs make many unem-

270

**DISCOVERING
IDEAS BY
COMPARING
AND
CONTRASTING
ALTERNATIVES**

ployable and even violent, legalization could backfire and actually increase crime in our society as the unemployable turn to stealing to survive, and the drug-crazed commit crimes they would not commit if they weren't under the influence of drugs. Furthermore the number of traffic injuries and deaths could increase dramatically with more drivers using drugs.

6   Certainly drug abuse in our nation is one of its most serious problems, but rushing into legalization of drugs is not the answer. We need to take time to study the problems created by the increasing numbers of addicts such legalization would create before we change current laws. A McDrug society is not the answer to our drug problem.   —Mark Eschler

10

ARGUMENT: DISCOVERING AND DEFENDING YOUR POINT OF VIEW

CONCEPTS TO LEARN

Argument as a tool in your writing

Creating a winning argument

Avoiding logical fallacies in your arguments

Writing an argument can be the most stimulating, satisfying form of essay writing you do. Because you must think carefully about your position on an issue well before you begin to write about it, you may often find that much of the writing task is surprisingly easy. For example, when you cluster, freewrite, or brainstorm to examine the various sides of the argument—including the points of view that do not agree with yours—you will discover additional points in favor of your own side. In addition, when you do research to find additional information, you may discover points in favor of your argument that you had not thought about.

When you learn to write a good argument, you also learn to argue well in any medium—in a conversation, in a formal debate, in a letter to the electric company, or in response to a question on a history exam. In fact, as you read this chapter, you will realize that argument is woven into the fabric of your life, and that you already possess many of the skills necessary for putting forth an effective argument.

272

ARGUMENT:
DISCOVERING
AND
DEFENDING
YOUR POINT
OF VIEW

A STRONG CONSTITUTION

Certainly, history has seen few people as proficient at putting forth an effective argument as Benjamin Franklin. Remarkably, he was able to do so under conditions that most people would have found intolerable.

When he was eighty-one years old, Benjamin Franklin attended the Constitutional Convention in Philadelphia, even though he had misgivings about the proceedings. While much younger men like Patrick Henry—who said about the deliberations that he "smelt a rat"—chose not to attend the convention at all, Ben Franklin, despite his doubts and frail health, remained throughout the sweltering summer months of 1787, to see the Constitution to its conclusion.

In Franklin's statement, which was addressed to George Washington on the day of the Constitution's signing, September 17, 1787, the elderly statesman expressed his concerns. He attributed his doubts, in part, to having lived long enough to see every side of an argument and to anticipate every possible outcome. Yet, can we say that he was wrong to worry—as he did—that some future United States president, acting apart from the legislative and judicial branches, might become corrupt?

> I confess that there are several parts of this constitution which I do not at present approve, but I am not sure I shall never approve them: For having lived long, I have experienced many instances of being obliged by better information or fuller consideration, to change opinions even on important subjects, which I once thought right, but found to be otherwise. It is therefore that the older I grow, the more apt I am to doubt my own judgment, and to pay more respect to the judgment of others.   —Benjamin Franklin

For Thought and Discussion

1. Benjamin Franklin is famous for a number of accomplishments besides his political activities. What were some of his other achievements?

2. Patrick Henry was noted for his ability to express himself convincingly, and he is best remembered for the revolutionary statement, "Give me liberty or give me death!" Why does this quote remain famous more than two centuries after it was uttered?

3. Brainstorm, with your classmates, a list of current public debates and disagreements.

4. Choose one such debate and freewrite on it for about ten minutes. When you are finished, discuss your ideas with a small group of your peers, in class.

ARGUMENT AND KEY QUESTIONS

273

ARGUMENT:
DISCOVERING
AND
DEFENDING
YOUR POINT
OF VIEW

Your freewriting about a well-known public debate undoubtedly included some arguments, pro and con. In exploring these issues, you may have convinced some people in the class to think about the debate in a new way—especially if you included concrete examples and illustrations in support of your ideas.

Because you have inherited from Benjamin Franklin and his colleagues the same kind of argumentative atmosphere that created the U.S. Constitution, you probably anticipated and answered some of your listeners' key questions without even thinking about the process you were involved in. Because you live in a society that depends on argument, you have become so accustomed to using this form of debate and discussion in your daily life that you may hardly notice that you often automatically provide thesis statements and support, even in everyday conversations.

Arguments come in all shapes and sizes. A song can be an argument: "You Ain't Nothin' but a Hound Dog" expresses a definite point of view, and the song's lyrics provide illustrations and examples as concrete support for that opinion—"Crying all the time" and "You ain't never caught a rabbit."

Cartoons can provide arguments. Think of some of the vigorous political debates in the Doonesbury cartoons, or the friendly arguments between Charlie Brown and Lucy in the Sunday comics when Lucy is trying to convince Charlie that he can succeed—this year—at baseball or football.

Likewise, poems present arguments. A love poem argues in favor of the lover's feelings about his or her beloved, as William Shakespeare does when he says, "Shall I compare thee to a summer's day?/Thou art more lovely and more temperate." Shakespeare argues that his beloved is lovelier and more pleasing than the most beautiful day he can think of. Emily Bronte argues for optimism and faith in the face of life's problems:

> No coward soul is mine,
> No trembler in the world's storm-troubled sphere:
> I see Heaven's glories shine,
> And faith shine equal, arming me from fear.

The Bright Side: Argument as a Tool

At the beginning of this chapter, you read a statement by eighty-one-year-old Benjamin Franklin about his misgivings with regard to the Constitution. Franklin acknowledged, however, that he had learned to value the opinions of others, as well as to listen to points of view that differed from his own.

274

ARGUMENT:
DISCOVERING
AND
DEFENDING
YOUR POINT
OF VIEW

The debate and discussion over questions such as those that confronted Franklin demonstrates the importance of argument in the political arena.

Unfortunately, the words *argue* and *argument* have gotten a lot of bad press; you may tend to associate them with unpleasant confrontations and fights. But when you look at their origins in Latin and Greek, you will understand them in a quite different way.

Argue comes from the ancient Indo-European root *arg-*, which meant to shine; it also came to mean white and silver. In Greek, this evolved into *arginoeis,* which means brilliant or bright-shining. And in Latin it became *arguere,* to make clear, to demonstrate. When you argue, you take great pains to make clear and demonstrate the points of an issue in order to explain them to another person or group of people. In this way, you hope that others will see the issue as you see it.

When you work to make an issue clear to others, you often clarify it for yourself as well. You discover that the questions become more sharply focused and that you eliminate extraneous information that may cloud the issue. As you examine all sides of a debate in preparing your own argument, you may find some problems with your point of view—perhaps you have forgotten to take some crucial piece of information into account. This examination gives you an opportunity to modify your argument accordingly.

But argument is important in our daily lives, as well. It provides us with a means to protect our own interests and the interests of people we care about. At home, for example, you might find yourself in a disagreement with your roommates or members of your family about your right to privacy. You may feel that once you close the door of your bedroom you should be left alone, undisturbed by other members of the household. They may feel, however, that since your room is in the house shared by all, you have no right to limit access to that space. Because you want to stay in the house— and your housemates want you to be there—you and they will settle this issue through the process of argument; you will offer your point of view, they will offer theirs, and between you, an agreement will be hammered out. Your argument need not degenerate into a battle; rather, it should provide a forum for you to exchange ideas in a civilized manner.

THE ART OF PERSUASION

Aristotle identified three strategies we use to persuade others of our point of view: (1) the *ethical appeal,* which depends on the reader's perception of the writer's character; (2) the *rational appeal,* which depends on the writer's use of logic and reason; and (3) the *emotional appeal,* which depends on the writer's ability to trigger certain emotional reactions in the reader.

The Ethical Appeal

275

ARGUMENT:
DISCOVERING
AND
DEFENDING
YOUR POINT
OF VIEW

The first attribute that you bring to any argument, whether it is written or spoken, is your own good sense, your character, and your consideration for the point of view of others. If you cannot persuade your audience that you are a thoughtful and fair-minded person, you will not persuade them of anything else. This fundamental characteristic of a good argument is what Aristotle called *ethos*; it is what we call the *ethical appeal*. In his discussion of the ethical appeal, Ohio State University composition professor Edward P. J. Corbett says:

> The *whole* discourse must maintain the "image" that the speaker or writer seeks to establish. The ethical appeal, in other words, must be pervasive throughout the discourse. The effect of the ethical appeal might very well be destroyed by a single lapse from good sense, good will, or moral integrity. A note of peevishness, a touch of malevolence, a flash of bad taste, a sudden display of inaccuracy or illogic could jeopardize a whole persuasive effort.

If you are discussing your right to privacy with your housemates, you know that they have already formed an opinion about your character and that they will automatically combine what they know of your honesty and integrity with the argument you put forth. When you write, however, you cannot depend on what people already know about you. Instead, you must create an image for yourself as you write by demonstrating, throughout your essay, the "good sense, good will," and "moral integrity" that Professor Corbett discusses by being fair-minded and polite, and by considering all sides of an issue.

The Rational Appeal

Your best chance to persuade your audience—whether it is composed of your readers or your housemates—is to appeal to their sense of reason and logic. If you can support your argument with evidence, if you can show your audience how and why your argument is logical and reasonable, and if you can anticipate and answer challenges to your argument with reasonable responses, you are appealing to the audience's rationality, or fundamental intelligence and good sense. According to Professor Corbett,

> Rationality is man's essential characteristic. It is what makes man human and differentiates him from other animals. Ideally, reason should dominate all of man's thinking and actions, but actually, man is often influenced by passions and prejudices and customs. To say that man often responds to irrational motives is not to say that he never listens to the voice of reason. We must have faith not only that man is capable of ordering his life by the dictates of reason but that most of the time he is disposed to do so.

276

ARGUMENT:
DISCOVERING
AND
DEFENDING
YOUR POINT
OF VIEW

Your housemates may be persuaded when you offer arguments that are based upon *well-defined terms, clear evidence,* and an *acknowledgment of possible opposing arguments.* When you write, you must include these elements; if you do not, you may find the proverbial "holes" shot through your argument by your readers.

The Emotional Appeal

Another powerful and influential factor in any argument is that of emotion. We like to think of ourselves as entirely rational creatures, but, in fact, we are heavily affected by the emotional content in any argument we must put forth or consider.

Aristotle did not have the advantage of seeing how emotional appeal is used in twentieth-century advertising, but he would not have been surprised. The effect can be instantaneous and overwhelming. Think about the emotional appeal of the ads in the 1988 presidential election when George Bush used the picture of convicted murderer Willie Horton to stir up voters' fears about crime and the "soft" treatment of criminals. Or think about the successful appeal to your emotions by TV ads which show adorable children playing with a certain brand of toilet tissue, eating a particular kind of hot dog, or spilling catsup on a special kind of carpet.

As a writer, you can use this favorite technique of advertisers to your advantage. When you use an example to illustrate a point, that example may very well contain within it an appeal to your readers' emotions. For example, if you are writing an essay about nursing homes, you might include an illustration in which you describe the daily life of eighty-three-year-old Nellie Ford, who spends her days sitting in a wheelchair, staring at a television screen:

> The home in which Nellie lives is clean, safe, and provides good medical care. Yet its staff, most of whom are paid minimum wage, never have the time to talk with the residents. Worse, the home does not provide its residents any recreational activities or intellectual stimulation.

Since your readers all know that they will someday grow old, and since they probably have relatives who are elderly, most are already emotionally involved in the issue of how one can best spend the last years of life. In a very real sense, it is not only Nellie Ford your readers are reading about; it is themselves or their loved ones. Here, the picture you provide has powerful emotional appeal because it triggers the question in a reader's mind, "Could this happen to my father?" "Could it happen to me?"

While the use of the emotional appeal is effective, you must be cautious when you employ it. The emotional appeal can quickly become—or appear to become—unethical. As a result, you can damage your credibility by appealing too obviously or too recklessly to your audience's emotions.

All the strategies for argument and persuasion, including the ethical and emotional appeals, are powerful tools which, when wisely and carefully used, can help you to strengthen your case. But when they are used carelessly or unwisely, they can damage or destroy your case.

277

ARGUMENT:
DISCOVERING
AND
DEFENDING
YOUR POINT
OF VIEW

For Thought and Discussion

1. With the class divided into two groups, have each group take one side of a currently "hot" topic of debate (your instructor may assign a topic, or you may decide on one as a class; suggested areas of discussion include abortion, nuclear defense, foreign relations, or environmental issues).

a. As a class, first decide on a "thesis" for the debate; in other words, find a focus before you begin to discuss specific issues. If, for example, the class decides to debate the issue of Medicare, narrow the focus by asking questions such as:

Should the government pay for all of the medical expenses of elderly citizens?

Should Medicare pay for long-term care at home?

Should the government have a strong voice in determining the amount and type of care received by Medicare recipients?

Is it fair for elderly people to have their medical expenses covered when younger people do not have this right?

How should the nation divide its medical care dollar between the very old and the very young?

Is it fair that people in their middle years are expected to pay for it all?

A glance will tell you that one of these topics will yield plenty of material for a debate of substance and that a broader topic would simply be too unwieldy.

b. Go to the library and find two articles on the chosen topic. These articles will provide you with statistics and examples to strengthen your argument. In addition, you may read some arguments that make the case for your opposition. Knowing the opposition's points will help you to strengthen your own case. As a class, reconsider the argument in light of your new insights.

2. Consider the cartoon on page 278. Obviously, the dinosaurs in the cartoon were unable to protect their long-term interests. So that you can begin to think about this issue before it's too late for your species (*Homo sapiens*), identify one issue currently facing elderly Americans that you view as critical. Discuss your answer.

3. Cluster, freewrite, or brainstorm about the issue you identified in number 2 and develop a thesis statement suitable for a 500- to 850-word essay that would argue your point.

278

ARGUMENT:
DISCOVERING
AND
DEFENDING
YOUR POINT
OF VIEW

ILLUSTRATION BY PETER STEINER

"I keep thinking we ought to be giving more thought to long-term care."

CREATING A WINNING ARGUMENT

If you think of arguing only in terms of discussions with other people, you may find it difficult to imagine yourself arguing to a piece of paper. Yet you will often be called upon to do just that, both in college and on the job, so it behooves you to think about the kinds of strategies you can call upon.

Focus on Your Central Point

The first and most important strategy in any good argument, as in all good writing, is to make certain that *you* know what your central point is. First, you will want to cluster, freewrite, or brainstorm to discover your topic; then ask questions about the topic so that you can focus on a central idea.

This is crucial: You must be clear in your own mind, or your readers will not understand the point you are trying to make.

Once you have identified the central point, experiment with the thesis. Even if the trial thesis is not the one you decide to adopt, you should try it out and see how it works. Clustering, brainstorming, and freewriting will help you discover what you think about the topic, and you will learn something from every experiment. Eventually, you will discover not only a thesis that expresses your point of view but one which you can support with material that will convince your readers.

Support Your Central Point

Once you have identified the central point, you need to come up with supporting points for the thesis. If you cannot, it helps to ask yourself questions about the topic:

What do I know about this issue?
What are the arguments for and against this issue?
Do I need to learn more about it before I attempt to formulate my argument?
Why have I chosen to argue about this issue?
What are the important factors for my readers to consider?
How can I best help them to see my point of view?

Take a Research Break

A research break at the library will help you discover the points on both sides of the argument, as well as additional support for your point of view. Read at least two articles on your topic. Try to find articles from opposing points of view. If your topic concerns events that are not current issues, check out books that have been written on the subject. A thorough knowledge of your subject is the best preparation you can make for a winning argument.

Prewrite Again

You might not know your position on an issue until you have researched it, then explored your thinking again through prewriting. Clustering, brainstorming, and freewriting will help you sort through the complexities of your topic so you can find a focus.

Additional prewriting will also help you to find supporting points for your thesis. For example, if you are writing about the problems of the elderly, you might focus on a thesis that states: "The retirement age in the United States should be raised to seventy." If you use prewriting techniques with this focus in mind, you will discover supporting ideas for your thesis, such as the following:

Raising the retirement age will increase the number of experienced workers.
It will reduce the cost of social security.

280

ARGUMENT:
DISCOVERING
AND
DEFENDING
YOUR POINT
OF VIEW

It will keep a large segment of the population active in the political
   and economic life of the nation.
It will keep older people healthy and active for a longer period.

Use an Essay Map

Once you have discovered the supporting points for your thesis, experiment
with creating an essay map—a brief summary of your supporting points
within your thesis statement. The essay map helps you to focus on the main
points you have chosen to discuss, and it helps you to avoid raising side
issues that might detract from your argument.

In an essay on raising the age of retirement, your thesis statement
might read as follows: "The retirement age in the United States should be
raised to seventy because this will increase the number of experienced
workers, reduce the cost of social security, and keep older people healthy
and active for a longer period."

The essay map within the thesis statement focuses attention—yours
and your readers'—on the *reasons* for your argument. While an essay map
is not a requirement for an effective argument, it can help you to organize
your points so that you do not become bogged down in irrelevant material
or accidentally wander away from your original intention.

Consider All Sides of the Issue

It is easy to become so involved with your own point of view that you forget
to consider the opposition; unfortunately, ignoring opposing arguments
does not make them go away. For example, you may feel strongly that raising
the retirement age to seventy is a good idea because it will benefit society
as a whole. Others may argue that such an increase in the age of retirement
will simply rob many people of the leisure years they had looked forward
to, forcing them to work until they are too old to enjoy the travel, the fishing
trips, and the time with their families they had hoped for. While your
argument focuses on what you perceive as a benefit to society, someone else
may view this issue quite differently, and in very personal terms.

When you are in a face-to-face encounter, of course, your opposition
will not allow you to forget his or her point of view. But when you are
writing, you have only the blank, neutral paper or computer screen in front
of you; it is all too easy under these circumstances to focus on your side of
the issue and ignore the opinions of others.

What is wrong with focusing exclusively on your own point of view?
Plenty. First, you may forget to include essential information in your argument if you are too one-sided in your thinking. Your readers, after all, may
not necessarily be on your side, and they will see a gaping hole where the

281

ARGUMENT:
DISCOVERING
AND
DEFENDING
YOUR POINT
OF VIEW

"other side's" points should be. Your readers will wonder why you have failed to address the questions and counterarguments that are obvious to them, and this could cause them to dismiss your argument.

The best reason for stating the opposition's case is a strategic one: You need to convince your readers that your side of the issue is the right side—just as you need to convince your roommates about why you should not have to do the dishes. One of the most convincing strategies is to acknowledge opposing arguments, then explain why they are not valid. You know from your own experience that your arguments become clearest when you have to respond to the opposition.

Organize Your Argument

Your best organizational tool may be your prewriting. Sound contradictory? After all, when you prewrite you are not supposed to be thinking about organization. Yet, as you look over your prewriting you will discover that certain key ideas seem to predominate. As a result, when you begin to organize your essay, those ideas are likely to emerge as the major elements in the argument.

As you begin to identify the major elements in the argument, think about how you can present your points most effectively using the organizational strategies we have discussed in this text. For example, the thesis statement "The retirement age in the United States should be raised to seventy because it will increase the number of experienced workers, reduce the cost of social security, and keep older people healthy and active for a longer period" sets up a *cause-effect* relationship, but your essay may lend itself more readily to *classification* or *comparison and contrast* as a dominant strategy. You will see in the following examples, however, that you are likely to use several strategies woven together as you construct your argument.

Decide on an Argument Strategy

Listed below are three models of organization that writers commonly use when writing an argument. These models focus on two key ideas, but the patterns can work no matter how long your essay or how many points you cover.

Model I

> *Thesis Statement:* "The retirement age in the United States should be raised to seventy."
>
> *Your First Point:* "Raising the retirement age will increase the number of experienced workers in a shrinking work force."

282

ARGUMENT:
DISCOVERING
AND
DEFENDING
YOUR POINT
OF VIEW

Your Second Point: "Raising the retirement age will reduce the cost of social security."

Your Rebuttal to the Opposition's First Point: "People who remain active in the work force are more likely to stay active and healthy longer."

Your Rebuttal to the Opposition's Second Point: "Older workers add stability and experience to a work force, and they can help to train and set an example for younger, less experienced workers."

Conclusion: "Society, industry, and individuals will all benefit from an increase in the retirement age to seventy."

Note the interplay between cause and effect throughout Model I. In addition, note how the writer compares and contrasts the opposing points. In the following sample paragraph, the writer also uses *description* and *narration* to illustrate and support one of the essay's points. Such support keeps readers interested and helps to convince them:

> While some people suggest that raising the retirement age would deprive older citizens of their chance to take trips, go fishing, or play bridge by pushing retirement to an age where they might be plagued by illness or disability, others point out that people who stay active at their work tend to live longer, more satisfying lives. A recent study of women in their eighties and nineties who were still active and alert found that the common denominator among them was their continued mental activity. They had never lost the sense that they still had much to learn and much to contribute to the world.

Model II

Thesis Statement: "The retirement age in the United States should be raised to seventy."

Opposition: "Older citizens will be cheated out of their chance to enjoy their retirement years, and they will rob younger workers of jobs that would otherwise be available."

Your Rebuttal to the Opposition's First Point: "People who remain in the work force are more likely to stay active and healthy longer."

Your Rebuttal to the Opposition's Second Point: "Older workers add stability and experience to a work force, and they can help to train and set an example for younger, less experienced workers."

Your First Point: "Raising the retirement age will increase the number of experienced workers in a shrinking work force."

Your Second Point: "Raising the retirement age will reduce the cost of social security."

Conclusion: "Society, industry, and individuals will all benefit from an increase in the retirement age to seventy."

ARGUMENT:
DISCOVERING
AND
DEFENDING
YOUR POINT
OF VIEW

Thesis Statement: "The retirement age in the United States should be raised to seventy."

Your First Point: Note that your first point also rebuts the opposition's first point: "Raising the retirement age will increase the number of experienced workers in a shrinking work force, as well as add stability and experience. Older workers can train and set an example for younger, less experienced workers."

Your Second Point: Note that your second point also rebuts the opposition's second point: "Raising the retirement age will reduce the cost of social security and keep older citizens active and healthy longer."

Conclusion: "Society, industry, and individuals will all benefit from an increase in the retirement age to seventy."

A STUDENT AT WORK

Student Steve Dominguez was intrigued with his topic, and he decided to develop the above points into a full-fledged essay. He decided to use the pattern in Model III to address each of the points in the essay map. Note that Steve avoided the temptation to "fill in the blanks"; that is, he did not give each point exactly the same amount of space, and he did not follow the pattern so rigidly that the reader is more aware of the pattern than the argument. Such an essay—and such a writing task—would be boring for both himself and his reader. As he developed this essay, Steve used the guidelines in "Creating a Winning Argument" beginning on page 278.

1   As he neared the age of one hundred, Paramount Pictures founder Adolph Zukor said, "If I'd known how old I was going to be I'd have taken better care of myself." As a nation, we may be saying something quite similar in the near future. With the approach of the twenty-first century, the proportion of older Americans to younger is changing dramatically, and as a consequence, the American work force is changing, as well. Because raising the retirement age will increase the number of experienced workers in a shrinking work force, reduce the cost of social security, and keep older people healthy and active for a longer period, the retirement age in the United States should be raised to seventy.

2   While the United States historically has been a nation dominated by the young, the largest age group in the nation will soon be composed of those who are middle-aged and older; in fact, according to Harry F. Rosenthal of the Associated Press, the fastest-growing segment of the U.S. population is now made up of persons who are over eighty-five years of age. This group is expected to grow from the present 2.7 million persons, to over sixteen million by the middle of the next century.

284

ARGUMENT:
DISCOVERING
AND
DEFENDING
YOUR POINT
OF VIEW

3   This dramatic demographic shift will require equally dramatic changes in the way we view the elderly. One of the most fundamental adjustments should be in the age of retirement, traditionally set at sixty-five. Because there will be fewer qualified younger workers, older workers should be retained longer, perhaps to the age of seventy or even seventy-five. Those who now expect to be "put out to pasture" in their sixties will look forward to five or ten more productive years, and they may have to postpone the "golden years" of retirement until their seventies or eighties. The economic benefit of this increase in the retirement age would be immediate. With fewer retirees drawing on Social Security, the spiraling costs of that benefit will begin to level off, protecting it for future generations and taking fewer tax dollars out of the pockets of today's younger workers.

4   While some people suggest that raising the retirement age would deprive older citizens of their chance to take trips, go fishing, or play bridge by pushing retirement to an age where they might be plagued by illness or disability, others point out that people who stay active at their work tend to live longer, more satisfying lives after sixty-five. A recent study of women in their eighties and nineties who were still active and alert found that the common denominator among them was their continued mental activity. They had never lost the sense that they still had much to learn and much to contribute to the world.

5   While they would personally benefit from being kept on the job, older workers are also likely to provide a sense of experience and stability that is lacking in many U.S. workplaces at the present time. Employers are having a difficult time finding workers who are both willing and qualified to do the work they have available. Younger workers are often not prepared for the available jobs, and employers do not have the time to train them. In addition, many younger workers have not had role models who can show them appropriate workplace behavior, and are likely to feel picked on if a boss suggests that they should not arrive late to work, or that they should dress in a manner that reflects well on the company. Older workers can set the tone and provide a positive example, for they have long since learned that certain kinds of behavior go along with succeeding on the job.

6   Some people may argue that older workers are depriving young people of available jobs, but in fact the opposite is true. There are jobs to be filled, but many workers are simply not well enough prepared to fill them. The experience, skills, and patience brought into the workplace by older workers could provide both employers and young workers with the resources they need to fill the gap between them.

7   "How strange that while we have spent the past 10,000 years trying to live long and grow old, now that we are having some success we don't know what to make of it," says gerontologist Ken Dychtwald in his book *Age Wave*. "Our nation has yet to figure out a positive and hopeful way to think about itself growing up." Perhaps we should begin by utilizing the resources available to us in the sixty-five- to seventy-year-old population, providing them with more active, healthy, productive years, saving the social security system from collapse, and making the workplace better for all.

285

ARGUMENT:
DISCOVERING
AND
DEFENDING
YOUR POINT
OF VIEW

For Thought and Discussion

This activity can be done individually or as a group exercise:

1. Decide on *one topic* for argument that is currently in the news, then discover the points on *both sides* of the argument, pro and con.

2. Arrange the points on both sides of the argument in each of the three patterns above.

3. If time permits, share your points with the class as a whole. If not, hand in the written pros and cons to your instructor.

 ## "SO'S YOUR OLD MAN!": LOGICAL FALLACIES

Argument is a highly civilized activity; when its rules are obeyed and its conventions followed, it saves a lot of bloodshed. The ancient Greek and Roman debaters understood this, but they were also aware that when things became hot and heavy, arguers would be tempted to try any strategies they could think of—fair or foul—to win audiences to their side.

There is a tendency among people when debating an issue to focus attention on the weaknesses of their adversaries. Even the most experienced debaters find themselves falling into this trap every once in a while—political campaigns are prime examples of this. Yet these veterans know that attacks on their *opponents* rather than on their opponents' *arguments* are unfair not only because they hit below the belt, but also because they often are ineffective and backfire, weakening the attacker's argument.

When a debater begins to deflect attention away from the issue, the central focus is lost and the argument too often degenerates into unpleasantness and hard feelings. These unfair strategies are called *logical fallacies,* and they are attempts to strengthen one's own argument by (1) attacking the opponent's character, (2) changing the subject, or (3) adding irrelevant material to the content of the argument.

The urge to use logical fallacies comes as naturally to us now as it did when Plato and his fellow Greeks were debating on Athens' streetcorners. The urge to punch one's opponent in the nose comes naturally, too, but we resist the temptation in favor of other, more effective methods of discussing our differences. We must, if we are to change anyone's thinking, train ourselves to avoid logical fallacies, just as we were trained as children to avoid hitting, kicking, and biting as ways of settling disputes.

It is also important to realize that some people's minds will change only a little—perhaps not at all—when they hear our arguments. Our arguments may only make small inroads, helping others to modify their views and become more tolerant of the other side; but even the most effective argument will not necessarily win them over. It is our job to do the best we

286

ARGUMENT:
DISCOVERING
AND
DEFENDING
YOUR POINT
OF VIEW

can to convince others of our point of view, yet it is equally important that we respect their right to hold a view that is different from ours.

ARGUING WITH CLASS: AVOIDING LOGICAL FALLACIES

Since a logical fallacy is an attempt to deflect the audience's attention away from the issue that is under debate, the best way to avoid any such tactics is to learn to identify the most common types.

Argument *Ad Hominem*

An *ad hominem* argument might attack an opponent's personal behavior, even though it has nothing to do with the issue—as when someone says, "I don't think Amelia Connor is a good doctor because she sent her kids to live with their father," or when a political opponent charges, "Peter Penney shouldn't be elected county treasurer because he buys expensive clothes."

Such charges are irrelevant, and they do not examine the reasons for the behavior or circumstances they attack: Amelia's ex-husband may be in a better position than she to care for their children full-time, or he may live near a school that the children want to attend. Peter may simply be a smart shopper who buys good clothes on sale, or he may in fact buy expensive clothes because they give him pleasure—just as other people derive pleasure from watching football games, going to parties, or working in the garden.

In politics, *ad hominem* (in Greek, "to the man" or "at the man") arguments may attack a candidate by raising issues about his or her affiliation with particular social, civic, or religious organizations, or they may attack more subtly by raising irrelevant questions about the candidate's family or ethnic background. Even though most thinking citizens abhor such attacks on candidates, these attacks are unfortunately effective, and unscrupulous political organizers will use them to their advantage.

Since it is not your purpose to attack the person who takes a different point of view from yours, avoid *ad hominem* arguments. Instead, take the time to make sure that your arguments have plenty of evidence to support your point of view.

Argument *Ad Populum*

Closely related to this is the argument *ad populum,* which means "to the people." Here, the argument slips into the use of terms that have predictable emotional appeal: "My opponent, Dorothy Baker, is against family values." By using such an appeal, her opponent may be hoping that he can avoid discussing specific issues in the campaign. He wants, instead, to divert voters' attention to their protective feelings about their own families; at the same time, he wants to imply that he is for "family values"—even though a survey of his voting record might indicate otherwise.

Other *ad populum* appeals likely to direct the audience's attention away from key issues focus on emotionally charged terms such as *God, American, motherhood, Communist, criminal,* or *radical.* Certainly we are accustomed to such appeals, not only in politics but also in advertising; however, a well-constructed argument does not rely on such devices in order to succeed.

The Red Herring

Another relative of *ad hominem* and *ad populum* is the "red herring." This is named after a tactic used by escaped prisoners who would drag a strong-smelling fish across tracks they were trying to cover so that pursuing dogs would be confused by the new scent and pursue the fish instead of the intended object. The tactic works as well on humans as it does on tracking dogs—only the "fish" is different.

By changing the subject in an argument and sending it off onto the wrong track, a writer hopes that he or she can divert the audience's attention to the phony issue and away from the real one. For example, a committee that opposes the construction of a new highway—because it will divert traffic away from a shopping center where many committee members own businesses—might try to "change the subject" by focusing the public's attention on a small cluster of trees that will have to be cut down (the red herring) rather than on the safety issues that prompted the planning of the new road in the first place.

The Bandwagon Appeal

Similarly, a "bandwagon appeal" hopes to draw the audience in by suggesting that the majority of people already believe in the argument. The appeal of this principle has been demonstrated by voter behavior in recent political campaigns: as one candidate begins to establish a lead in preelection polls, undecided voters tend increasingly to favor that candidate; many people are simply more comfortable siding with the majority, and persuasive debaters understand this.

The highway issue discussed under red-herring arguments may also take advantage of the bandwagon appeal. Since no one wants to be against trees, the committee that opposes the new highway may mount a "save-our-trees" campaign, gathering in new members who may have legitimate con-

288

ARGUMENT:
DISCOVERING
AND
DEFENDING
YOUR POINT
OF VIEW

cerns about the safety of the highway, but who want to be on the side that is for motherhood, apple pie—and trees.

Misuse of Authorities, "Common Knowledge," and Statistics

When you use information from outside sources for your argument, you certainly can bolster its credibility. However, this information can backfire if you are not careful to check that (1) the authority you cite is an authority in the field you are discussing, (2) the authority's ideas are used precisely and not applied too loosely, (3) an idea "everyone knows" is true *is*, in fact, true, (4) the statistics you use are timely and not out of date, and (5) your source for statistics draws conclusions that can be supported by the statistics.

For Thought and Discussion

1. Find an example of an advertisement in a newspaper or magazine that uses one or more of the logical fallacies described above. Bring the ad to class and describe how the advertisers have used logical fallacies.

2. In class, brainstorm to discover a current controversy in which the participants are employing the kinds of tactics we have discussed above. Newsmagazines, television news interviews, and daily newspapers should provide many examples of logical fallacies used on both sides of the issue.

A POETIC ARGUMENT

The following poem by Dylan Thomas argues against the graceful acceptance of aging and death. Though he lived only to the age of thirty-nine (1914–1953), the Welsh poet wrote passionately about the feelings of fear, anger, and regret that people are likely to experience as they feel themselves grow older and watch their powers diminish. He wrote "Do Not Go Gentle into That Good Night" shortly before his own untimely death.

Do Not Go Gentle into That Good Night

Do not go gentle into that good night,
Old age should burn and rave at close of day;
Rage, rage against the dying of the light.   3

Though wise men at their end know dark is right,
Because their words had forked no lightning they
Do not go gentle into that good night.   6

Good men, the last wave by, crying how bright
Their frail deeds might have danced in a green bay,
Rage, rage against the dying of the light.   9

Wild men who caught and sang the sun in flight,
And learn, too late, they grieved it on its way,
Do not go gentle into that good night.   12

Grave men, near death, who see with blinding sight
Blind eyes could blaze like meteors and be gay,
Rage, rage against the dying of the light.   15

And you, my father, there on the sad height,
Curse, bless, me now with your fierce tears, I pray.
Do not go gentle into that good night.
Rage, rage against the dying of the light.   —Dylan Thomas   19

289

ARGUMENT:
DISCOVERING
AND
DEFENDING
YOUR POINT
OF VIEW

For Thought and Discussion

1. Is Thomas's poem an argument or simply a protest? What is the difference between the two? What, in your own words, is Thomas's thesis in this poem?

2. What adjectives does Thomas use to describe the people about whom he writes?

3. What is the predominant *image* (mental picture) that comes to you as you read the poem? Discuss, in class, why Thomas chose this rather than some other kind of image.

4. Why, in your opinion, does Thomas suggest *rage* instead of acceptance for the inevitable process of dying? What kind of emotional response do you feel is appropriate for those facing death?

A PROFESSIONAL WRITER AT WORK

In the following excerpt from her book *In the Fullness of Time: The Pleasures and Inconveniences of Growing Old*, eighty-year-old Avis D. Carlson argues that, like teenagers, elderly people face an "identity crisis" of their own. Carlson finds a number of parallels between the problems that confront adolescents and those that confront their grandparents, as members of both groups find themselves at a stage in life about which they know little and understand less. Carlson is arguing against society's preconceptions and stereotypes of aging, and she is arguing for an understanding of what it is like to grow old in a culture that values youth and energy over wisdom and acceptance.

We Too Have an Identity Problem

1   Every literate person is familiar with and probably somewhat bored by Erik Erikson's phrase, "Identity crisis." In the past decade it has been tossed about ad nauseam—with about as many connotations as users. Thus a mother may apologize for a troublesome teenager, "He's having a hard time finding

290

ARGUMENT:
DISCOVERING
AND
DEFENDING
YOUR POINT
OF VIEW

himself.'' The teenager himself, if sufficiently verbal, may ask the world to understand how painful it is not to know "who I am."

2   As commonly used, the phrase applies to youngsters on the threshold of adulthood, or, if there has been some unfortunate blockage in personal development, to young adults. In either case, it applies to the *young,* who are held to be engaged in a "search for identity."

3   What has not been so clearly recognized is that entrance into old age, like entrance into adulthood, also sets up an identity crisis, in which the individual becomes *uncertain in his image of himself and of the role or roles expected of him.* Because it is so little understood, this uncertainty is one of the hardest features of growing old.

4   According to Erik Erikson, identity is the result of a constant interplay between ourselves and (a) our thinking about ourselves and (b) what we feel others feel we are or (c) should be. As he also says, this three-fold process mostly takes place unconsciously and without too much stress.

5   It is my observation and, more importantly, my *experience* that there is an identity crisis attending entrance into old age and that it is every bit as full of uncertainty and emotional distress as the one we went through a half century earlier.

6   As I watch my adolescent grandchildren it sometimes seems to me that they and I have a great deal in common. (Naturally, *they* don't think so!) Both they and I are emerging from a familiar stage of life into an unknown one where we must be constantly feeling for a new footing. Both of us belong to an age-group commonly regarded as a social problem, if not a downright nuisance. Growing up is scary business, but so is growing old. At times childhood seems a poor preparation for the stresses imposed by changes in bodies and emotions of the adolescent. But believe me, the elder often feels that *his* past was not a very good preparation for the stresses imposed by his changing body and emotions—not to mention the furiously changing world around him.

7   But, of course, the analogy can't be pushed very far. There are great differences. The adolescent is changing at a great pace, usually much faster than the one laid out for his grandparents. Within a few years he must have acquired enough maturity to function independently. His body is developing rapidly, his muscles growing stronger. If all goes well, his horizon widens from month to month as new experiences pour in. He is, or should be, rapidly gaining independence, that is, the ability to make his own decisions and live without the supporting prop of his parents.

8   We, on the other hand, find our physical strength diminishing, our muscles and sense organs weakening. And worse, from having been the strong, supporting force in the family all during our mid-years, we are very apt to find ourselves becoming dependent in various ways, even if not financially. As the years go on, health and other problems will almost certainly force us to depend on others for many services. This can be galling, especially if we do not feel genuine affection in those who serve us. In any case, even under the best of circumstances, such as when those upon whom we must depend obviously respect and love us, the new situation is a severe comedown. Literally, old age is the only period of life when a loss of role does not almost auto-

matically usher one into a new role. In American life old age is a time *without a future.* If we try to cling to the roles we had, we become nuisances and society is not slow to let us know.

291

ARGUMENT:
DISCOVERING
AND
DEFENDING
YOUR POINT
OF VIEW

9   In old age we have not only to create our own new roles (and not just any old roles, but roles that allow us to feel useful and interested) but to create a set of values that in some ways go against the grain of general American values.

10   If we can't create those roles and values, we are lost. A great many of us are lost. The elderly psychiatrist, Olga Knopf, declares: "I am convinced that no old person is entirely free from at least occasional depressions." Depression in old age differs from that in youth in one respect, however. In the aged, the anger is directed more against himself than against anyone in the outer world. This self-hatred and self-rejection explain in part the high rate of suicide among the older generation.

11   To experience changes like this, over however many years, is to experience an "identity crisis." One of its most exasperating features is that, like the earlier crisis, it is very hard to pin down in one's mind exactly where one is at the moment. Am I old or am I not? (Am I grown up or am I not?) What is expected of me? (What am I supposed to be doing in this new period in my life?) If, as seems clear, many of my age group are not much approved of, how do I set about winning approval? (Do I say, "To heck with them all"?) How can I live on good terms with myself and with a society that has grave misgivings about the value of most people my age? All this when I'm not yet even sure that I'm old!

12   The folk wisdom is not much help. There was a time, I think, when old people more or less *knew* how they were expected to behave.

13   But now, about the best the folk wisdom can do is to wheel out some old saws, such as: "You're as old as you feel," or "Some people are older at forty than others at seventy." Much help such platitudes offer a sixty-year-old trying to place himself!

14   Remembering what his sixteen-year-old self felt about sexagenarians, he likely devotes some time on or around his sixtieth birthday to examining himself for signs of decrepitude. (At least *I* did.) What he probably finds is that he "feels" no different than he did at fifty. Indeed, he may even "feel" considerably better, because he has finished with many of the responsibilities that then weighed him down. So, temporarily, he relaxes, assuring himself that of course he will be old sometime, but the time is certainly not yet. Meanwhile, he will just not concern himself too much with what he sees in the mirror.

15   Joan Walsh Angland has said, "My mind never tells me—only the mirror speaks of the passing years." Very nice. But the fact is that most of us get to be quite clever at dealing with that mirror. Smiling at it, we find, will wipe off several years because the lines then run up instead of down. Or we may discover with one of my sisters that leaving off one's glasses also helps.

16   But at some time around seventy or seventy-five, even the lucky of us are forced to begin running through our surprised minds the astounding thought: "*It has happened. I am old.*" We have known all along that time was sliding by and that eventually, if we managed to avoid death, we would be

292

ARGUMENT:
DISCOVERING
AND
DEFENDING
YOUR POINT
OF VIEW

old. But the time was always somewhere in the misty future. How can it possibly be *now*? No matter how well we think we have prepared ourselves for old age, it is almost sure to come as the surprise described in the couplet by an unknown author:

> I have always known that at last I would take that road,
> But yesterday I did not know that it would be today.

17   What finally convinces us is not so much the candles our children tactfully leave off our birthday cakes or the shock in the eyes of an old friend who has not seen us for several years as it is in the evidence within ourselves. We suddenly observe that the muscles in an arm have gone stringy. Or that we have unconsciously begun to sit or lean against something when putting on slacks. Or that clothing that once fit perfectly is now fitting badly. Or that a finger has begun to quiver uncontrollably. Or that our digestion has become so cranky that some foods must be forgone and none of them seems to have much flavor anymore. Or that our eyes or ears are markedly duller than they were only a few years ago, and that chores we were doing without thinking are now tiring.

18   Worse, oh much worse, the names of people and places are evading us. Suddenly, in the very middle of a sentence or an introduction of someone we've known for years, a word or a name is gone. Eventually we remember it, but the experience is a little frightening as well as very embarrassing. *These are the events that let us know.*

19   But the recognition is badly complicated by the fact that while the symptoms of age are being perceived, the "I" that sits behind every face feels itself to be just what it has always been. So it cannot really *believe* that what is appearing in the mirror or in the embarrassing memory lapses can be itself. Because the perpetually watchful "I" is incredulous, the person in the process of being brought to concede that he has become old has a real psychological problem on his hands. Like the little old woman who lost her petticoat, one is shocked by the primal question of identity: "Can this really be I?"

20   The problem is compounded by two facts of elderly life today: one, that the crisis is usually met in solitude; the other, that the general attitude of American society toward its old is one of profound disrespect.

21   What is needed, of course, is what has come to be called "consciousness raising." But who is around to help us with it? Within the last few decades there has evolved a whole professional class of counselors for the young. Also marriage counselors and vocational counselors and psychiatrists and "mind expanders" of assorted denominations, all dealing with the young and the middle-aged. But outside a handful of psychiatrists specializing in the problems of the elderly and a few overworked geriatricians (most of whom are barely middle-aged, so new is this medical specialty), who is around to help us with our special problems of identity? A well-married old couple who long ago learned to communicate their deepest feelings can greatly help each other, but many if not most old couples have never learned to enter the needed level of communication. And besides, there are all of the elderly singles—especially us widows, who in our younger days were actively discouraged from talking too freely about our deepest feelings.

22   So most of us going into the stage of life known as old age must do it alone and without much understanding or support. We don't even talk about it much among ourselves. Such talk as we have usually takes the form of wry jokes like, "I'm in the metallic stage, gold in my teeth, silver in my hair, and lead in my feet." Or the corny old, "My get-up-and-go has got-up-and-went."

23   Occasionally, when the arthritis gets too bad or money too scarce, we may let go and moan about our condition—whereupon everyone who decently can makes a quick departure from our presence, and we have had another good lesson in not talking about the problems.

24   As for sitting down to discuss seriously among ourselves the bewildering and overwhelming fact of having become old and of death waiting who knows how close, we just don't do it. Or at least we are only beginning to do it in some of the better senior citizen centers. It's as if we ourselves subscribe to the general notion that there is something *improper* about the subject. In such reticence, we tend to accept the general myths about us, one of which is that we are all alike and, therefore, all of us are helpless and need protection. Other myths are that we are demanding and set in our ways, lonely because we are not living with our families, on our way to an institution if not already there, and sooner or later going to become senile.

25   The best literary statement I have seen of this phase of the identity problem of the old is a quotation by Beauvoir from Gide's *Journal*, which is to say, from the most solitary of writing, the journal of a professional writer:

> If I did not keep telling myself my age over and over again, I am sure I should scarcely be aware of it. Nevertheless, even by repeating, "I am over sixty-five" like a lesson to be learnt by heart I can hardly persuade myself of it: all I manage to do is to convince myself of this—that the space in which my desires and my delights, my powers and my will can still hope to spread out is very narrow.

26   Or again, in words that have the ring of personal experience to many a senior not sufficiently gifted with words or self-analysis to have written them for himself:

> My heart has remained so young that I have the continual feeling of playing a part, the part of the seventy-year-old that I certainly am; and the infirmities and weaknesses that remind me of my age act like a prompter, remind me of my lines when I tend to stray. Then, like the good actor I should like to be, I go back into my role and I pride myself on playing it.

Only by taking careful note of the physical and mental changes that are happening in us can we realize that the time is finally *now*.

27   The other tangle of facts making the acceptance of one's having become old (that is, identifying oneself as one of the old) very difficult is the attitude of our culture toward its old. To return to Erikson's definition, the second part of identity formation consists of the individual's judging himself "in the light of what he perceives to be the way others judge him in comparison to themselves and to a typology significant to them."

28   If the first phase of identifying oneself as old was subjective and hazy, this one is brutally clear. In a culture whose basic value is productivity, we are first

294

ARGUMENT:
DISCOVERING
AND
DEFENDING
YOUR POINT
OF VIEW

pushed out of employment and then either judged useless or tolerated for our sentimental value. Though perhaps not as completely as it was two decades ago, social esteem still largely depends on productivity. Today, as always, he who does not produce is felt to be a weight to be borne, gracefully or grudgingly, by society.

29   Particularly for those who come to it without financial reserves, old age can be a time of great cruelty. And never let it be forgotten that around 5,000,000 (or a good fourth) of us are below the poverty line. Just as the Eskimo grandmother, left to freeze in her igloo, was a side effect of her culture, these millions of old people are at least partly a side effect of our culture. They are the end result of a lifetime of lacks: too little money, too little education, too few stimulating jobs and experiences, inadequate diet and medical care, limited interests, and limiting emotions. If some of them are cantankerous or senile, who knows what they might have been under less grinding circumstances? The wonder is that so many have made of themselves interesting, lovable human beings in spite of all the limitations they met.

30   When people say, "Old age is so pathetic," they are usually thinking of the elderly sick and poor. We need to remember, however, that there are many kinds of old people in this country. Many are "comfortably situated." A few are rich, and they as well as the poor have special problems. A Florida psychiatrist has remarked about some of her patients who were buying $100,000 condominiums, "Unless the people in those buildings can find ways to get really involved with other people, those buildings might as well be called pre-burial vaults."

31   So far as cultural attitudes go, the plight of the elderly poor and lonely differs only in degree from that of the not-poor and not-lonely. The tiny percentage of old people who have won fame or general applause through a sizable contribution to the common good does not, of course, have this problem of social disrespect. (What they may get is a somewhat patronizing celebration of what they *were*.) But for all the rest of us the attitude of our society toward the old is one of the hard facts we must confront in forming our new self-identification, our sense of "I am" and "I have a right to be." In his poem "Provide, Provide," Robert Frost said it for all time:

> No memory of having starred
> Atones for later disregard,
> Or keeps the end from being hard.

32   To return to Erikson again:

> An optimal sense of identity, on the other hand, is experienced merely as a sense of psycho-social well-being. Its most obvious concomitants are a feeling of being at home in one's body, a sense of "knowing where one is going," and an inner assuredness of anticipated recognition from those who count.

33   Nothing I ever read or heard spoken more completely sums up the difficulties we face in thinking, "I've grown old." How can one "feel at home" in a body that every week and every year changes for the worse? And how can one have a sense of "knowing where one is going" when, if there is anything

295

ARGUMENT:
DISCOVERING
AND
DEFENDING
YOUR POINT
OF VIEW

certain to the elder, it is that he *can't* know where he will be or in what "shape" he will be in a year or a decade hence—or even if he will *be* at all. And how can he feel assured of recognition when every year those who "count" for him personally dwindle in number and finally become so few that he feels almost denuded?

34   Any way one looks at it, the process of identifying oneself as old is not easy. No wonder our ambition tends to be to "stay young" rather than to *become* the best possible old person. To become the "best possible" elder is a very difficult, highly creative undertaking and should be so regarded by both the old person and those around him.

For Thought and Discussion

1. What is an identity crisis?

2. Avis Carlson draws a number of parallels between teenagers and elders. Using your own experience as a guide, think of some additional similarities that the two groups have in common.

3. In addition to using outside sources for this essay, Carlson uses her own personal experience. Cite five examples of her use of outside sources, either quotes from other reading or statistics.

4. What does Carlson say about the "I" that lives inside of each person? What is its nature? How does it respond to the changes that occur as one grows older?

5. At what point, according to Carlson, does a person realize that he or she has become "old"?

6. If you had to advise someone on how to "grow old gracefully," what five suggestions would you make?

WRITING ASSIGNMENT

Argument is stimulating, whether you are writing or talking. Not only does argument require that you take a position and defend it, but it also requires that you avoid the tendency to drift into logical fallacies or wander off into side issues that distract the reader from the topic at hand.

This kind of discipline can be exciting. As you formulate your argument in your prewriting, you will discover new ways of approaching the topic and new kinds of examples and illustrations; as a result, you may decide that you want to reorganize your strategy several times before you're satisfied. With each new discovery your argument takes on added definition, and you become more confident in your ability to discuss your point of view.

Formulating and writing an argument is a *process,* and it is one that requires time, testing, and (in many cases) research. Below is a process that you and your peers may follow as you develop and polish your argument.

296

**ARGUMENT:
DISCOVERING
AND
DEFENDING
YOUR POINT
OF VIEW**

1. In a peer group, take turns describing the topics and arguments that each person has formulated so far. As you listen to and discuss your peers' arguments, you will find yourself sharpening your own focus and coming up with examples and illustrations to back up your argument. In addition, their questions about your topic and arguments will provide you with ideas and supporting points that you had not considered before.

2. You may not have felt strongly one way or another on this issue before researching it; even after doing some research you may be uncertain about how you feel about some aspects of the issue. In addition, you may find that you agree with one side of the debate on some points, and with the other side of the debate on other points. That's okay! Examine all of the sides of the argument, and develop a point of view that is uniquely your own.

3. After you have read about and discussed your topic, set aside the articles and any notes you have taken (you'll return to them later) and simply cluster or freewrite on the topic until you have run out of points on both sides.

4. Now, evaluate your cluster or freewriting and organize key points into one of the patterns we have discussed in the chapter. If the pattern does not seem to be working for you, shift to another. If you need additional arguments or supporting points, do some more research on your topic.

5. Develop each of the points you wish to make, using examples and illustrations, and make certain that your points and the opposition's points are roughly parallel (though you need not give the opposition equal time). This is where you may wish to refer to the articles you have read on the topic, quoting examples or authorities in support of one or another of your points.

6. Write a finished essay of at least 800 words in length.

Suggestions for Topics

For this assignment, take a stand on an issue that is current in the news. Inform yourself on both sides of the issue and make a point to find as many newspaper and newsmagazine articles on the issue as you can. Be sure to hang on to copies of your sources. Your instructor may ask that you hand in clippings and photocopies of articles on your topic, along with your essay.

Peer Editing Checklist

Each peer editing group should respond to the following points for the student essay "The Problems of Taking Care of Elderly People" in the next section. When the group has practiced peer editing on this essay, it should go to work on the papers written by group members. Be sure to make enough photocopies of your essay for your peer editing group so that everyone has access to a paper.

297

ARGUMENT:
DISCOVERING
AND
DEFENDING
YOUR POINT
OF VIEW

1. First, read the essay through once without stopping.

2. Indicate any ideas, passages, imagery, allusions, or other aspects of this essay you found effective. Positive reinforcement is a powerful tool.

3. What is the central point of the essay's argument?

4. List the concrete details that develop the central point.

5. Ask the author about any concrete details you would like to know to strengthen or clarify the central point for you.

6. Determine which argument pattern the writer has used. Read through the essay to see if the pattern is consistent throughout.

7. Point out any logical fallacies.

8. Check to see if the writer acknowledges opposing points of view.

9. What is your reaction to the essay's title? To the introduction? To the conclusion? Do they help you better understand the author's point, or do they pique your interest in reading the essay?

When writers have revised the content of the essay to their satisfaction and are ready for feedback about mechanics, point out but do not correct any problems you suspect exist with spelling, grammar, and punctuation. It is the writer's responsibility to make such corrections.

Help! For Further Work

Read the following student draft as if you were its peer editor. Then answer the questions in the peer editing checklist.

The Problems of Taking Care of Elderly People

1   Sam and Ethel Green are in their mid-seventies, and they live in a comfortable section of Chicago, Illinois. They have raised three children, and ran a successful business (selling furniture and appliances, but the best part of their business was selling TVs) until Sam became ill with Alzheimer's disease.

2   Like millions of other elderly Americans, Sam and Ethel were suddenly faced with the problem of how to take care of Sam's needs while avoiding putting him in a rest home. You see, the government's Medicare and Medicaid programs only pay for care in hospitals or nursing homes. They won't pay for care at home.

3   Ethel didn't want to send Sam to a nursing home, because she had heard horror stories about people getting bedsores, lying in their own feces, and they were deprived of proper nutrition. Everybody knows that nursing homes don't really care about their patients. Also, Sam didn't want to leave home. He knew if he went into a nursing home he would never come out.

298

ARGUMENT:
DISCOVERING
AND
DEFENDING
YOUR POINT
OF VIEW

4   Medicare and Medicaid were programs past by the government to help elderly people when they had large medical expenses. The government thought everyone would be happy going to a nursing home instead of staying at home, but this hasn't turned out to be the case. Instead, many seniors groups are putting pressure on their congressmen to pass a law that would help people take care of their families at home, but it won't do any good, because politicians are not interested in ordinary people's problems. They only want to help big business, and many nursing homes are owned by large corporations.

5   Sam and Ethel and their children all want Sam to stay at home, so they have gone into debt to pay for professional nursing care. This costs the Greens over $1000 a month, and their Social Security and retirement checks only add up to $1500 a month. They might actually have to sell their home, just to keep Sam home—but, then, he wouldn't *have* a home. Yet if Sam went to a nursing home tomorrow, the government would pick up the tab to the tune of as much as $2000 a month. The Greens are mad. They don't think the government knows how to do simple math.

STUDENT STARS

The students who wrote these essays did the following:

1. Prewriting

2. Writing

3. Revision of content

4. Proofreading and revision of mechanics.

Whose Life Is It, Anyway?

1   The members of my generation have been scolded and held up to ridicule by countless critics for being materialistic, mindless, and spineless. We are scoffed at because we wear designer labels, we are despised because we don't know as much as our parents' generation (or do as well on tests as students in other countries), and the older generation worries that if there were a war, we wouldn't show up.

2   I think this is unfair. In the first place, the members of no other generation can know what it's like to grow up now, because they didn't—they grew up in other times with other priorities and problems. For example, my grandparents were teenagers during the Great Depression, and for them, the major concern was to earn enough money to buy food and pay the rent. Some ten million out of the 122 million Americans in 1932 were out of work, and there were few social programs to help them. Many people resorted to selling apples and pencils on streetcorners as a way to survive. My grandparents were "materialistic" as teenagers, but in a sense very different from the way we use the word today: they thought about little else than the "material" goods that would keep them alive—food and shelter. Even if designer labels had been

299

ARGUMENT:
DISCOVERING
AND
DEFENDING
YOUR POINT
OF VIEW

readily available to them back then, my grandparents wouldn't have had the money or time to shop for them. As a result, of course, they don't really understand what all the fuss is about when my sisters and I shop for just the "right" clothes.

3   The members of my generation, on the other hand, have grown up in a prosperous world that seems dedicated to marketing and packaging. As babies we were placed in front of the TV where we watched ads for toys that we soon learned to acquire for ourselves—either by using our very own baby charm, or by working on our parents' guilt. But we also watched *Sesame Street,* where we were "sold" numbers and letters by the most persuasive salespeople of our era: Big Bird and Kermit the Frog. We learned early about marketing and packaging, and it was only natural that as we grew older and more independent, we would begin to market and package ourselves.

4   It takes a lot of time, energy, and savvy to put together a successful "package" that a consumer will "buy," and don't think for a moment that we aren't conscious of the fact. We know what our society really wants from us, and we are doing our best to measure up: It wants us to be perfect—physically and mentally perfect. The physical part is the easiest, the showiest, and the most fun to put together, so many of us concentrate first on that aspect of ourselves, hoping that it will deflect attention from our other deficiencies long enough for us to go through the arduous and awkward process of "finding" ourselves.

5   Our parents and teachers tell us that we will find ourselves through our studies—and as long as we get A's and B's, they figure we must be learning something. We know that making the Dean's list certainly enhances the package, but this, apparently, is no longer enough. Dozens of surveys, reports, and books have come out that tell us how dumb we are; yet here are most of us, living up to the school's requirements, working hard at our studies, and wondering why the world around us keeps upping the ante on our lives.

6   The members of my parents' generation were teenagers in the fifties and sixties, and they remember their college days as the happiest time in their lives; in fact, that's what my parents keep saying to me: "Enjoy yourself! This is the best time of your life." For them, it probably was. They didn't have to work while they were in school, they looked forward to secure jobs after graduation no matter how they were "packaged," and they were living in the richest, most powerful, most optimistic nation on earth.

7   My life isn't like that, nor are the lives of most of my friends. We worry a great deal about the kinds of jobs we'll be able to find after graduation, and virtually all of us have to work while we're in school. In addition, we worry about the kind of nation we'll be living in when we're our parents' age. Will it be even more crime- and drug-ridden than it is now, and will there be even more homeless people? Will it be possible for the members of my generation to buy homes, and will we be able to afford to have children? And if we do succeed in having homes and families, will they—and we—be wiped out in a second by a nuclear weapon?

8   I guess you could call us materialistic, mindless, and spineless, but the challenges that lie ahead are as serious as those of any generation that has gone before, and we know it. We may be taking a little longer to recognize what we must do in order to respond to the challenges, but that doesn't mean

300

ARGUMENT:
DISCOVERING
AND
DEFENDING
YOUR POINT
OF VIEW

we won't. After all, many of the problems facing us are unlike any that mankind has faced before, and it's going to take us a little more time to figure out what to do. We have been prepared by our elders to inherit a very different world than the one that is actually heading toward us, and it will be a test of our generation's courage and creativity to decide how best to meet the challenges.

9   I believe that, at some point, the members of my generation will decide to put aside the packaging and marketing modes, because for us, they're nothing new. And since we like excitement and action (remember, we're the TV generation that wants everything solved within thirty minutes, including commercials), we may decide to fight a war—one that's against nuclear weapons, against the poverty that holds so much of the world's population hostage, and against the degradation of our environment. Don't worry, Mom and Dad, those are wars we're sure to show up for, because we're beginning to realize that unless those problems are solved, there is no future for any of us.

—Bobbie Chrisney

Drinking and Driving

1   It happened a couple of years ago when my girlfriend and I were leaving a party. I asked her to drive home because I was intoxicated. She responded, "I can't because I don't know how to drive a five-speed." So I drove home seeing double lines, swerving on the highway and creeping along at a snail's pace because I knew my reactions were slow. I was not too drunk to be terrified at what I was doing.

2   Fortunately I did not hurt myself, my friend, or any innocent fellow drivers. Once we made it home, I promised myself I would never drive drunk again. I had learned my lesson. Unfortunately, many other people are not aware of how alcohol affects their abilities. Many even believe that after a few drinks they can handle situations better than when they are sober.

3   Other misconceptions about drinking further increase the danger of drunk driving. Some believe that beer and wine do not have the same effect as hard liquors. In fact, an eighty-proof whiskey, gin, or vodka has the same alcohol content as four to five ounces of wine or twelve ounces of beer—about half an ounce of alcohol.

4   The most problematic connection between drinking and driving is that the intoxicated person fails to recognize how much alcohol impairs behavior. The higher the blood-alcohol level, the more the driver's reaction time is slowed, and the more his or her ability to distinguish between the levels of light or sound and to estimate the speed and distance of moving objects is impaired. In addition, the driver's coordination is reduced.

5   These alcohol-induced physiological effects mean, for example, that people driving at night have more difficulty with glare, since their eyes are slow to adapt to changes in the light. As the blood-alcohol level increases, performance decreases, impairing the ability to perform driving tasks such as stopping, driving at a consistent speed, and steering steadily. The drunk driver is an erratic driver who makes frequent adjustments in speed, direction, and following distance.

301

ARGUMENT:
DISCOVERING
AND
DEFENDING
YOUR POINT
OF VIEW

6 While the driving performance in individual, simple tasks may seem acceptable, the many minor deviations or errors drunk drivers make and then correct (or over-correct) increases their vulnerability to accidents. Driving requires people to do several things at once, such as maintaining a constant speed while responding to signals and monitoring the speed and location of other vehicles.

7 People with a blood-alcohol level of .08% (the legal level defining intoxication in California) can perform one or two simple maneuvers, such as driving along a road and turning at a predictable point. However, real driving can be a much more complex task: a car suddenly turns in front of a driver, someone runs a red light, oncoming traffic shifts into a driver's lane. Now drivers must divide their attention between simple steering, recognizing new situations, making decisions about what to do, and carrying out the proper driving maneuvers. During these typical driving situations, the intoxicated driver often cannot respond quickly or accurately enough to avoid an accident.

8 Even more frightening is the fact that once behind the wheel, the intoxicated driver feels excessively confident and takes more risks than when sober. The result? More than half of all fatal accidents involve a drunk driver. That night I stupidly drove when I was drunk. I was very lucky. I wonder if my fellow drivers knew how lucky they were to get home safely that night.

—Natalie Ushakoff

11

THINKING ON YOUR FEET: EXTEMPORANEOUS WRITING

CONCEPTS TO LEARN

The importance of extemporaneous writing

Key factors in successful extemporaneous writing

Grading standards for extemporaneous writing

In a world as competitive as ours, the ability to respond to ideas and situations quickly—both in person and on paper—is often crucial; yet you may be unsure about how to acquire the necessary skills. Some lucky people seem to have been born with the ability to prepare organized arguments readily and effortlessly, but most of us seem to be more talented at coming up with the perfect argument or response two days after it is needed. This chapter will give you an opportunity to think about and work on your *extemporaneous*—that is, on-the-spot—writing skills.

Everything you have learned so far in *Writing Wisely and Well* has been preparation for this chapter. All the tools you have acquired for generating ideas, identifying key questions, organizing information, and presenting coherent arguments will come into play when you are asked to create an extemporaneous piece of writing in class. This is the kind of writing you have to do for essay exams in many of your classes, as well as for entrance and exit exams in college; most certainly it is the kind of writing that you will have to do on the job. In fact, in both your academic and professional life, you will probably be asked to produce more extemporaneous writing than any other kind.

Before the advent of the printing press or paper or pencils, most people had no choice but to communicate extemporaneously; they were forced—literally—to "think on their feet." In the following passage, the Greek biographer Plutarch (A.D. 46–120) describes how the philosopher Socrates (470–399 B.C.) formulated and put forth his arguments and ideas while he was busy with everyday activities. Although Socrates focused his attention on fundamental, hard questions about the nature of human knowledge and human behavior, he did not sit in an isolated room while the "real world" swirled outside the walls around him; rather, he formed and put forth his arguments wherever he happened to be, combining his passion for ideas with his everyday activities, some of which were mundane and even disagreeable.

> They are wrong who think that politics is like an ocean voyage or a military campaign, something to be done with some particular end in view, something which leaves off as soon as that end is reached. It is not a public chore, to be got over with. It is a way of life. Politics and philosophy are alike. Socrates neither set out benches for his students, nor sat on a platform, nor set hours for his lectures. He was philosophizing all the time—while he was joking, while he was drinking, while he was soldiering, whenever he met you on the street, and at the end when he was in prison and drinking the poison. He was the first to show that all your life, all the time, in everything you do, whatever you are doing, is the time for philosophy. And so also it is of politics.

For Thought and Discussion

1. In what way does Plutarch suggest that politics is connected with daily life?

2. What is our society's attitude toward politics?

3. Discuss what is likely to happen to a democratic system if politics is left only to a few interested, involved individuals.

4. The quotation from Plutarch describes Socrates integrating his philosophical ideas with his daily activities. Give specific examples of actions in your life that reflect your own beliefs and philosophy.

5. Socrates committed suicide in prison by drinking hemlock. Why did he choose to die in this manner? (Remember, this information is as close as your encyclopedia.)

6. Find at least three examples of parallelism in the above passage by Plutarch.

 ## STATING YOUR CASE

A democratic political system like ours depends on the ability of its citizens to be able to express their opinions extemporaneously—at the spur of the moment—no matter where they are or what they are doing. "People who want to understand democracy," says Simeon Strunsky, "should spend less time in the library with Aristotle and more time on the buses and in the subway" listening to others' opinions and speaking their own minds.

In our political system, we expect people to speak up for themselves and their communities if they feel that an injustice has been done. If, for example, your city decides to develop a toxic waste dump near your home, you have not only the right as a citizen but the obligation as a member of your community to make your feelings known about the project. You may have to discuss the issue with a number of your neighbors, speak at city council meetings, and write a number of letters. In addition, you must be ready to present your case within a matter of days—perhaps even hours or minutes—if you want to be successful.

W. H. Auden, the author of the following poem, was far from quiet as a citizen; he spoke out during his lifetime (1907–1973) on issues ranging from economics and socialism to religion and psychology. As you read Auden's poem, think about the criticism he is leveling at our society, and ask yourself if the unknown citizen reflects behavior of people you know.

The Unknown Citizen
(To JS/07/M/378
This Marble Monument Is Erected by the State)

He was found by the Bureau of Statistics to be   1
One against whom there was no official complaint,
And all the reports on his conduct agree
That, in the modern sense of an old-fashioned word, he was a saint,
For in everything he did he served the Greater Community.   5
Except for the War till the day he retired
He worked in a factory and never got fired,
But satisfied his employers, Fudge Motors Inc.
Yet he wasn't a scab or odd in his views,
For his Union reports that he paid his dues,   10
(Our report on his Union shows it was sound)
And our Social Psychology workers found
That he was popular with his mates and liked a drink.
The Press are convinced that he bought a paper every day
And that his reactions to advertisements were normal in every way.   15
Policies taken out in his name prove that he was fully insured.
And his Health-card shows he was once in hospital but left it cured.
Both Producers Research and High-Grade Living declare
He was fully sensible to the advantages of the Installment Plan
And had everything necessary to the Modern Man,   20
A phonograph, radio, a car and a frigidaire.
Our researchers into Public Opinion are content
That he held the proper opinions for the time of year;
When there was peace, he was for peace; when there was war, he went.

He was married and added five children to the population,   25

Which our Eugenist says was the right number for a parent of his generation,

And our teachers report that he never interfered with their education.

Was he free? Was he happy? The question is absurd:

Had anything been wrong, we should certainly have heard.

—W. H. Auden

For Thought and Discussion

1. Compare the Unknown Citizen to a member of the animal kingdom (for example, a bird, a lion, or an ant); what animal would seem most like him? Why?

2. What is a "scab"? Why would his union be pleased to know that the Unknown Citizen wasn't one?

3. Using the clues provided in the poem, can you ascertain during what period of time the Unknown Citizen lived, worked, and raised his family?

4. "The Unknown Citizen" is intended to be a comment, not only on the life of its subject, but also on the society in which he lived. What do you think Auden's opinion is of this society?

5. Name some citizens who are currently not willing to be quiet and unknown. What kind of effect have they had on the world in which you live?

▍ FLEXING YOUR MENTAL MUSCLES

There are few professions in this age of instant communication that do not require their members to write numerous letters, reports, and memos. As a student, you have probably already written a good many extemporaneous, in-class essays; they often appear in the form of essay exams, and they strike fear into the hearts of many college students. As a result, when your English instructor assigns an in-class essay, you are likely to react as if the essay were a test rather than an opportunity to work on a very important skill. Yet in-class writing is a skill that you need to practice if you are to become a capable and confident extemporaneous writer, both for college and in your professional life.

Most jobs, even in small businesses, now require that you create a "paper trail"—a written record of your activities, transactions, and com-munications. As a professional, you will be required to supply frequent updates to your employers and supervisors, not to mention suppliers and clients; also, you will often have to do background research in order to write proposals that argue for new projects and suggest new ways of doing things. While you will be able to revise and correct such reports, letters, and pro-

posals some of the time, the reality of most jobs is that there is little time for rethinking what you write. Often, you will have to depend on your extemporaneous writing skills.

Many professionals now find themselves turning to the computer and hastily composing a letter or report which may, in turn, travel instantly by computer link or fax machine across the city, across the country, or halfway around the world. As you look around the typical office of the 1990s, you may be amazed, as Charlene is in the accompanying cartoon, at the enormous investment in machines to facilitate instant communication. Yet, those machines are worthless if the person who uses them is unable to write quickly, effectively, and efficiently.

For Thought and Discussion

1. Take five minutes in class to make a list of the kinds of extemporaneous writing you have had to do in the past. Now imagine what kinds of extemporaneous writing you will have to do in the future, and list them.

2. Discuss your lists with other members of the class, and have one person write on the board all the kinds of extemporaneous writing situations that come up in the discussion.

3. Choose three or four items from that list and discuss the nature of each situation: What kinds of successes have writers had with each? What kinds of difficulties?

EXTEMPORANEOUS WRITING IN COLLEGE

In-class essays are an ever-present reality in your life as a college student. It is likely that before you entered your first year of college, you were required to write at least one extemporaneous essay. This essay gave teachers and counselors an opportunity to assess your ability to think quickly and to express yourself effectively on paper—a skill that your college considers vital for your continuing success as a student.

Yours may be one of the growing number of colleges and universities that require periodic essay exams as a measure of your readiness to progress to the next class level; in addition, most schools now require that you write an extemporaneous essay as a prerequisite for admission to your major department. You may feel that such tests are unfair because you have not had much practice with extemporaneous writing. You realize that there is simply no substitute for experience: It is true that students who have had extensive opportunities to write in class invariably come away feeling more capable in every extemporaneous writing situation they encounter.

The Creator-Critic Revisited

In Chapter 1 of this text you learned about the two parts of your brain, the creator and the critic. You learned techniques to help you temporarily "turn off" the critic in order to allow new ideas to surface by clustering, brain-storming, and freewriting. You can use these techniques to get ideas down on paper for an extemporaneous in-class essay, as well. While freewriting may be impractical for an in-class essay where time is limited, five minutes of clustering or brainstorming may provide you with all the ideas you can use for the rest of the hour. In addition, once you have put your ideas down on paper in a cluster or brainstorm, you can relax a bit. They are where you can get to them when you need them. But there is another advantage to allowing your creative brain a chance to help you with extemporaneous writing.

Writing teachers who assign and read a great deal of extemporaneous writing notice a curious phenomenon. When students are writing in their journals, not really thinking about creating an introduction, thesis, and conclusion, very often these elements appear—as if by magic. But there is a logic at work, and you can use it to your advantage when you are under pressure to write. Your creative brain stores pictures and patterns while your critical brain stores words and rules. The latter are essential, of course, for any writing process, but the pictures and patterns can help, as well. When you are receptive to the creative brain's resources, and when you learn methods for letting those resources work for you, you will discover that extemporaneous writing is not as frightening as it seemed.

Your turn

To help you discover your own ability to organize naturally, try writing on the following topics in ten- or fifteen-minute writing periods:

308

**THINKING ON
YOUR FEET:
EXTEMPO-
RANEOUS
WRITING**

Why [your topic] has had a profound influence on my life

What my community can do about its drug problem

The decision to have an abortion is/is not the right of every woman

Sixteen-year-olds should/should not be allowed to drive

Coed dorms are a good/bad idea

Public school students should/should not be required to wear uniforms

The minimum wage should/should not be raised

A traffic signal is needed at a certain intersection because . . .

If the air quality in our city is to be improved, we must take these
measures . . .

Here are some helpful hints for on-the-spot writing:

1. Read the topic first for *meaning*. Then read it a second time to determine exactly what the topic asks you to do. For example, does it ask you to explain a process? Does it ask for an analysis? Does it ask you to formulate a judgment?

2. Next, read for *organization*. Determine how many parts there are to the topic. Does it ask you first to explain, then discuss the topic? Does it ask you to address a series of subtopics?

3. At this point, *prewrite*. Take two or three minutes to create a cluster, brainstorm, or rough outline of the topic, and scan your prewriting for possible approaches.

4. You may wish to restate the topic, or parts of the topic, in your *opening sentence*. This helps get you started on the essay and it gives you another chance to think about the topic and what it is asking you to do.

5. As you move through the *body of the essay*, be sure that you are providing enough facts and examples to support your ideas and conclusions. Also be sure that you have addressed all parts of the assignment.

6. Once you have discussed the topic and/or answered the question to your satisfaction, write a brief *conclusion* and *stop*. Your grade will not be enhanced by more words, merely because you have pages left in the blue book or time left on the clock.

7. Be sure to leave enough time at the end to *proofread* your essay. Five minutes should give you enough time to check for misspellings and correct unclear sections of the essay.

Some Tips from an Expert

Study skills expert Harry Shaw points out three common serious errors students make when taking an exam or writing an in-class essay: they panic, they are careless, and they don't think. In order to avoid falling into these traps, remember the following steps:

1. When you feel panicked, take three very deep breaths, counting to ten for each breath. This will calm you and reactivate your paralyzed brain. If you are well rested and properly fed (avoid eating carbohydrates and fats before an exam—they make you sleepy), your confidence will be quickly restored.

2. To avoid careless errors, look for key words in the essay topic, provide concrete support for any abstract ideas in your essay, and leave enough time at the end to proofread.

3. Focus exclusively on the task at hand. If there is noise in the room, ignore it by concentrating on your writing ideas.

4. Avoid looking at what anyone else is doing, as you may worry that the one paragraph you have written is no match for the full page written by the person next to you. Since you don't know whether that person is writing anything worth reading, you cannot possibly make a comparison.

Essay exams in courses such as astronomy, history, political science, biology, psychology, and philosophy often require that you use one or more of the organizational patterns we have already discussed in this text: *process* (Chapter 6), *classification* (Chapter 7), *cause and effect* (Chapter 8), *comparison and contrast* (Chapter 9), and *argument* (Chapter 10). Your psychology professor may ask you, for example, to compare and contrast Freud's psychoanalytic theory with Jung's analytical psychology, while your biology professor may ask you to describe the characteristics of the kingdom Fungi, or your political science professor may ask you to classify economic theories.

If the exam question does not suggest a particular pattern (often it is implied in the question), you should quickly review patterns that might work by clustering or brainstorming around the question and asking yourself if you can spot a cause-effect relationship, if you can classify the main points you want to discuss, or if there is a process involved. Be especially alert for opportunities to compare and contrast.

Often, students report success using the comparison-contrast pattern in essay exams, as it is an easy pattern to set up and keep track of. In a history class, for example, you might be asked to "Compare and contrast the leadership styles of Grant and Lee or of Nixon and Carter," while in an environmental science class you could be asked to "Contrast the characteristics of land that is suitable for cultivation with those of land that is not." In a cultural anthropology class you might "Compare and contrast the characteristics of men's and women's associations in the United States prior to 1950."

Of course, you will always remember that no matter what organizational pattern you use, your essay must contain an *introduction,* a *thesis,* and a *conclusion.*

310

THINKING ON
YOUR FEET:
EXTEMPO-
RANEOUS
WRITING

A REAL-WORLD OPPORTUNITY

The following extemporaneous writing topic comes from the University of California at Berkeley, where it was administered to entering freshmen who achieved a score below 600 on the verbal portion of the SAT. A passing score on the following examination admitted students to the university's freshman composition course. Those who did not pass this examination were required to take an additional course in English composition before they were admitted to freshman composition.

Students were given two hours to read the passage and complete their essays using the following guidelines:

1. Read the passage and essay topic carefully.

2. Underline significant portions of the passage and make marginal notes.

3. Plan the essay before beginning to write.

4. When you write the essay, be certain that it is controlled by a central idea and that it is developed using specific illustrations and examples.

5. Be sure to allow time for proofreading and revising the essay.

These guidelines are good to remember for *any* extemporaneous writing situation you may face in college.

Examination Topic

Introductory Note: Sissela Bok has taught philosophy and ethics at Harvard and Brandeis. The following passage is adapted from her 1978 book *Lying: Moral Choice in Public and Private Life.*

1   What if all government officials felt free to deceive provided they believed the deception genuinely necessary to achieve some important public end? The trouble is that those who make such calculations are always susceptible to bias. They overestimate the likelihood that the benefit will occur and that the harm will be averted; they underestimate the chances that the deceit will be discovered and ignore the effects of such a discovery on trust; they underrate the comprehension of the deceived citizens, as well as their ability and their right to make a reasoned choice. And, most important, such a benevolent self-righteousness disguises the many motives for political lying which could *not* serve as moral excuses: the need to cover up past mistakes; the vindictiveness; the desire to stay in power. These self-serving ends provide the impetus for countless lies that are rationalized as "necessary" for the public good.

2   Consider the following situation and imagine all the variations on this theme being played in campaigns all over the United States, at the local, state, or federal level:

3   A big-city mayor is running for reelection. He has read a report recom-

mending that he remove rent controls after his reelection. He intends to do so, but believes he will lose the election if his intention is known. When asked, at a news conference two days before his election, about the existence of such a report, he denies knowledge of it and reaffirms his strong support of rent control.

4   In the mayor's view, his reelection is very much in the public interest, and the lie concerns questions which he believes the voters are unable to evaluate properly, especially on such short notice. In all similar situations, the sizable bias resulting from the self-serving element (the desire to be elected, to stay in office, to exercise power) is often clearer to onlookers than to the liars themselves. This bias inflates the alleged justifications for the lie—the worthiness, superiority, altruism of the liar, the rightness of his cause, and the inability of those deceived to respond "appropriately" to hearing the truth.

5   These common lies are now so widely suspected that voters are at a loss to know when they can and cannot believe what a candidate says in campaigning. The damage to trust has been immense. Many refuse to vote under such circumstances. Others look to appearance or to personality factors for clues as to which candidate might be more honest than the others. Voters and candidates alike are the losers when a political system has reached such a low level of trust. Once elected, officials find that their warnings and their calls to common sacrifice meet with disbelief and apathy, even when cooperation is most urgently needed. Lawsuits and investigations multiply. And the fact that candidates, should they win, are not expected to have meant what they said while campaigning, nor be held accountable for discrepancies, only reinforces the incentives for them to bend the truth the next time, thus adding further to the distrust of the voters.

6   Political lies, so often assumed to be trivial by those who tell them, rarely are. They cannot be trivial when they affect so many people and when they are so peculiarly likely to be imitated, used to retaliate, and spread from a few to many. When political representatives or entire governments arrogate to themselves the right to lie, they take power from the public that would not have been given up voluntarily.

Essay Topic

For centuries, some political writers have argued that leaders must be willing to deceive, even lie, to govern effectively. Sissela Bok argues otherwise. What do you think about the position she takes here? Draw on your reading, personal experience, or observation of others to develop your essay.

Grading Standards for Extemporaneous Essays

Students are often mystified by the process of extemporaneous writing because they have only a foggy notion of what the readers or graders are looking for. The following scale is one that college composition instructors throughout the nation use when they read in-class essays, placement exams, and entrance or exit exams.

312

**THINKING ON
YOUR FEET:
EXTEMPO-
RANEOUS
WRITING**

Excellent (6): This paper will satisfy all the requirements of the assignment. It will contain a significant central idea that is clearly stated
and developed with concrete, convincing, and relevant details. In
addition, it will display excellence in organization, provide ample
support for its arguments, and display persuasive reasoning. It may
exhibit some flaws, such as minor errors in punctuation and spelling,
but it will demonstrate a high degree of skill, as well as a sense of
style.

Competent (5): A 5 paper is clearly competent. It presents a thoughtful
analysis of or response to the text, elaborating that response with
appropriate examples and sensible reasoning. A 5 paper may be less
complex or fluent than a 6, and it may have a few more errors and
be less well organized, but it does show that its writer can usually
choose words accurately, vary sentences effectively, and observe the
conventions of written English.

Satisfactory (4): A 4 paper presents an adequate analysis of or response
to the text, elaborating that response with sufficient and acceptable
reasoning. This writer may become too general in his or her argument, providing less development for the topic than the 5 or 6
papers. Nevertheless, a 4 paper will exhibit overall competence and
fulfill all parts of the assignment, choosing words of sufficient precision, controlling sentences of reasonable variety, and observing the
conventions of written English.

Unsatisfactory (3): A 3 paper is unsatisfactory in one or more of the
following ways. It may analyze or respond to the text illogically;
it may lack coherent structure or elaboration with examples; it
may reflect an incomplete understanding of the text or the topic.
Its prose is usually characterized by at least one of the following:
frequently imprecise word choice, little sentence variety, occasional major errors in grammar and usage, or frequent minor
errors.

Very Poor (2): A 2 paper shows serious weaknesses, ordinarily of several
kinds. It frequently presents a simplistic, inappropriate, or incoher-
ent analysis of or response to the text, one that may suggest some
significant misunderstanding of the text or the topic. Its prose is
usually characterized by at least one of the following: simplistic or
inaccurate word choice, monotonous or fragmented sentence structure, or many repeated errors in grammar and usage.

Unacceptable (1): A 1 paper suggests severe difficulties in reading and
writing conventional English. It may disregard the topic's demands,
or it may lack any appropriate pattern of structure or development.
It may be inappropriately brief. It often has a pervasive pattern of
errors in word choice, sentence structure, grammar, and usage.

The following essays were written at Berkeley in response to the passage by Sissela Bok. Read the first two essays and respond to the questions that follow.

Score: 3

1   Sissela Bok believes that if our government and the politicians decide to lie, they will be taking away power from the public. She explains that they are making a lie to cover up a previous mistake in order to stay in power. This will actually make the situation worse. I completely agree with her.

2   The people who tell lies think that they are actually doing the right thing. They think that no one will find out. In reality, the lies are usually found out and a lot of people lose their trust in them. The politicians need to realize that it is to their advantage to tell the truth from the beginning.

3   Many voters look for the candidates that they believe are the most honest. If they find that the candidates do not do what they promised, the voters will distrust our government even more. This will lead them into not voting again because they are afraid it will happen over and over.

4   If people do not vote anymore, then our whole idea of democracy will be shattered. The government will control our lives and the idea of laissez-faire will be forgotten. This is why it is very important that the people have trust in each other.

5   The people that tell lies have to realize that they will hurt someone no matter how trivial they feel the lie is. It will be to their benefit to choose not to lie to anyone. This applies to everyone, not just our government and the politicians. Our lives would be much easier if we had trust in each other.

For Thought and Discussion

1. In the opening paragraph of this essay, does the writer accurately explain Sissela Bok's argument? Discuss your answer.

2. At what points in the essay could the writer have illustrated her argument with specific examples?

3. The sentences in the last two paragraphs of this essay are very short. How could the writer combine her ideas in order to make them more effective, while at the same time making the sentences more readable?

4. Why was this essay given a 3?

Score: 2

1   Sissela Bok's argument on political lying is a very important topic which deals and affects us morally and maybe physically. The thought of political lying is morally unacceptable, but has been going on for centuries and is still being praised by our political runner and sometimes staff. Political writer's

314

**THINKING ON
YOUR FEET:
EXTEMPO-
RANEOUS
WRITING**

view on this topic is for it or supporting it, which they include "to govern more effectively."

2   The view of Sissela Bok portrays the thought of millions of U.S. men and woman, but hasn't been a topic too big a deal. This shows us that the public has adopted it and hasn't tried to make a change and speak their mind. In my opinion it should be treated at court as fraud instead of just another joke. "They underrate the comprehension of the deceived citizens, as well as their ability and their right to make a reasoned choice." In this quote Sissela tells us we are morally being deceived, by want of understanding and making that choice on who to pick. Maybe that is why people are choosing candidates that have a good appearance and a good voice, instead of someone who is right for the job. This statement is reinforced with the fact of Ronald Reagan's office term. Ronald Reagan was a smart actor who showed us through his campaign that he had presidential qualities. But as we now know he deceived in some ways, such as the tax rate, military spending and Nicaragua. The view of a political writer is very disunderstandable.

3   They quote it makes government run more effectively, but is very untrue because "we the people" are the supposably ones that make up the laws. Political runners lie so that people will like what they hear instead telling the actual truth. When people like what they hear of course they will go out and vote for him. In the long run though its the people the one's that are hurt.

4   In conclusion, political lying is acceptable but should be the opposite as Sissela states. This topic *needs* to be taken more seriously, maybe a bill should be written against political lying. Because with political lying all we get is unreasoned choices which are no good for our society. Sissela's position is very righteous, because she took it more seriously, which enforces us to take it more seriously.

For Thought and Discussion

1. What specific example does the writer use to illustrate the dangers of political lying? In what way is the example effective in helping the writer to make his or her case? How could the writer have used it more effectively?

2. What is the student writer's central point?

3. It is generally not considered appropriate to refer to the writer of a published work by his or her first name, as the student does in this essay. Why do you think this is the case? How should this student have referred to the author?

4. Why was this essay given a 2?

 STUDENT STARS

The students who wrote the following essays took the time to do the following during the two hours allotted:

Prewriting: twenty to thirty minutes
Essay writing: sixty to ninety minutes
Proofreading: ten to fifteen minutes.

315

**THINKING ON
YOUR FEET:
EXTEMPO-
RANEOUS
WRITING**

Score: 6

1   In the early 1970s, in a sleeping Washington D.C., several men crept noise-lessly through an office building made empty by the night and looted some files. When the break-in was discovered, a small man in a large white house made a decision. He would simply pull some strings and erase the crime from history. He had the power. He was President of The United States. He was the government official who "felt free to deceive provided he believed the deception genuinely necessary to achieve some important public end," that end being salvaging the reputation of his own political party. Contrary to arguments that support the deception of the public as an effective means for working the machinery of politics, there is no proof that in contemporary society a leader must deceive the public in order to achieve a goal. Nixon's attempt to deceive the public brought him spiralling down to obscurity from the power he lied for.

2   Sissela Bok supports the theory that the public must not be steered by reins of dishonesty held by elected officials. Bok's "big city mayor" tried to justify his deceit by claiming a lack of knowledge among his constituents. But it is much too difficult to consider the people naive enough to believe everything they hear in our society, where information is readily available by the turn of a dial or a flip of a switch. Thus a lie cannot be justified by claiming the inability of the people to make an informed decision.

3   A politician that makes false campaign promises may suffer the same con-sequences as the little boy who cried "Wolf!" Just as the little shepherd boy lied about a wolf among his flock, so Sissela Bok's "big city mayor" lies about a rent control issue. Just as the shepherd boy lost credibility among the people who came to his aid only to find no wolf, so the mayor loses credibility when he promises what the people want to hear and delivers something else. What a politician who makes false campaign promises must remember is that, when the shepherd boy called "Wolf!" when a wolf indeed threatened his flocks, not one villager came because his credibility had been destroyed.

4   While the media has provided a forum for making the general public aware of political issues, it has also become a weapon in the hands of campaigning politicians. As Bok says, "voters are at a loss to know when they can and cannot believe what a candidate says in campaigning." Sitting through one set of campaign commercials will provide the viewer with percentages, facts, and figures that will sing the glories of a candidate, figures that in the next sixty second spot will be turned around to become bleeding black marks on the very same candidate's record. It is no wonder that the percentage of registered voters who actually go to the polls declines steadily each year. A politician should not base a campaign on dishonest prostitution of the English language, twisting words into phrases that seduce a listener's ear. Widespread truth warping in the media leads only to low voter participation, taking power from the candidates in their search to find greater amounts of it. Exaggera-

316

**THINKING ON
YOUR FEET:
EXTEMPO-
RANEOUS
WRITING**

tions, false campaign promises, and crooked politics will lead not to greater power, but further decomposition of a political system in which the people have already lost faith.

For Thought and Discussion

1. The writer of this essay compares Sissela Bok's "big city mayor" with two well-known illustrations, one real and one fictional, in which lying back-fired. What episodes are they? Which episode is fictional?

2. In what way does the writer of this essay expand on Bok's original argument about the public's loss of faith in the political system?

3. Does the writer agree or disagree with Bok? Which part of the student essay is most effective in making the writer's point?

4. Locate at least one example of parallelism in this essay.

5. In what way could this essay be improved?

6. Why was this essay given a 6?

Score: 5

1   There is no acceptable reason for public officials to deceive the American people. Unfortunately, lying has become an expected part of the political system. Officials feel they have to lie to protect national security, to insure that they are elected, or even to meet their own personal interests. These lies should in no way be allowed, for eventually they cause harm to the public and to our image as a nation.

2   Deception is not necessary for the protection of national security. Granted, there are subjects that the general population should not be aware of. If the public should somehow catch wind of classified information, the concerned officials can deny comment or prepare a statement that is one-hundred per-cent true, that stops inquiry yet gives no real information. Lies used as a cover-up only bring more trouble down the road.

3   Lies used as cover-ups, when revealed, create scandal that is detrimental to all of America. The most recent example of this is the Iran-Contra affair. This whole arrangement was illegal, and the people involved knew that from the start. Still they kept it secret, put the money in Swiss bank accounts, and diverted funds so that the money could not be easily traced, nor the situation easily discovered. When the Iran-Contra affair was finally revealed everyone concerned denied knowledge of its existence. Soon they were pleading the Fifth, and eventually confessing. Even in their confessions, however, they covered for each other. These lies, compounded upon each other, created a nationwide scandal. Faith in the current administration was reduced, America was scandalized in the eyes of foreign nations, and American foreign policy regarding terrorism and Central America was questioned. Perhaps the saddest result of the deception, however, is that people were forever denied the knowledge of what really happened.

317

THINKING ON
YOUR FEET:
EXTEMPO-
RANEOUS
WRITING

4   The campaign process is also plagued with lies. Officials so desperately
want to be elected that they will do nearly anything to be elected. As a result,
they tell half-truths and outright falsehoods to get votes. This undermines the
whole reason for campaigning. People are not sure who or what to believe. It
often seems that the one who puts up the best facade wins. Charisma is
becoming more important than the issues thanks to television and radio
campaigning. The best case of this is the Kennedy-Nixon debate. Those who
listened to the radio believed Nixon to have won the debate, but Nixon's
uneasy appearance on television made viewers believe that Kennedy had won.
This uncertainty of who or what to believe has also increased voter apathy.
People do not vote because they are not sure what to believe. The right to
vote is perhaps one of the greatest of American freedoms, but only a great
minority of the people vote because there is a general lack of faith in the
system, due to widespread deception.

5   Our forefather envisioned a government that was untarnished by corruption. The traditional values of integrity, honesty, and "may the best man win"
no longer seem to apply today. A candidate or official may have a perfectly
legitimate excuse for lying in his own mind, but a lie is a lie. In theory, the
Constitution of the United States sets up a nearly perfect system of government, but in practice, corruption and deception have prevented our government from achieving its full potential.

For Thought and Discussion

1. With what example does the writer of this essay illustrate his point
about lying in American political life?

2. The writer discusses the issue of "charisma." How does he connect
it with political lying? Does the writer make this connection clear?

3. In his essay and the one preceding, the writers illustrated their
arguments with concrete examples: one with a fable and both with episodes
from American politics. In class, brainstorm a list of some other stories or
incidents that could be used to illustrate the dangers of lying.

4. Why was this essay given a 5?

Score: 4

1   In her passage on political lying, Sissela Bok argues that this practice is
very serious and intrinsically bad. I am in complete agreement with Ms. Bok.
Political lying, as seen throughout history, is more detrimental than useful
and should never be implemented in a society. Myself and the people of the
United States know this idea all too well due to our knowledge of the Watergate and Iran-Contra scandals.

2   In the early 1970's Richard Nixon proved to America that intentional
political deception is harmful. The basis for Mr. Nixon's lies occurred in the
Watergate apartment complex where Republican party members illicitly took
and reviewed Democratic party plans. President Nixon denied that this inci-

318

**THINKING ON
YOUR FEET:
EXTEMPO-
RANEOUS
WRITING**

dent took place, believing that no harm would come to him because the American people would not be concerned. This was Nixon's folly because as soon as he lied certain taped conversations of this event were discovered. The Congress of the United States thus sought to impeach Nixon but he resigned instead. Nixon believed a lie would help him out of a difficult situation. His deception, however, resulted in his loss of a job and more importantly a loss of confidence in the President of the United States.

3   Another obvious example of the fallacy of political lying, and perhaps more pertinent to a person of my age, concerns the Iran-Contra scandal. This is a most complex event, but as I understand it the United States, or more specifically the National Security Council, sold to the government of Iran military arms for the purpose of freeing hostages and obtaining Contra rebel supplies. The men involved in this multi-faceted scheme were Colonel Oliver North, Phillip Hakim, Admiral Poindexter, Mr. Secord, the Iranian Parliament leader (Rafsanjani?), perhaps the President, and also the Contras. An attempt was made to cover up this elaborate plan (a lie) from the "shallow" minds of the people. This caused perhaps the biggest scandal of the 1980's. Colonel North admitted he lied, thus destroying the prestige of himself as well as the Marines. Admiral Poindexter had been damaged. The Contras are probably less popular now because they are related to this scandal. Most importantly, Ronald Reagan became a "lame duck" president because of his ambiguous role in this affair.

4   Political lying is never beneficial, only harmful. Politicians of today and the past are learning the hard way about this simple fact. Senator Gary Hart believed his extra-marital relationship would not hurt him if he denied it. He had to drop out of the race for the presidency. The American people are not naive to deception, and as long as they remain educated they will not succumb to scandal. This country has had two classical examples of how lying is destructive in ourselves and our country, I hope our president avoids this evil practice.

For Thought and Discussion

1. Compare this writer's account of the Iran-Contra affair with the account in the preceding essay. Do these accounts focus on the same details? Which account is more credible? Why?

2. How would you suggest to this writer that the essay be improved?

3. Suggest patterns of development the writer could have used to develop the key ideas in the essay.

4. Why was this essay given a 4?

 WRITING ASSIGNMENT

Read the following passage, then respond to it in writing. You may write for fifty minutes, but take care to observe the following guidelines:

Spend about ten minutes on prewriting.
Write for approximately thirty-five minutes on the essay topic.
Proofread for five minutes.

This essay should be written in class.

Very important note:
Do not, under any circumstances, attempt to write a complete rough draft and then make a neat copy. *You don't have time.* If you need to cross something out, simply do so. If you have to add a passage to a section that has already been written, simply indicate that you have done so with an asterisk or an arrow.

Topic

What is the purpose of a university education? Should it simply be a stepping stone toward a career and a comfortable, middle-class lifestyle, or should it provide students with an understanding of the history, philosophy, literature, and languages that are the building blocks of our culture?

In his essay on "How to Fix the Premedical Curriculum," Lewis Thomas worries that unless the trend toward pre-professional training in the undergraduate years is reversed, "all the joy of going to college will have been destroyed [for] all the students and all the faculty as well." He proposes that every undergraduate student, no matter what his career goal, be required to follow a core curriculum, including classical Greek, "English, history, the literature of at least two foreign languages, and philosophy." Thomas suggests that such training will, in the end, produce doctors and other professionals who will be of much greater benefit to society than they are at present, for they will "have learned as much as anyone can learn about how human beings have always lived their lives."

Thomas is not the only one who is concerned about the lack of a broad education for students aiming at the professions. Writing in the San Jose State University *Spartan Daily,* Frank Lopez points out that most SJSU students have little or no interest in "the frightening questions of existence" which are posed by philosophy. Most find intellectual endeavors "just really boring."

Should we, as a society, continue to encourage university students to pursue only the training that will lead directly to good jobs? Do we have an obligation to them, and to ourselves, to ask that they understand more about their world before they become involved in shaping its direction and, ultimately, our own future?

Assignment

Discuss this issue, both from the perspective of a university student and from the perspective of a citizen living in a troubled world.

Obviously, a peer editing session of the kind you are accustomed to is not appropriate for an extemporaneous essay. However, once the essay has been returned to you by your instructor, meet with a peer group of three or four students and discuss the following questions:

1. What did your instructor like about your essay?

2. What kinds of problems did you discover as you wrote? What do you still need to work on?

3. Point out both positive and negative aspects of each essay presented to your peer editing group.

4. How will you capitalize on what you have learned when you encounter extemporaneous writing situations in the future?

12

THE FORMAL RESEARCH PAPER

CONCEPTS TO LEARN

Using formal documentation in the research paper

Parenthetical notations

List of works cited

"The future," Henry Lauder wrote, "is not a gift—it is an achievement." In our increasingly complex world, ensuring a safe future is the focus of a great deal of activity in disciplines as diverse as agriculture, medicine, and oceanography. As knowledge has grown more and more specialized, wisely evaluating the alternatives available to us requires an ever increasing amount of information. In the following excerpt from "One Vote for This Age of Anxiety," anthropologist Margaret Mead discusses the impact of this information explosion on our world. Increasing knowledge makes a better world possible. However, as this knowledge brings us the possibility of a less physically threatening world, it increases the potential not just for our happiness, but for our anxiety as well.

As for the populations of a great part of the world, they aren't so much anxious as hungry. They aren't anxious about whether they will get a salary raise, or which of the three colleges of their choice they will be admitted to, or whether to buy a Ford or Cadillac, or whether the kind of TV set they want is too expensive. They are hungry, cold and, in many parts of the world, they dread that local warfare, bandits, political coups may endanger their homes, their meager livelihoods and their lives. But surely they are not anxious.

For anxiety, as we have come to use it to describe our characteristic state of mind, can be contrasted with the active fear of hunger, loss, violence and death. Anxiety is the appropriate emotion when the immediate personal

321

terror—of a volcano, an arrow, the sorcerer's spell, a stab in the back, and other calamities, all directed against one's self—disappears.

This is not to say that there isn't plenty to worry about in our world of today. The explosion of a bomb in the streets of a city whose name no one had ever heard before may set in motion forces which end up by ruining one's carefully planned education in law school, half a world away. But there is still not the personal, immediate, active sense of impending disaster that the [Third World] knows. There is rather the vague anxiety, the sense that the future is unmanageable.

This is the world out of which grows the hope, for the first time in history, of a society where there will be freedom from want and freedom from fear. Our very anxiety is born of our knowledge of what is now possible for each and for all. The number of people who consult psychiatrists today is not, as is sometimes felt, a symptom of increasing mental ill health, but rather the precursor of a world in which the hope of genuine mental health will be open to everyone, a world in which no individual feels that he [or she] need be hopelessly brokenhearted, a failure, a menace to others or a traitor to himself [or herself].

For Thought and Discussion

1. How does Margaret Mead use contrast to help define *anxiety*?

2. Point out two passages in which Mead uses irony. Then explain what impact that irony has.

3. List three predictions supporting the idea that the future is unmanageable.

4. Explain why you agree or disagree that the future is unmanageable.

5. Will *Homo sapiens* be better or worse off in fifty years than now? In a hundred years? Support your answers.

6. Make a list of the changes in the world you would like to make now for the benefit of the future.

7. Compare your list with the list made by your classmates. Then compile a list of the most frequently desired changes.

8. Make a list of three items the class feels should get top priority in helping to create a better future.

9. Make a list of any suggestions for change about which your class cannot agree.

Save the lists you have made, as we will use them again in this chapter.

 DISTANT DREAMS

Looking into the future, whether that view be through the intellectual lens of the scientist or through the eyes of the ancient oracles at Delphi, is a human activity that predates recorded history. One goal that many of those seeking a view of the future have in common is expressed in Margaret Mead's words: "a society where there will be freedom from want and freedom from fear." It is about his dreams for such a future that Irish poet William Butler Yeats, winner of the 1923 Nobel prize for literature, writes in the following poem.

While Yeats' poetry is relatively traditional in its rhythm and rhyme schemes, his subject matter is contemporary. His poetry is especially relevant for current and future readers. Like many modern writers, Yeats drew images from everyday life to express his search for a better world.

He Wishes for the Cloths of Heaven

Had I the heavens' embroidered cloths,
Enwrought with golden and silver light,
The blue and the dim and the dark cloths
Of night and light and the half-light,
I would spread the cloths under your feet:
But I, being poor, have only my dreams;
I have spread my dreams under your feet;
Tread softly, because you tread on my dreams.

—William Butler Yeats

For Thought and Discussion

1. Explain how the dreams of Yeats' poem are related to the idea of managing the future.

2. Return to the lists you made in response to the "For Thought and Discussion" questions in the preceding section. Give two examples of literal ways other people are treading on your dreams for the future.

3. What steps would you have to take to convince others of the changes you feel should be made to ensure a better future?

WHY WRITE THE FORMALLY DOCUMENTED RESEARCH PAPER?

If your priorities for the future are to get the go-ahead (see the figure on page 324), you will need to be well informed about your subject and to communicate that information clearly and logically to others. In this chapter you will learn how to convince others of your ideas by writing a formally documented research paper. In such papers you must use a specific, standardized method of writing parenthetical citations, and you must create a list of works cited to credit your sources.

You will need to write formal research papers for a variety of college classes. For example, for an astronomy class you might write about the effect of recent research on our knowledge of the planet Venus. For a political science class you might write about the role of the Supreme Court on a

R. Chast

particular body of laws such as those governing abortion or affirmative action. For a history class, you might discuss the causes of the Civil War or of World War I. In writing such papers, sometimes you will be able to use the informal documentation discussed in Chapter 5. Very often, however, you will be asked to use the documentation style used in the professional journals that cover your particular subject.

The formal documentation discussed in this chapter allows readers to quickly trace the source of your idea or information. Knowing what your source is helps your readers to decide upon the validity of what you write. If your source is a venerable journal such as *Nature* or a respected newspaper such as the *Washington Post,* your readers will accept your information and ideas more readily than they will if they find your source less credible. When your source is one respected for its veracity, your own ideas gain credibility. Think about your own reaction to ideas and information. How often do you ask, "Where did you find [hear, read] that?"

In addition to evaluating the credibility of your source, your readers may want to learn more about your topic to obtain or evaluate the additional information they can get by reading that source.

"Anxiety," according to Arthur Somers Roche, "is a thin stream of fear trickling through the mind. If encouraged, it cuts a channel into which all other thoughts are drained." When we face a large task, we can stifle our creative thought processes by feeling overwhelmed by the task. However, if we divide the task into steps, it becomes less formidable. Before we discuss how and when to write formally documented papers, let's look at how to divide the process of writing research papers into unintimidating steps. If you have not already done so, you should read Chapter 5 before you tackle your research project.

Step 1: Identifying Your Topic

Sometimes you will be assigned a specific topic for your research paper, but more often you have to find your own topic. First you must decide upon a general area of interest—for example, nuclear energy or problems with the environment.

These broad topics are far too complex to cover in a book, so your first step is to limit your subject. To do this you should read a general background article about your topic in an encyclopedia or magazine. (See Chapter 5 for instructions on how to find such an article.) Your initial reading will help you understand the issues involved in your subject. The list of subdivisions under your general topic in *Reader's Guide to Periodical Literature* or its on-line equivalent or a comprehensive encyclopedia article may be useful in limiting your topic.

Once you have done some background reading, try clustering, freewriting, or brainstorming to help find a focus for your topic. Record the questions that pop into your mind during prewriting; the answers often lead to a thesis.

Discussing your topic is another means of generating ideas and discovering a thesis. Even when you disagree with others involved in a discussion, their ideas will help you think of and clarify your own ideas.

Step 2: Taking Notes

Review how to take notes and keep track of your sources on pages 137–141 in Chapter 5. Once you have done enough background reading (the "presearch" discussed in Chapter 5), you are ready to explore your own thoughts through freewriting. Your initial prewriting will help you create an informal, flexible preliminary outline to use as you take notes.

So that you can find information quickly and efficiently, it is best to subdivide your notes as you do your research. Carol Elster, author of the student star research paper at the end of this chapter, used the following informal outline to guide her research into the impact of pornography on violent crimes:

> Pornography: definition
>
> Is there a difference between sexually explicit material and pornography?
>
> Statistics: research into the impact of pornography on behavior
>
> Current research
>
> Freedom of speech: First and Fourteenth Amendments and the legality of limiting pornography
>
> Current legislation
>
> The views of feminists
>
> Solutions

As you do your initial research and note-taking, you will loop back and forth between your critic and your creative brain. The ideas you read will help you generate additional ideas about your topic, but these ideas should also inspire your critical brain to analyze and evaluate them. Is a particular source accurate? What are the credentials of its authors or the authorities they cite? Is the evidence convincing? How do the ideas or evidence in your sources affect your own ideas? Remember the following Ralph Waldo Emerson quotation as you do research: "A foolish consistency is the hobgoblin of little minds." As you learn more about your topic, evaluate both your sources and your own ideas. After all, the process of research should not merely confirm what you already know; it should give you new insights.

Step 3: Putting Your Ideas Together

If you followed Chapter 5's note-taking suggestions, your paper is well on its way to being organized as you take notes.

To develop the ideas in your preliminary outline, try one or more of the idea-generating techniques from Chapters 1 through 10. Let's say, for example, you are writing a paper about the problems the United States faces in disposing of the mountain of garbage it produces daily. Using clustering and directed freewriting, you have discovered a thesis. As you consider how to organize your ideas and information, use your critical brain to help you plan an attack. Using the classifying techniques from Chapter 7, you could categorize the types of garbage and the types of disposal techniques available. Using the process techniques of Chapter 6, you could explain the impact of disposal techniques on the current and future environment. Using the cause-effect techniques from Chapter 8, you could support your thesis by presenting arguments showing the impact current waste production and disposal have on the environment.

To support your points, you, like most writers, will use a variety of development techniques. As you read through your preliminary outline, jot down the ideas for development techniques that occur to you. Then add this list of techniques to your informal outline. Remember, however, that this outline is merely a guide. The outline will help you guard against going off on a tangent. However, as you continue to discover ideas about your topic, integrate valuable new insights within your informal outline. If you triple-space the outline, you will have room to add ideas. If you are writing on a computer, you can merely jot down your new ideas in an appropriate place within your outline.

At this point, you are ready to begin writing. If you get stuck, try clustering, brainstorming, freewriting, or asking questions about your topic. When you write most effectively, your critical and creative brains work as a team passing the ball back and forth. If your critical brain becomes too active, put it in its place with a prewriting technique. Or try one of the development techniques such as comparison and contrast or classification to help get your ideas flowing.

Remind yourself that the actual process of writing eliminates writer's block. When you have a large writing project to complete, dread of that project can stymie you. Instead of dreading the task, simply sit down and start writing. You don't even have to begin at the beginning of your informal outline. Begin writing about the area with which you feel most confident. Remember that your initial writing is not etched in a stone tablet placed in the center of your campus to haunt you forever. You are simply (and perhaps roughly) getting ideas onto paper—or on screen.

Also remember Chapter 5's step 5: You may have to return to the library to find additional information as you write.

Step 4: Documenting Your Paper

There are three instances when you must cite your sources:

1. When you use someone's exact words
2. When you use someone's idea
3. When you use a fact or statistic that is not common knowledge.

Deciding what is common knowledge or what is your original idea requires judgment on your part. If you have any doubts, play it safe: cite your source.

Your turn

Turn to the student star essay at the end of this chapter; find one example of each of the three reasons listed above for which the student star author cited her sources.

THE RULES OF FORMAL DOCUMENTATION

Several slightly different sets of rules exist to guide authors when they are required to formally document their sources. Like so much else in writing, the set of documentation rules you select will be determined by your audience. In this chapter's professional essay, author Milton Russell wrote for *Environment,* which uses a modified version of *The Chicago Manual of Style* rules. When you write for the humanities, you will generally use a similar set of rules designed by the Modern Language Association (MLA), so with Russell's permission, we have changed his documentation format to that recommended by the MLA.

Why do such rules for documentation exist? Because they help your reader to determine where you got your information. As you learned in Chapter 5, *where* you got your information is important for three reasons:

1. Some sources are more reliable than others.

2. Your reader might want to verify that you have genuine sources and that you have interpreted them correctly.

3. Your reader may want to find out more about your research by reading your sources.

The sources you include in your list of works cited show where you got the information you actually cite. Often when you do research, the information you read gives you a better understanding of your topic, but you do not actually use that information in your paper. The sources that appear on your list of works cited must actually be cited within your paper; those sources may include someone's exact words, someone's idea, or a fact or statistic that is not common knowledge.

For Thought and Discussion

1. Turn to the list of works cited on the last page of this chapter. How is this list organized?

2. In what publication does an article by Gloria Steinem appear?

3. How does the format of the Works Cited list help readers quickly locate the Steinem article? Notice the indentation of lines after the first line in each entry.

4. What article was published anonymously (without an author listed)?

5. Which article has more than one author? How are their names arranged?

WORKS CITED LISTS AND PARENTHETICAL NOTATIONS

In writing your research paper, you need to know the format for citing your sources, both in your list of works cited and in the text of the paper itself. The following sections contain detailed information on how to write a Works Cited list and how to use parenthetical notations in your paper. Lines after the first are indented, as you will note.

When Your Source Is a Book

1. For a book with a single author:

> Shackleton, Ernest. *South.* New York: Macmillan, 1920.

Parenthetical notation: (Shackleton 127).

If you are referring to the entire work, omit the page number. In this case, the parenthetical notation would be simply (Shackleton).

2. For a book with two or three authors:

> Block, Haskell M., and Robert G. Shedd. *Masters of Modern Drama.* New York: Random, 1962.

Parenthetical notation: (Block 283).

3. For a book with more than three authors:

> Spiller, Robert, et al. *Literary History of the United States.* New York: Macmillan, 1960.

Parenthetical notation: (Spiller 216).

4. For a selection from an edited collection:

> Elbow, Peter. ''Embracing Contraries in the Teaching Process.'' *The Writing Teacher's Sourcebook.* 2nd edition. Ed. Gary Tate and Edward P. J. Corbett. New York: Oxford, 1988.

Parenthetical notation: (Elbow 220).

If the parenthetical notation is for a selection for which you have credited the author within your text, simply list the page number in your parenthetical notation (220).

5. For a selection from an encyclopedia:

> Rothschild, Miriam Louisa. ''Siphonaptera.'' *Encyclopaedia Britannica: Macropaedia.* 1984 ed.

Parenthetical notation: (Rothschild).

When Your Source Is a Periodical

1. For a magazine article with one author:

Kunzig, Robert. "Earth on Ice." *Discover* Apr. 1991: 54–61.

Parenthetical notation: (Kunzig 58).

2. For a magazine article with two or three authors:

Deigh, Robb, Jill Rachlin, and Amy Saltzman. "How to Keep from Getting Fired." *U.S. News and World Report* 25 Apr. 1988: 76–80.

Parenthetical notation: (Deigh 77).

3. For a magazine article with more than three authors:

Lamar, Jacob V., et al. "Kids Who Sell Crack." *Time* 9 May 1988: 20–33.

Parenthetical notation: (Lamar 24).

4. For a magazine article with an anonymous author:

"How to Tackle Japan Inc." *Time* 9 May 1988: 64.

Parenthetical notation: ("How to Tackle Japan" 64).

5. For a journal:

Rico, Gabriele. "Daedalus and Icarus Within: The Literature/Art/Writing Connection." *English Journal* 78 (1989): 14–23.

Parenthetical notation: (Rico 21).

When Your Source Is a Government Document

Often government documents list no specific author; when no author is identified, cite the government agency as the author. Your entry should begin with the name of the government (county or state, for example) followed by the name of the agency.

United States. Fish & Wildlife Service. "Southern Sea Otter Recovery Plan." 3 Feb. 1982.

Parenthetical notation: (U.S. 14).

When Your Source Is a Pamphlet

What Makes Ticks Tick and Fleas Flee. Dallas: Zoecon Corp., 1983.

Parenthetical notation: (*What Makes* 5).

When Your Source Is an Interview

Cailliet, Gregor. Personal interview. 5 May 1993.

Parenthetical notation: (Cailliet).

When Your Source Is a Television or Radio Program

MacNeil, Robert. *The MacNeil-Lehrer News Hour.* PBS-TV, 12 May 1993.

Parenthetical notation: (MacNeil).

Reminder: Your Authority's Credentials

Be sure to explain why the source you cite is or represents an authority—unless, of course, your source's credentials would be known to your audience. For example:

> With the growing importance of the shark industry, scientists believe there are a number of important facts they need to learn about these animals. Dr. Gregor Cailliet, Professor of Marine Biology at Moss Landing Marine Laboratories, points out that scientists do not know how much sharks need to eat, how often they eat, how much they rest, how fast they grow, exactly where they live, or how many of them there are in U.S. coastal waters. Cailliet says that if scientists are to assess the impact of the burgeoning shark fishery, they must know more about the life cycles of sharks.

 A PROFESSIONAL WRITER AT WORK

In the following article from *Environment,* author Milton Russell discusses his own wish list for the future.

As you read, note how and when Russell credits his sources in parentheses. Also note that Russell himself is an authority on his subject matter. He was assistant administrator for Policy, Planning, and Evaluation at the U.S. Environmental Protection Agency from 1984 to 1988. He is currently professor of economics and senior fellow in both the Energy, Environment, and Resource Center and the Institute for Waste Management and Education at the University of Tennessee in Knoxville. In addition, he is a senior economist at Oak Ridge National Laboratory.

Environmental Protection

1   Bob Dylan's ''The Times They Are A-Changin' '' was a theme song for the generation that heralded the environmental awakening in the United States

of two decades ago. Given the point at which we find ourselves with many environmental questions, it might well be an appropriate anthem again.

2   Four basic changes are taking place now, but will be even more important in the future. The first change is in the types of environmental problems that will absorb most of our talents and efforts. In brief, the environmental enterprise will become more concerned about toxic substances and more conscious of ecological impacts that often accompany—and sometimes outweigh—public health problems.

3   The second change is in the targets of efforts to improve the environment. The importance of changing the behavior of a few industrial polluters will decline, to be replaced by the need to alter the ways in which literally millions of private citizens go about their daily lives. Third, the role of environmental professionals will shift, and the tools with which they traditionally sought beneficial environmental results will have to be augmented to reach those new targets. Finally, there will be profound change in the roles of the federal government on the one hand, and of states, communities, and private citizens on the other.

4   To understand these changes, it is useful to look back and see where this country has been with regard to the environment, and to access where it is now. There are features in this experience much different from those that molded the European reaction to environmental concerns. Better understanding of these differences may improve the ability of countries to borrow wisely from each other in meeting the environmental challenges we face.

How We Got Here

5   As Calvin Coolidge put it, "The business of America is business," and for most of our history that has been true. That business meant converting a virgin land to the most productive economy ever known. The national treasure awaiting exploitation included not only the raw materials needed for industrial supremacy, but also the natural sinks of great rivers and lakes, tidal bays, seas, vast skies, and, most of all broad stretches of land in which to dispose cheaply of the waste products of industry and of life itself. The nest we fouled was indeed our own. But it was enormous, and for those who did not choose to push on to fresh frontiers, the stench was overpowered by the stronger perfume of money.

6   Pockets of despoliation were always present. They showed up first in the industrial East, where, for example, salmon disappeared from some streams early in the 19th century (Netboy 169–182). They existed in the coal regions where a combination of strip-mining and acid drainage turned productive streams into silt-laden, lifeless sewers sacrificed to America's industrial juggernaut. The pockets showed up as choking, lung-searing air in our richest cities. But there were still many other streams and lakes, and at least those better off could escape the foul air by repairing to the surrounding hills and suburbs. It is sobering to reflect on a near-ubiquitous institution that began a couple of generations ago—the "fresh air funds" that took poor children from the city. "Fresh air" was not a cute name for a life-enriching rural experience: fresh air *was* the experience, and the goal.

7   In short, the vastness of our country sustained the reality that there was an

"away" to which pollution could be shunted; that ecological insults did not threaten the fabric of natural life on which we all depended and which we valued; and that a nest too fouled could be abandoned, to start afresh.

8   The historian Frederick Jackson Turner marked the end of the first phase of American life with the closing of the geographic frontier around 1890. His thesis was that the closing of that safety valve brought a profound change in the way Americans thought of themselves, their country, and the rest of the world (Turner). It took decades for the full implications of a closed geographic frontier to sink in and to change the American outlook. We have only recently come to realize that our environmental frontier has likewise closed, and we are still sorting out the meaning for the way we behave and relate to each other and natural systems.

9   The environmental frontier—the sense that there is an "away"—sealed up when Americans began to see that the pustules of environmental degradation were no longer isolated, but instead threatened the land with a consuming rash. That recognition was a long time coming. It was presaged by the recurrent motif of environmental disaster found in post-World War II science fiction. The popularity of John Kenneth Galbraith's *The Affluent Society* in the 1950s suggests that people identified with his outrage at expansive private consumption in the presence of public squalor. *Silent Spring* caused many to question whether progress was a bargain when bought at the cost of birthright pleasures such as the song of a bird in the wild (Carson). The Donora disaster of 1948, where twenty people died and almost half a town was stricken with illness from polluted air, altered forever the vision of belching smokestacks as an acceptable nuisance ("Delayed Effects"). Buckminster Fuller's compelling image of Spaceship Earth dramatized that there really was no "away"— that "here" was all there was. The flaming Cuyahoga River emptying into the dying Lake Erie was a graphic reminder that the waste sink of the industrial Midwest was finally spilling over.

10   The realization dawned that Mother Earth was being abused by her children. She was reaching the point where she could no longer absorb the punishment and benignly forgive. That realization was given form and substance by Earth Day in 1970. Millions of Americans found that their concerns and outrage were shared by others. No longer was environmental degradation a local issue or the province of an alienated few, but a national issue that engaged the energy and dedication of Main Street America ("Nation").

11   With congressional elections impending and a presidential election on the horizon in 1972, suddenly the environment was a hot political issue. Scarcely two months after Earth Day, President Richard Nixon proposed to Congress the establishment of the Environmental Protection Agency (EPA) as an umbrella organization at the national level to manage the national effort to heal the environment (Nixon).

12   Although industry was largely skeptical of this seeming fad, political and environmental leaders were aware of deep grassroots support and used that support to launch and maintain a decade-long surge of environmental activism. That support has been maintained and even grown (Dunlap). Congress passed several sweeping new statutes in quick succession, giving EPA the power and responsibility to reverse the worst excesses of pollution.

13   The problems were gross and the solutions appropriately crude. There was little need and no patience for careful science, discriminating regulations, or a weighing of the costs. The mission was to blanket the nation with a consistent set of requirements that would keep major pollutant streams out of the air and water. Industrial polluters were the obvious target. Theirs were the largest and most visible waste streams and the most susceptible to rough-and-ready control.

14   Despite the enormous odds against it, the hell-bent-for-leather strategy worked quite well on the whole. The environment is cleaner now than it would have been had the nation not responded. For example, air quality is generally better now than in 1970, despite a growth in gross national product of 50 percent and an increase of 17 percent in population (U.S. EPA "National Air" 246, 279). As a dramatic example, ambient lead concentrations in urban areas dropped by 79 percent from 1976 to 1985 (3–38). Most of our rivers are cleaner now, or at least are holding their own (U.S. EPA *National Water* 15). Private activism and government regulation unquestionably have turned the advancing tide of the most visible and repulsive pollution.

15   So much is history. Through those efforts major environmental risks to health have been substantially reduced. People live longer; they have safer air, water, and food; and they enjoy more pleasing surroundings than before.

16   But the focus here is on the future, and the job yet undone. The sobering evidence is that this country will not be able to continue environmental progress and achieve its goals by simply maintaining or even intensifying current efforts. The challenges for the 1990s are fundamentally different from those of 1970, and new approaches will be necessary to meet them and to maintain the progress already achieved. At the same time, no backsliding can be permitted on past progress. The premise of what follows is that the baseline of success from existing efforts will be maintained.

Change in Environmental Threats

17   The perceived threats to environmental quality have now changed as compared with those of a generation ago. Then one could see, smell, and taste the problem to be attacked. When the battle was going well, human senses knew it. Now attention has shifted to toxic chemicals, some of which can pose subtle threats at concentrations almost mystically small, discernible only through advanced technology. And toxic chemicals are everywhere—in the ambient air, in the home, in the food chain, and in the water. Unlike the case with smoke or sewage, however, to find a toxic chemical is not to define a course of action. There may be a hazard—but unless it is harmful at relevant doses and unless people or ecological systems are exposed at those levels, there is no *risk*. It is the amount of risk and what can be done about it that are the important aspects in guiding action.

18   The problem of toxic chemicals is exacerbated when suspected carcinogens are involved. For the pollutants of major consequence in the 1970s, there were natural stopping places for control because, below some concentrations, natural systems were capable of absorbing the insult or rendering the pollutant harmless. Similarly, for many of these pollutants, human health thresholds exist so that few if any harmful effects are observed below a certain level. For most carcinogens, however, current scientific theory holds that any dose can

be assumed to have some probability of harm, although perhaps only very small. Zero risk does not imply zero smoke in the air or zero sewage in the water, but it does imply zero exposure to most carcinogens (U.S. *51 Federal*).

19   Yet, it is a delusion to set a goal of eliminating toxic chemicals in the same way that the goal of "swimmable, fishable" water was set. That is a prescription for frustration. There are not the scientists, engineers, and technicians to study every chemical and devise controls to eliminate all risks. And if there were, and even if it were physically possible, there is not the social and political will to pay the price in reduced consumption of goods and services that zero risk would entail. Therefore, added to the technical enterprise of reducing toxic pollution is a demanding social and political task. That task is to select from a near infinity of potential targets which toxic chemicals should get priority attention and to determine how far to go in controlling those selected (U.S. EPA "Risk").

20   Making these choices is information-intensive. In addition, it demands the highest level of leadership and public involvement. This is because the public will be faced with explicit tradeoffs between reducing toxic risks still further and reducing yet more personal freedom and consumption of other goods and services—including risk reductions elsewhere. Such choices are inherently cruel, and the temptation to simply turn them aside is great. Indeed, the political system has mostly succeeded until now in casting a rhetorical veil between such choices and the public when it comes to the environment. It has done so by promising progress toward perfection, by asserting that the cost would be paid by others, or disingenuously, by simply fuzzing or denying the tradeoffs present. But that time is passing.

21   Another change in focus is toward greater concern with protection of ecological systems. Protection of health was understandably the early priority. Fortunately, many of the actions of the first generation of pollution controls protected natural systems as well. It has become clear, however, that this is not enough to assure that future citizens will enjoy the birds, the fish, the diversity of plants, and the vistas this generation enjoys. Indeed, even *within* this generation subtle but significant losses have occurred.

22   Public attention has been drawn to the plight of endangered species such as the California condor, the black-footed ferret, and the dusky seaside sparrow, the latter of which apparently became extinct in June 1987. But more telling, perhaps, has been the almost imperceptible draining away of habitat and the subsequent diminution in size and diversity of animal and plant populations. It is striking to read accounts such as Edwin Way Teale's classic *Autumn Across America,* based on observations in the late 1940s. He depicts as commonplace flights of birds in places where they are now nowhere to be found, at least in the numbers he described. Not that success stories are lacking, as the expansion and extension of the wild turkey population demonstrates strikingly. The growth of white-tailed deer populations and the expansion of the coyote range are also notable.

23   Captive breeding programs and intensive management have brought back a sustainable population of whooping cranes. The bald eagle population is growing and extending its range as DDT is purged from the system, and through active intervention to protect nesting sites and to transplant young birds to new areas. Protection of special habitats has preserved, at least for

now, the grizzly and the wolf. But the common vision of the ecological legacy we want to leave is not one reduced to open zoos and wilderness preserves, as important as they are, but of healthy, productive ecological communities, thriving along with a human population in a common setting. To achieve that legacy will take action—to protect the wetlands, to preserve greenbelts, to improve water quality, and to avoid ecological insults even beyond those injurious to human health.

Change in Subjects to Control

24   When it comes to formulating the next generation of environmental controls, environmental professionals will soon learn sympathy for General Charles Cornwallis. He was trained and equipped to fight set battles against neat columns of brightly dressed soldiers, only to find himself peppered with fire from colonial rebels behind every tree in the woods.

25   In the old days the polluter was big industry, easy to identify, easy to paint as the culprit, and relatively easy to control. Perhaps as important, it was easy to pass off the cost of cleaning up as someone else's problem, although in truth it was borne by all of us as workers, investors, consumers, and taxpayers. For the future, however, much of the remaining pollution that will cause the most risk is from widely dispersed sources whose control will depend on changing the behavior of individual citizens (U.S. EPA "Unfinished" 97–100). Here the cost in dollars, inconvenience, and lost amenities cannot be passed off or hidden.

26   People want clean air, in general, but few want the nuisance or expense of an annual automobile inspection. Still less do they want to reduce driving or give up favored consumer goods. Toxic air emissions from industry are pretty well controlled; the evidence is that most risk now comes from individually small but cumulatively large sources, such as dry cleaners and woodstoves (U.S. EPA Office of Air and Radiation). The air indoors is more hazardous than that outside, but homeowners want clean ovens, painted walls, and inexpensive warmth in the winter. Today's tight home construction that brings down fuel bills ironically exacerbates risks from everything from smoking to naturally occurring radon.

27   Modern sewage treatment plants mean sharply higher, and very unpopular, monthly household bills, especially now that the federal government will be paying less of the cost under the Water Quality Act of 1987 (Pub. L.). The major threat to wetlands is not from large conversions sponsored by big corporations but from small changes imposed by householders who wanted to bulkhead their shorelines or farmers who want to drain and plow a prairie pothole or convert hardwood bottomlands to soybean production (Odum). Rivers and lakes are threatened by run-off from streets, farms, and forests and by the do-it-yourself motorist who dumps used oil down the storm sewer (U.S. EPA Office of Water). People want streams and estuaries to support fish, game, and recreation, but they also want shirts clean, and so the phosphorous continues to flow into the water. They want industrial hazardous waste properly managed, but few support a facility to do just that if there is a chance it might be located in their neighborhood.

28   The litany goes on. The problems are obvious; the solutions are commensurately murky. Certainly they are not the traditional ones. The tool kit of

environmental protection that got us this far does not have the wrenches and levers to fix the remaining problems. New tools are needed, and environmental professionals will have to learn to use them.

Change in Roles

29   Devising and applying those tools represents the third change needed for effective environmental protection for the 1990s and beyond. Here the waters are scarcely charted, but the general course appears clear.

30   First of all, the people who are to provide the solution must understand and accept the problem as theirs. Unless the health risks are understood and judged unacceptable, unless the environmental implications of life as usual are seen as intolerable, it is fruitless to expect behavior to change. In this new phase of environmental progress, action comes only when the polluters choose to impose change on themselves and their fellows. Those who are part of the problem are also those who must agree upon and carry out the solution. This is not a situation amenable to command and control; it is one that demands coalition and consensus.

31   In this new era, the role of the environmental professional is one of assessing risk—defining the nature, scope, and magnitude of the problem. It is also one of communicating that risk assessment to the affected public and of laying out possible fixes to the problems discovered. Then an informed community can make its choice and find a way to bear fairly the burdens any actions impose. The risks identified can be weighed against the cost of reducing them, and a balance struck based on prevailing values.

32   Individuals will be making the risk management decisions for themselves and with their fellows, for each other. Questions such as these will be posed: Is avoiding that herbicide risk worth tolerating dandelions in the neighborhood lawns? Do I want to test my home for radon? If I find it, will I pay to cut my risk of lung cancer? Should I put a catalytic converter on my woodstove to avoid harmful emissions in my house—and how much pressure will I withstand from my neighbors who don't want those emissions in their back yard? Will I support land-use control to protect wetlands if that means that a marina is further away, or that the longed-for beach house cannot be built on the already-purchased lot? Or that jobs will not be created here because lack of wharfage means that a plant will be located elsewhere? Will I vote in or out a mayor who supports an incinerator to transform my garbage safely, knowing that the facility may be sited in my neighborhood?

33   Environmental professionals who have joyfully worn the cloak of philosopher kings, forcing some people to clean up their act for the good of others, will have to change their clothes. The new message is: We are all in this together. Here are the facts. What should we do about it?

34   In brief, this means opening up the process of environmental decision making to those who must bear the consequences and pay the costs. And then accepting their judgment. This is a new way of doing things, and for those steeped in the past and concerned about the future, it may seem dangerous. But Thomas Jefferson did not think so. He said:

> I know no safe depository of the ultimate powers of the society but the people themselves; and if we think them not enlightened enough to

exercise their controls with a wholesome discretion, the remedy is not to take it from them, but to inform their discretion.

Besides, when it comes to most of the environmental problems left on our plate, there is no realistic option except to share control.

Change in Institutions

35   Three types of change have been addressed so far: change in types of environmental problems, change in who causes them, and change in how they must be fixed.

36   The final change must come in institutions by which our society achieves and assures environmental quality. The roles and relationships among the parties that have been traditionally entrusted with environmental protection—the federal government, the states, the communities, and the private sector—have changed and will change still more.

37   In many respects states are better equipped than EPA to carry out the everyday work of environmental protection. Twenty years of building have brought this country to the point where most states have competent, highly professional institutions to ensure consistent and responsible environmental protection within their own borders. A few years ago, EPA acknowledged that fact as it issued a new policy on state and federal roles (U.S. "EPA Policy").

38   That policy, negotiated between EPA and state participants, defined a new partnership for environmental protection, one that assigned to each party the functions it is best fit to perform. Briefly, states take on the lion's share of responsibility for field-level program operations, such as permitting, inspecting, and enforcing. EPA, on the other hand, acts as sort of national franchiser—an environmental McDonald's. EPA has principal responsibility to provide national leadership, evaluation, and support to state environmental programs; to issue national standards and regulations; to undertake research and information collection; to back up states on the odd occasion when they cannot perform; and to represent the needs of both partners before Congress and within the administration. This system was well conceived and it is essential that it continue to provide the national framework and baseline for environmental protection.

39   This partnership, however, has far to go to reach success in treating even traditional environmental concerns. For EPA and Congress, which prescribes its behavior through statutes, the realization that states and localities must be trusted, or built to a position of trust, requires a leap of faith that many have been unable to make. Just as telling, the states and localities are sometimes reluctant to accept responsibility for tough actions when they can turn to their less locally constrained Uncle Sam to play the gorilla in the closet. It is a lot easier for a local or state official to hold voters to a federally mandated standard than to achieve the same goals first by getting local legislation passed and then by enforcing this close-to-home-grown decision.

40   The points outlined above suggest, however, that these ongoing institutions must also be enriched to meet the challenges of the future. The direction of the needed change seems clear: states, communities, and citizens will require organizations to diagnose local problems, to find acceptable solutions, and to

induce behavioral change. And on the other side, EPA will need to back off on the micromanagement that places a straitjacket on those who need to deal with their special problems in ways they find acceptable. Finally, Congress will need to provide flexibility in the statutes to allow states and communities more freedom to determine for themselves at least the "how," and in some cases the "what" and the "when." Again, none of these changes will be easy. But some are already under way.

41   States are adjusting to the new realities by rethinking their approach to environmental planning. Several states have joined with EPA in developing new ways of diagnosing their specific multimedia environmental problems and in planning for their correction. In Maryland, for example, a state task force has identified twenty of the most troublesome environmental issues, such as indoor air pollution and groundwater contamination, and held workshops on each to define appropriate goals and recommendations for action. While the process is being carried out by state agencies, there has been extensive involvement by citizen experts and other nongovernment participants. In Delaware the governor has organized a broadly representative Environmental Legacy Program to define a desired environmental future and design an action program to ensure it. In Pennsylvania state government and private citizens have joined the federal EPA in an effort to determine where the most risks are and to establish priorities in addressing them.

42   The role of communities is expanding as well. EPA has been at work with several localities in providing technical support for their evaluation of complex environmental conditions at the local level. These "Integrated Environmental Management Projects" have been set up in places as diverse as Philadelphia; Baltimore; Santa Clara, California; West Virginia's Kanawah Valley; and most recently, in Denver. Although each project has been different, all of them have organized local interests in the collection of empirical information on pollution, its location, its attendant risks, and the options available for reducing those risks. The focus is on what risks are left *after* the safety net of national controls is imposed (U.S. EPA "Baltimore" 809–815).

43   Based on quantitative risk assessments when possible and qualitative ones otherwise, these local communities are coming up with priorities and plans for action. The data and technical assistance provided to the communities by EPA empowers local residents to decide which risks are acceptable and which are not.

44   In other places, grassroots movements have grown up to meet environmental needs. One instance involves Oregon's Tillamook Bay, an area famous for both oysters and cheese. Coastal Oregon gets about one hundred inches of rain a year. The attendant run-off washes dairy cattle waste into the bay in such volumes that in 1977 the Food and Drug Administration threatened to close the bay to oyster harvesting under a little-used federal regulation that would have replaced state authority. To preserve their local environment and economy, local oystermen and dairy operators have voluntarily joined to institute the best available management practices at over half of the area's dairies. They sought and received help from the state, the Soil Conservation District, the Department of Agriculture, and EPA. But the solution was ini-

tialed and implemented by local citizens and industry. Oysters and cheese production now happily coexist, and local institutions see to it that neighbors do not impose on one another (Jackson 184).

45   In short, there is a world of creativity in our communities that our previous over-reliance on federal regulations has left untapped. Federal regulations are powerful but limited tools—like the driver in a golf bag that has its place at the tee but not on the putting green. States, localities, and private citizens have at their command many more subtle devices that are properly denied at the federal level. Prudent zoning and other land-use controls come to mind as particularly incisive tools for handling specific problems. In an increasing number of environmental situations, EPA would do best to stay at the tee while others more effectively play on the green.

Where We Are Going

46   Daniel Boone wanted to move west when he could smell another's wood-smoke. He could. We cannot. The environmental frontier is closed. With no "away," the output and consumption that meet people's wants, and the dark underside of attendant environmental risks, must be managed in a closed system.

47   For example, pesticides and herbicides will continue to be needed, but more careful attention to the way they are used and to their true benefits and environmental dangers can lead to the use of safer, more selective, and less persistent ones and to less of them being released. Hazardous waste will continue to be produced, but its volume can be reduced, more of it can be destroyed or recycled, and the risk from the remainder can be lessened by selecting wisely where it finally comes to rest. Or again, pressing social wants will lead to destruction of habitat, but there will be less destruction when ecological damages are put into the equation, and most of the loss can be offset by proper attention to mitigation and enhancement of habitat elsewhere. The issue is balance. The questions to be posed are how our constrained space and limited resources are to be used, for what ends, and who is to decide.

48   Great progress has been made under the statutes, regulations, and institutions that grew up over the past generation, and that hard-won progress must be protected. Yet the seemingly well-marked though arduous road to environmental quality that has been followed must be rerouted to deal with new realities:

• The illusion that safe can mean risk-free has been dispelled with better understanding of cancer and by the ubiquity of toxic chemicals that are essential to daily life.

• The recognition that protecting people does not automatically protect ecological systems came as we discovered that power plant emissions that meet health standards are implicated in reducing the biological diversity of lakes.

• The belief that it was others who had to clean up has been replaced by the reality that "the enemy is us," even as we sort our garbage for the incinerator and take our cars to have their emissions checked.

- The view that solutions could be devised, enunciated, and policed from on high has evaporated as communities wrestle with siting hazardous waste facilities and choosing how to cut down on the hydrocarbon emissions that create local smog.

- The reflexive posture of "leave it to the feds" has come up against the diversity of problems, the complexity of local solutions, and the need for outcomes that communities can accept as fair.

49   The easy part of meeting the environmental challenge of the 1990s will be scientific and technical. This society knows how to mobilize and use its talent to gain the knowledge it needs. All it takes is the will to devote the needed resources to the task, and time. The hard part lies in accomplishing the shifts in attitude, behavior, and institutions needed to comport with this stage of the American quest for a safe, healthy, ecologically secure environment.

50   Bob Dylan was the troubadour of a great period of spontaneous change in America. But as he noted, the times are changing indeed. Today's environmental professionals will not be true to their mission unless they take a leadership role in fostering the daunting but essential changes that will mold an environmental legacy they will be proud to leave to the twenty-first century.

Works Cited

Carson, Rachel L. *Silent Spring*. Boston: Houghton, 1962.

Coolidge, Calvin. Speech to the American Society of Newspaper Editors. 17 Jan. 1925.

"Delayed Effects of Smog Studies," *New York Times* 30 Nov. 1958: 68.

Dunlap, Riley E. "Public Opinion on the Environment in the Reagan Era." *Environment* July/Aug. 1987: 7.

Galbraith, John Kenneth. *The Affluent Society*. Boston: Houghton, 1958.

Jackson, John E. "Shellfish Sanitation in Oregon: Can It Be Achieved Through Pollution Source Management?" in EPA Office of Regulations and Standards. "Perspectives on Nonpoint Source Pollution." EPA 440/5-85-001. Washington: GPO, 1985.

Jefferson, Thomas. Letter to William Charles Jarvis. 28 Sep. 1820.

"Nation Set to Observe Earth Day." *New York Times* 21 Apr. 1970: 36.

Netboy, A. *The Salmon: Their Fight for Survival*. Boston: Houghton, 1974.

Nixon, Richard. "Message to Congress Transmitting Reorganization Plan 3 of 1970: Environmental Protection Agency." *Public Papers of the President*. Washington: GPO, 1970.

Odum, William E. "Environmental Degradation and the Tyranny of Small Decisions." *BioScience 32* 1982: 728–29.

Public Law. No. 100-4, 1987.

Teale, E. W. *Autumn Across America*. New York: Dodd Mead, 1956.

Turner, F. J. *Frontier in American History*. New York: Holt, 1920.

United States. Environmental Protection Agency. "Baltimore Integrated Environmental Management Project: Phase 1 Report." Washington: GPO, May 1987.

United States. Environmental Protection Agency. "National Air Quality and Emissions Trends Report, 1985." Washington: GPO, 1985.

United States. Environmental Protection Agency. *National Water Quality Inventory: 1984 Report to Congress*. EPA 440/4-85-029. Washington: GPO, 1985.

United States. Environmental Protection Agency Office of Air and Radiation, Office of Policy, Planning and Evaluation. "The Air Toxics Problems in the United States: An Analysis of Cancer Risks for Selected Pollutants." EPA 450/1-85-001. Washington: GPO, 1985.

United States. Environmental Protection Agency Office of Water Program Operations. *Report to Congress: Nonpoint Source Pollution in the U.S.* Washington: GPO, 1984.

United States. Environmental Protection Agency. "Risk Assessment and Management: Framework for Decision Making." Washington: GPO, Dec. 1984.

United States. Environmental Protection Agency. "Unfinished Business: A Comparative Assessment of Environmental Problems, Overview Report." Washington: GPO, 1987.

United States. "EPA Policy Concerning Delegation to State and Local Governments." Internal policy document. 4 Apr. 1984.

United States. *51 Federal Register.* 33992–34003, Washington: GPO, 1986.

For Thought and Discussion

1. What is the thesis of "Environmental Protection"?

2. Early in the article author Milton Russell provides us an outline to help us follow his complex idea. Summarize that outline.

3. How does Russell justify including historical background since his thesis focuses on the future?

4. What do the thesis ideas of *The Affluent Society* and *Silent Spring* have in common? How do these ideas tie in with Russell's thesis?

5. Give an example of the progress Russell says we have made in cleaning up our environment.

6. Explain how the future focus of environmental protection measures will differ from the focus in the past.

7. In the future, how will communications skills play an important role in helping environmental professionals?

8. List three examples of sacrifices individuals may be required to make in the interest of a healthier environment. How would you feel about making these sacrifices?

9. Give three examples of imagery Russell uses to add interest and concreteness to this article.

10. Explain why this article did or did not convince you of its thesis.

11. Review Russell's introduction, and then explain how he tied his ideas together in his conclusion.

 WRITING ASSIGNMENT

Write a paper of approximately 1,800 words about a current controversial issue. Use parenthetical notations and a list of works cited to document your sources.

Use at least three different *kinds* of sources (for example, magazine, newspaper, professional journal, government document, personal interview, television documentary). Use at least six different sources to document your paper.

Review the steps earlier in this chapter that help break this essay into stages.

Suggested Topics

Review the lists you made in response to discussion topics 6 to 9 at the beginning of this chapter to see if one of the items would interest you as a research topic. Alternatively, choose a topic from the following list, which consists of general subject areas that need to be more narrowly focused for a paper of the assigned length.

Nuclear power plants
Arms control
Acid rain
The greenhouse effect
The ozone problem
Toxic wastes
Reducing pollution through conservation of energy
Pesticides
The impact of pollution on the economy
The death penalty
Mercy killing (euthanasia)
Reducing the risk of heart attack
Reducing the risk of cancer (select a specific type)
The impact of the balance of payments on the economy

Peer Editing Checklist

After you have completed the prewriting and the first draft of your essay, meet with a peer editing group so that you can assess the reaction of an audience to your writing. Make enough photocopies of your essay for your peer editing group.

1. Point out the positive qualities of the paper such as effective words or phrases, figurative language, allusions, alliteration, or the subject of the essay. Positive reinforcement is a powerful tool.

2. Tell the writer what you think the thesis is. (If you are not sure what the thesis is, indicate this.)

3. What is your reaction to the essay's introduction? Does the introduction help you better understand the author's point or pique your interest in reading the essay?

4. List the technical terms the paper uses. Circle any terms that need further explanation.

5. Point out any section of the paper in which you are confused about the ideas or their development.

6. Point out any places where you are not clear about the credentials of the authorities cited.

7. Point out any details or passages that do not seem relevant to the author's point. The author can then decide whether a transition could clarify the connection with the thesis or if the point is truly irrelevant.

8. Point out any places where you are not clear about the source of the ideas, facts, or information cited.

9. What is your reaction to the essay's title? Does it help you to better understand the author's point, or does it pique your interest in reading the essay?

10. What function does the essay's conclusion serve? Does the conclusion contain any new ideas not developed within the essay?

When writers have revised the content of the essay to their satisfaction and are ready for feedback about mechanics, point out but do not correct any problems you suspect exist with spelling, grammar, and punctuation. It is the writer's responsibility to make such corrections.

 STUDENT STAR

While the examples thus far in this chapter have centered around challenges of the future, it is important to note that the methods discussed in this chapter apply to many other subjects.

The author of the essay in this section has done the following:

1. Prewriting
2. Writing
3. Revision
4. Correction of mechanical errors.

The reprinted journal entries reflect the preliminary thinking and research for the student star essay that immediately follows them. As you read the journal entries, note the looping back and forth between the author's critical and creative brains.

After you read the journal entries and the final polished draft, note that the student did not actually use some of her preliminary research in her Works Cited list. Rather the initial background reading helped to focus her thesis and direct her later research.

For my research project, I'd like to explore the whole question of pornography. I consider myself to be a rather liberal person; of course I'm all for the First and Fourteenth Amendment protection of freedom of speech and of the press. However, I am disgusted, shocked, repulsed by the kinds of pornography that gets protected by these amendments. After all, don't we have the right not to be assaulted by pornography? Much pornography is violent—especially violence against women and children. It seems to me that such violence could inspire other violence. If what we read and see doesn't have any impact on our behavior, what's the whole point of advertising, for example?

I guess with advertising, we are not actively resisting what we see, but how many people who are exposed to pornography are actively resisting its message? What I need to do is to read a general article about pornography, maybe even in such a general source as an encyclopedia. I guess my next steps should be to the library to see if I can find an overview to help me clarify my thinking.

Entry Two

General encyclopedias helped me clarify my thinking. The *Encyclopedia Americana* said: "Under the assumption that pornography tends to deprave or corrupt and to lead to sexual crimes, it is forbidden in most nations of the world. See also *Obscenity.*"

This encyclopedia says that in most nations pornography is forbidden because of the assumption that it corrupts. That corruption is what I'm interested in. In fact does pornography sometimes cause criminal behavior? What evidence can I find about this?

The "obscenity" section of *Encyclopedia Americana* contained some interesting material on the history of obscenity laws, but my critic brain pointed out that such history isn't directly relevant to my central point except for the sections that traced the pertinent Supreme Court decisions. There was also a paragraph on the 1970 Commission on Obscenity and Pornography: this report contended that no evidence exists to support the idea that pornography causes antisocial behavior. That was disappointing news. However, there are commissions and there are commissions. The fact that a commission in 1970 came up with a conclusion does not mean that conclusion was The Truth.

Entry Three

Next I turned to the *Academic American*. Like *Encyclopedia Americana,* it cited the 1957 *Roth v. United States,* but this encyclopedia was more helpful in its analysis. In *Roth,* for the first time the Supreme Court said that pornography is "not within the area of constitutionally protected speech." Making this decision even more useful for my paper, this ruling defined obscenity as: (1) matter that appeals to prurient interests, (2) offends current standards, (3) has no redeeming social value.

It occurred to me right away that "offends current standards" was pretty wishy-washy (abstract) as society has changed what it considers offensive a lot over the years. In the 1973 case *Miller v. California* the court said the individual states could decide what material was pornography.

Another great tip I got from this encyclopedia was the following information:

> . . . although the national Commission on Obscenity and Pornography in 1970 could find no link between the consumption of pornography and antisocial behavior, the depiction of violence directed against women in pornographic material was then comparatively rare. Recently, psychologists have begun to establish connections in some men between exposure to such violence—usually in films, and often in films without overt sexual content—and both sexual stimulation and negative changes in attitudes toward women. Some observers see the upsurge in rape and sexual abuse of women and children as a result of the increase in sadistic pornography.

Clearly the research I have wondered about does exist. My next step is to try to find the recent research referred to in the *Academic American.*

Entry Four

One of my problems in this paper is obviously going to be how to limit my topic. As I read the entry "Erotic and Pornographic Literature" in *Academic American,* it occurred to me that there is pornography and there is pornography. What I mean is that there is a big difference between material that is merely sexy but not violent. I did a computer search for information that turned up a great article by Gloria Steinem called "Erotica and Pornography: A Clear and Present Difference." This article makes a point which in retrospect seems very obvious: there is a big difference between what Steinem defines as *erotica*—material she says depicts mutually pleasurable sexual expressions that are loving and sensual. *Pornography* Steinem defines differently. Pornography has a message of violence and domination of women and often even of children. This is precisely the stuff I think should be illegal.

Early in my paper, I need to borrow Steinem's definition. This will help me limit my topic, and it should also help me not infringe on First Amendment rights. After all, when rights clash—as they do with the issue of pornography—then these rights must be modified to protect other rights. That's the nifty allusion in Steinem's title; it refers to Justice Holmes' decision in which he limits the freedom of speech. This freedom does not mean we can yell "fire" in a crowded hall—I think. I'd better look up "Clear and Present Danger" to see if I'm right about that. I somewhat remember it from my political science class.

There are several more questions I need to have answered: Is there any research that shows that being exposed to pornography increases the likelihood of a violent crime? If I could find such research, it would be a major help in supporting my point.

I wonder if feminist organizations such as NOW [National Organization for Women] have a stand on pornography. I remember reading about a source that lists addresses—maybe even phone numbers—of organizations. I found it: the four-volume *Encyclopedia of Associations: National Associations of the United States.*

I wonder how much laws vary concerning pornography. I need to check for a source that discusses any local or state ordinances that attempt to limit pornography.

Hi ho, hi ho, it's back to the library I go. But this time, I think I know what I'm looking for. I'm ready to dig in and begin my paper.

The final draft of this essay follows.

The Pornography Debate

1   The legality of violent pornography poses a perplexing social problem in modern America. The real issue is whether or not pornography causes the degradation and subordination of women. The debate has divided feminists, brought together a large faction of right-wing activists calling for the elimination of pornography, and caused outcries from civil rights activists such as the American Civil Liberties Union (ACLU), who claim that moves to criminalize pornography violate First Amendment guarantees of free speech.

2   Many people consider pornography to be violence disguised as sex. In fact, feminists such as Gloria Steinem make an effort to distinguish pornography from erotica. Steinem defines *erotica* as images of mutually pleasurable sexual expressions that have a sense of loving and sensuality. The message of pornography, on the other hand, is violence against and domination of women and often of children (Steinem 37).

3   In the legal sense, there are three types of pornography: (1) soft-core materials fully protected by law; (2) certain medium-core materials which may be regulated and isolated to commercially undesirable areas; and (3) hard-core pornography which is obscene in the strict legal sense. Distribution of hard-core materials is forbidden and punishable by law (Allen, "Case"). In this paper, I will define as *pornography* depictions of sex in which unequal power or obvious force are shown.

4   Pornography has many forms: typical are rape, beatings, dismemberment, and simulated murder. A *Penthouse* feature that exemplifies pornography depicted nude Asian women bound like turkeys (Press 61).

5   Although pornography depicts blatant violence such as bruises, torture, or obvious humiliation, it may be more subtle; for example, it may show unequal nudity—one person nude and vulnerable while the other is fully clothed. Pornography uses sex to portray inequality. Pornography implies that pain and humiliation are the same as sensual pleasure (Steinem 38).

6   On July 9, 1986, the Attorney General's Commission on Pornography delivered its report asking for a nationwide attack on the pornography industry. The report called for a combined effort of more vigorous law enforcement and increased vigilant efforts by community citizens' groups (Pear B1). The commission based its findings upon public hearings in six cities, a review of published articles on pornography, staff investigations, and views of more than 3,000 public letters (B7).

7   The commission found that a causal relation does exist between violent

pornography and sexually violent acts. Since sexually explicit materials in which adult participants appeared fully willing to participate comprise a small category, according to the report, the report's main focus was on violent pornography, not the types of materials previously designated as *erotica*.

8   Evidence in this report strongly supports attitudinal changes in subjects with substantial exposure to sexually violent materials. For example, viewers of such material are much more likely to see rape victims as having suffered minimally and having been more responsible for their assault. According to this report, evidence also suggests that enough exposure to pornography leads to acceptance of the "Rape Myth" whereby women are believed to enjoy rape, and the rapist is only acting in accord to the woman's desires (B7).

9   It is true that a 1970 Presidential Commission on Pornography concluded that pornographic materials were not a significant cause of sexual deviance. However, this commission explains its very different conclusion by pointing out that the abundance of sexually violent material has risen dramatically since that time. In fact, this new commission called the old panel's findings "starkly obscene." The 1986 commission did affirm that there is no scientific evidence of a connection between nonviolent, nondegrading materials and acts of sexual violence; such materials were the chief focus of the 1970 panel (B7).

10   The 1986 commission said that current laws on obscenity should be adequate to control violent pornography, but that these laws went unenforced by local, state, and federal prosecutors. For this reason, the commission asked citizens to form "watch groups" to file complaints, pressure their local prosecutors, and boycott establishments selling pornography (B1).

11   In fact, the Supreme Court has already ruled that obscene materials are not protected by the First Amendment, and that judges may apply community standards in deciding what is obscene. Despite the commission's conclusion that adequate clinical evidence exists supporting a causal relation between sexually violent materials and an increase in aggressive behavior towards women, the commission has come under fire from the ACLU. The ACLU believes that the report is no more than moralizing, and that no scientific basis for suppressing pornography exists (B7).

12   But the fact remains that pornography encourages at least attitudinal changes in its viewers, which may result in behavioral changes. Although the National Organization for Women (NOW) does not support vigilant enforcement of obscenity laws, many feminists say that pornography imitates life. Women are sexually abused and raped in astounding numbers, and evidence points to a connection between this abuse and pornography (Press 65).

13   In 1980, Diana Russell conducted a survey of college women in which 10% reported being either forced or asked to imitate sex acts which came out of pornograhy. Diana Scully, a sociologist at Virginia Commonwealth University, after interviewing 114 rapists, concluded that scenes depicted in pornography are replicated in rapists' accounts of their crimes (65).

14   Furthermore, laboratory research conducted by Edward Donnerstein at the University of Wisconsin shows that young men who view sexually violent films and are then asked to judge a simulated rape trial are less likely to convict than those who did not view the film. Donnerstein reports that these

viewers became more callous toward and trivialized rape (62). A 1984 study of 200 prostitutes undertaken by researcher Mimi Gilbert found 193 cases of rape. In approximately 25% of these crimes, the rapist was apparently acting out a pornographic script. "I seen it in all the movies," said one to his victim. "You love being beaten" (65).

15   Yet Donnerstein continues to contend that nobody can prove a causal link between exposure to pornography and effects on behavior (Pally 795). But he affirms that pornography does indeed change attitudes. The way in which it does so is called "misattribution"—when exposure to eroticism is followed by violence, the viewer misattributes his arousal from the sex to the violence, and after awhile, they simply merge, according to Donnerstein (Press 62). Attitudes do affect behavior; it is naive to assume otherwise.

16   Some makers of pornographic material argue that pornography actually prevents crimes against women by acting as a catharsis. However, statistics indicate otherwise; the legalization of pornography in Denmark actually precipitated an increase in rape (Griffin 83). Other pornographers simply do not care about the impact of their materials. Al Goldstein, publisher of *Screw,* says, "Frankly, I don't think it matters whether porn is degrading to women. It's a society of many voices and I don't want any of them silenced." Some porn stars contend that controlling pornography violates their civil rights by telling them they can't make movies "about making love" (Press 66). But love and sex are not what most anti-porn activists object to: images of people making love implies erotica, not the violence and distortion of power implicit in pornography.

While most Americans find pornography repugnant, they assume it harms nobody. One reason for this acceptance is the 1970 commission's conclusions—which were based primarily on erotica, not pornography (61). However, the Gallup organization conducted a poll for *Newsweek* in 1985 which showed two-thirds of those surveyed supported a ban on materials of sexual violence (58). Thus it appears that when people fully understand what is meant by pornography, they oppose it.

18   Exactly how to deal with pornography is controversial. At the 1982 Barnard Conference, even feminists were divided on how to treat pornography. Some feminists are determined to fight it, but some are convinced that the right to explore sexuality must not be threatened (Blakely 38). According to Sol Gordon, Professor of Child Studies at Syracuse University, Americans need sex education because many people are so uneducated they think that to rape is better than to masturbate. Gordon believes proper sex education in schools could have a great impact (Allen, "Pornography" 29).

19   Lester Kirkendall, voted Humanist of the Year by the American Humanist Association in 1983, believes that the bottom line in dealing with pornography is to create a relationship between men and women that stresses equality. Kirkendall emphasizes that men and women must respect each other—a respect that could be fostered through proper education (24). However, the alleviation of sexual brutality through sex education is a long process that will not help those who currently fall victim to violence.

20   Andrea Dworkin, co-author of a revolutionary anti-porn ordinance in Minneapolis, says, "We will know that women are free when pornography no

longer exists'' (25). She and attorney Catherine MacKinnon created in 1985 what they hope will become an exception to the First Amendment protections. They believe that any woman is a potential target for the brutality of pornography. Under their ordinance, a woman who is assaulted as a result of pornography can sue not only the perpetrator, but the maker and distributor of the pornographic material as well. The ordinance was written with a special concern: zoning ordinances legitimize pornography by allowing it in given areas. This ordinance, which was passed by the Minneapolis City Council but vetoed by the mayor, would have included pornography as sex discrimination (Press 66).

21 The case for discrimination is made on the basis that pornography keeps women subordinate, promotes violence against women, and inhibits women's access to equal opportunities (Blakely 40). The case pits a woman's right to freedom from sexual discrimination against a pornographer's right to freedom of speech. However, as Justice Holmes pointed out a century ago, the freedom of speech is not an absolute freedom. It does not include the freedom to yell ''fire'' in a crowded hall; it does not include the freedom to wreak violence upon one segment of our population.

22 Ordinances modeled after that of Minneapolis were subsequently introduced in a number of other locations, but thus far, I can find no press reports of any of these ordinances passing. The ordinances have been defeated by a combination of factors. Right-wing coalitions try to transform such ordinances into censorship of any sexually suggestive materials—even literary works considered classics such as *Lolita* by Vladimir Nabokov (44).

23 Other opposition comes from two factions: those who claim the ordinances threaten First Amendment guarantees and feminists who don't believe the elimination of pornography will make a significant impact on violence directed against women. The Feminist Anti-Censorship Task Force questions whether pornography causes violence and whether laws are the best way to change misogynist attitudes (Blakely 38). Barry Lynn, a lobbyist for the ACLU, doubts pornography influences action and fears ordinances will threaten freedom of speech (Press 66).

24 Yale Professor Burke Marshall believes the ordinances would be more feasible if the authors could define pornography more narrowly, so a book like *Slaughterhouse Five* would not be jeopardized (66).

25 Clearly something must be done about pornography. We cannot permit its continuation with a clear conscience in the face of evidence that shows its violent impact on many of its viewers—and their victims. Pornographic films known as ''snuff'' movies are the recent rage. In them women are murdered and often dismembered on camera. What do such films have to do with sexuality? How does it protect society's interests to allow such ''freedom of expression''?

26 A combination of efforts is needed to combat pornography. Sex education must be promoted so people are not taught about ''sexuality'' in the distorted terms of the pornographer. It is vital to teach the ignorant that women do not derive sexual pleasure from abuse. Obscenity laws must be enforced more stringently. And *pornography* must be defined more narrowly so as not to

endanger all sexually suggestive materials. Pornography is like a cancer; neglected it will not get better—left unchecked it will have grave consequences.
—Carol Elster

Works Cited

Allen, Gina, Annie Gaylor, and Sol Gordon. "Pornography: A Humanist Issue." *The Humanist* July/Aug. 1985: 23–44.

Allen, Gina. "The Case Against Pornography." *America* 15 Mar. 1986: 198.

Blakely, Mary. "Is One Woman's Sexuality Another's Pornography?" *Ms.* Apr. 1985: 37–47.

Griffin, Susan. *Pornography and Silence.* New York: Harper 1981.

Pally, Marcia. "Ban Sexism, Not Pornography." *The Nation* 29 June 1985: 794–97.

Pear, Robert. "Panel Calls on Citizens to Wage National Assault on Pornography." *New York Times* 18 July 1986: B1, B6–B7.

Press, Eric, Tessa Namut, and Susan Agrest. "The Case Against Pornography." *Newsweek* 18 Mar. 1985: 58–67.

Steinem, Gloria. "Erotica and Pornography: A Clear and Present Difference." *Take Back the Night.* Ed. Laura Lederer. New York: Morrow 1980.

ACKNOWLEDG-MENTS

354
ACKNOWLEDG-MENTS

Excerpt from *Albert Einstein: Creator and Rebel* by Banesh Hoffman with Helen Dukas. Copyright © 1972 by Helen Dukas and Banesh Hoffman. Used by permission of the publisher, Dutton, an imprint of New American Library, a division of Penguin Books USA Inc.

"November Surf" from *The Selected Poetry of Robinson Jeffers* by Robinson Jeffers. Copyright 1932 and renewed 1960 by Robinson Jeffers. Reprinted by permission of Random House, Inc.

"Toads," by Philip Larkin, from *Philip Larkin: Collected Poems,* The Marvell Press, 1989.

From *The Far Side,* two cartoons by Gary Larson. Copyright © 1985 and 1984 Universal Press Syndicate. Reprinted with permission. All rights reserved.

Drawing by Levin; © 1984 The New Yorker Magazine, Inc.

"Newsreel," by C. Day Lewis. Reprinted by permission of Sterling Lord Copyright © 1938 by C. Day Lewis.

"Shoe" cartoon by Jeff MacNelly, reprinted by permission: Tribune Media Services.

Drawing by Martin; © 1985 The New Yorker Magazine, Inc.

Excerpt from "One Vote for This Age of Anxiety," by Margaret Mead, in *The New York Times,* May 20, 1956. Copyright © 1956 by The New York Times Company. Reprinted by permission.

"Love Poem," from *Selected Poems* by John Frederick Nims. Copyright © 1947. Reprinted by permission of The University of Chicago Press.

Drawing by D. Reilly; © 1987 The New Yorker Magazine, Inc.

Drawing by Richter; © 1987 The New Yorker Magazine, Inc.

Excerpt from "Environmental Protection," by Milton Russell, in *Environment,* September 1987. Reprinted with permission of The Helen Dwight Reid Educational Foundation. Published by Heldref Publications, 1319 18th Street, NW, Washington, D.C. 20036. Copyright © 1987.

Excerpt from *Cosmos* by Carl Sagan. Copyright © 1980 Carl Sagan. Reprinted from *Cosmos* by permission of the author.

"The Ocean," by Laura St. Martin. Reprinted by permission of the author.

Excerpt from "Air Pollution," by Kirk R. Smith, in *Environment,* October 1988. Reprinted with permission of The Helen Dwight Reid Educational Foundation. Published by Heldref Publications, 1319 18th Street, NW, Washington, D.C. 20036. Copyright © 1988.

"The Recoloring of Campus Life," by Shelby Steele. Copyright © 1989 by *Harper's Magazine.* All rights reserved. Reprinted from the February issue by special permission.

"Uncle Ed" from "Ruth's Song (Because She Could Not Sing It)" from *Outrageous Acts and Everyday Rebellions* by Gloria Steinem. Copyright © 1983 by Gloria Steinem. Copyright © 1984 by East Toledo Productions, Inc. Reprinted by permission of Henry Holt and Company, Inc.

Cartoon by Peter Steiner. Reprinted from the AARP Bulletin with permission.

"TV Families: Packaged Dreams," by Ella Taylor, from *Prime Time Families,* as it appeared in *The Boston Review,* 1989. Reprinted by permission of the author.

"Do Not Go Gentle Into That Good Night," by Dylan Thomas: *Poems of Dylan Thomas.* Copyright 1952 by Dylan Thomas. Reprinted by permission of New Directions Publishing Corporation.

"On Societies as Organisms," copyright © 1971 by the Massachusetts Medical Society, from *The Lives of a Cell* by Lewis Thomas. Used by permission of Viking Penguin, a division of Penguin Books USA Inc.

"Quantum Physics' World: Now You See It, Now You Don't," by James Trefil, in *Smithsonian,* August 1987. Reprinted by permission of the author.

"Ex-Basketball Player" from *The Carpentered Hen and Other Tame Creatures* by John Updike. Copyright © 1954, 1955, 1956, 1957, 1958, 1982 by John Updike. Reprinted by permission of Alfred A. Knopf, Inc.

Excerpt reprinted by permission of the publishers from *One Writer's Beginnings* by Eudora Welty, Cambridge, Mass.: Harvard University Press, copyright © 1983, 1984 by Eudora Welty.

Excerpts from *Children Without Childhood* by Marie Winn. Copyright © 1981, 1983 by Marie Winn. Reprinted by permission of Pantheon Books, a division of Random House, Inc.

"He Wishes for the Cloths of Heaven" from *The Poems of W. B. Yeats: A New Edition,* edited by Richard J. Finneran (New York: Macmillan, 1983).

INDEX